Food Law

Second Edition

Barry Atwood LLB, Solicitor

Former Under-Secretary (Legal), Ministry of Agriculture, Fisheries and Food

Tottel publishing

Published by
Tottel Publishing Ltd
Maxwelton House
41-43 Boltro Road
Haywards Heath
West Sussex
RH16 1BJ

ISBN 13: 978-1-84592-591-8
ISBN 10: 1-84592-591-2

Formerly published by LexisNexis Butterworths

This edition reprinted by Tottel Publishing Ltd 2007

British Library Cataloguing-in-Publication Data.
A catalogue record for this book is available from the British Library.

Typeset by M Rules, London
Printed and bound in Great Britain by
Marston Book Services, Abingdon, Oxfordshire

Food Law

Preface to the second edition

Since the first edition of this book there have been significant developments in food law. Radical measures have been required not only to combat dangers from bovine spongiform encephalopathy, E coli 157 and chemical contamination of food and feed, but also to tighten controls on genetically modified organisms and other technological innovations. Most fundamental of the consequent changes have been those wrought by the establishment of the United Kingdom Food Standards Agency and the plans for parallel provision in the European Community. Major initiatives have also been implemented to modernise rules on labelling, hygiene, additives and contaminants and to raise the quality of agricultural products, while reducing unnecessary restrictions in the harmonised rules for specific processed foodstuffs.

Nor have relevant developments been restricted to food law alone. Practitioners must additionally have regard to the reordering of the United Kingdom constitutional arrangements by the Government of Wales Act 1998 and other devolution legislation, the amplification of enforcement requirements by provisions such as the Criminal Procedure and Investigation Act 1996, and the extension of civil law remedies by amendments to the sale of goods and product liability legislation.

Substantial revision of the first edition has thus been necessary to explain the current rules, including now those on feeding stuffs. An attempt has been made to place them clearly in their Community and English law framework. There has also been some reordering and amalgamation of material, in particular to give more prominence to the food safety requirements, to reflect the modern structure of hygiene law and to gather together all regulations on the chemical safety of food. Nevertheless, the aim has always been to honour Tony Painter's objective of providing a concise guide to a big and complex subject. Until recently he edited *Butterworths Law of Food and Drugs* and to him (and indeed to his predecessor the late John O'Keefe) I owe a particular debt. In preparing the second edition of this book, as throughout most of my professional life, I have relied greatly on that comprehensive work.

I am certainly glad to have this opportunity to acknowledge the generous help I have received from many busy people. My thanks are particularly due to Roland Rowell who made time to read and give informed and practical comment on the draft text; to my new colleagues at Butterworths, as well as to many former ones in the Civil Service, for so quickly responding to my importunate demands for information; to Margaret and Emrys Powell for access to the Internet; and to my wife Jenny, without whose patient support and encouragement this second edition would never have been completed.

Errors and shortcomings in this edition are my responsibility. The law of England and Wales is stated as at 31 January 2000, although it has been possible to take account of some subsequent amendments.

Barry Atwood
Croydon
January 2000

Preface to the first edition

As a consultant on food law, and editor of *Butterworths Law of Food and Drugs* and *O'Keefe's Law of Weights and Measures*, it has been apparent to me for some time that there is a need for a concise book on food law drawing attention to new developments, discussing matters of particular difficulty and identifying all the legislation applying to food. Quite independently, my colleagues in Butterworth Law Publishers Ltd had come to the same conclusion and this book is our attempt to fulfil that need.

It has proved to be a daunting task, for the ever widening and constantly changing scope of food law has made it difficult to decide what to include and what to omit. Another difficulty has been that there will be further important developments during the next year or two as the EC Single Market is established.

My approach has been to draw an outline portrait of food law and then to concentrate on important and long-established provisions which have been re-enacted in the Food Safety Act 1990, to explain the new provisions of that Act, and to clarify the role and influence of EC law. I have been influenced in my choice of topics by my experience as a consultant which suggests the issues which continue to give rise to difficulties of interpretation and implementation.

Another problem facing the author of a book on food law is that so much of it is new. The Food Safety Act 1990 is, of course, the most portentous source of new law and many EC developments also break entirely new ground. With only a limited period of operation, and without the benefit of judicial interpretation, I have felt it necessary to be cautious in offering opinions on new law, and I have tried to make my summaries of it as accurate as possible. However, the fact remains that this is a small book dealing with a huge subject and I have been obliged to seek a balance between essential principles and detail.

Food law is a fascinating subject. It has an infinite capacity to surprise; it poses the most intractable of problems; it attempts to control an ever changing and highly technological industry; and it can be most rewarding. If this modest book stimulates an interest in the subject I will be well satisfied.

Finally, I freely and gratefully acknowledge the help I have received and the collective wisdom I have enjoyed from trading standards and environmental health officers, from lawyers I have worked with over the years, from my friends in science and technology and from my colleagues in Butterworth Law Publishers Ltd.

AA Painter
Aldwick, West Sussex
January 1992

Contents

Abbreviations

A&HA 1964	Agriculture and Horticulture Act 1964
AA 1970	Agriculture Act 1970
ACAF	Advisory Committee on Animal Feeding Stuffs
ACMSF	Advisory Committee on Microbiological Safety of Food
ACNFP	Advisory Committee on Novel Foods and Processes
ACRE	Advisory Committee on Releases to the Environment
ACP	Advisory Committee on Pesticides
AHA 1981	Animal Health Act 1981
ATP	Agreement on the International Carriage of Perishable Foodstuffs
BA 1990	Broadcasting Act 1990
BSDA	British Soft Drinks Association
BSE	Bovine Spongiform Encephalopathy
C&EMA 1979	Customs and Excise Management Act 1979
CA 1985	Companies Act 1985
CAA 1968	Criminal Appeal Act 1968
CAP	Common Agricultural Policy
CCDC	Consultant in communicable disease control
CCPs	Critical Control Points
CJA 1988	Criminal Justice Act 1988
CJA 1991	Criminal Justice Act 1991
CJD	Creutzfeld-Jakob Disease
CMO	Chief Medical Officer
COC	Committee on Carcinogenicity of Chemicals in Food, Consumer Products and the Environment
COM	Committee on Mutagenicity of Chemicals in Food, Consumer Products and the Environment
COMA	Committee on the Medical Aspects of Food and Nutrition Policy
COT	Committee on Toxicity of Chemicals in Food, Consumer Products and the Environment
CP&IA 1996	Criminal Procedure and Investigation Act 1996
CPA 1987	Consumer Protection Act 1987
D&COA 1994	Deregulation and Contracting Out Act 1994
DBES	Date Based Export Scheme
DH	Department of Health
DTI	Department of Trade and Industry
EC	European Community Treaty
ECA 1972	European Communities Act 1972
ECHS	Export Certified Herd Scheme
ECJ	European Court of Justice
EEA	European Economic Area
ELISA Test	Enzyme-Linked Immunosorbent Assay Test

EPA 1990	Environmental Protection Act 1990
F&EPA 1985	Food and Environment Protection Act 1985
FA 1984	Food Act 1984
FAC	Food Advisory Committee
FAO	Food and Agriculture Organisation
FSA 1990	Food Safety Act 1990
FSA 1999	Food Standards Act 1999
GMO	Genetically Modified Organism
GWA 1998	Government of Wales Act 1998
H&SWA 1974	Health and Safety at Work Act 1974
HACCP	Hazard Analysis and Critical Control Points
HAS	Hygiene Assessment System
IA 1978	Interpretation Act 1978
LACOTS	Local Authorities Co-ordinating Body on Food and Trading Standards
LGA 1992	Local Government Act 1992
MA 1968	Medicines Act 1968
MAFF	Ministry of Agriculture, Fisheries and Food
MCA 1980	Magistrates' Courts Act 1980
MFS Prescription	Medicated feeding stuffs prescription
MHS	Meat Hygiene Service
MRM	Mechanically recovered meat
nvCJD	New variant Creutzfeldt-Jakob disease
OIE	International Office of Epizootics
OVS	Official veterinary surgeon
PARNUTS	Food intended for particular nutritional uses
PA 1974	Prices Act 1974
PACE	Police and Criminal Evidence Act 1984
PDO	Protected designation of origin
PGI	Protected geographical indication
PHLS	Public health laboratory service
QUID	Quantitative ingredient declarations
RASFF	Rapid Alert System for Food
RSA 1993	Radioactive Substances Act 1993
S&SGA 1994	Sale and Supply of Goods Act 1994
SA 1998	Scotland Act 1998
SEAC	Spongiform Encephalopathy Advisory Committee
SFCC	Scottish Food Co-ordinating Committee
SGA 1979	Sale of Goods Act 1979,
SPS Agreement	World Trade Organisation Agreement on the Application of Sanitary and Phytosanitary Measures
TDA 1968	Trade Descriptions Act 1968
TEU	Treaty on European Union
TNE	Tolerance negative error
UKROFS	United Kingdom Register of Organic Food Standards
VAT	Value Added Tax
VPC	Veterinary Products Committee
W&MA 1985	Weights and Measures Act 1985
WHO	World Health Organisation

Chronological table of statutes

Chronological table of statutory instruments

Table of European Communities legislation

Table of cases

PARA

Decisions of the European Court of Justice are listed below numerically. These decisions are also included in the preceding alphabetical list.

PARA

98, 99/75: Carstens Keramik GmbH v Oberfinanzdirektion Frankfurt am Main [1976] ECR 241, ECJ 1.5.7
41/76: Criel (née Donckerwolke) v Procureur de la République [1976] ECR 1921, [1977] 2 CMLR 535, ECJ 1.3.2
5/77: Tedeschi v Denkavit Commerciale srl [1977] ECR 1555, [1978] 1 CMLR 1, ECJ 16.3.1
31/78: Bussone v Italian Ministry for Agriculture and Forestry [1978] ECR 2429, [1979] 3 CMLR 18, ECJ 7.3.6
120/78: Rewe-Zentral AG v Bundesmonopolverwaltung für Branntwein [1979] ECR 649, [1979] 3 CMLR 494, CMR 8543, ECJ 1.3.1
88/79: Ministère Public v Grunert [1980] ECR 1827 ..... 1.6.4
788/79: Gilli and Andres [1980] ECR 2071, [1981] 1 CMLR 146, ECJ 1.6.4
27/80: Fietje [1980] ECR 3839, [1981] 3 CMLR 722 ..... 7.1.2
56/80: Weigand v Schutzverband Deutscher Wein eV [1981] ECR 583, [1983] 1 CMLR 146, ECJ .. 7.3.9
193/80: EC Commission v Italy [1981] ECR 3019, ECJ 1.6.2, 7.1.2
8/81: Becker v Finanzamt Münster-Innenstadt [1982] ECR 53, [1982] 1 CMLR 499, ECJ 1.5.5
124/81: EC Commission v United Kingdom [1983] ECR 203, [1983] 2 CMLR 1, ECJ 1.6.2
261/81: Walter Rau Lebensmittelwerke v De Smedt PvbA [1982] ECR 3961, [1983] 2 CMLR 496, ECJ 1.3.1
40/82: EC Commission v United Kingdom [1984] ECR 283, ECJ 1.6.2
126/82: D J Smit Transport BV v Commissie Grensoverschrijdend Beroepsgoederenvervoer [1983] ECR 73, [1983] 3 CMLR 106 ..... 1.2.1
14/83: Von Colson and Kamann v Land Nordrhein-Westfalen [1984] ECR 1891, [1986] 2 CMLR 430, 134 NLJ 473, ECJ 1.2.1
281/83: EC Commission v Italy [1985] ECR 3397, [1987] 1 CMLR 865, ECJ 1.6.3, 7.1.2
96/84: Vereniging Slachtpluimvee-Export eV v REWE-Zentral-Aktiengesellschaft [1985] ECR 1157 ..... 15.4.1
178/84: EC Commission v Germany [1987] ECR 1227, [1988] 1 CMLR 780, ECJ 1.3.1, 1.6.2, 7.1.2
130/85: Wulro BV v Tuchtgerecht Van De Stichting Scharreleieren-Controle [1986] ECR 2935, [1988] 1 CMLR 496, ECJ 7.3.6
407/85: Drei Glocken [1988] ECR 4233, ECJ 1.6.4, 7.1.2
286/86: Ministère Public v Déserbais [1988] ECR 4907, [1989] 1 CMLR 516, ECJ 6.5.5, 7.1.2
91/87: Erzeugergemeinschaft Gutshof-Ei GmbH v LandRheinland-Pfalz [1988] ECR 2541, [1990] 1 CMLR 96, ECJ 7.3.6
298/87: Re Smanor SA [1988] ECR 4489, ECJ 1.6.4, 6.5.5
25/88: Ministère Public v Bouchara (née Wurmser) and Norlaine SA [1989] ECR 1105, [1991] 1 CMLR 173, ECJ 19.3.2
C-131/88: EC Commission v Germany [1991] ECR I-825, ECJ 1.5.5
C-204/88: Ministère Public v Paris [1989] ECR 4361, [1991] 1 CMLR 841, ECJ 7.3.6
322/88: Grimaldi v Fonds des Maladies Professionnelles [1989] ECR 4407, [1991] 2 CMLR 265, [1990] IRLR 400, ECJ 1.5.7
C-332/88: Alimenta SA v Doux SA [1990] ECR I-2077 ..... 1.5.7
C-106/89: Marleasing SA v La Comercial Internacional de Alimentación SA [1990] ECR I-4135, [1992] 1 CMLR 305, [1993] BCC 421, 135 Sol Jo 15, ECJ 1.2.1
C-196/89: Italy v Nespoli [1990] ECR I-3647, [1992] 2 CMLR 1, ECJ 1.6.4
C-210/89: Re Low-Fat Cheese: EC Commission v Italy [1990] ECR I-3697, [1992] 2 CMLR 1, ECJ 1.6.4
C-241/89: Société d'application et de recherches en pharmacologie er phytithèrapie, SARL (SARPP) v Chambre syndicale des raffineurs et conditionneurs de sucre en France [1990] ECR I-4695, ECJ 1.6.4
C-372/89: Gold-Ei Erzeugerverbund GmbH v Überwachungsstelle für Milcherzeugnisse und Handelsklassen [1991] ECR I-43, ECJ 7.3.6
C-6, 9/90: Francovich and Bonifaci v Italy [1991] ECR I-5357, [1993] 2 CMLR 66, [1995] ICR 722, [1992] IRLR 84, ECJ 1.6.5
C-203/90: Erzeugergemeinschaft Gutshof-Ei GmbH v Stadt Bühl [1992] ECR I-1003, [1994] 1 CMLR 397, ECJ 7.3.6
C-236/91: EC Commission v Ireland [1992] ECR I-5933, sub nom Re Directive on Animal Semen: EC Commission v Ireland [1993] 1 CMLR 320, ECJ 13.1.5
C-17/93: Re Van de Veldt [1994] ECR I-3537, sub nom C-17/93: Openbaar Ministerie v van der Veldt [1995] 1 CMLR 621, ECJ 7.1.2
C-144/93: Pfanni Werke Otto Eckart KG v Landeshauptstadt München [1994] ECR I-4605, [1995] 2 CMLR 345, ECJ 6.5.12

Chapter 1

The development of modern food law

1.1 THE ORIGINS OF FOOD LAW

1.1.1 Although from the Middle Ages onwards rules in respect of particular foodstuffs were from time to time enacted by central government, it was not until the nineteenth century that general legislation as now understood was put into place. Two statutes of the same year established a food safety and consumer protection framework still recognisable in current British law. The Sale of Food and Drugs Act 1875 laid the foundations of modern provisions controlling the composition of food. Added to an existing ban on injurious ingredients[1] was the key prohibition on selling food not of the nature, substance and quality demanded by the purchaser[2] together with the important supplemental procedures relating to sampling, analysis and legal proceedings[3]. The main protection against chemical contamination of food was thus established. Basic control on biological (bacterial) contamination began with the Public Health Act 1875 which provided an offence of selling unfit food, as well as powers for its inspection, seizure and condemnation[4].

It is beyond the scope of this book to describe the origins of other food safety and consumer controls which it considers[5]. However, it might usefully be noted that quantity marking powers were removed from food legislation by the 1963 predecessor of the Weights and Measures Act 1985 (W&MA 1985), that price marking rules are essentially a modern development and that the late nineteenth century source of current feeding stuffs legislation is briefly mentioned in para **16.1.1** below.

1 See now Food Safety Act 1990 (FSA 1990), ss 7 and 8(1) and (2)(a).
2 See now FSA 1990, s 14.
3 See now FSA 1990, Pt III and the Food Safety (Sampling and Qualifications) Regulations 1990.
4 See now FSA 1990, ss 8 and 9.
5 See in particular ch 15 (quantity and price marking requirements) and ch 16 (feeding stuffs).

1.1.2 Modern British food law has developed on the bases described, supplemented in particular by statutory powers[1], which have enabled ministers to make a multiplicity of regulations on the composition, labelling and hygiene of food. These are both 'vertical' (applying to specific foods) and 'horizontal' (dealing generally with matters such as labelling, additives and contaminants). When in 1973 the United Kingdom acceded to what is now the European Community[2], the subordinate legislative powers were extended so that provisions implementing Community food Directives and Regulations could be integrated into the existing national structure[3]. This was further reinforced by the FSA 1990 which augmented the core food safety provisions[4], strengthened controls in respect of food businesses[5], food premises[6] and emergencies[7] and added powers to regulate food sources, novel foods, genetically modified food sources and food contact materials[8]. The FSA 1990 extends to England, Wales and Scotland. Northern Ireland has its own parallel legislation.

1.1.2 *The development of modern food law*

As we shall see below, while powers to make food regulations in respect of Scotland and Wales have now also been devolved, the new Food Standards Agency has been given responsibility for watching over and developing policy for the safety and standards of food and feeding stuffs throughout the United Kingdom.

1 See now FSA 1990, s 16.
2 The 'European Economic Community' was redesignated the 'European Community' by TEU, Art G(A)(1).
3 See now FSA 1990, s 17.
4 See FSA 1990, ss 7–9.
5 See FSA 1990, ss 10–12.
6 See FSA 1990, s 19.
7 See FSA 1990, ss 12–13.
8 See FSA 1990, ss 16–18.

1.1.3 The James Report[1] confirmed that the FSA 1990 was generally acknowledged to be a good tool for ensuring food safety. However, it identified significant weaknesses in the organisation responsible for applying the Act. As a result the Food Standards Agency was established by the Food Standards Act 1999 (FSA 1999) as the central United Kingdom food department and ministerial responsibility was concentrated in the Secretary of State for Health and the devolved authorities in Scotland, Wales and Northern Ireland[2].

1 'Food Standards Agency: An interim proposal by Professor Philip James: 30 April 1997'.
2 See ch 2.

1.1.4 In recent years there has been a tendency in food legislation to return to reliance on general duties. For example, the provisions in respect of food safety have been strengthened by section 8 of the FSA 1990 and sundry specific rules were removed or simplified by the Food (Miscellaneous Revocations and Amendments) Regulations 1995.

Nevertheless, the amount of detailed provision in the current body of law remains formidable[1].

1 See Appendix A, which also includes feeding stuffs legislation.

1.2 THE NATURE OF COMMUNITY LAW

1.2.1 The European Community Treaty constitutes a special order of international law which has two essential and complementary features. First, the subjects of Community law are not only Member States but also individual citizens who may, if a Community provision has 'direct effect' (that is, essentially if it is unconditional and sufficiently precise) and has not been properly implemented, rely on it before a national court[1]. Secondly, in case of conflict with Member States' national law, Community law is supreme[2].

It must also be borne in mind that, even where Community provisions do not have 'direct effect', the Community principle of consistent interpretation requires national legislation, whether subsequent or precedent, to be interpreted so as to give effect to them[3]. An important example of this principle relates to the enforcement provisions in and under the FSA 1990 which are considered in chapter 17. As noted in para **17.3.1**, it is essential that these provisions be read in the light of food control Directives 89/397/EEC and 93/99/EEC.

Despite the fundamental importance of these principles, Community law has as yet required little ostensible change to the general framework of British food law in the FSA 1990. Thus, although specific provision was included in section 15 of the FSA 1990 in order to adapt it to Article 2 of the general food labelling Directive 79/112/EEC, sections 8 and 14 have evidently been regarded as wide enough as they stood to implement Article 3 of the food contaminants framework Regulation 315/93/EEC. In practice, most Community food law has to date been quite suitable for detailed implementation by regulations under the FSA 1990 or, where appropriate, under the W&MA 1985, the Consumer Protection Act 1987, Part II, the Food and Environment Protection Act 1985, Part III or the European Communities Act 1972. The lack of impact on the FSA 1990 itself may be about to change. The Commission White Paper of 12 January 2000 on Food Safety, described in section **1.8** below, is proposing a general food law Directive to establish food safety as the primary objective of European Union food law and to lay down the common principles underlying food legislation[4]. It remains to be seen how far the FSA 1990 will need to be adapted to meet this Community imperative.

Certainly, despite an unjustified reputation as the odd-man-out in Europe, the United Kingdom has loyally complied with its obligation to harmonise national food legislation with Community law and today most new food law in this country derives from Community Directives and Regulations[5].

1 Case 26/62 *NV Algemene Transport en Expeditie Onderneming Van Gend en Loos v Nederlandse Administratie der Belastingen* [1963] ECR 1. Case 126/82 *D J Smit* [1983] ECR 73, [1983] 3 CMLR 106, ECJ.
2 Case 6/64 *Costa v ENEL* [1964] ECR 585. See also on direct effect, para **1.5.2** below.
3 See case 14/83 *Von Colson and Kamann v Land Nordrhein-Westfalen* [1984] ECR 1891; and case C-106/89 *Marleasing SA v La Commercial de Alimentation SA* [1990] ECR I-4135.
4 COM (1999) 719, final paras 66–68.
5 See further section **1.5** below.

1.3 FOOD REGULATION AND THE FREE MOVEMENT OF GOODS

1.3.1 As might be expected, food is subject to the fundamental Community law principle of free movement of goods which aims at the abolition of all state commercial and tariff barriers to intra-Community trade[1]. For national food legislation the most significant aspect of this principle has been the prohibition imposed by Article 28 (ex-Article 30) EC on measures having effect equivalent to quantitative restrictions on imports from other Member States. Until the celebrated *Cassis de Dijon* judgment by the European Court of Justice (ECJ) in 1979[2], it was assumed that this prohibition was confined to measures which discriminated against such imports. The judgment made clear that the prohibition extends to any measure applying to imports and home products alike, if it restricts imports of products lawfully produced and marketed in another Member State. The measure will only escape this prohibition if it is shown to be necessary in order to satisfy a compelling public interest requirement (a 'mandatory requirement') such as the protection of public health, the fairness of commercial transactions or the defence of the consumer. To be justified on one of these grounds, the measure must be proportionate to its objective[3]. For example, the Court has taken the view that it was unnecessary for consumer protection and therefore illegal to impose a national beer standard on imports: compulsory labelling with the nature of the product would be sufficient for the purpose[4].

1 Articles 23–31 (ex-Arts 9–37) EC. The provisions of the EC Treaty were amended and renumbered by the Amsterdam Treaty. For a more general survey of EC trade law, see Lasok and Bridge *Law and Institutions of the European Union* (6th edn, 1994) ch 17.
2 Case 120/78 *Rewe-Zentral AG v Bundesmonopolverwaltung für Branntwein* [1979] ECR 649, [1979] 3 CMLR 494, ECJ.
3 Case 261/81 *Walter Rau Lebensmittelwerke v De Smedt* [1982] ECR 3961 (margarine packaging).
4 Case 178/84 *EC Commission v Germany* [1987] ECR 1227.

1.3.2 Since 1979 the *Cassis de Dijon* doctrine (which is also sometimes called the 'rule of reason' or the 'mutual recognition principle') has been well established by application in numerous ECJ cases[1]. The Member States' obligation is moreover not only confined to acceptance, in the normal way, of adequately labelled products which have been lawfully manufactured and marketed in the Community: they must likewise normally accept third country products which have been put in free circulation there[2]. As interpreted in these judgments, Article 28 (ex-Article 30) EC has significantly limited the scope for a Member State to enact its own national food compositional standards. Unless a national standard can be justified in the way described in para **1.3.1** or under the narrowly interpreted derogation in Article 30 (ex-Article 36) EC[3], the State must either exempt Community imports from the standard or forego it altogether.

The pressure exerted by the *Cassis de Dijon* doctrine was an added stimulus to deregulation in the United Kingdom and sundry national food standards were revoked by instruments such as the Food (Miscellaneous Revocations) Regulations 1991 and the Food (Miscellaneous Revocations and Amendments) Regulations 1995.

However, as we shall see in chapter 7, others survive albeit in simplified forms. In these cases it has been necessary, by a 'mutual recognition clause'[4], to exempt products from other Member States where either they are lawfully produced and marketed or, in the case of third country imports, they are in free circulation. An example of such an exemption is to be found in regulation 3(2) of the Bread and Flour Regulations 1998 which contains food standards of wholly national inspiration. Less obvious examples are in regulation 3 of the Spreadable Fats (Marketing Standards) (England) Regulations 1999 and regulation 3(1) of the Food Labelling Regulations 1996[5]. Although these instruments are mainly concerned with the implementation of Community law, both also contain national standards (see, in regulation 4 of the former, the margarine vitamin content provisions and, in regulation 42 of the latter, the national controls to prevent misleading descriptions).

As explained in para **1.9.1** below, these exemptions also take account of Article 8 of the European Economic Area Agreement, which provides for free movement between contracting States of goods originating in those States.

1 For a fuller consideration of the *Cassis de Dijon* doctrine, see Vaughan *Law of the European Communities*, Pt 12, paras 422–445: the rule of reason.
2 See Case 41/76 *Criel (née Donckerwolke)* [1976] ECR 1921. As to 'free circulation', see Art 23.2 (ex-Art 9.2) EC.
3 In particular Art 30 (ex-Art 36) EC permits 'restrictions on imports, exports or goods in transit justified on the grounds of . . . the protection of health and life of humans . . .' provided that such 'prohibitions or restrictions shall not . . . constitute a means of arbitrary discrimination or a disguised restriction on trade between Member States'.
4 See case C-184/96 *EC Commission v France* [1998] ECR 1-6197.
5 See *Hackney London Borough Council v Cedar Trading Ltd* (1999) 163 JP 749.

1.3.3 As a result of the *Cassis de Dijon* case, the Commission completely reviewed its policy on the harmonisation of foodstuffs legislation. In 1985 it presented a

Communication[1] to the Council and the European Parliament proposing that Community food legislation should henceforth be limited to the harmonisation of national rules justifiable in terms of the mandatory requirements identified by the Court. To ensure free movement of foodstuffs, reliance would otherwise be placed on the *Cassis de Dijon* doctrine with reinforcement of the labelling rules to guarantee consumer information and fair trading. In addition, the Commission encouraged the food industry to develop quality policies based on the use of voluntary instruments, such as codes of practice.

By another Communication of 1989[2], the Commission reiterated its view, in the light of the *Cassis de Dijon* doctrine, as to the rules applicable in the absence of Community provisions and as to the measures which must continue to be subject to Community legislation: it also confirmed its intention to bring forward proposals for labelling to identify specific quality products. This was supplemented in 1991 by a controversial interpretative Communication[3] giving the Commission's opinion about the conditions under which Member States of destination might impose on a product a name different from that under which it is marketed in the producing Member State[4].

The Community approach to quality promotion is further explained in para **7.4.1** below.

On 16 June 1999 the Commission published a further Communication proposing ways of improving mutual recognition in the single market. This revealed that food remains the area most affected by mutual recognition infringements.

1 Communication (COM (85) 603 final) on the completion of the internal market in the foodstuffs sector.
2 Communication (89/C271/03) on the free movement of foodstuffs within the Community.
3 Interpretative Communication (91/C270/02) on the names under which foodstuffs are sold.
4 See further para **6.5.5** (iii) below.

1.4 COMMUNITY NOTIFICATION PROCEDURES

1.4.1 Since 1 January 1989 the capacity of a Member State to make national food rules has also been restricted by measures designed to anticipate threats to the free movement of goods within the Community. An augmented procedure is now laid down by Council Directive 98/34/EC, as amended. In particular, this requires prior notification to the Commission of any draft technical regulation proposed by a Member State. Since the equivalent Community obligation in superseded Directive 83/189/EEC was held by the ECJ to be directly effective[1], it may reasonably be assumed that failure to notify a draft national food standard under Directive 98/34/EC would likewise render the resulting national legislation unenforceable against individuals.

Additionally for food, specific Community notification procedures apply to proposed national legislative initiatives in respect of labelling[2], contaminants[3] and hygiene[4].

1 Case C-194/94 *CIA Security International SA v Signalson SA* [1996] All ER (EC) 557.
2 Directive 79/112/EEC, as amended, Art 16(2).
3 Regulation 315/93/EEC, Art 5(3)(b).
4 Directive 93/43/EEC, Art 7(3).

1.5 COMMUNITY FOOD LEGISLATION

1.5.1 The Community impacts most conspicuously on national food law through its substantial body of vertical and horizontal legislation which Member States must implement in response to the general duty of loyal cooperation in Article 10 (ex-Article 5)

EC[1]. Three kinds of binding Community secondary legislative acts are prescribed by Article 249 (ex-Article 189) EC. These are the Regulation, the Directive and the Decision. The Article also specifies Recommendations and Opinions which are non-binding Community acts but may nonetheless have practical effects. The respective features of these various acts are briefly considered below.

It will be observed that in relation to food these acts are essentially made under two different Treaty powers; that is, Article 37 (ex-Article 43) EC where the subject falls within the common agricultural policy, and Article 95 (ex-Article 100a) EC in relation to internal market matters. As briefly explained in section **1.7** below, different legislative procedures apply in respect of Articles 37 and 95 EC. More important, however, for those with the sometimes difficult task of interpreting ambiguous Community texts, is the need to adopt the ECJ approach and keep in mind the context and objectives of the legislation.

1 For a list of the principal Community food and feeding stuffs law and related measures, see Appendix B.

The Regulation

1.5.2 The chief characteristic of a Community Regulation is that it is part of national law without specific incorporation: in the words of Article 249 (ex-Article 189) EC, a Regulation is 'directly applicable'. Provisions of a Regulation may also be 'directly effective' and confer rights on individuals[1]. In the United Kingdom the European Communities Act 1972 section 2(1) gives effect both to the direct applicability of Community Regulations, and to the rights conferred on individuals by directly effective Community provisions. Most Regulations concerned with food are made as part of the common agricultural policy under Article 37 (ex-Article 43) EC either immediately or via subordinate powers derived from it. This is true, for example, of marketing standards for such foods as milk and milk products, eggs, poultrymeat, fruit and vegetables, wine, olive oil and fish and provisions in respect of organic products, the protection of geographical indications and designations of origin and certificates of specific character[2].

Legislation for approximation of food law under Article 95 (ex-Article 100a) EC has so far seldom been in the form of a Regulation. However, in recent years Member States seem to have been prepared to concede a move in this direction as regards subjects like contaminants (in Regulation 315/93/EEC) and novel foods (in Regulation 258/97/EC) and the Commission is certainly eager to use Regulations in future for provisions which leave little margin of discretion to Member States in their implementation[3].

1 As to 'direct effect' generally, see para **1.2.1**.
2 As to the principal Regulations relating to these products, see sections **7.3** and **7.4** below.
3 Commission Green Paper COM (97) 176 on 'the General Principles of Food Law in the European Union', Pt III.3.

1.5.3 Although Community food Regulations are directly applicable, most of their provisions are intended to impose obligations on citizens and need to be supplemented by national law imposing penalties for non-observance and providing for enforcement. This supplementation is achieved in a variety of ways. Thus, fruit and vegetable marketing standards are enforced by special provision adapting the agricultural grading legislation in the Agriculture and Horticulture Act 1964, Part III[1]. Sometimes reliance for enforcing sanctions is temporarily placed on the pre-existing general offences in the FSA 1990 and Trade Descriptions Act 1968. Examples of this interim approach to implementation may be seen from paras **7.3.7**, **7.4.2** and **7.4.3** in relation to the poultrymeat marketing standards and provisions for the protection of geographical indications, designations of origin and certificates of specific character. For the majority of Regulations however, provision for enforcement is made without delay by bespoke subordinate legislation under the FSA 1990[3] or the European Communities Act 1972, section 2(2)[3].

1 See the Grading of Horticultural Produce (Amendment) Regulations 1973.
2 See for example the Milk and Milk Products (Protection of Designations) Regulations 1990.
3 See for example the Olive Oil (Marketing Standards) Regulations 1987.

The Directive

1.5.4 The Directive is the form which has most frequently been employed by the Community for the harmonisation of national food law. From the Member States' point of view it is more flexible than the Regulation since, although binding on national authorities as to the result to be achieved, it leaves to them the choice of form and methods. Moreover, until the Single European Act added Article 95 (ex-Article 100a) to the EC Treaty, it was, under Article 94 (ex-Article 100), the only kind of measure that could be taken specifically for the approximation of laws.

Although Directives under Article 37 (ex-Article 43) EC have been made as part of the common agricultural policy on subjects such as pesticide and veterinary medicine residues and on hygiene of products of animal origin, they have mainly been used for internal market food legislation under the powers in Article 95 (ex-Article 100a). They have covered a wide range of matters including labelling and advertising, additives, specific product categories, residues in food, enforcement and product liability.

1.5.5 A time limit is normally laid down in a Directive within which it must be implemented by Member States. Provisions of Directives will often be directly effective[1]. Those which create rights and obligations for individuals must be incorporated into national law with the precision and clarity necessary in order to satisfy fully the requirement of legal certainty[2]. In Great Britain, provisions of food Directives are transposed into national law by subordinate legislation under the FSA 1990 or other statutes cited in para **1.2.1**.

1 See, for example, case 8/81 *Becker v Finanzamt Münster-Innenstadt* [1982] ECR 53. As to 'direct effect' generally, see para **1.2.1**.
2 Case C-131/88 *EC Commission v Germany* [1991] ECR I-825.

The Decision

1.5.6 A Decision is binding in its entirety on those to whom it is addressed. Decisions addressed to Member States may, like Directives, be directly effective and require implementation[1]. As will be seen in chapter 13, Decisions are used to impose health conditions on the import of products of animal origin, specific examples being the Decisions on animal health and certification, approved establishments and non-importation implemented by the Fresh Meat (Import Conditions) Regulations 1996 and described in para **13.2.2**.

1 Case 9/70 *Franz Grad v Traunstein* [1970] ECR 825. As to 'direct effect' generally, see para **1.2.1** above.

The Recommendation, the Opinion and other non-binding acts

1.5.7 Other Community acts may have practical effects even though they do not impose formal legal obligations[1]. Article 249 (ex-Article 189) EC provides specifically that 'recommendations and opinions shall have no binding force', but national courts may have to take into consideration a recommendation which is capable of clarifying the interpretation of national or Community law[2]. Moreover, a veterinary expert's opinion under Article 10 of Directive 71/118/EEC as to whether imported meat is unfit for human consumption was held to represent an important factor to be taken into account by national authorities or courts before which proceedings may be brought[3].

A particular influence on Member States' food law has been exercised by Commission Communications described in para **1.3.3** above relating to the completion of the internal market in implementation of the *Cassis de Dijon* judgment. Following that decision, the Commission confined harmonisation to those national rules which were justifiable on the public interest grounds identified by the ECJ and took action in the Court against those rules which in its view were not.

1 Joined cases 98 and 99/75 *Carstens Keramik v Oberfinanzdirektion* [1976] ECR 241.
2 Case 322/88 *Grimaldi v Fonds des Maladies Professionelles* [1989] ECR 4407.
3 Case C-332/88 *Alimenta v Doux* [1990] ECR I-2077.
4 Under Article 226 (ex-Article 169) EC, see para **1.6.2**.

1.6 ENFORCEMENT OF COMMUNITY LAW

1.6.1 ECJ judgments to enforce Community law against Member States may be obtained both through actions by the Commission or other Member States and through proceedings begun in national courts by individuals.

Infraction proceedings

1.6.2 The EC Treaty enables the Commission under Article 226 (ex-Article 169) EC, or another Member State under Article 227 (ex-Article 170) EC, to bring infraction proceedings against a Member State for failure to fulfil a Community law obligation. Proceedings by Member States are rare, but the Commission has proved itself to be both diligent and generally successful in pursuing infractions. Article 226 proceedings in relation to food seem to have been provoked less by Member States' failure to implement Community rules than by their obstruction of the free movement of goods, as described in para **1.3.1** above. Under what is now Article 226, notable ECJ decisions striking down national import restrictions have related to UHT milk[1], poultrymeat[2], wine vinegar[3], beer[4] and bearnaise sauce[5].

1 Case 124/81 *EC Commission v United Kingdom* [1983] ECR 203.
2 Case 40/82 *EC Commission v United Kingdom* [1984] ECR 283.
3 Case 193/80 *EC Commission v Italy* [1981] ECR 3019.
4 Case 178/84 *EC Commission v Germany* [1987] ECR 1227.
5 Case C-51/94 *EC Commission v Germany* [1995] ECR I-3599.

1.6.3 In the event of an adverse infraction ruling by the European Court, Article 228 (ex-Article 171) EC has always required the defaulting State to take the necessary steps to comply with the judgment[1] and, since the Maastricht Treaty[2], has laid it open to the possibility of a financial penalty imposed by the ECJ.

1 See, for example, Case 281/83 *EC Commission v Italy* [1985] ECR 3397 (wine vinegar).
2 TEU Article G(E)(51).

Preliminary rulings

1.6.4 Proceedings begun by individuals in national courts have been an alternative means of enforcing Community law which has direct effect, ever since the ECJ expounded that principle in 1963[1]. The national court or tribunal may under Article 234 (ex-Article 177) EC refer the Community law issues to the ECJ for interpretation and must do so where there is no judicial remedy against its decision under national law. Through Article 234 references, successful challenges have been mounted against the defective implementation of various Community provisions related to food. Particular examples have concerned the use of preservatives and antioxidants[2] and the labelling of deep frozen yoghurt[3] and artificial sweeteners[4]. However, as with Article 226 actions by the Commission, the most significant ECJ decisions resulting from Article 234 references have related to Member States' national laws which hindered free trade. Among the many examples of foods that have formed the subject of such proceedings are the low alcohol blackcurrant liqueur 'Cassis de Dijon' (in the leading case noted in para **1.3.1** above), wine vinegar[5] and pasta products[6].

Sometimes a Member State's dubious import restriction has been attacked in the ECJ through a 'pincer movement' which involves both an Article 226 action by the Commission and an Article 234 reference resulting from proceedings by disgruntled traders in the national court. For example, an Italian minimum fat standard for cheese imposed on imports from other Member States was declared illegal by the ECJ on 11 October 1990 not only in infraction proceedings by the Commission, but also in a reference from the Pretore di Milano[7].

1 See para **1.2.1** text and n 1.
2 Case 88/79 *Ministére Public v Grunert* [1980] ECR 1827.
3 Case 298/87 *Smanor* [1988] ECR 4489.
4 Case C-241/89 *SARPP v Chambre Syndical des Raffineurs et Conditionneurs de Sucre de France* [1990] ECR I-4695.
5 Case 788/79 *Gilli and Andres* [1980] ECR 2071.
6 Case 407/85 *Drei Glocken* [1988] ECR 4233.
7 See respectively case C-210/89 *EC Commission v Italy* [1990] ECR I-3697 and case C-196/89 *Italy v Nespoli and Crippa* [1990] ECR I-3647.

1.6.5 Since 1991 the scope for individuals to take action in national courts has been extended by the ECJ's decision that compensation can in principle be obtained from a Member State for damage caused by breach of Community law whether or not the provision in question is directly effective[1]. Compensation may, in particular, be awarded for failure to implement a Directive[2] and for obstructing the free movement of goods[3]. The conditions for reparation are (i) that the rule of law infringed must have been intended to confer rights on individuals; (ii) that the breach must be sufficiently serious; and (iii) that there must be a direct causal link between the breach of the obligation resting on the State and the damage sustained by the injured parties[4].

This Community law based remedy is additional to an English law action for misfeasance in a public office which would lie where, in an exceptional case, the breach of Community law was found to be a deliberate abuse of power. Such an action was brought by French turkey importers to reclaim damages suffered as a result of a UK poultrymeat import ban[5]. As indicated in para **1.6.2** above, the ban had been declared illegal in case 40/82.

1 As to 'direct effect' generally, see para **1.2.1**.
2 Joined cases C-6 and 9/90 *Francovich v Italy* [1991] ECR I-5357.
3 Case C-5/94 *R v Ministry of Agriculture, Fisheries and Food, ex p Hedley Lomas* [1996] ECR I-2553.
4 Joined cases C-178/94, C179/94 and C-188/94 to C-190/94 *Dillenkofer v Germany* [1996] ECR I-4845.
5 *Bourgoin SA v Minister of Agriculture, Fisheries and Food* [1986] QB 716.

1.7 THE MAKING OF COMMUNITY SECONDARY LEGISLATION ON FOOD

1.7.1 Community legislative procedures are complex and it will suffice to highlight the main features of those which normally apply in respect of food. In addition to the co-decision and the consultation procedures briefly considered below, the principal law-making processes include the co-operation procedure which is now specified in Article 252 (ex-Article 189c) EC and which formerly applied to Article 95 (ex-Article 100a) EC. For a fuller description of all the legislative processes, the reader is referred to Lasok and Bridge *Law and Institutions of the European Union* (6th edn, 1994), chapters 7 and 8.

1.7.2 The Council, the European Parliament and the Commission are all involved in EC law-making. The process is initiated by proposals for draft legislation formulated by the Commission through working groups made up of nominees from national governments.

The co-decision procedure

1.7.3 As indicated in para **1.5.4** above, the principal Community food legislative measures are made under Article 95 (ex-Article 100a) EC. For this power, the legislative procedure prescribed by the Maastricht Treaty[1] is specified in Article 251 (ex-Article 189b) EC. It is commonly known as the co-decision or joint legislative procedure because it aims at legislation adopted jointly by the Parliament and the Council. A Conciliation Committee of the two institutions is convened if agreement is not otherwise reached.

1 TEU, Art G(E)(61).

The consultation procedure

1.7.4 Paragraphs **1.5.2** and **1.5.4** above noted that food legislation is also made as part of the common agricultural policy under Article 37 (ex-Article 43) EC. In this case what is sometimes called the consultation or basic procedure applies. Dating back to the Treaty of Rome, this confers on the Council the power to make the legislation. The European Parliament is entitled only to be consulted before the decision is taken.

The Commission's delegated powers

1.7.5 Whether made under Article 95 or 37 EC, food legislation often delegates to the Commission power to make detailed measures. These are subjected to a prescribed procedure requiring their submission to a committee of officials from Member States.

The current rules are in 'Comitology' Decision 99/468/EC. Leaving aside special provision in relation to the taking of safeguard measures, the Decision continues to prescribe three basic procedures for the exercise of implementing powers by the Commission. In ascending order of the restrictions placed on Commission freedom of action, they are the advisory procedure, the management procedure and the regulatory procedure. In the foodstuffs sector proper, the Council has systematically imposed the regulatory procedure which requires a favourable opinion from a qualified majority[1] of the committee before the Commission can take a decision. In common agricultural policy legislation prescribing marketing standards, the Council has resorted to the management procedure whereby the Commission's decision may be overruled by the Council unless it follows the committee's opinion.

In simplifying the options and conferring functions on the European Parliament, Decision 99/468/EC confirmed that the existing approach should continue in future legislation. The regulatory procedure is to be followed as regards measures of general scope designed to apply essential provisions of basic instruments, including measures concerning the protection of the health or safety of humans, animals or plants. The management procedure should be followed as regards management measures relating to the application of the common agricultural policy.

While acknowledging Decision 99/468/EC, in its White Paper on Food Safety[2] the Commission has advocated the streamlining and simplification of the procedures laid down by Community food legislation in order to ensure efficacy, transparency and rapidity.

1 See the Commission Green Paper COM (97) 176 on 'the General Principles of Food Law in the European Union', Pt III 4. The vote weighting and numbers for adoption of measures by qualified majority are specified in Art 205(2) (ex-Art 148(2)) EC.
2 COM (1999) 719 final, paras 81–84. See further para **1.8.1** below.

Draft Community legislation

1.7.6 Although the Secretary of State and devolved authorities are required by section 48(4) to consult before making regulations under the FSA 1990, there is no statutory consultation duty in relation to proposed Community legislation. In practice, UK Government departments are generally diligent in issuing to consumer, enforcement and trade interests detailed consultative papers on proposals received for new Community food legislation.

When submitting views on these proposals to government, interested parties must keep in mind that they are dealing with the negotiators, not with the legislators. Ministers and officials have proved themselves willing and able to comprehend the views put to them and skilful in taking account of those views in Brussels.

Most sectors of the food industry and consumer interests have also established trade representative offices close to the Commission in order to argue the case for their members directly.

1.8 FUTURE COMMUNITY DEVELOPMENTS

1.8.1 On 12 January 2000 the Commission published radical and far-reaching plans in a White Paper on Food Safety[1]. The main proposal is for the establishment by 2002 of an independent European Food Agency with the tasks of risk assessment through scientific advice to Community legislators, of gathering and analysing information, of informing consumers and of running a rapid alert system to deal with crises. If this proposed Agency is to prevent the kind of dispute that has arisen between national agencies over implementation of Community law on UK beef exports[2], it will need rapidly to establish the independence and scientific pre-eminence that the White Paper envisages.

An action plan is included in the White Paper to improve food safety legislation. At its core is to be a general food law embodying food safety principles relating to the responsibilities of feed manufacturers, farmers and food operators; traceability; risk analysis; and, where appropriate, the precautionary principle. The White Paper is complemented by a Commission Communication of 2 February 2000 setting out guidelines on the use of the precautionary principle[3].

The White Paper also contemplates that all parts of the feed and food supply chain are to be subject to official control run by national authorities.

1 COM (1999) 719 final.
2 See para **13.8.5** below.
3 COM (2000) 1 final.

1.9 THE EUROPEAN ECONOMIC AREA

1.9.1 The European Economic Area Agreement is a treaty between the 15 Member States of the European Community and Norway, Iceland and Liechtenstein, which is basically implemented in the United Kingdom by the European Economic Area Act 1993.

The EEA Agreement is of concern to food law because, as between contracting States, it provides for the application of the EC Treaty and secondary legislation rules on the free movement of goods. By contrast with Community law, however, the freedom of trade established by Article 8(1) of the Agreement is generally limited to products originating in the contracting States: by virtue of Article 8(2), it does not extend to products from third countries unless otherwise specified. Moreover, the EEA Agreement did not adopt the common agricultural policy.

The products covered by the EEA Agreement are principally specified in Article 8(3). Agricultural products (including prepared foodstuffs) are not generally caught, but some are specified in Protocol 3 to the Agreement and a substantial group of food products is brought in through EEA adoption of Community harmonising provisions by Article 23 and Annex II, Part XII.

Within its limits, the EEA closely shadows the European Community. The Agreement adopted pertinent rulings of the European Court, EFTA countries are consulted on relevant proposals for Community legislation and, when this has been enacted, the EEA Joint Committee implements parallel EEA rules. The EFTA Surveillance Authority and EFTA Court have functions akin to those of the European Commission and the European Court.

Two specific implications of the EEA Agreement for national food Regulations might usefully be mentioned. First, the *Cassis de Dijon* doctrine described in section **1.3** above applies with the result that the scope for national imports controls on food originating in the EEA contracting States is limited. Secondly, the food control Directive 89/397/EEC, considered in section **17.2** below, is specifically covered by the EEA Agreement, Annex II, Part II, paragraph 50. In consequence, products intended for consignment to contracting States must be inspected with the same care as those intended for marketing in the United Kingdom.

1.10 THE INTERNATIONAL DIMENSION

The Community and international organisations

1.10.1 Chapter 8 of the recent Commission White Paper on Food Safety[1] notes that the international framework as regards food safety has developed significantly through the enhanced role of international organisations such as the Codex Alimentarius and the International Office of Epizootics (OIE) under the World Trade Organisation Agreement on the Application of Sanitary and Phytosanitary Measures (the SPS Agreement), the World Health Organisation (WHO) and the Food and Agriculture Organisation (FAO). The Community plays an active role in the SPS Committee and is eager to accede to Codex Alimentarius and OIE in which, although the Member States participate, it has only observer status. Codex Alimentarius is explained in the following paragraph: OIE is concerned with study and research into diseases of cattle.

1 COM (1999) 719 final.

The Codex Alimentarius Commission

1.10.2 The Codex Alimentarius Commission was jointly set up in 1962 by the FAO and WHO to protect the health of consumers, to ensure fair practices in the food trade and to draw up international food standards. It now has a membership of 165 countries. The Codex Alimentarius Commission is supported by a series of committees which have developed a significant number of vertical and horizontal food standards. Although not binding on member countries, a considerable influence has in practice been exercised over national and Community law by provisions such as the Codex Standard for the labelling of prepackaged food[1] and the Codex Guidelines for Nutrition Claims[2].

1 See Codex STAN-1985 (Rev 1-1991).
2 See Codex CAC/GL 23-1997 and para **8.5.3** below.

1.11 SOURCES OF INFORMATION

1.11.1 For busy practitioners, the problem often is to be able check quickly the latest developments on a particular aspect of food law. A list of useful addresses and numbers is to be found in Appendix C.

Chapter 2

Central and local government control of food

2.1 FOOD STANDARDS ACT 1999 AND DEVOLUTION

2.1.1 Responsibility for administration of food law was essentially laid down when modern legislation began to be enacted in the second half of the nineteenth century[1]. Prior to the Food Standards Act 1999 (FSA 1999) and recent devolution changes, central government responsibilities for policy and legislation were primarily borne by the Minister of Agriculture, Fisheries and Food, who took the lead on food composition and chemical safety, and by the Secretary of State for Health, who led on hygiene and biological safety except in respect of the hygiene of meat, milk, eggs and egg products which were perceived to fit most readily with the minister's agricultural responsibilities. The Scottish and Welsh Secretaries also shared responsibility under the Food Safety Act 1990 (FSA 1990). The bulk of enforcement work was in the hands of county councils and district councils where the division between the composition and the hygiene of food was reflected in the respective responsibilities of their trading standards officers and environmental health officers.

A decade of food problems, and above all the BSE/CJD crisis, had eroded public confidence in this structure. Three main weaknesses in it were identified by the James Report of 30 April 1997. They were—

(1) the conflict between the functions of the Minister of Agriculture, Fisheries and Food under the food legislation and his promotional responsibilities for the agricultural, fishing and food industries;
(2) the fragmentation and lack of coordination between the different bodies involved in food policy and in the monitoring and control of food safety; and
(3) the uneven enforcement of food law.

As a solution, the Report proposed a Food Standards Agency, which was fully established on 1 April 2000 by the FSA 1999[2]. This chapter explains the FSA 1999 and devolution legislation as it relates to food and feeding stuffs. In summary, the Agency is responsible for the development of United Kingdom food policy to the Secretary of State for Health and devolved authorities, who have taken over food functions from the Minister of Agriculture, Fisheries and Food. The Agency is however, a non-ministerial government department with the important power to make public the advice it has given to the Secretary of State and others. It is able to survey the full range of activities connected with the production and supply of food and feeding stuffs, to sponsor necessary regulations and to set standards for, and monitor the performance of, local authority food law enforcement. A number of other public bodies inevitably remain involved in food matters and enforcement, but in the Agency there is at last a central department dedicated to and capable of safeguarding public health and protecting consumer interests in relation to food and feeding stuffs.

The Food Standards Act 1999 (Transitional and Consequential Provisions and Savings) (England and Wales) Regulations 2000 transfer to the Agency former enforcement functions under meat hygiene and other secondary legislation of the Minister of Agriculture, Fisheries and Food. Other provisions (a) save the minister's power under the 1990 Act to join with the Health Secretary in regulating veterinary residues in food and related inspection charges (see further para **2.1.2**); and (b) enable the Heath Secretary with or without the minister to regulate feeding stuffs under the Agriculture Act 1970 (AA 1970), Part IV (see further para **2.2.3**).

1 See para **1.1.3**.
2 Food Standards Act 1999 (Commencement No 1) Order 2000; and Food Standards Act 1999 (Commencement No 2) Order 2000.

2.1.2 The establishment of the Scottish Parliament and the National Assembly for Wales has also had significant effects on central government food and feeding stuffs control.

Since Scotland has a jurisdiction separate from that in England and Wales, the law there falls outside the scope of this book. It should, however, be observed that among the subjects included in the general devolution to the Scottish Parliament by the Scotland Act 1998 (SA 1998) are food, food contact materials, feeding stuffs and agricultural and horticultural produce[1]. On the other hand, consumer protection, product standards, safety and liability and weights and measures are generally reserved matters[2] and outside legislative and devolved competence[3].

In Wales, the National Assembly has inherited ministerial food and feeding stuffs and other agricultural functions, including the power to make to make secondary legislation. Ministerial functions exercisable under specified enactments are devolved by the National Assembly for Wales (Transfer of Functions) Order 1999, SI 1999/672, made under the Government of Wales Act 1998 (GWA 1998)[4]. The long list of functions thus transferred to the Assembly include in particular, and subject to minor exceptions, not only those under the FSA 1990, but also those under the AA 1970, the Food and Environment Protection Act 1985, Part I, the Agriculture and Horticulture Act 1964, the Animal Health Act 1981 and the Eggs (Marketing Standards) Regulations 1995[5]. So that the SA 1998 and the National Assembly for Wales (Transfer of Functions) Order 1999 take account of changes made in other legislation by the Food Standards Act 1999, these changes are treated as having preceded the devolution provisions[6].

Certain further points should be noted about legislative responsibilities in respect of Wales. First, subordinate legislative powers transferred to the Welsh Assembly continue to be exercisable by the transferor minister for the purpose of implementing Community obligations or dealing with matters arising out of or related to them[7]. This continuing power in relation to Wales was, for example, invoked by the Minister of Agriculture, Fisheries and Food in making the Food (Animal Products from Belgium) (Emergency Control) (England and Wales) Order 1999 referred to in para **11.6.4** below.

Secondly, the Transfer of Functions (Agriculture and Food) Order 1999, SI 1999/3141, assigns to the Minister of Agriculture, Fisheries and Food and the Health Secretary functions under the FSA 1990, which were formerly exercisable by the minister, the Health Secretary and Welsh Secretary. The prime example of such a function is the power to regulate veterinary residues in food and related inspection charges considered further in para **2.2.5** below. Paragraph **2.1.1** above noted that this joint power is saved by the Food Standards Act 1999 (Transitional and Consequential Provisions and Savings) (England and Wales) Regulations 2000.

Thirdly, section 29 of the GWA 1998 makes provision to enable the Assembly, like Ministers of the Crown, to be designated to exercise the power conferred by section 2(2) of the European Communities Act 1972 (ECA 1972) to make regulations to implement Community law. Subject to specified restrictions and conditions, the Assembly has been designated by the European Communities (Designation) (No 3) Order 1999, SI 1999/2788, in relation to measures relating to the common agricultural policy of the European Community, except measures concerning feeding stuffs containing medicinal products (including growth regulators) or medicinal products when destined for use in feeding stuffs. As a result, the Assembly will, for example, have the full range of powers to implement, in respect of Wales, Community common agricultural policy food standards of the kind described in para **2.2.7** and section **7.3** below.

1 SA 1998, ss 29 and 53 and Sch 5, s C8.
2 SA 1998, s 30 and Sch 5, ss C7, C8 and C9. There seem to be some anomalies: for example, trade descriptions and misleading and comparative advertising specifically in relation to feeding stuffs are evidently reserved matters.
3 SA 1998, ss 29 and 54.
4 GWA 1998, s 22.
5 As to the relevance of these statutes in the present context, see below respectively at section **16.2**; section **11.7**; paras **7.3.18** and **7.3.19**; paras **16.9.2** and **16.9.3**; and para **7.3.6**.
6 See FSA 1999, ss 18(2) and 40(2) and (3).
7 GWA 1998, s 22(5) and Sch 3, Pt II, para 5. For the kindred power in relation to Scotland, see SA 1998, s 57.

2.1.3 The Food Standards Agency thus reports to the Secretary of State for Health and his counterparts in the devolved administrations, but operates at arm's length from them in developing policy and in carrying out its other other functions. In consequence, there is a rather complex network of central government responsibilities, the main elements of which are described in sections **2.2** and **2.3** below. The Agency will need to work closely with the Department of Health, the Ministry of Agriculture, Fisheries and Food and equivalent authorities in Scotland, Wales and Northern Ireland. To facilitate 'joined up government', the reciprocal administrative relationships and respective responsibilities are to be recorded in 'administrative concordats'[1]. Each concordat will set out an overview of the agreed operational and policy responsibilities of the Agency and the other relevant organisations and specify how they will relate to each other on particular issues. The concordats are, however, non-statutory documents and cannot override the duties and powers of the Agency. In accordance with the modern policy of open government, the concordats will be publicly available.

1 See para 22 of the Reply by the Government to the Report from the Food Standards Committee, Session 1998–99, 'Food Standards Draft Bill' (HC 276).

2.2 MINISTERIAL RESPONSIBILITIES

The Secretary of State for Health and the Food Safety Act 1990

2.2.1 If the complexities of devolution are discounted, ministerial responsibility under the FSA 1990 has generally been simplified by the FSA 1999. By section 26(1)(b) of the FSA 1999, functions under the FSA 1990 have generally ceased to be exercisable by the

Minister of Agriculture, Fisheries and Food: and through a series of detailed amendments set out in Schedules 3 and 5, his former responsibilities have essentially passed to the Secretary of State for Health.

The powers of the Secretary of State under the FSA 1990 thus amended are set out in Appendix D. In particular, it is the Secretary of State and the devolved authorities, not the Food Standards Agency, who have the power to make regulations under the FSA 1990. Although the protection of public health is paramount, political judgments on legislation must take account of economic and other factors beyond the Agency's remit. However, as indicated in para **2.3.2***(a)* below, the Agency will be the primary source of policy advice on food safety and standards and will, in particular, draft necessary subordinate legislation. Moreover, the Government will not be able to brush aside Agency recommendations. Using the power explained in para **2.3.6***(d)* below, the Agency can publish its advice to ministers who in consequence will have to justify publicly any decision to reject it.

The Secretary of State for Health and other primary legislation

2.2.2 The FSA 1999 transfers other functions related to food from the Minister of Agriculture, Fisheries and Food to the Secretary of State for Health. Paragraph 4 of Schedule 5 to the 1999 Act amends the Trade Descriptions Act 1968 (TDA 1968) so that orders made under the latter Act concerning food or feeding stuffs are henceforth to be made jointly by the Health Secretary with the President of the Board of Trade[1].

More important, however, are functions in respect of making emergency orders under Part I of the Food and Environment Protection Act 1985 (F&EPA 1985)[2]. The enabling powers in section 1 have already been amended by the Scotland Act 1998 (Modification of Functions) Order 1999, SI 1999/1756, so that the Secretary of State for Scotland acts in relation to Scotland and the sea within British fishery limits adjacent to Scotland[3]. In relation to England, now the FSA 1999 is fully in force, the 1985 Act Part I functions, by virtue of section 26(1)(a), have ceased to be exercisable by the Minister of Agriculture, Fisheries and Food and have been conferred, by Schedule 5, paragraph 6, on the Secretary of State. In addition to being able to make emergency orders[4], the Secretary of State has power, shared with the Food Safety Agency, to consent to the doing of things which would otherwise contravene an emergency order and to give directions in relation to an emergency order[5], as well as power to confer authority on investigation and enforcement officers[6]. In relation to Wales, the functions under the 1985 Act, Part I, are transferred to the National Assembly but those under section 1(1) and section 3(1) and (2) are exercisable concurrently with the Secretary of State[7].

1 TDA 1968, s 38(2A).
2 As to emergency orders under the F&EPA 1985, Pt I, see further section **11.7** below.
3 See the definition of 'Scottish zone' in section 126(1) of the Scotland Act 1998.
4 F&EPA 1985, s 1.
5 F&EPA 1985, s 2.
6 F&EPA 1985, s 3.
7 See the National Assembly for Wales (Transfer of Functions) Order 1999, SI 1996/672, art 2(a) and (b) and Sch 1.

The Minister of Agriculture, Fisheries and Food and feeding stuffs

2.2.3 Special provisions apply in relation to the responsibilities for the composition and labelling of feeding stuffs under Part IV of the AA 1970. In Scotland and Wales[1] the subject is a devolved matter: in England it is passing through a transitional phase. Although the Minister of Agriculture, Fisheries and Food retains powers to make regulations under Part IV, the relevant administrative unit has transferred from his department to the Food Standards Agency. Moreover, for England and Wales the Secretary of State and the minister are expected in the near future to exercise the further powers, conferred by section 30 of the FSA 1999 and described in para **2.3.8***(e)* below, to establish by order provisions for the regulation of feeding stuffs based on the FSA 1990. In the meantime, regulation 14 of the Food Standards Act 1999 (Transitional and Consequential Provisions and Savings) (England and Wales) Regulations 2000 confers power on the Secretary of State for Health to make regulations under Part IV of the AA 1970 jointly with or instead of the minister.

The powers of the Secretary of State will evidently be further strengthened in relation to the control of feeding stuffs because, as described in para **4.1.4** below, Schedule 5, paragraph 23 of the FSA 1999 extends the regulatory powers of the FSA 1990 to cover the production of food sources.

The Minister of Agriculture, Fisheries and Food will retain lead responsibility for feeding stuffs matters of a veterinary nature mentioned in paras **2.2.4** and **2.2.5**.

1 See the National Assembly for Wales (Transfer of Functions) Order 1999, Sch 1. See also the SA 1998, ss 29 and 53 and Sch 5, s C8.

The Minister of Agriculture, Fisheries and Food and zoonoses

2.2.4 In view of the veterinary expertise and responsibilities of his department, the Minister of Agriculture, Fisheries and Food, with the devolved authorities[1], retains primary responsibility under the Animal Health Act 1981 (AHA 1981) in respect of reducing the risk to human health from any disease of animals or organism carried in them, such as salmonella[2]. Probably the most significant measures of this kind have been orders under the AHA 1981 to combat bovine spongiform encephalopathy[3], such as the Bovine Spongiform Encephalopathy (No 2) Order 1996, as amended, and the Specified Risk Material Order 1997[4].

The Food Standards Agency and the ministry will co-operate closely on feeding stuffs matters affecting human and animal health and arrangements will be put in place to ensure that they do 'not' duplicate work in this area. The arrangements for sharing information on food-borne zoonoses are explained in para **2.3.8***(c)*.

1 See the National Assembly for Wales (Transfer of Functions) Order 1999, Sch 1. See also the SA 1998, ss 29 and 53.
2 See AHA 1981, s 29 and SI 1989/285.
3 See AHA 1981, s 29 and SI 1988/2264, as amended.
4 Paragraphs **16.9.2** and **16.9.3** respectively below. See further as to BSE, section **13.8** below.

The Minister of Agriculture, Fisheries and Food and veterinary residues, zootechnical products and medicated feeding stuffs

2.2.5 Through his executive agency, the Veterinary Medicines Directorate, the Minister of Agriculture, Fisheries and Food continues to play a key role in the control of veterinary products which is not a devolved matter[1]. The FSA 1999 provides for the Food Standards Agency to be consulted on subordinate legislation under the Medicines Act 1968 and on general policy[2]. Veterinary residues in food[3] are controlled under the FSA 1990, responsibility for which is devolved as explained in paras **2.1.2** and **2.2.1** above.

In England, the Minister will evidently continue to join with the Secretary of State for Health in making regulations on veterinary residues and related inspection charges under the FSA 1990 notwithstanding that in general the Minister's access to the 1990 Act has been ended by section 26(1)(b) of the 1999 Act[4]. Paragraph **2.1.2** above noted that he acquired this power through the Transfer of Functions (Agriculture and Food) Order 1999. Paragraph **2.1.1** noted that the power is saved through the Food Standards Act 1999 (Transitional and Consequential Provisions and Savings) (England and Wales) Regulations 2000.

The Minister's Veterinary Medicines Directorate also continues to take the lead responsibility for zootechnical products and medicated feeding stuffs described in sections **16.6** and **16.8** below.

1 See the National Assembly for Wales (Transfer of Functions) Order 1999 SI 1999/672. See also the SA 1998, Sch 5, section J4.
2 See respectively **2.3.6***(c)(i)* and **2.3.8***(d)* below.
3 As to veterinary residues, see section **10.8** below.
4 See paras **2.2.1** above and **2.3.8***(a)* below.

The Minister of Agriculture, Fisheries and Food and pesticide residues

2.2.6 Pesticides and pesticide residues[1] are controlled under Part III of the F&EPA 1985 in respect of which the Minister of Agriculture, Fisheries and Food (through his executive agency, the Pesticides Safety Directorate) continues to have a central responsibility. Under the 1985 Act, regulations on pesticide residues in food and feeding stuffs are made jointly in England by the Minister and the Secretary of State and in Wales by the Minister and the National Assembly[2], while in Scotland the function is wholly devolved[3].

The 1985 Act has been amended by the FSA 1999 to provide, in particular, for the Food Standards Agency to be consulted about regulations and about the general approach to the giving, revocation or suspension of approvals and the imposition of conditions on approvals[4].

1 As to pesticide residues, see section **10.7** below.
2 See the National Assembly for Wales (Transfer of Functions) Order 1999, SI 1999/672, Sch 1.
3 See the Scotland Act 1998, ss 29 and 53 and Sch 5 section C8.
4 See section **2.3.6***(c)(ii)* below.

The Minister of Agriculture, Fisheries and Food and CAP food standards

2.2.7 Yet another class of legislation for which distinct responsibilities should be noted is comprised of those European Community Regulations that, as part of the common agricultural policy (CAP), prescribe marketing standards or quality marks[1]. Given the framework in which this legislation is made, the Minister of Agriculture, Fisheries and Food retains primary responsibility, in conjunction (since agriculture is a devolved matter[2]) with authorities in Scotland and Wales and Northern Ireland. It appears that pragmatic arrangements are to be applied so that functions such as inspecting fruit, vegetables and bananas to ensure compliance with marketing standards[3], liaising with the Commission over the registration of protected food names[4] and supporting the United Kingdom Register of Organic Food Standards[5] will continue to be carried out by ministry staff on behalf of responsible authorities outside England.

The Food Standards Agency manifestly has a direct interest in CAP food standards legislation by virtue of its consumer protection objective[6]. Before removal of the functions of the Minister of Agriculture, Fisheries and Food under the FSA 1990, the bespoke subordinate legislative powers of the Act[7] were often used to implement CAP marketing standards Regulations[8]. Now that those powers rest with the Health Secretary it remains to be seen how far this practice will continue.

1 See respectively sections **7.3** and **7.4** below.
2 See SA 1998, ss 29 and 53 and Sch 5, s C8; and National Assembly for Wales (Transfer of Functions) Order 1999, Sch 1.
3 See paras **7.3.18** and **7.3.19** below. The MAFF Horticultural Marketing Inspectorate acts in England and Wales.
4 See paras **7.4.2** and **7.4.3** below.
5 See para **7.4.4** below.
6 FSA 1999, s 1(2).
7 FSA 1990, s 17(2).
8 See section **7.3** below.

2.3 THE FOOD STANDARDS AGENCY

Constitution of the Agency

2.3.1 The Food Standards Agency is a Crown department established by the FSA 1999 for the purposes of carrying out the specific functions conferred by or under the Act[1]. The way in which these functions will be carried out is limited by subsequent requirements in the Act, particularly sections 22 and 23 which relate to the Agency's general objectives[2].

The Agency's main objective in carrying out its functions is to protect public health from risks which may arise in connection with the consumption of food (including risks caused by the way in which it is produced or supplied) and otherwise to protect the interests of consumers in relation to food[3]. Consonant with the scope of the FSA 1990, the Agency is thus concerned with protecting the public not only from unhealthy food, but also from fraudulent food trading.

The Agency consists of a chairman and deputy chairman and not less than eight or more than twelve other members of whom—

- one member is appointed by the National Assembly of Wales[4];
- two members are appointed by the Scottish Ministers[5];
- one member is appointed by the Department of Health and Social Services for Northern Ireland[6]; and
- the others are appointed by the Secretary of State (in practice, the Secretary of State for Health)[7].

Defined as 'the appropriate authorities' by section 36(1) of the FSA 1999, these authorities also jointly appoint the chairman and deputy chairman and must consult before appointing other members of the Agency[8].

Particular considerations are specified which the authorities are required to take into account before making appointments[9]. They must have regard to the desirability of securing that a variety of skills and experience is available among the Agency's members (including experience in matters related to food safety or other interests of consumers in relation to food). They must also consider whether prospective appointees have financial or other interests which are likely to prejudice the exercise of their duties. Such interests will not automatically disqualify a person from appointment as a member. Under paragraph 9 of Schedule 1, the Agency is obliged to establish a register of private interests and, although not specifically required by the Act, the Agency's procedural rules are expected to prevent members from participating in discussion of matters in which they have such interests.

The Agency is a body corporate, detailed provision being made by FSA 1999, section 2(4) and Schedule 1 for tenure, remuneration and parliamentary disqualification of members, for the appointment of staff, for proceedings and execution of documents, and for delegation of powers. Paragraph 12(2) of Schedule 1 preserves the rule in *Carltona Ltd v Works Comr*[10] whereby officials of central government may exercise the powers of their minister or Agency without formal delegation of authority.

Provision is also made for appointment of a chief executive and Directors for Wales, Scotland and Northern Ireland, who are responsible for securing that the Agency is run efficiently and effectively within their own respective remits[11].

Three main groups make up the Agency's headquarters in London. They are the Food Safety Policy Group; the Enforcement and Food Standards Group; and the Corporate Resources and Strategy Group. Scottish, Welsh and Northern Irish Executives have been established to develop and implement policies on food issues that are specific to each country, within the framework set by the Agency as a whole. They provide support to their respective Parliaments, Assemblies and Ministers on the Agency's local activities, and prepare legislation, modified to meet local needs, as required to implement the Agency's policies. The Agency is accountable to the relevant devolved legislatures for its activities within and for their geographical areas. The other main element of the Agency is its Meat Hygiene Service (MHS). As explained more fully in para **13.1.4** below, the MHS's main function is to provide an inspection service in respect of all licensed meat plants.

The Agency's annual report must be laid before Parliament, the National Assembly of Wales, the Scottish Parliament and the Northern Ireland Assembly[12]. It is intended that the annual report should indicate progress against indicators of the Agency's performance[13].

The FSA 1999, section 5 and Schedule 2 provide for the establishment of advisory committees which must be set up to advise the Agency in particular on food safety and standards matters related to Wales, Scotland and Northern Ireland respectively. A committee may also be established by the Secretary of State, after consulting the Agency, for England or any English region. The Agency may, after consultation, set up other advisory committees, mechanism being provided for it to be assigned responsibility for existing non-statutory advisory committees[14].

Financial provision for the Agency is made by the FSA 1999, section 39 and Schedule 4.

1 FSA 1999, s 1(1) and (3).
2 See para **2.3.7***(a)* and *(b)* below.
3 FSA 1999, s 1(2).
4 Under the GWA 1998, powers are vested in the National Assembly as a whole. In practice, that part of the Assembly which takes responsibility for health matters would lead on the Agency in Wales.
5 'Scottish Ministers' is a collective term for the members of the Scottish executive of the devolved administration. See SA 1998, s 44(2).
6 In Northern Ireland, powers are vested in departments, acting on behalf of ministers, or when the Northern Ireland Act 1998 is in force, the NI Executive.
7 FSA 1999, s 2(1).
8 FSA 1999, s 2(2).
9 FSA 1999, s 2(3).
10 [1943] 2 All ER 560.

11 FSA 1999, s 3.
12 FSA 1999, s 4.
13 See para 23 of the Reply by the Government to the Report from the Food Standards Committee, Session 1998–99, 'Food Standards Draft Bill' (HC 276).
14 As to the existing non-statutory advisory committees, see section **2.4** below.

General functions of the Agency in relation to food

2.3.2 The general functions in relation to food summarised below are conferred on the Agency by sections 6–8 of the FSA 1999.

(a) Development of food policy and provision of advice etc to public authorities

The Agency has the function of (i) developing policy on food safety and standards and (ii) providing advice, information and assistance to public authorities. Within government it will be under a duty to provide such advice, information and assistance on request, unless it is not reasonably practicable for it to do so (for example, because the costs of providing any particular item of information would be disproportionate). Such advice, information and assistance could, for example, include detailed recommendations to ministers on the need for primary legislation or proposing subordinate legislation to improve food safety and standards. It will also represent the UK at working level in relevant European Community and other international fora.

It is intended that the Agency as a UK body will be the primary source of policy advice in relation to food safety and standards to the Government as a whole, and to the devolved authorities. Most of the relevant expertise on these subjects will therefore reside with the Agency and will not be duplicated in other departments. It will also be able to advise other departments on matters for which it is responsible, such as the Ministry of Agriculture, Fisheries and Food about food hygiene relating to farms or the Department of Trade and Industry about relevant consumer protection matters.

(b) Provision of advice, information and assistance to other persons

The Agency also has the function of providing advice, information and assistance in respect of matters connected with food safety or other interests of consumers in relation to food to the general public and to anyone other than public authorities. The general public must be kept adequately informed about matters which the Agency considers significantly affect their capacity to make informed decisions about food. The power allows for information to be given to particular sections of the public including groups representative of food industry sectors. It may therefore be expected to undertake a whole range of public information activities from running information campaigns to giving advice to those with food allergies and issuing food hazard warnings.

(c) Acquisition and review of information

To furnish it with sufficient information for the taking of informed decisions and the effective performance of its tasks, the Agency has the function of obtaining, compiling and keeping under review information about matters connected with food safety and standards. This function includes monitoring scientific developments and undertaking or commissioning research. The Agency will take over existing research and development projects which fall within its mandate and which are financed by the Ministry of Agriculture, Fisheries and Food and the Department of Health.

General functions of the Agency in relation to feeding stuffs

2.3.3 Section 9 of the FSA 1999 provides for the Agency to have the same general functions in relation to matters connected with the safety of animal feeding stuffs and other interests of users of animal feeding stuffs, as are summarised in para **2.3.2** above in relation to matters connected with food safety and other interests of consumers in relation to food.

Although the Minister of Agriculture, Fisheries and Food retains the responsibilities in respect of feeding stuffs specified in paras **2.2.3–2.2.5** above, the subject is of importance to the Agency because of the safety implications for humans consuming meat and animal products. This concern is essentially covered by the Agency's main objective in section 1 and by its advice and information functions in sections 6–8[1], but power to deal with certain related matters is required. In particular, the Agency must be in a position to deal with pet food (responsibility for which cannot readily be separated from that for animal feed), to protect the interests of purchasers of feed and to ensure that the safety or health of the animals themselves is not damaged.

1 See paras **2.3.1** and **2.3.2** above.

Observations by the Agency with a view to acquiring information

2.3.4 For the purposes of its functions, noted at para **2.3.2***(c)* read with **2.3.3** above, of obtaining and keeping under review information relevant to its work, sections 10 and 11 of the FSA 1999 confer powers enabling the Agency to carry out observations. They replace previous more limited powers of section 25 of the FSA 1990[1] which enabled orders to be made concerning the provision of information and the taking of samples. The Agency is authorised to carry out observations with a view to acquiring information about any aspect of the production or supply of food or food sources, or any aspect of the production, supply or use of animal feeding stuffs. The information may include information about (a) food premises, food businesses or commercial operations being carried out with respect to food, food sources or contact materials[2], (b) agricultural premises, agricultural businesses or agricultural activities[3] and (c) premises, businesses or operations involved in the production, supply or use of animal feeding stuffs.

The term 'observations' is intended to describe the gathering of general information on food safety and standards through surveillance programmes or other appropriate means. It does not relate to the investigation of particular alleged offences. For these, safeguards of the kind in the Police and Criminal Evidence Act 1984 apply and the FSA 1990 provisions and other enforcement powers will continue to be used by enforcement authorities[4].

Supplementary powers are provided by section 11 which enable the Agency to authorise its staff or agents to enter premises, take samples and inspect records, including health records of food industry workers.

1 See FSA 1999, Sch 5, para 15.
2 By FSA 1999, s 36(4), the expressions 'food', 'food source', 'contact material', 'food premises', 'food business' and 'commercial operation', have the same meanings as in FSA 1990 (ss 1 and 53(2)). See further ch 4.
3 As to 'agricultural activity', 'agricultural business' and 'agricultural premises', see FSA 1999, s 10(3).
4 See further chs 17 and 18.

Monitoring by the Agency of enforcement action

2.3.5 The Agency's function of monitoring performance of enforcement authorities[1] in enforcing relevant legislation is conferred by section 12 of the FSA 1999 as supplemented by sections 13–16.

A major weakness in previous arrangements identified by the James Report was the uneven enforcement of food law (see section **2.1** above). Accordingly, the Agency has the function of monitoring and setting standards[2] for the performance of enforcement authorities in enforcing the provisions in and under—

(a) the FSA 1990;
(b) the Food Safety (Northern Ireland) Order 1991; and
(c) Part IV of the AA 1970 relating to matters connected with animal feeding stuffs.

The Agency's monitoring function is extended by the Food Standards Act 1999 (Transitional and Consequential Provisions and Savings) (England and Wales) Regulations 2000 so as also to cover a specified list of Regulations made under the ECA 1972.

Each annual report of the Agency[3] must give an account of its own performance as an enforcement authority. Initially this will relate in particular to its role in enforcing meat hygiene legislation through the Meat Hygiene Service and its enforcement of Dairy Products Hygiene Regulations[4].

The Agency may make a report to any other enforcement authority as to their performance including guidance as to improvement. Further, it may direct the authority to arrange for publication of the report and to notify the Agency of action they have taken or propose to take in response.

For the purpose of monitoring enforcement action, the Agency may require specified information from enforcement authorities, their officers and employees and from persons subject to duties enforceable by authorities. Provision is made for powers of entry, sampling, inspection and copying of records and the requiring of assistance. These powers apply to enforcement authority premises, laboratories at which enforcement authority work has been carried out and premises in respect of which the authority powers are or have been exercisable.

Paragraph **2.3.6***(b)* below notes how the FSA 1990 has been amended to confer other enforcement powers on the Agency. It may be specified as an enforcement authority for regulations or orders; it may be directed to discharge an enforcement authority's duty; and it may take over the conduct of proceedings either with the consent of the person who instituted them or when directed to do so by the Secretary of State. It may also require the submission of reports and returns by food authorities and be empowered by order to discharge any duty of a defaulting food authority.

In discharge of its function of monitoring enforcement performance, the Agency is to introduce a scheme for setting and auditing local authority enforcement standards. Its proposals, developed following extensive discussions with local authority organisations, consumer groups and food industry representatives, comprise four main elements. They are (a) food law enforcement service planning guidelines; (b) a food law enforcement standard; (c) a scheme to monitor local authority food law enforcement activity; and (d) a scheme to audit local authority food law enforcement activity. After public consultation, the Agency aims to issue the service planning guidance to local authorities in September 2000 and to establish the new monitoring and audit arrangements in April 2001.

1 'Enforcement authority' is defined in FSA 1999, s 15(2).

2 As to setting standards for enforcement authorities, see further paras 10 and 12 of the Reply by the Government to the Report from the Food Standards Committee, Session 1998–99, 'Food Standards Draft Bill' (HC 276).
3 See para **2.3.1** above.
4 See paras **13.1.4** and **13.9.1** below.

Other functions of the Agency

2.3.6 Sundry further functions are conferred on the Agency by the FSA 1999. Thus, paragraph 4 of Schedule 5 amends the TDA 1968 to require that the Agency be consulted by the Board of Trade before the making of any order of the kind described in para **2.2.2** above[1]. However, the main block of other functions is conferred on the Agency by sections 17–21 of and Schedule 3 to the FSA 1999. These functions are summarised below.

(a) Delegation of powers to make emergency orders

The Secretary of State (or appropriate devolved authority) may delegate to the Agency the power to make emergency orders under section 1(1) of the F&EPA 1985 and section 13(1) of the FSA 1990[2]. It is envisaged that the Agency will be authorised to act only when the Secretary of State (or appropriate devolved authority) is unavailable.

(b) Functions of the Agency under the Food Safety Act 1990

The FSA 1999, section 18 and Schedule 3, Part I specify the functions conferred on the Agency by the FSA 1990, as amended.

Section 18(2) provides that any amendment made by Schedule 3 which extends to Scotland is to be taken as a pre-commencement enactment for the purposes of the SA 1998. Although much of the legislation in question has been devolved, the provisions of the SA 1998 and orders made under it do not generally amend the texts of Acts of Parliament to show what has been done. In consequence when the FSA 1999 amends an Act which has been subject to Scottish devolution, it does not attempt to alter the text to reflect the post devolution responsibilities. Instead the amendments are deemed to pre-date the SA 1998 which automatically makes the transfer to the relevant Scottish authority and attracts the powers to make further provision.

As to enforcement, the Agency may be directed to discharge the duties of enforcement authorities under section 6(3) of the FSA 1990[3], may be specified as an enforcement authority for regulations or orders and may take over the conduct of proceedings either with the consent of the person who instituted them or when directed to do so by the Secretary of State.

As to emergency control orders, the Agency has power, shared with the Secretary of State, to grant consent to the doing of anything prohibited by an emergency control order and give directions to prevent commercial operations with respect to food, food sources or food contact materials to which an emergency control order applies[4].

As to codes of practice under section 40[5], the Agency may, after consulting the Secretary of State, give directions to food authorities as to steps to be taken in order to comply with codes and enforce those directions. It may also undertake consultation with representative organisations regarding proposals for such codes of practice.

Moreover, the Agency may require the submission of reports and returns by a food authority (under section 41)[6], may be empowered by order to discharge any duty of a food authority (under section 42)[7] and may undertake consultation with representative organisations regarding proposals for regulations or orders under the FSA 1990 (under section 48)[8].

(Provision parallel to Schedule 3, Part I is made by Part II in respect of the Food Safety (Northern Ireland) Order 1991.)

(c) Functions of the Agency under other Acts besides the Food Saftey Act *1990*

The FSA 1999, section 18 and Schedule 3, Part III specify functions conferred on the Agency by the provisions of other Acts, as amended. These provisions are summarised below. As explained at *(b)* above, amendments which extend to Scotland are taken as pre-commencement enactments for the purposes of the SA 1998.

(i) Medicines Act 1968

Where a committee is established under the Medicines Act 1968 (MA 1968) for purposes including the consideration of veterinary medicinal products, one member must be appointed on the nomination of the Agency. This provision will in practice apply to the Veterinary Products Committee[9]. As with the Advisory Committee on Pesticides, it is expected that the Agency will also provide an adviser to this committee and its sub-committee. The Agency must be consulted on any regulations or orders applying to veterinary drugs or medicated feeding stuffs. As to consultation with the Agency on the general policy in relation to veterinary products, see para **2.3.8***(d)* below.

(ii) Food and Environmental Protection Act 1985

In relation to emergency orders under Part I of the Food and Environmental Protection Act 1985 (F&EPA 1985)[10], the Agency has the power to give consents and directions and to recover expenses.

In relation to the control of pesticides under Part III[11], ministers (that is, essentially the Minister of Agriculture, Fisheries and Food through his executive agency, the Pesticides Safety Directorate) must consult the Agency on regulations and as to the general approach to the giving, revocation or suspension of approvals and the imposition of conditions on approvals. The Advisory Committee on Pesticides[12] must also include one member on the nomination of the Agency.

The Agency also has certain functions in respect of deposits in the sea under Part II of the F&EPA 1985.

(iii) Environmental Protection Act 1990 (EPA 1990)

Functions are conferred on the Agency by amendment to the provisions relating to the control of genetically modified organisms ('GMOs') in Part VI of the EPA 1990. The Secretary of State for the Environment, Transport and the Regions and the devolved authorities have lead responsibility for these provisions. In England and Wales, the Minister of Agriculture, Fisheries and Food acts jointly in the making of regulations and the exercise of other functions concerning his continuing interest in the economic and environmental implications of GMOs for the farming and food industries. In considering applications for consent to release GMOs, the Government is advised by an independent statutory committee, the Advisory Committee on Releases to the Environment (ACRE).

To reflect the Agency's responsibilities for food safety and consumer protection, Part VI has been amended so that—

- as regards matters with which it is concerned, the Agency acts jointly with the Secretary of State (and, if appropriate, the minister) in requiring persons to apply for authorisation to release, market, import or acquire GMOs or in prohibiting persons from doing any of these things;

- the Agency may be appointed by regulations, jointly with the Secretary of State, to grant exemptions from risk and notification requirements or from the requirement for consent to release, market, import or acquire GMOs;
- the Agency must be consulted before regulations are made (other than those on fees and charges) or consents are granted or varied.

(iv) Radioactive Substances Act 1993 (RSA 1993)
The Agency has the right to be consulted on the grant or variation of authorisations to dispose of radioactive waste in the case of nuclear sites. As to the ending of the functions of the Minister of Agriculture, Fisheries and Food under the RSA 1993, see para **2.3.8***(a)* below.

(d) Publication by the Agency of information and advice

Section 19 of the FSA 1999 empowers the Agency to publish advice given by it in accordance with its general functions of developing food policy and providing advice etc to public authorities (paras **2.3.2***(a)* and **2.3.3** above) and providing advice, information and assistance to other persons (paras **2.3.2***(b)* and **2.3.3** above) or information obtained by it as a result of its observations or enforcement monitoring (paras **2.3.4** and **2.3.5** above).

The Agency's power to publish the advice it gives to ministers will be important to its influence and independence. There will obviously be strong moral pressure on ministers to produce convincing reasons if they contemplate rejecting Agency advice.

There are certain express limitations on publication. The power cannot be exercised where publication is prohibited by an enactment[13], is incompatible with any Community obligation or would constitute contempt of court. Before deciding to exercise the power, the Agency is required to consider whether publication of the advice or information in question is outweighed by any considerations of confidentiality attaching to it. Subject to these limitations, the Agency may also disclose information to other public authorities, which would, for example, assist them in carrying out their enforcement responsibilities.

An example of information published under section 19 is given in para **2.4.4** below. Companies submitting novel food applications are now required to permit the routine disclosure of the non-confidential information that they provide in support of such applications.

(e) Power to issue guidance on control of food-borne diseases

Supplementing its general function of giving advice, information and assistance, the Agency has the specific function of issuing general guidance to local authorities and other public authorities (for example, health authorities) on matters connected with the management of outbreaks of 'food-borne disease'. This expression refers to diseases of humans which are capable of being caused by the consumption of infected or otherwise contaminated food. It includes, for example, salmonella, E coli 0157 and campylobacter. Guidance issued under the power might in particular relate to tracing the food-related source of any outbreak, or to the speed with which action needs to be taken to limit the spread of food poisoning[14].

(f) Supplementary powers

The Agency also has power to do anything which is calculated to facilitate, or is conducive or incidental to, the exercise of its functions. In particular it may carry on educational or training activities, give financial or other support to activities carried on by others, acquire and dispose of property and, in England and Wales and in Northern Ireland, to institute criminal proceedings. It may charge for facilities and services it provides.

1 TDA 1968, s 38(2B).
2 See sections **11.7** and **11.6** below.
3 See para **2.5.2** below.

4 See para **11.6.3** below. The Agency also has power shared with the Secretary of State, to recover certain expenses incurred in respect of emergency control orders — see FSA 1990, s 13(7) as amended by FSA 1999, Sch 5, para 11(4).
5 See para **2.5.3** below.
6 See para **2.5.3** below.
7 See para **2.5.4** below.
8 See para **4.1.4** below.
9 See SI 1970/1304, establishing the Veterinary Products Committee, and para **2.4.13** below.
10 As to emergency orders under the F&EPA 1985, Pt I, see section **11.7** below.
11 As to the control of pesticides, see para **10.7.1** below.
12 As to the Advisory Committee on Pesticides, see para **2.4.12** below.
13 However, see para **2.3.7***(d)* below as to the power to relax or lift statutory prohibitions.
14 As to the current Food Hazard Warning System, see section **11.5** below.

General provisions relating to the functions of the Agency

2.3.7 Sections 22–25 of the FSA 1999 make the following general provisions relating to the functions of the Agency.

(a) Statement of general objectives and practices

The Agency is required to prepare and publish (with the approval of the appropriate authorities) a statement of the general objectives it intends to pursue, and general practices it intends to adopt, in carrying out its functions. The statement must remain within the scope of the Agency's main objective set out in section 1(2)[1].

The Government evidently has in mind that the statement should encompass key features of the 'guiding principles' set out in chapter 2 of the White Paper[2]. The aim is to ensure that the Agency will act in a reasonable, balanced and impartial way, taking full account of the requirements of democratic accountability.

The statement must specifically include objectives (i) securing consultation with interested parties, (ii) promoting links with government departments, local authorities, other public authorities and devolved authorities to ensure that the Agency is consulted on food safety and standards matters, (iii) securing that its decisions and their bases are recorded and available so that the public can make informed judgments, and (iv) any other objectives notified to the Agency by the appropriate authorities acting jointly. The Agency must publish the objectives after approval by the appropriate authorities, who may (subject to consultation with the Agency) modify them.

(b) Consideration of objectives, risks, costs and benefits etc

In carrying out its functions, the Agency must have due regard for its statement of objectives and practices. It must also take account of the nature and size of the risks relevant to a decision; the likely costs and benefits associated with the action under consideration; and relevant advice or information from an advisory committee[3]. This duty does not apply where it would be unreasonable or impractical for it to do so (eg in relation to decisions on appointments) and does not affect the Agency's obligation to discharge other duties (eg those over which it has no discretion).

(c) Directions relating to breach of duty or to international obligations

The Secretary of State (or devolved authorities) may give the Agency directions if it appears there has been a serious failure by the Agency to pay due regard to its statement of objectives and practices or to take into consideration specified risks, costs and benefits, advice and information (subparas *(a)* and *(b)* above), or to perform any other duty.

The Secretary of State (or devolved authorities) may also give the Agency directions for the implementation of UK obligations under the Community Treaties[4] or any international agreement of the United Kingdom. Ministers bear ultimate responsibility for the performance of international obligations but resort to this power is hardly likely to be frequent since, as indicated at para **2.3.2** *(a)* above, the Agency will represent the UK at working level in the relevant international discussions and will thus be well informed of most relevant obligations.

The authority giving directions must first have consulted the Agency and other authorities and, if the Agency fails to comply, may give effect to them by exercising the Agency's powers. In the event of non-compliance by the Agency, the Secretary of State may also (with the agreement of the other appropriate authorities) remove all the members of the Agency from office and make other arrangements for carrying out the functions until new appointments are made. Resort to these powers is most unlikely to be needed. Informal methods might generally be expected to secure necessary action.

(d) Power to modify enactments about disclosure of information

Power is conferred on the Secretary of State enabling him by order to remove or relax any statutory prohibition in so far as this appears to prevent disclosure to the Agency of information that would facilitate the carrying out of its functions, or to prevent the Agency from exercising its function of publishing information described in para **2.3.6***(d)* above.

1 See para **2.3.1**.
2 'The Food Standards Agency: A Force for Change' (Cm 3830) January 1998.
3 See paras **2.3.1** and **2.4.1**.
4 See Interpretation Act 1978, Sch 1 and ECA 1972, s 1.

Miscellaneous provisions

2.3.8 Sections 26–35 of the FSA 1999 enact certain miscellaneous provisions which are summarised below.

(a) Statutory functions ceasing to be exercisable by the Minister of Agriculture, Fisheries and Food

In pursuance of the policy of removing the conflict with the promotional responsibilities of the Minister of Agriculture, Fisheries and Food for the agricultural, fishing and food industries, his functions under the FSA 1990[1], Part I of the F&EPA 1985[2] and the RSA 1993[3] generally cease to be exercisable. Detailed provision for transfer of responsibilities to the Secretary of State, the devolved authorities and the Agency are to be found in Schedules 3 and 5 to the FSA 1999.

(b) Notification of tests for food-borne disease

The Secretary of State and the devolved authorities are empowered to make regulations requiring the notification of information about tests on samples taken from individuals (whether living or dead) for the presence of (i) organisms of a description specified in the regulations or (ii) any substances produced by or in response to the presence of organisms of a description so specified. The organisms specified must be capable of causing disease in humans and commonly transmitted to humans through the consumption of food.

Information collected under these powers will enable the Agency better to understand the patterns of the incidence and prevalence of food-borne disease. The pathogens initially expected to be covered by a notification scheme are salmonella, E coli 0157 and campylobacter.

(c) Arrangements for sharing information about food-borne zoonoses

The Agency and the ministers and devolved authorities with responsibility for any matter connected with food-borne zoonoses are required to make arrangements for sharing information about food-borne zoonoses and may make arrangements for coordinating their activities. 'Food-borne zoonosis' is defined[4] as any disease of, or organism carried by, animals which constitutes a risk to the health of humans through the consumption of, or contact with, food.

The White Paper[5] envisaged that the Agency and the Ministry of Agriculture, Fisheries and Food and devolved authorities for animal health will establish a joint committee to coordinate information on the surveillance of pathogens. These arrangements will assist the Agency in developing a strategy for control of food-borne zoonoses, which has customarily been effected under the AHA 1981 (see para **2.2.4** above).

(d) Consultation on veterinary products

The Agency's position is further strengthened in relation to the protection of food from chemical contamination by veterinary residues. Ministers responsible for the regulation of veterinary products (principally the Minister of Agriculture, Fisheries and Food through his executive agency, the Veterinary Medicines Directorate) must consult the Agency on the general policy in relation to this subject[6].

(e) Animal feeding stuffs

In relation to animal feeding stuffs, the Agency has the general functions conferred by sections 6 and 7 (by virtue of the effect feeding stuffs can have on food safety) and section 9 (in relation to the general safety of animal feed and the interests of users of feed)[7]. As a result, the Agency is concerned with the controls on the chemical composition and biological safety of animal feeding stuffs. The relevant legislation (currently to be found in Part IV of the AA 1970 and regulations and orders under that Act, the ECA 1972 and the AHA 1981[8]) would benefit from updating and improvement, not least in the light of the establishment of the Agency. The FSA 1999, therefore, confers on the Secretary of State and the Minister of Agriculture, Fisheries and Food, acting jointly, power by order to make new provision in England and Wales[9] for the regulation of feed based on the FSA 1990. In particular, the order might be expected to establish a general requirement for the safety of feeding stuffs similar to the 'food safety requirements' prescribed by section 8 of the FSA 1990[10].

The provisions of the order need not be confined to protecting human health, but may also be made with a view to protecting animal health or any other purpose which appears to the ministers to be appropriate.

(f) Miscellaneous devolution provisions

Further miscellaneous provisions are made by sections 32–35 of the FSA 1999 consequent upon devolution.

A 'Henry VIII' section provides powers, by Order in Council subject to prior consultation with the Agency, to modify the Act to deal with changes which might be required in the light of the unprecedented experience of operating a UK body (the Agency) in a devolved area (essentially, food safety and standards).

Power to act by Order in Council is also provided to deal with the consequences of any legislation by the Scottish Parliament or Northern Ireland Assembly withdrawing functions from the Agency.

The Agency has a duty to take account of activities of the Food Safety Promotion Board for which provision was made as an all-Ireland implementation body following the Belfast Agreement between the United Kingdom and the Republic of Ireland.

Detailed provisions are also made concerning devolution in Scotland.

1 But see para **2.2.5** above.
2 See para **2.3.6**(*c*)(*ii*) above and para **11.7.1** below.
3 See para **2.3.6**(*c*)(*iv*) above.
4 FSA 1999, s 28(5).
5 'The Food Standards Agency: A Force for Change' (Cm 3830) January 1998.
6 As to veterinary medicines, see further paras **2.2.5** and **2.3.6**(*c*)(*i*) above and section 10.8 below.
7 See paras **2.3.2**(*a*) and (*b*) and **2.3.3** above.
8 See ch 16.
9 The Scottish ministers act in relation to Scotland.
10 See section **9.2** below.

2.4 EXPERT ADVISORY COMMITTEES

2.4.1 For many years it has been the practice of ministers to appoint non-statutory committees of eminent independent specialists to inform their decisions under the FSA 1990 and related legislation by providing advice on matters of food safety and standards. Expert advisory committees are at last integrated into the statutory framework by the FSA 1999. The Food Standards Agency is empowered to establish them[1] and, in exercise of its powers, must take into account relevant advice and information from advisory committees[2].

Of the current committees, those described in paras **2.4.2** to **2.4.5** will evidently be taken over by the Agency which will provide their secretariats and may vary their terms of reference or, if it chooses, wind them up.

In addition, advice will be available to the Agency from the committees described in paras **2.4.6–2.4.11**. It will contribute to the work of the secretariats of the Spongiform Encephalopathy Advisory Committee (SEAC), the Committee on the Medical Aspects of Food and Nutrition Policy (COMA) and the Committee on Toxicity of Chemicals in Food, Consumer Products and the Environment (COT) together with other interested departments (that is, MAFF and the Department of Health in the case of SEAC and the Department of Health in the case of COMA and COT). It is also proposed that the Agency shall have a key role in supporting the new Advisory Committee on Animal Feeding stuffs (ACAF).

The COT and associated committees on Mutagenicity of Chemicals in Food, Consumer Products and the Environment (COM) and Carcinogenicity of Chemicals in Food, Consumer Products and the Environment (COC) support other committees with advice on the subjects within their respective remits.

To be distinguished from other committees are the Advisory Committee on Pesticides (ACP) and the Veterinary Products Committee (VPC) described in paras **2.4.12** and **2.4.13** respectively. Although having an interest in food safety, they are statutory committees established under different legislation. The MAFF Pesticides Safety Directorate and Veterinary Medicines Directorate respectively continue to provide secretariat services, but the Agency has the right to nominate a member to each committee[3] and is expected to contribute to their safety assessment and surveillance work.

Advisory Committees have important functions in relation to the Government's chemical and microbiological food surveillance programmes, which are now the responsibility of the Agency[4].

1 FSA 1999, s 5 and Sch 2; and see para **2.3.1**.
2 FSA 1999, s 23; and see para **2.3.7***(b)*.
3 See para **2.3.6***(c)(i)* and *(ii)*.
4 FSA 1999 s 10: see para **2.3.4** above.

2.4.2

Food Advisory Committee (FAC) The FAC was set up by ministers in 1983 to continue to advise them on the composition of food in succession to the Food Standards Committee and the Food Additives and Contaminants Committee. It is the most venerable advisory committee in origin: recommendations of the FAC and its predecessors have always been influential in the formulation of UK food legislation. As a result, their reports have often provided useful guidance to this legislation[1].

The Committee is now specifically charged with assessing the risk to humans of chemicals which are used in or on food and with advising central Government on the exercise of powers in the FSA 1990 relating to the labelling, composition and chemical safety of food. In particular it became responsible for oversight of chemical surveillance when the Steering Group on Chemical Aspects of Food Surveillance was disbanded at the end of 1995.

The FAC also advises central Government on general matters relating to food safety. This special role was given to it in the run-up to the establishment of the Food Standards Agency. As well as advising on various aspects of the arrangements for setting up the Agency, the FAC took on responsibility for overall presentation of the food safety machinery to the general public, general risk assessment and any other questions which cut across different areas of food safety policy and went beyond the remit of any one expert committee.

In exercising its functions the Committee takes into account the advice and work of other relevant advisory committees including the Committee on Toxicity of Chemicals in Food, Consumer Products and the Environment, the Advisory Committee on Novel Foods and Processes and the Advisory Committee on Microbiological Safety of Food.

From November 1997 the FAC was made more open to the public. Amongst other initiatives to increase public awareness of its activities have been the publication of a quarterly newsletter 'Food for Thought' and, in October 1998, the organisation of its first open conference 'Food Controls — Past, Present and Future'.

1 See *Butterworths Law of Food & Drugs*, Div D.

2.4.3

Advisory Committee on Microbiological Safety of Food (ACMSF) The ACMSF was established in December 1990 to assess the risk to humans of microorganisms which are used, or occur, in or on food, and to advise central Government on the exercise of powers in the FSA 1990 relating to the microbiological safety of food. It has been particularly concerned with the causes of and remedies for the increase in microbiological illnesses of food-borne origin from pathogens such as salmonella, listeria, campylobacter and E coli. Since 1995 the committee has been responsible for advice on the forward strategy and general direction of the Government's microbiological food surveillance programme.

2.4.4

Advisory Committee on Novel Foods and Processes (ACNFP) The ACNFP is required to advise central Government on any matters relating to the irradiation of food or to the manufacture of novel foods or foods produced by novel processes having regard, where appropriate, to the views of relevant expert bodies.

In particular advice is given on initial safety assessments and on other Member States' assessments under Novel Foods Regulation 258/97/EC[1]. A move was recently made to increase the openness of the ACNFP. All companies submitting novel food applications are now required to permit the routine disclosure of the non-confidential information that they provide in support of such applications. As a temporary means of authorising disclosure, the Novel Foods and Novel Food Ingredients (Amendment) (England) Regulations 1999 were enacted. General powers for the Food Standards Agency to publish such information are now provided by section 19 of the FSA 1999[2].

1 See para **7.2.12** below.
2 See para **2.3.6**(*d*) above.

2.4.5

Consumer Panel The Consumer Panel's role is to bring to the attention of central Government food issues of concern to consumers; to advise on the transparency for consumers of Government food policies; and to advise on the transmission to consumers of advice and information relating to Government policies on food safety, diet and nutrition. Although different in kind from the scientific committees, the potential importance of the Panel is nevertheless emphasised by the fact that it has customarily been chaired by the Minister of Food.

2.4.6

Spongiform Encephalopathy Advisory Committee (SEAC) SEAC was reconstituted as a permanent expert committee in 1990, from the Tyrrell Committee on research into spongiform encephalopathies. In 1998 the membership was revised and widened, and the terms of reference were clarified. SEAC is now charged with providing scientifically-based advice to central Government on matters relating to spongiform encephalopathies, taking account of the remits of other bodies with related responsibilities.

2.4.7

Committee on the Medical Aspects of Food and Nutrition Policy (COMA) COMA was established in 1963. It comprises experts in the fields of nutrition, health and other relevant fields. It is required to consider and advise the Chief Medical Officer (CMO), and through the CMO the Government, on (a) the medical and scientific aspects of policy in relation to nutrition; (b) at the request of, or in association with, appropriate Advisory Committees, the medical and nutritional aspects of developments in the agricultural and food industries including the production and processing of food; and (c) at the request of the Department of Health, matters falling within these terms of reference.

2.4.8

Committee on Toxicity of Chemicals in Food, Consumer Products and the Environment (COT) On request, the COT assesses and advises central Government on the toxic risk to humans of substances which are—

(a) used or proposed to be used as food additives, or used in such a way that they might contaminate food through their use or natural occurrence in agriculture, including horticulture and veterinary practice or in the distribution, storage, preparation, processing or packaging of food;
(b) used or proposed to be used or manufactured or produced in industry, agriculture, food storage or any other workplace;

(c) used or proposed to be used as household goods or toilet goods and preparations;
(d) used or proposed to be used as drugs, when advice is requested by the Medicines Control Agency, a section 4 Committee or the Licensing Authority[1];
(e) used or proposed to be used or disposed of in such a way as to result in pollution of the environment.

The COT also advises on important general principles or new scientific discoveries in connection with toxic risks, coordinates with other bodies concerned with the assessment of toxic risks and presents recommendations for toxicity testing.

1 These bodies are established under the MA 1968: the 'section 4 Committees' include the Veterinary Products Committee (VPC) described at para **2.4.13**.

2.4.9

Committee on Mutagenicity of Chemicals in Food, Consumer Products and the Environment (COM) The COM is related to the COT and assesses and advises central Government on the mutagenic risk to man of substances described in para **2.4.8** as well as advising, coordinating and presenting recommendations in connection with mutagenic risks, as the COT does in connection with toxic risks.

2.4.10

Committee on Carcinogenicity of Chemicals in Food, Consumer Products and the Environment (COC) The COC is also related to the COT and assesses and advises central Government on the carcinogenic risk to man of substances described in para **2.4.8**, as well as advising, coordinating and presenting recommendations in connection with carcinogenic risks as the COT does in connection with toxic risks.

2.4.11

Advisory Committee on Animal Feeding Stuffs (ACAF) The ACAF was set up in 1999 because of concerns about the integrity of animal feeds, particularly over the implications of bovine spongiform encephalopathy and the use of genetically modified feed ingredients. It advises central Government on the safety and use of animal feeds and feeding practices, with particular emphasis on protecting human health and with reference to new technical developments. In carrying out its functions, the ACAF liaises with other relevant advisory committees as appropriate.

2.4.12

Advisory Committee on Pesticides (ACP) The ACP advises ministers on regulations for the control of pesticides, as to approval of pesticides which they contemplate giving, revoking or suspending and any conditions which should attach to approvals[1]. Similar advisory functions are undertaken for central Government in respect of active substances and authorisation of plant protection products under the EC plant protection products Directive 91/414/EEC[2].

Together with the FAC, the ACP also receives and considers reports on Government food surveillance for pesticide residues.

1 F&EPA 1985, s 16(7) and (8) and the Control of Pesticides (Advisory Committee on Pesticides) Order 1985, SI 1985/1516.
2 OJ L 230, 19.8.91, p 1 and see the Plant Protection Products Regulations 1995, SI 1995/887, as amended.

2.4.13

Veterinary Products Committee (VPC) By virtue of the MA 1968, section 4 and the Medicines (Veterinary Products Committee) Order 1970[1], the VPC is required (a) to advise central Government on safety, quality and efficacy in relation to veterinary use of any substance or article (which is not an instrument, apparatus or appliance) to which any provision of the MA 1968 is applicable, and (b) to promote the collection and investigation of information relating to adverse reactions, for the purpose of enabling such advice to be given. This mandate has been adapted to the European Community context[2]. The VPC considers applications for authorisations and appeals in respect of veterinary medicinal products and provides advice on European applications and scientific matters.

1 SI 1970/1304.
2 See in particular, the Marketing Authorisations for Veterinary Medicinal Products Regulations 1994, SI 1994/3142, as amended.

2.5 FOOD AUTHORITIES

Definition

2.5.1 In implementation of the James Report and subsequent White Paper, the FSA 1999 makes provision, summarised in para **2.3.5** above, for firmer co-ordination and oversight to reinforce the effectiveness of food law enforcement. However, the work continues to be undertaken primarily by local authorities.

In the FSA 1990, the responsible local authorities are designated 'food authorities'. By section 5(1) of that Act, in England they are the London boroughs, the district councils, the non-metropolitan county councils, the Common Council of the City of London, the appropriate Treasurer of the Inner Temple or of the Middle Temple and, as respects the Isles of Scilly, the Council of the Isles of Scilly[1]. By section 5(1A) of the FSA 1990 food authorities in Wales are the county councils and the county borough councils[2].

By section 5(3), where functions under the FSA 1990 are assigned by order, in England and Wales, to a port health authority[3] or joint board for a united district[4] or, in England, to a single authority for former metropolitan counties[5], that authority is deemed to be the food authority in relation to those functions. Section 5 makes parallel provision for Scotland.

1 FSA 1990, s 57(1) and SI 1990/2486, art 20.
2 Local Government (Wales) Act 1994, s 22(3) and Sch 9, para 16.
3 Public Health (Control of Disease) Act 1984, ss 2 and 7.
4 Public Health Act 1936, s 6.
5 Local Government Act 1985, Sch 8, para 15(6).

Enforcement responsibilities under the 1990 Act

2.5.2 By section 6(1) of the FSA 1990, the authority which is to enforce and execute any provision in or under the Act is 'the enforcement authority' with powers to institute proceedings[1] and, through its authorised officers[2], to sample[3], enter and inspect[4].

So far as the Act itself is concerned, every food authority is required by section 6(2) to enforce and execute its provisions within their area except where that duty is expressly or by necessary implication imposed on some other authority[5].

The Local Government Act 1992 made provision for structural change in England as a result of which certain single tier unitary authorities have been created. Generally however, as a result of the definition described in para **2.5.1**, two tiers of local authority are 'food authorities' in most English areas. This is so where there are both non-metropolitan county and district councils, as well as in the Inner and Middle Temples in the City of London. In such areas the authorities potentially have concurrent enforcement authority functions by virtue of section 6(2). A local authority may arrange for another local authority to discharge functions on its behalf[6], but, in the absence of such an arrangement, the possibility still exists for confusion over which authority is to act in any particular case. To avoid this, provision of two kinds was made. First, the Food Safety (Enforcement Authority) (England and Wales) Order 1990[7] provides in relation to such areas that the functions in respect of emergency prohibition notices and orders[8] shall be exercised only by the district councils (or, within the Temples, by the appropriate Treasurer) and that the provisions as to false presentation and description of food[9] shall be enforced solely by the county councils (or, within the Temples, by the Common Council of the City of London). Secondly, clarification for cases of concurrent jurisdiction is provided by Statutory Code of Practice no 1 (Responsibility for Enforcement of the Food Safety Act 1990)[10]. The Code stresses the need for adequate liaison arrangements between district and county councils to ensure full cooperation in enforcement and the passing of information between authorities. It further recommends that district councils should investigate and take legal proceedings in all cases of contamination by micro-organisms or their toxins such as salmonella, listeria or botulism and all cases of mould or foreign matter in or on food. County councils should undertake routine checks and analysis of food for chemical contamination and improper use of additives and should normally investigate and take legal proceedings in cases of contamination by chemicals, subject to proper liaison with the district councils where there are public health implications. County councils should also investigate and take legal proceedings in cases of compositional offences, adulteration and misleading claims.

In relation to a particular case or cases the Secretary of State has power to direct that an enforcement duty imposed on food authorities by section 6(2) shall be discharged by the Secretary of State, the Minister of Agriculture, Fisheries and Food or the Food Standards Agency[11].

The enforcement authorities for Regulations under the Act are specified by those Regulations[12]. The division of responsibility generally adheres to the principles described in Statutory Code of Practice no 1[13], but Regulations on the hygienic production of fresh meat and milk and certain other foods are central government responsibilities[14] which have been transferred to the Food Standards Agency by the Food Standards Act 1999 (Transitional and Consequential Provisions and Savings) (England and Wales) Regulations 2000.

The Secretary of State may take over proceedings instituted by some other person[15] or may direct the Food Standards Agency to do so[16]. Unless so directed, the Agency may take over proceedings only with the consent of the person who instituted them[17].

1 FSA 1990, s 6(5).
2 See para **2.6.1**.
3 FSA 1990, s 29.
4 FSA 1990, s 32.
5 As to food authority liaison, LACOTS and the Home Authority principle, see para **17.3.2** below.
6 Local Government Act 1972, s 101.
7 SI 1990/2462 made under FSA 1990, s 5(4).
8 FSA 1990, s 12.
9 FSA 1990, s 15.
10 As to Codes of Practice, see para **2.5.3**.
11 FSA 1990, s 6(3) and FSA 1999, Sch 3, para 2(a).
12 FSA 1990, s 6(4) and FSA 1999, Sch 3, para 2(b).

13 In specifying enforcement authorities, Regulations not enforced by central government exclude from the concept of a food authority, district councils or county councils, as appropriate. Following the creation of unitary authorities in Wales by the Local Government (Wales) Act 1994, art 2 of the Local Government Reorganisation (Wales)(Consequential Amendments) Order 1996, SI 1996/525, updates these references in preexisting subordinate legislation.
14 See, for example, ch 13, in particular at paras **13.1.4** and **13.9.1**.
15 FSA 1990, s 6(5A).
16 FSA 1990, s 6(5B) and FSA 1999, Sch 3, para 2(c).
17 FSA 1990, s 6(5C) and FSA 1999, Sch 3, para 2(c).

Statutory codes of practice and food authority returns

2.5.3 The Secretary of State is empowered to issue Codes of Practice for the guidance of food authorities as regards the execution and enforcement of the Act and of regulations and orders made under it[1]. Food authorities are required to have regard to the relevant provisions of any such Code and must comply with any direction which is given to them by the Food Standards Agency to take any specified steps to comply with a code[2]. Any such direction is specifically enforceable in England and Wales, on the Agency's application for judicial review, by the order known as *mandamus* commanding the authority to perform its public duty[3]. Before exercising its power to give or enforce a direction, the Agency must consult the Secretary of State.

At the time of writing, amendment of six of the Codes of Practice is being considered. They are Codes no 5 (the use of improvement notices), no 6 (prohibition procedures), no 7 (sampling for analysis or examination), no 8 (food standards inspections), no 9 (food hygiene inspections) and no 19 (qualifications and experience of authorised officers and experts). It is expected that the Food Standards Agency will carry out a longer term review of the Codes.

The Agency may also require reports and returns from food authorities[4] in order to monitor their activities.

1 FSA 1990, s 40 (1). The Codes of Practice are listed at Appendix E.
2 FSA 1990, s 40(1A) and (2) and FSA 1999, Sch 3, para 4(1)(a).
3 FSA 1990, s 40(3) and FSA 1999, Sch 3, para 4(1)(b).
4 FSA 1990, s 41 and FSA 1999, Sch 3, para 5.

Default of food authorities

2.5.4 As noted in para **2.5.2**, section 6 of the FSA 1990 enables central government to take over enforcement duties imposed on food authorities by the FSA 1990 or proceedings instituted by persons other than the Secretary of State. These powers apply whether or not a food authority is in default. Where a local authority fails to fulfil a public function or acts illegally, judicial review may well lie. Additionally however, the FSA 1990 makes express provision for any case in which the Secretary of State is satisfied that a food authority has failed to discharge a duty imposed by or under the FSA 1990 and that the authority's failure affects the general interests of consumers of food. In such a case he may by order empower another food authority, the Food Standards Agency or one of his officers to discharge the duty in place of the authority in default. He may, but is not obliged to, cause a local inquiry to be held where he believes a food authority is in default[1].

Given the Food Standards Agency's responsibility monitoring enforcement performance[2], it would be surprising if the Secretary of State did not, in the normal way, follow its advice when deciding under section 6 or 42 of the FSA 1990 to remove functions from an enforcement authority.

1 FSA 1990, s 42 and FSA 1999, Sch 3, para 6.
2 See para **2.3.5** above.

2.6 AUTHORISED OFFICERS

2.6.1 The statutory duties of enforcement under the FSA 1990 are generally carried out by 'authorised officers'[1]. An authorised officer 'in relation to a food authority' means, in essence, any person, whether or not an officer of the authority, who is authorised by them in writing, either generally or specially, to act in matters arising under the Act[2]. In much the same terms, 'authorised officer' is now also defined 'in relation to an enforcement authority'[3], which may be specified, for the purposes of subordinate legislation, from a list including not only food authorities, but also the Minister of Agriculture, Fisheries and Food, the Secretary of State, the Food Standards Agency or, in regulations, the Commissioners of Customs and Excise[4]. It should also be noted that provisions of the Act itself often apply to 'an authorised officer of an enforcement authority'[5].

Most authorised officers of district councils are environmental health officers and most authorised officers of county councils, trading standards officers. Veterinarians and other appropriately qualified officers are employed by the Meat Hygiene Service to carry out inspections in accordance with European Community requirements as to trade in meat and for the inspection of slaughterhouses and meat cutting premises[6].

1 As to 'proper officers' and others authorised to authenticate documents, see FSA 1990, s 49.
2 FSA 1990, s 5(6).
3 FSA 1990, s 6(6) as amended by the Deregulation and Contracting Out Act 1994, s 31 and Sch 9 and s 76 and Sch 16.
4 FSA 1990, s 6(4).
5 See FSA 1990, ss 10, 12, 29, 30 and 32.
6 See para **13.1.4** below.

2.6.2 There are virtually no regulations prescribing qualifications for food authority authorised officers[1]. The additional food control measures Directive 93/99/EEC requires Member States to ensure 'that the competent authorities have, or have access to, a sufficient number of suitably qualified and experienced staff, in particular in areas such as chemistry, food chemistry, veterinary medicine, medicine, foodmicrobiology, food hygiene, food technology and law' so that the controls referred to in Directive 89/397/EEC can be carried out adequately[2]. This Community obligation is implemented in Great Britain by Statutory Code of Practice no 19 on the qualifications and experience of authorised officers and experts. In essence, the Code requires authorised officers to be qualified in food hygiene or in food standards or in both. It specifies the food hygiene and food standards qualifications respectively considered suitable. Should a food authority require other expertise listed in Directive 93/99/EEC, they must ensure that the expert engaged has a recognised qualification in the area for which he is required. As to qualifications for food analysts and food examiners, see section **2.8**.

1 The Authorised Officers (Meat Inspection) Regulations 1987, SI 1987/133, which continue in force under FSA 1990, s 5(6), concern qualifications to undertake work which in 1995 essentially passed to the Meat Hygiene Service (ie inspections in respect of meat). See further para **13.1.4** below.
2 As to Directives 89/397/EEC and 93/99/EEC, see section **17.2** below.

2.6.3 By section 44 of the FSA 1990, an authorised officer of a food authority is not personally liable for anything done by him for the purpose of the execution or purported execution of the Act and within the scope of his employment, if he acted in the honest belief that his duty under the Act required or entitled him to do it. Further, if an action is brought against an officer of a food authority in respect of an act done by him in the execution or purported execution of the Act but outside the scope of his employment, his food authority may indemnify him in whole or in part against any damages or costs which he may be ordered to pay if they are satisfied that he acted in the honest belief that the act complained of was within the scope of his employment.

On the authority of sections 5(6) and 6(6), there is a growing trend for food authorities to use the services of consultants or freelance staff for the enforcement of provisions in and under the Act. Since their relationship to the authority is not one of employment, it is questionable whether they would fall within the protection of section 44.

2.7 PUBLIC ANALYSTS

2.7.1 The public analyst has been the key figure in the enforcement of law relating to the composition of food since the beginnings of the modern legislation in the second half of the nineteenth century. While acting as principal scientific adviser to the food authority on this subject, the public analyst holds a public office with a certain independence of status[1]. Over the years the expert evidence of public analysts has been influential in helping courts establish the standards of food demanded by purchasers under what is now section 14 of the FSA 1990[2] and important for the purposes of determining whether chemically contaminated food is unfit for human consumption for the purposes of section 9 of the Act. For certain additive and contaminant Regulations, the public analyst's certificate that food does not comply is evidence that the food may be treated as unfit and seized and destroyed on the order of a justice of the peace[3].

Food authorities are required to appoint one or more public analysts[4] who must be qualified in accordance with regulations under section 27(2) of the FSA 1990[5]. In October 1998 the Report on the Review of Public Analyst Arrangements in England and Wales endorsed retention of the requirement that food authorities appoint public analysts and recommended continuing professional development as part of their qualifications.

The authority must pay to the public analyst such remuneration as may be agreed and may also appoint a deputy public analyst. For the purposes of the provisions protecting officers acting in good faith described at para **2.6.3**, the public analyst is deemed to be an officer of the food authority whether or not his is a whole-time appointment[6].

1 See FSA 1990, ss 27–31.
2 *Bowker v Woodroffe* [1927] All ER Rep 415. As to s 14, see further section **5.3** below.
3 See, for example, the Miscellaneous Food Additive Regulations 1995, as amended, reg 6 and the Lead in Food Regulations 1979, as amended, reg 5.
4 FSA 1990, s 27. 'Food authority' here does not include the council of a non-metropolitan district and the appropriate Treasurers of the Temples.
5 Food Safety (Sampling and Qualifications) Regulations 1990, as amended, reg 3.
6 FSA 1990, s 44(4).

2.7.2 Some public analysts are employed by a food authority and work from laboratories provided by that authority. Others are independent. They may be appointed by more than one food authority and engage in commercial consultancy work. However, a person is prohibited by the Act from acting as a public analyst for an area if he is engaged directly or indirectly in any food business in that area[1] and a director, owner or employee of a food business, or partner in a food business, is prohibited by regulations from acting as a public analyst for the area in which that business is situated[2]. Breach of these prohibitions might be expected to invalidate the public analyst's appointment and render inadmissible any evidence he gave.

1 FSA 1990, s 27(2).
2 Food Safety (Sampling and Qualifications) Regulations 1990, as amended, reg 5(1).

2.8 FOOD EXAMINERS AND FOOD ANALYSTS

2.8.1 The FSA 1990 introduced the concept of a food examiner and a food analyst. In the Act, 'examination' means microbiological examination[1] and 'food examiner' is defined[2] as a person who possesses the requisite qualifications to carry out examinations for the purposes of the Act. Food authorities are not obliged to appoint a food examiner.

'Analysis' includes microbiological assay and any technique for establishing the composition of food[3] and 'food analyst' is defined[4] as a public analyst or other person having the requisite qualifications to carry out analyses for the purposes of the Act. In October 1998 the Report on the Review of Public Analyst Arrangements in England and Wales recommended continuing professional development as part of the qualification for food analysts.

The qualifications for food analysts and food examiners are prescribed by regulations 3 and 4 respectively of the Food Safety (Sampling and Qualifications) Regulations 1990, as amended. Evidently with the object of avoiding conflicts of interest[5], regulation 5 prohibits a director, owner or employee of a food business, or partner in a food business from analysing or examining any sample which he knows was taken from that business.

Certificates of analysis and examination given by food analysts and food examiners have evidential status[6].

1 FSA 1990, s 28(2).
2 FSA 1990, s 30(9).
3 FSA 1990, s 53(1).
4 FSA 1990, s 30(9).
5 FSA 1990, s 31(1)(g).
6 See para **17.4.7** below.

2.9 THE GOVERNMENT CHEMIST

2.9.1 Recourse to the Government Chemist as a referee analyst in the event of dispute has been part of food standards law since 1875 and the mechanism, in modern form, appears in and under the FSA 1990. An authorised officer who has retained part of a sample is required to submit it to the Government Chemist, or such other food analyst as the Government Chemist may direct, for analysis if he and the owner agree or if a court so orders[1].

Although the laboratory of the Government Chemist is now in private hands, it is subject to contractual constraints so that the Government Chemist can fulfil the regulatory role imposed on that office which remains an independent appointment. (See further para **17.4.8** below, as to the recommendations in October 1998 of the Report on the Review of Public Analyst Arrangements in England and Wales.)

1 FSA 1990, s 31(1)(h) and Food Safety (Sampling and Qualifications) Regulations 1990, as amended, reg 7. See further para **17.4.8** below.

Chapter 3

Consumer remedies

3.1 INTRODUCTION

3.1.1 In laying the foundations of modern consumer protection legislation, Victorian statutes took account of existing contractual relations between buyer and seller. Even today, an offence under what is now section 14 of the Food Safety Act 1990 (FSA 1990), depends on the nature, substance or quality demanded by the purchaser[1]. Moreover, for the purpose of providing protection for purchasers of feeding stuffs, Part IV of the Agriculture Act 1970 still relies in part on implying warranties into the contract for sale[2].

The requirements enforced by criminal law that have progressively been imposed have not reduced the need for civil remedies available to consumers. In fact those remedies have themselves been augmented over the years. In addition to improvements to the contractual route, tortious and Community-law based avenues are also now open to aggrieved consumers. Most will no doubt decide to report defective food to a food authority for investigation and possible prosecution. A court by or before which a person is convicted of an offence may make an order requiring him to pay compensation for any personal injury, loss or damage resulting from the offence[3]. However, the consumer who has suffered significant loss may wish to bring an action against the retailer or supplier for damages instead of or in addition to seeking to initiate criminal proceedings.

It might usefully be noted here that the standard of proof in criminal proceedings is higher than that in civil proceedings[4]. In the former, the prosecution's case must be proved 'beyond reasonable doubt'[5]. In the latter, the plaintiff has simply to satisfy the court 'on the balance of probabilities', even where in the civil proceedings commission of a crime is alleged[6].

To avoid prejudicing a fair trial, civil proceedings will normally[7] be deferred until a prosecution arising from the same facts is completed. There is, in any event, practical advantage to the plaintiff in waiting because, by section 11(1) of the Civil Evidence Act 1968, the fact that a person has been convicted of an offence by or before any court in the United Kingdom is admissible in evidence where relevant in civil proceedings to prove that the offence was committed.

Sections **3.2**, **3.3** and **3.4** below respectively summarise the remedies that may be pursued by the consumer for breach of contract, tort or strict product liability in respect of a defective food product. In contemplation of civil proceedings, sections **3.5** and **3.6** note some elementary precautions for consumers and producers. These are merely indicators and should in no way be treated as a substitute for full legal advice on the specific circumstances of a particular trade or incident.

It should also be borne in mind that civil actions relating to food may be brought by others besides consumers. Two sorts warrant brief mention here. The first is an action against the food authority. In *Welton v North Cornwall District Council*[8] an environmental health officer negligently required the owner of food premises to undertake works which were unnecessary to secure compliance with the FSA 1990 and food hygiene regulations. The owner incurred substantial and unnecessary expenditure in executing the works and sued the local food authority. The authority was held by the Court of Appeal to be under a common duty of care to the owner and liable in damages for the economic loss sustained.

Secondly, there are civil actions pursued by food manufacturers to protect their products against misrepresentation. The scope of the present work does not admit more than a brief reference to this subject. It might usefully be noted, however, that the tort of passing off, the main kind of injurious falsehood, provides an important safeguard where it can be established that the public are being deceived into believing that another trader's food products are those of the plaintiff. Recent conspicuous cases concerning champagne[9], whisky[10], chocolate[11] and chocolate biscuits[12] have also involved interpretation of Community Regulations or trade mark disputes.

1 See section **5.3** below.
2 See section **16.2** below.
3 Powers of Criminal Courts Act 1973, s 35, as amended; Magistrates' Courts Act 1980, s 40.
4 *Miller v Minister of Pensions* [1947] 2 All ER 372 at 373–374.
5 See further para **18.2.2** below.
6 *Hornal v Neuberger Products Ltd* [1957] 1 QB 247, [1956] 3 All ER 970.
7 *Harris v Crisp* [1992] 33 LS Gaz R 36, CA.
8 [1997] 1 WLR 570.
9 *Taittinger v Allbev* [1994] 4 All ER 75, [1993] 2 CMLR 741 (the Elderflower champagne case).
10 See *Scotch Whisky Association v Glen Kella Distillers* [1997] 16 LS Gaz R 29, [1997] Sol JO LB 91 ('Manx whiskey'); *Matthew Gloag and Son Ltd and Another v Welsh Distillers Ltd and Others* [1998] FSR 718, [1998] 2 CMLR 203 (1998) Times, 27 February, ('Welsh whisky').
11 *Chocosuisse Union des Fabricants Suisses de Chocolat v Cadbury Ltd* [1998] RPC 117.
12 *United Biscuits (UK) Ltd v Asda Stores Ltd* [1997] PRC 513.

3.2 SELLER'S LIABILITY FOR BREACH OF CONTRACT

3.2.1 A shopper seeking to sue a shopkeeper in contract for supply of defective food clearly first needs to show the existence of that contract. The extended meaning of 'sale' in section 2 of the FSA 1990[1] does not apply to the law of contract. In English law a bare promise is not legally binding. Besides an intention to create legal relations, an enforceable contract requires that there be an offer by one party and acceptance of the offer by the other, so that the plaintiff can show that there has passed from him to the defendant 'valuable consideration', that is to say, a benefit to the defendant or detriment to the plaintiff by which the defendant's promise was obtained.

For the contract for sale of food to fall within the ambit of the Sale of Goods Act 1979 (SGA 1979)[2], it must be one by which the seller transfers or agrees to transfer the property in goods to the buyer for a money consideration called the price[3].

The normal contract for sale of food in a supermarket will be formed when the offer to purchase the food is accepted at the check-out[4]. The purchase price paid to the shop assistant constitutes the consideration passing from the shopper.

1 See para **4.6.1** below.
2 See para **3.2.3** below.
3 SGA 1979, s 2(1).

4 *Pharmaceutical Society of Great Britain v Boots Cash Chemists (Southern) Ltd* [1952] 2 QB 795, [1952] 2 All ER 456.

3.2.2 At common law, a contract generally confers rights and imposes obligations only on persons who are parties to it, this relationship between them being known as 'privity of contract'. An action by the purchaser of a defective food product claiming damages for breach of contract may be brought only against the immediate vendor (ie normally the retailer). Unless buying direct, a retail purchaser has no action against the manufacturer or processor of a defective food product for breach of contract. However, each seller in the supply chain may in turn be liable to his buyer for breach of the contract by which he sold the defective food until the party responsible for the defect is reached[1].

The privity of contract relationship also means that a stranger to the contract cannot sue on it: the vendor is liable only to the purchaser of the food. Although a purchaser may, for example, be able to recover damages suffered by his whole family as a result of defective food sold to him by a restaurant[2], in general a stranger to the contract would have to proceed for damages in tort as described in section **3.3** below.

It should be noted that the Law Commission has recommended a new statutory exception to the privity of contract rule which would allow a third party to take the benefit of a contract made for this purpose[3].

1 *Kasler and Cohen v Slavouski* [1928] 1 KB 78; *Dodd and Dodd v Wilson and McWilliam* [1946] 2 All ER 691.
2 *Jackson v Horizon Holidays Ltd* [1975] 3 All ER 92.
3 See most recently privity of contract – contracts for the benefit of third parties (1996) (Law Commission No 242: Cm 3329).

3.2.3 Terms are implied into contracts of sale of goods by the SGA 1979, as amended by the Sale and Supply of Goods Act 1994 (S&SGA 1994).

The most important of these are—

(a) where there is a contract for sale of goods by description, that the goods will correspond with the description[1];
(b) where the seller sells goods in the course of a business, that the goods are of satisfactory quality[2]; and
(c) where the seller sells goods in the course of a business and the buyer makes known the particular purpose for which the goods are being bought, that the goods supplied under the contract are reasonably fit for that purpose[3].

A retail sale of food may give rise to an action for breach of the condition as to compliance with description ((a) above) so long as it is sold not merely as the specific thing but as a thing corresponding to a description[4], or for breach of the condition as to the fitness for purpose ((c) above)[5], except where there was no reliance on the skill and judgment of the seller or such reliance would have been unreasonable. However, most relevant today is likely to be the condition noted at (b) above, that goods be of satisfactory quality. As modernised by the S&SGA 1994, goods are of satisfactory quality for the purposes of the 1979 Act if they meet a standard that a reasonable person would regard as satisfactory, taking account of any description of the goods, the price (if relevant) and all other relevant circumstances[6]. The quality of goods includes their state and condition and, among other aspects, their fitness for all the purposes for which goods of the kind in question are commonly supplied, their freedom from minor defects and their safety[7]. The implied quality condition is excluded in the case of defects specifically drawn to the buyer's attention or defects which ought to have been revealed by examination by the buyer[8].

These provisions will evidently need further amendment by 1 January 2002 in implementation of European Parliament and Council Directive 1999/44/EC on certain aspects of the sale of consumer goods and associated guarantees.

1 SGA 1979, s 13.
2 SGA 1979, s 14(2).
3 SGA 1979, s 14(3).
4 *Grant v Australian Knitting Mills Ltd* [1936] AC 85, 100 per Lord Wright. See also SGA 1979, s 13(3).
5 See, for example, *Wallis v Russell* [1902] 2 IR 585, CA (unfit crabs); *Chaproniére v Mason* (1905) 21 TLR 633 (stone in a bun).
6 SGA 1979, s 14(2A).
7 SGA 1979, s 14(2B).
8 SGA 1979, s 14(2C)(a) and (b).

3.2.4 By section 6 of the Unfair Contract Terms Act 1977, liability for breach of the obligations arising from the implied terms summarised in para **3.2.3** above cannot be excluded or restricted by contract as against a person dealing as a consumer. 'Deals as a consumer' is defined by section 12. A party to a contract does so provided that he neither makes the contract in the course of a business nor holds himself out as doing so, that the other party does make the contract in the course of a business and that, in the case of a contract governed by the law of sale of goods, the goods in question are of a type ordinarily supplied for private use or consumption.

In parallel with these provisions are the Unfair Terms in Consumer Contracts Regulations 1999 which implement Council Directive 93/13/EEC. The Regulations apply, with certain exceptions, to unfair terms in contracts concluded between consumers and sellers or suppliers[1]. An unfair term is one which has not been individually negotiated and which contrary to the requirement of good faith, causes a significant imbalance in the parties' rights and obligations under the contract to the detriment of the consumer[2]. More specifically, it appears that a provision excluding the legal rights of the consumer described in para **3.2.3** above would be caught by the indicative and non-exhaustive list in Schedule 2 of terms which may be regarded as unfair and would in consequence not be binding on the consumer[3].

1 Unfair Terms in Consumer Contracts Regulations 1999, reg 4.
2 Unfair Terms in Consumer Contracts Regulations 1999, reg 5.
3 Unfair Terms in Consumer Contracts Regulations 1999, reg 8.

3.3 MANUFACTURERS' LIABILITY FOR THE TORT OF NEGLIGENCE

3.3.1 Until 1932 a consumer damaged by a defective product generally had no civil remedy other than in contract as a buyer. That year it was established that a manufacturer of products owes the consumer a duty of care which, if breached with resulting damage to the consumer, will render him liable for the tort of negligence. This major change was brought about by the landmark House of Lords' decision in *Donoghue v Stevenson*[1]. In this case, a young woman claimed to have suffered gastro-enteritis as a result of drinking a bottle of ginger beer contaminated by the remains of a decomposed snail. The bottle had been bought from the retailer by her companion thus depriving her of action in contract. In his judgment, Lord Atkin said—

'A manufacturer of products, which he sells in such a form as to show that he intends them to reach the ultimate consumer in the form in which they left him with no reasonable possibility of intermediate examination, and with the knowledge that the absence of reasonable care in the preparation or putting up of the products will result in an injury to the consumer's life or property, owes a duty to the consumer to take reasonable care.'

1 *Donoghue v Stevenson* [1932] AC 562, HL.

3.3.2 Negligence soon became one of the most important torts, actionable duties of care having been recognised by the courts in a whole range of human activities beyond the manufacture of foodstuffs[1]. In 1977 the consumer's position was further strengthened in respect of contracts or notices excluding or restricting liability for negligence. Henceforth, such provisions were absolutely prohibited when in respect of liability for death or personal injury and, in the case of other loss or damage, acceptable only if reasonable[2]. Yet there remained a demand for a regime of strict product liability.

1 For a particular example relating to food hygiene enforcement, see *Welton v North Cornwall District Council* noted at para **3.1.1** above.
2 Unfair Contract Terms Act 1977, s 2.

3.4 STRICT LIABILITY

3.4.1 In 1978 the Royal Commission on Civil Liability and Compensation for Personal Injury (the Pearson Commission)[1] recommended that producers should be strictly liable for death or personal injury caused by a defect in their products. But it was not until 1985 that Council Directive 85/374/EEC (on the approximation of the laws, regulations and administrative provisions of the Member States concerning liability for defective products) finally introduced a strict product liability regime. The purpose of the Directive is to reduce distortions in competition between Member States by giving similar protection to consumers throughout the Community against defective products.

1 Cmnd 7054 — 1978.

Liability for defective products

3.4.2 Council Directive 85/374/EEC is implemented in Great Britain by Part I of the Consumer Protection Act 1987 (CPA 1987). Subject to what is said below, section 2 provides that producers, those holding themselves out as producers[1] and those importing into a Member State from outside the Community are liable for damage caused wholly or partly by defects in their products. It is for the injured person to prove the damage, the defect and the causal relationship between defect and damage[2]. Where two or more persons are liable for the same damage, their liability is joint and several[3]. Section 2 is without prejudice to any liability otherwise arising[4], so actions in contract and negligence remain available in appropriate cases.

'Product' is defined as including a product which is comprised in another product whether by virtue of being a component part or raw material or otherwise[5]. However, as enacted, section 2 did not apply to persons in respect of defects in game or agricultural produce which they supplied before it had undergone an industrial process[6]. This exemption for unprocessed primary agricultural products must be removed by 4 December 2000 in implementation of an amendment to Directive 85/374/EEC by Directive 1999/34/EC. The amendment is aimed at helping to restore consumer confidence in the safety of unprocessed primary agricultural products, in particular following the BSE scare[7].

In response to this crisis, the Commission has also recently issued a Green Paper COM (1999) 396 final, on 'liability for defective products', to establish whether Directive 85/374 /EEC is achieving its objectives and whether any further amendment is needed.

1 Ie suppliers who market the products of others as their 'own-brand' or who fail to identify the producer, importer or own brander when asked to do so by an injured person.
2 Directive 85/374/EEC, Art 4.
3 CPA 1987, s 2(5).
4 CPA 1987, s 2(6).
5 CPA 1987, s 1(2).
6 CPA 1987, s 2(4).
7 See in particular the Commission Green Paper COM (97) 176 on 'the General Principles of Food Law in the European Union' Pt IV.8.

Meaning of 'defect'

3.4.3 For the purposes of the legislation, there is a defect in a product where the safety of that product is not such as persons generally are entitled to expect. In order to decide what persons generally are entitled to expect, regard must be had to all relevant circumstances, including the manner in which the product is marketed, any instructions or warnings given with it, what might reasonably be expected to be done with it and the time when the product was supplied by the producer[1].

On this basis it appears, for example, that the failure of a food, in some unsafe way, to meet the expectations of a particular nutritional use[2] for which it had been marketed, would constitute a defect. On the other hand, scrupulous compliance with statutory requirements as to warnings and use instructions is important as a means of limiting liability under the CPA 1987 as is advocated at para **3.6.1** below.

Further comment on this definition is to be found in Miller's *Product Liability and Safety* Butterworths, Vol III, at paragraphs 118–121 and 256.

1 CPA 1987, s 3.
2 See section **8.6** below.

Damage giving rise to liability

3.4.4 'Damage' is defined in section 5 of the CPA 1987. It means death, personal injury or specified loss or damage to property. Liability for property under section 2 is excluded in respect of—

(a) the defective product;
(b) property not of a description ordinarily intended for private use or consumption;
(c) property not intended by the injured person for his or her own private use or consumption; and
(d) damage valued at no more than £275.

No limit is set to the damages which may be awarded by a court.

According to the Commission's 1999 Green Paper on liability for defective products[1], 'non-material damage (any damage not affecting property, moral damage, mental suffering etc) is not at present covered' by Directive 85/374/EEC. Assuming that the European

Court would embrace this limited interpretation, it is apparent that Part I of the CPA 1987 extends beyond the Directive in this particular, notwithstanding that it generally purports to have 'effect for the purpose of making such provision as is necessary in order to comply with the product liability Directive and shall be construed accordingly'[2]. Miller notes that 'personal injury' is defined in section 45(1) of the Act to include 'any disease and any other impairment of a person's physical or mental condition' and concludes that 'nervous shock in the form of recognised psychiatric illness is within the range of compensation'[3].

1 Commission Green Paper COM (1999) 396 final on 'liability for defective products', p 31.
2 See CPA 1987, s 1(1).
3 *Product Liability and Safety* Butterworths, Vol III, para 81.

Defences

3.4.5 Section 4 of the CPA 1987 prescribes six defences to civil proceedings by virtue of Part I of the Act in respect of a defect in a product. They are—

(a) that the defect is attributable to compliance with a Community or national law requirement. The defendant must show that the defect was the result of compliance. In an action by a consumer for injury caused by food containing a damaging additive, the manufacturer would be unable to sustain the defence unless he had been required by law to incorporate it[1];
(b) that the defendant did not supply[2] the product. This is important in cases where counterfeit or out-of-date foods are sold by unauthorised retailers;
(c) that the defendant did not supply the product in the course of a business and would be caught by the Act only by virtue of things done otherwise than with a view to profit. This, for example, excludes private individuals making food at home;
(d) that the defect was not in the product at the time it was supplied. This may be important in cases of bad storage of food by a retailer or where a consumer fails to observe storage instructions on a label or simply keeps the food too long before eating it;
(e) that the state of scientific and technical knowledge at the time the product was supplied was not such that a producer of products of the same description as the product in question might be expected to have discovered the defect if it had existed in his products while they were under his control[3]. This so-called 'development risks' defence may be of value in regard to novel foods[4];
(f) in the case of an ingredient of a food, that the defect constituted a defect in that food and was wholly due to its design (ie recipe) or to compliance by the ingredient producer with instructions given by the producer of the food.

1 For examples of regulations which require the incorporation of ingredients, see para **7.5.1** below.
2 See CPA 1987, s 46.
3 See case C-300/95 *EC Commission v United Kingdom* [1997] ECR I-2649.
4 See para **7.2.12** below.

Prohibition on exclusions from liability

3.4.6 Liability under Part I of the CPA 1987 to a person who has suffered damage caused wholly or partly by a defect in a product, or to a dependant or relative of such a person, may not be limited or excluded by a contract term, notice or any other provision[1].

1 CPA 1987, s 7.

Limitation of actions

3.4.7 An action must be commenced not later than three years from the date of injury to the plaintiff by the defective product or, if later, the date when the plaintiff knew he had a claim against the defendant. The right of action is extinguished upon expiry of a period of ten years from the date on which the defective product was supplied by the producer unless the injured person has in the meantime instituted proceedings against the producer[1].

1 Limitation Act 1980, s 11A, inserted by CPA 1987, Sch 1.

3.5 SOME ELEMENTARY PRECAUTIONS FOR CONSUMERS

3.5.1 Where injury to a person or death or damage to property has resulted from a defective food product, procedural mistakes at an early stage can have an adverse effect on any proceedings which may follow. The following points might be borne in mind—

(a) ensure that any remains of the food and its container are retained and kept safely;
(b) in the event of illness, seek advice from your doctor, ensure that stool and/or other samples are obtained as soon as possible and keep the results;
(c) report the matter to the environmental health department of the local food authority (see section **2.5** above). This is most important in cases where contaminated or defective food may still be on sale. Make it clear to the officer that civil proceedings may follow and that the evidence may be required in court;
(d) if the environmental health officer wishes to take remnants of the food and/or its container away, ask for a written receipt giving details of the food and other evidence taken;
(e) in cases of injury to a person or death, ask the doctor attending the injured person to certify in writing the nature and extent of the injury or the cause of death;
(f) unless the injury to a person or damage to property is trivial, and in all cases of death, seek early advice from a solicitor;
(g) with the assistance of the solicitor, where instructed, prepare a written statement as soon as possible of the time, date and place of purchase of the food and the events leading up to and immediately following the injury, death or damage;
(h) through the solicitor, where instructed, notify the retailer and the producer (where his identity is known) in writing of the incident, its seriousness, and the intention to seek damages;
(i) do not risk prejudicing the proceedings by statements to the press, radio or television about the incident.

3.6 SOME ELEMENTARY PRECAUTIONS FOR PRODUCERS

3.6.1 To minimise the risk from actions for damages, the following elementary precautions might be considered by food producers—

(a) ensure that the food control and management systems[1] take account of the possibility of civil as well as criminal liability;
(b) ensure full compliance with statutory requirements as to warnings and use instructions[2] which may also serve to limit liability under the CPA 1987[3];

(c) make appropriate arrangements for product liability insurance;
(d) ensure that staff responsible for handling consumer complaints are properly trained in dealing sensitively with the public and in the basic principles of criminal and civil liability;
(e) on receipt of a complaint, seek full details, preferably in writing, with the object in particular of establishing—
  (i) whether or not there has been any death, personal injury or damage to property and of determining the nature and extent of injury or damage;
  (ii) the name, pack size and code number of the product alleged to have caused the problem;
  (iii) the name and address of the retailer (if any) who sold the product;
(f) obtain from the retailer—
  (i) in appropriate cases, a full report on the incident; and
  (ii) if possible, samples for testing of the batch from which the product was drawn;
(g) if the injured person claims to have been medically examined, request a copy of the doctor's report;
(h) if the complaint is of a serious nature and suggests that other products may be defective, implement the product recall procedures;
(i) comply with the notification obligations etc under the product liability insurance;
(j) if at any stage there appears to be substance to the complaint, refer the matter to the producer's lawyers;
(k) except on the advice of lawyers, make no admission of any kind or offer of compensation. A chance remark such as 'Oh, we have had several complaints about that', might seriously affect liability.

1 See para **19.3.9** below.
2 See for example para **6.5.17** and **6.5.19** below.
3 CPA 1987, s 3(2).

Chapter 4

Food Safety Act 1990: extent, subordinate legislative powers, interpretation and presumptions

4.1 THE ACT

4.1.1 Chapters 1 and 2 explained the importance of the Food Safety Act 1990 (FSA 1990) as the principal measure for food control in Great Britain. They also noted the important changes made by the Food Standards Act 1999 (FSA 1999) to place central government responsibility essentially in the hands of the Food Standards Agency and the Secretary of State for Health, subject to the devolution of functions effected by the Scotland Act 1998 (SA 1998) and under the Government of Wales Act 1998 (GWA 1998).

Extent

4.1.2 This book is concerned with the FSA 1990 and food law applying in England and Wales, but it is important to understand the position elsewhere in the United Kingdom. Although section 29 of the SA 1998 has conferred legislative competence in this field on the Scottish Parliament, for the present at least, the FSA 1990 still also continues to apply to Scotland. With the exception of the power in respect of oil and gas installations referred to below, the substantive provisions of the FSA 1990 have never applied to Northern Ireland which has its own parallel legislation[1]. In practice, the food law rules of the various parts of the United Kingdom are unlikely to diverge very much because they are mostly made in implementation of common Community obligations.

Power to make special provision for the Isles of Scilly has now been removed from the FSA 1990 which applies there as it does to the rest of England[2].

Her Majesty may, by Order in Council, direct that any of the provisions of the Act shall apply to any of the Channel Islands with such exceptions and modifications as may be specified[3].

For the purposes of the FSA 1990, territorial waters of the United Kingdom adjacent to any part of Great Britain are treated as situated in that part[4]. There is also power, for the purposes of the FSA 1990 and subordinate legislation, to provide, by Order in Council, for oil and gas installations and safety zones to be treated as if they were situated in a specified part of the United Kingdom[5].

1 Food Safety (Northern Ireland) Order 1991, SI 1991/762 (NI 7).
2 FSA 1999, Sch 5, paras 9 and 22.
3 FSA 1990, s 57(2).
4 FSA 1990, s 58(1).
5 FSA 1990, s 58(2)–(4); Oil and Gas (Enterprise) Act 1982, s 23.

Enforcement of provisions in and under the Food Safety Act 1990

4.1.3 Chapters 17, 18 and 19 below describe the important provisions of the 1990 Act on food inspections, sampling, analysis and examination, on prosecutions of — the generally strict liability — offences and on the statutory defences which reduce their severity.

Regulations and orders

4.1.4 The FSA 1990 confers on the Secretary of State for Health and devolved authorities wide-ranging powers to make regulations and orders[1] by statutory instrument subject to annulment in pursuance of a resolution of either House of Parliament[2]. With specified exceptions[3], there is an obligation to consult organisations representative of interests likely to be substantially affected before making regulations or orders[4]. Consultation undertaken by the Food Standards Agency may be treated as effective for this purpose[5], there being in any event an obligation to have regard to relevant advice given by the Agency[6].

Powers in previous legislation to regulate food composition, labelling and hygiene and to provide for enforcement of Community obligations were extended in what are now section 16, Schedule 1 and section 17 to enable provision also to be made for food sources, contact materials and microbiological standards. Subordinate legislative capacity was further strengthened by powers to make emergency control orders (section 13) and to regulate novel foods and food sources, genetically modified foods and food sources, to prohibit imports of specified food classes (section 18) and to apply regulations to commercial operations (section 26), as well as to enable food premises to be registered or licensed (section 19) and enforcement authorities to make charges (section 45)[7].

Additionally, substances and activities relating to farm production of food sources may now be regulated under a power inserted by the FSA 1999. This new power extends the scope of the FSA 1990 to complete the cover of relevant on-farm activity which might result in the chemical or biological contamination of food. However, it is expected to be used only where the powers of the Agriculture and Environment Ministers prove inadequate[8].

It may be helpful to mention here specific powers which are the respective sources of two familiar provisions in regulations. First, section 48(1)(a) is the authority for applying specified provisions of the FSA 1990 for the purposes of regulations[9]. Secondly, section 26(1)(b) is the authority for the provision, traditionally included in certain addictive and contaminant regulations, for certified non-compliant food to be treated as failing to comply with the food safety requirements[10] and so liable to condemnation under section 9 of the Act[11].

1 See para **2.2.1** and Appendix D.
2 FSA 1990, s 48(3).
3 The exceptions are regulations under s 17(2) or 18(1)(c) and any order not made under Pt I.
4 FSA 1990, s 48(4).
5 FSA 1990, s 48(4B).
6 FSA 1990, s 48(4A).
7 See further section **4.4** below as to food sources and contact materials, and section **4.5** as to commercial operations.
8 FSA 1990, Sch 1, para 6A.
9 See, for example, Food Labelling Regulations 1996, reg 48, as amended.
10 See, for example, the Miscellaneous Food Additives Regulations 1995, as amended, reg 6 and the Lead in Food Regulations 1979, as amended, reg 5.
11 As to condemnation of food, see section **9.3** below.

4.1.5 Regulations and orders made under the Food Act 1984 or earlier legislation continue in force as if made under equivalent provisions of the FSA 1990[1]. Modifications were made to that subordinate legislation to adapt it to the provisions of the FSA 1990[2]. Regulations made under the European Communities Act 1972 which referred to the previous food legislation were also adapted to the provisions of the FSA 1990[3].

1 FSA 1990, s 59(3) and Sch 4, para (2).
2 Food Safety Act 1990 (Consequential Modifications) (England and Wales) Order 1990, SI 1990/2486.
3 Food Safety Act 1990 (Consequential Modifications) (No 2) (Great Britain) Order 1990, SI 1990/2487.

Application to the Crown

4.1.6 The National Health Service (Amendment) Act 1986[1] applies food legislation to NHS hospitals. By section 54 of the FSA 1990, the provisions of the FSA 1990 and regulations and orders made under it became binding on other Crown establishments[2]. As a result, food supplied in military bases, HM prisons, public service canteens and the like are subject to provisions in and under the Act. The Crown is not criminally liable, but, on the application of an enforcement authority, the High Court may declare unlawful a Crown act or omission which constitutes a contravention. The provisions of the Act and subordinate legislation apply to persons in the public service of the Crown as they apply to others.

Similar provision is made by section 38 of the FSA 1999 to apply that Act to the Crown.

1 As amended by FSA 1990, s 59(1) and Sch 3, para 36(1).
2 For guidance on the practical implications of s 54, see Code of Practice no 13 on the enforcement of the FSA 1990 in relation to Crown premises.

4.2 CONSTRUCTION OF SUBORDINATE LEGISLATION

4.2.1 Expressions used in regulations and orders made under the FSA 1990 have the meaning which they bear in the Act unless the contrary intention appears[1]. Definitions in regulations and orders apply only to the regulations or order in which they appear, in the absence of express provision to the contrary. It is a common misunderstanding in the food industry to assume that definitions in, for example, food labelling regulations apply to regulations concerning particular classes of food and vice versa. They do not unless, of course, the regulations themselves so provide.

1 Interpretation Act 1978, s 11.

4.3 FOOD FOR HUMAN CONSUMPTION

4.3.1–2 Food is defined in the FSA 1990 as including drink; articles and substances of no nutritional value which are used for human consumption; chewing gum and other products of a like nature and use; and articles and substances used as ingredients in the preparation of food. Food does not include live animals or birds, or live fish which are not used for human consumption while they are alive; fodder or feeding stuffs for animals, birds or fish; controlled drugs; or (subject to such exceptions as may be specified in an order made by the Secretary of State for Health) medicinal products or articles or substances which are licensed under the Medicines Act 1968[1].

By contrast with previous food statutes, the FSA 1990 does not exclude water from the definition of 'food', although water supplied to premises by a water undertaker or by means of a private supply is subject not to the substantive provisions of the FSA 1990[2] but to the Water Industry Act 1991 and regulations made thereunder[3].

1 FSA 1990, s 1. As to the meanings in particular of 'animal', 'article', 'fish' and 'substance', see s 53(1).
2 FSA 1990, s 55.
3 See Water Supply (Water Quality) Regulations 1989, as amended; and Private Water Supply Regulations 1991, as amended.

4.3.3 The term 'human consumption' is important because most offences prescribed in and under the FSA 1990 are concerned with food which has been sold, or is intended for sale, for human consumption. Human consumption is defined[1] as including use in the preparation of food for human consumption and thus encompasses food ingredients, but more important are three presumptions specified in section 3 for the purposes of the Act. The presumptions are that—

(a) any food commonly used for human consumption if sold or offered, exposed or kept for sale, shall be presumed, until the contrary is proved, to have been sold or, as the case may be, to have been or to be intended for sale for human consumption;
(b) any food or article or substance commonly used for human consumption or in the manufacture of food for human consumption which is found on premises used for the preparation, storage or sale of that food shall, until the contrary is proved, be presumed to be intended for sale or for manufacturing food for sale for human consumption; and
(c) any article or substance capable of being used in the composition or preparation of any food commonly used for human consumption which is found on premises on which that food is prepared shall, until the contrary is proved, be presumed to be intended for such use.

1 FSA 1990, s 53(1).

4.3.4 These presumptions place on the defendant the burden of proving, as the case may be, that the food, article or substance in question was not intended for sale or for manufacturing food for sale for human consumption, or that the article or substance in question was not intended for use in the composition or preparation of food commonly used for human consumption. The standard of proof is less than is generally required of the prosecution[1]: the defendant has simply to 'prove' his case[2], but positive evidence is required[3]. It would therefore, for example, be prudent for a manufacturer clearly to identify any food at the factory that has been rejected for human consumption. The same is no doubt also true of food that is not yet ready for sale for human consumption, or food that is awaiting acceptance and introduction to the manufacturing process, even though in these cases the presumptions may be easier to rebut.

1 See para **18.2.2** below.
2 *Cant v Harley & Sons Ltd* [1938] 2 All ER 768.
3 *Hooper v Petrou* (1973) 71 LGR 347, [1973] Crim LR 198.

4.4 FOOD SOURCES AND CONTACT MATERIAL

4.4.1 In response to the sophistication of modern food production and the requirements of Community obligations, the scope of powers for regulating food was not only strengthened by extending the definition of 'food' in the FSA 1990, but also by applying them additionally to food sources and contact material. 'Food source' is defined as any growing crop or live animal, bird or fish from which food is intended to be derived (whether by harvesting, slaughtering, milking, collecting eggs or otherwise): 'contact material' is defined as any article or substance which is intended to come into contact with food[1].

1 FSA 1990, s 1(3). As to regulations on contact materials, see further section **10.6** below. As to an example of provision in respect of food sources, see the now revoked Food (Animals and Animal Products from Belgium) (Emergency Control) Order 1999, SI 1999/1542.

4.5 COMMERCIAL OPERATIONS

4.5.1 For the reasons given in section **4.4** above, the thresholds at which the requirements of regulations can be imposed were also increased and systematised by the FSA 1990. Where specified contraventions have occurred, section 26(1)(a) enables provision to be made for prohibiting or regulating the carrying out of any 'commercial operation'. This term is very widely defined by the Act[1]: in relation to any food or contact material, it means, any of the following, namely—

(a) selling, possessing for sale and offering, exposing or advertising for sale;
(b) consigning, delivering or serving by way of sale;
(c) preparing for sale or presenting, labelling or wrapping for the purpose of sale;
(d) storing or transporting for the purpose of sale;
(e) importing and exporting;

and, in relation to a food source, means deriving food from it for the purpose of sale or for purposes connected with sale.

1 FSA 1990, s 1(3).

4.6 SALE

4.6.1 The point of sale, however, is the threshold at which British food controls have traditionally been imposed and it remains the principal one employed in and under the 1990 Act. Most of the prohibitions and restrictions imposed on sale in and under the Act are couched so as to bear also on offer, exposure and having in possession for sale. The general meaning of 'sale' has been summarised in section **3.2** above, but the FSA 1990 extends this to include the supply of food, otherwise than on sale, in the course of a business, and any other thing which is done with respect to food and is specified in an order made by the Secretary of State for Health[1]. The Act also applies to food which is offered as a prize or reward or is given away in similar specified circumstances[2].

As to the term 'business', see para **4.8.1** below.

1 See *Swain v Old Kentucky Restaurants* (1973) 138 JP 84.
2 FSA 1990, s 2.

4.6.2 Exposure for sale means exposure to view in a context where sales are carried out or anticipated[1]. Margarine has been held to be exposed for sale even though wrapped in paper and so not visible to the purchaser[2].

Offer for sale should not be confused with an invitation to do business. The mere display of food in a self-service store does not constitute an 'offer for sale': it is merely an invitation to the customer to offer to buy[3].

1 *McNair v Terroni* [1915] 1 KB 526; *Keating v Horwood* (1926) 90 JP 141.
2 *Wheat v Brown* [1892] 1 QB 418.
3 *Pharmaceutical Society of Great Britain v Boots Cash Chemists (Southern) Ltd* [1952] 2 QB 795, [1952] 2 All ER 456.

4.6.3 The term 'possession for sale' has acquired an increased importance with the extension of previous provisions on unfit food by the FSA 1990 section 8 (on non-compliance with the food safety requirements) and section 9 (on inspection and seizure of suspected food)[1] and with the Community obligation to extend enforcement inspections to all stages of production, manufacture, import into the Community, processing, storage, transport, distribution and trade[2].

The term 'possession' as used in the context of the Act appears to mean possession by the defendant or his agent in fact and should be given a popular and not a narrow construction[3]. Physical possession of food by an agent does not divest the owner of possession[4]; but food left for collection by a buyer at a place determined in the contract of sale may not be in the possession of the vendor[5].

1 See sections **9.2** and **9.3** below.
2 See Council Directive 89/397/EEC, Art 4 and para **17.2.2** below.
3 *Webb v Baker* [1916] 2 KB 753, 80 JP 449.
4 *Towers & Co Ltd v Gray* [1961] 2 QB 351, [1961] 2 All ER 68; *City Fur Manufacturing Co Ltd v Fureenbond (Brokers) London Ltd* [1937] 1 All ER 799; *R v Sleep* (1861) 25 JP 532, CCR.
5 *Oliver v Goodger* [1944] 2 All ER 481.

4.7 IMPORTS AND EXPORTS

4.7.1 Import and export are obvious thresholds for food control, but common market rules have in practice largely confined their application for this purpose to third country trade[1] notwithstanding that, in the FSA 1990, the terms still relate to all goods entering and leaving the United Kingdom.

By section 53(1) of the FSA 1990, 'exportation' and 'importation' have the same meanings in the Act as they have for the purposes of the Customs and Excise Management Act 1979 (C&EMA 1979) and 'export' and 'import' must be construed accordingly.

The terms are not actually defined in the C&EMA 1979. However, 'importer' is defined by section 1(1), in relation to any goods at any time between their importation and the time when they are delivered out of charge, as including any owner or other person for the time being possessed of or beneficially interested in the goods and, in relation to goods imported by means of a pipe-line includes the owner of the pipe-line, and Part IV provides for reporting inwards and otherwise for the control of importation of goods from places outside the United Kingdom. Likewise, 'exporter' is defined, in relation to goods for exportation or for use as stores, as including the shipper of the goods and any person performing in relation to an aircraft functions corresponding to those of a shipper, and Part V provides for entry outwards and otherwise for the control of exportation of goods for a destination outside the United Kingdom[2].

The European Community legislation imposing conditions for import of products of animal origin for human consumption is implemented by regulations under the European Communities Act 1972[3].

1 See, for example, Imported Food Regulations 1997 noted in para **13.1.1** below.
2 Generally, goods removed to the UK from the Isle of Man are deemed not to be imported into the UK and goods removed to the Isle of Man from the UK are deemed not to be exported from the UK: see Isle of Man Act 1979, ss 8 and 9.
3 As to these import conditions, see para **13.1.5** below.

Defences in relation to exports

4.7.2 In laying down the general principles for the performance of official control of foodstuffs, Council Directive 89/397/EEC[1], as extended by the European Economic Area Agreement[2], imposes two particular obligations concerning exports. Member States must ensure that products intended for consignment to another EEA State are inspected with the same care as those intended for marketing on their own territory[3]; and they must also not exclude a product from appropriate control on the grounds that it is intended for export outside the EEA[4]. In general, British food Regulations had previously exempted exports so as to avoid conflict with the rules of importing countries. Existing exemptions were revoked by the Food Safety (Exports) Regulations 1991 and food for export is required to comply with the Regulations unless the defendant proves that it complies with the importing country's domestic legislation[5].

In more recent food Regulations[6], the defence has been restricted to exports to countries having legislation—

(a) which is analogous to the Regulations in question; and
(b) where a substantive Community obligation is being implemented and the export is to another State bound by that obligation, which complies with those provisions.

In these Regulations, Directive 89/397/EEC is essentially implemented by limb (a), which alone appears in the rare instances where the enacted rules are of purely national inspiration[7]. It aims at preventing low grade exports to the third world, while not imposing British rules on sophisticated Western importing countries.

Limb (b) acknowledges that the underlying Community obligations must be respected: the defence will be unavailable if the importing state has failed to implement them. The scope of limb (b) will differ according to whether or not the substantive Community obligation in question has been extended to the European Economic Area: if so, it should consequentially be extended to apply to EEA States.

Whatever its particular form, the defence in relation to exports must evidently be established on the balance of probabilities[8] and, so as to be ready if necessary to discharge the onus which it imposes, the prudent food exporter should no doubt seek the help of the overseas buyer in making advance preparations. He will evidently need to obtain written evidence of the foreign legislation, satisfying himself that it is analogous to the English provisions, that his product complies with it and, where appropriate, that the foreign legislation complies with the substantive Community obligation in question.

1 As to the implementation of other provisions of Council Directive 89/397/EEC, see section **17.2** below.
2 See para **1.8.1** above.
3 Article 2(2).
4 Article 3.

5 For an anomalous form of the defence in relation to exports, see Food (Control of Irradiation) Regulations 1990, reg 8.
6 See, for example, Food Labelling Regulations 1996, reg 47.
7 See, for example, Bread and Flour Regulations 1998, reg 9.
8 See *Cant v Harley & Sons Ltd* [1938] 2 All ER 768 and para **4.3.4** above.

4.8 FOOD BUSINESS AND PREMISES

4.8.1 For the purpose of protecting consumers, particularly in relation to hygiene, controls are required not only on food itself, but also on the undertakings which deal with it and on the places where they operate. Substantive provisions of this kind are noted in chapter 11, as regards unhygienic businesses, and in chapters 12 and 13, as regards licensing and hygiene regulations.

In support of these important provisions, section 1(3) of the FSA 1990 contains a number of other definitions. A 'food business' is defined as meaning 'any business in the course of which commercial operations with respect to food or food sources are carried out'[1] and a 'business' as including 'the undertaking of a canteen, club, school, hospital or institution, whether carried on for profit or not, and any undertaking or activity carried on by a public or local authority'.

'Food premises' means 'any premises used for the purposes of a food business', while 'premises' includes 'any place, any vehicle, stall or moveable structure, and for such purposes as may be specified in an order made by the Secretary of State, any ship or aircraft of a description so specified'.

It might usefully be recalled that 'premises' and 'business' are also of importance to the powers of entry in section 32 of the FSA 1990[2] and that the latter term is relevant to sections 2[3] and 22[4].

1 See *Salford City Council v Abbeyfield (Worsley) Society Ltd* [1993] COD 384.
2 See section **17.5** below.
3 See para **4.6.1** above.
4 See para **19.4.1** below.

Chapter 5

Food composition: general safety and quality

5.1 INTRODUCTION

5.1.1 This chapter successively considers the offence of rendering food injurious to health, which now appears in section 7 of the Food Safety Act 1990 (FSA 1990), and the offence of selling food not of the nature, substance or quality demanded, now to be found in section 14 of that Act. As indicated in para **1.1.1** above, their predecessors were enacted in 1875 as the main controls on the chemical composition of food with the result that there is a substantial body of case law relevant to section 14 in particular.

It is important to note, however, that the FSA 1990 modified the previous structure of the legislation. On the face of things at least, the chemical and biological control provisions had remained separate. The FSA 1990 acknowledged and extended an integration that had in practice taken place over the years. In particular, it classified the prohibition on rendering food injurious to health provision under a 'food safety' heading, together with key provisions aimed at the biological control of food and originated in the Public Health Acts. These biological control provisions are the prohibition on selling unfit food and the powers for the inspection and seizure of suspect food which are now respectively contained in sections 8 and 9 of the FSA 1990. The modification was no mere formal change. The prohibition on selling, or offering or exposing for sale of food rendered injurious to health was incorporated into section 8 with the prohibition on sale etc of unfit food, by the inclusion of both in a new wider concept of 'food safety requirements'. Food failing to comply with the food safety requirements was likewise subjected to the section 9 powers to inspect and seize suspect food. This amalgamation, within sections 8 and 9, of chemical with biological food safety controls is considered further in para **5.3.1** and in chapter 9.

At the same time, the prohibition, in what is now section 14 of the Act, on selling food not of the nature, substance or quality demanded was classified under a 'consumer protection' heading. It should not be assumed, however, that this prohibition covers only selling which threatens the purchaser's pocket. As explained below, it most certainly also continues to extend to the selling of food which threatens the purchaser's health.

5.2 RENDERING FOOD INJURIOUS TO HEALTH

5.2.1 Food law owes its origins to the reprehensible practice of adding substances to food to make it go further or the abstraction of substances which may have an alternative use. The addition of water to milk and other drinks, sawdust to bread, sand to pepper and many similar practices were common in the mid-nineteenth century. The abstraction of fat from milk, lean from meat and similar practices, although perhaps not as frequent because they involved more effort, were also practised. In more recent times the use of harmful additives in food has posed a danger to the public.

5.2.2 Modern law prohibiting the sale of adulterated food in fact dates back to the Adulteration of Food and Drink Act 1860 and, by the time of the Sale of Food and Drugs Act 1875, the prohibition on rendering food injurious to health by adulteration becomes recognisably like section 7 of the FSA 1990. Section 7 makes it an offence for any person to render food injurious to health by means of the addition of any article or substance to food, or the use of any article or substance as an ingredient in the preparation of food, or abstracting any constituent from food and subjecting food to any other process or treatment, with intent that it shall be sold for human consumption[1]. In requiring proof of intent, section 7 is exceptional. In the 1990 Act, offences are generally strict liability[2].

1 FSA 1990, s 7(1).
2 See para **19.1.1** below.

5.2.3 To secure a conviction under section 7 of the FSA 1990, it is necessary to establish that the food was in fact injurious to health[1]. In determining whether food is injurious to health, a court is required to have regard not only to the probable effect of that food on the health of a person consuming it, but also the probable cumulative effect of food of substantially the same composition on the health of a person consuming it in ordinary quantities[2]. The effects of exceptional long term consumption is thus to be discounted as, it seems, are the effects on exceptional individuals. The food in question must be injurious to a substantial portion of the community, such as invalids and children[3]. However, the prohibition was extended by the inclusion in the FSA 1990 of section 7(3). This provides that 'injury', in relation to health, includes any impairment, whether permanent or temporary.

1 *Hull v Horsnell* (1904) 68 JP 591.
2 FSA 1990, s 7(2).
3 *Cullen v McNair* (1908) 6 LGR 753, 72 JP 280; and *Haigh v Aerated Bread Co Ltd* [1916] 1 KB 878.

5.2.4 Positive action by way of addition to, subtraction from or treatment of food is necessary for an offence to have been committed. The section does not, therefore, apply to food which has become injurious to health by reason of decomposition. Moreover, illegal residues of pesticides and veterinary medicines are not, it is submitted, caught by this provision, because the substances in question are added not to 'food', but to 'food sources'. In food, such residues are properly to be regarded as contaminants, rather than additives[1].

1 See ch 10.

5.2.5 The term 'abstract' has given rise to difficulties in the past. A failure to correct the natural tendency of a constituent of a fluid to rise to the top or sink to the bottom of a container may amount to abstraction[1] as, presumably, would the failure to prevent the escape of an evanescent constituent. However, reducing the proportion of a constituent by dilution is not abstraction[2].

1 *Penrice v Brander* 1921 JC 63; *Bridges v Griffin* [1925] 2 KB 233.
2 *Dearden v Whiteley* (1916) 85 LJ KB 1420.

5.2.6 There is a lack of modern judicial authority on the section 7 prohibition since deliberate adulteration of food by producers with injurious substances is rare today. Deliberate contamination by food terrorists and the illegal use of food additives are practices covered by more specific offences[1]. However, as is shown by examples like the detection in 1985 of di-ethylene glycol in certain German wines, adulteration by producers has not been entirely eradicated and section 7 remains as a threat to any who contemplate committing this grave form of dishonest practice.

1 See respectively Public Order Act 1986, s 38 and the various regulations considered in section **10.2** below.

5.3 FOOD NOT OF THE NATURE OR SUBSTANCE OR QUALITY DEMANDED

5.3.1 As indicated in paras **1.1.1** and **5.1.1**, what is now section 14 of the FSA 1990 has been the principal protection for the consumer from unsatisfactory food since 1875. It is an offence for a person to sell to the purchaser's prejudice any food which is not of the nature or substance or quality demanded by the purchaser[1]. The section is thus responsive to a bespoke stipulation by the purchaser, but where, as in the normal way, there is none and where there is no statutory standard for the food, the court must decide from the evidence what was demanded. This is considered further in para **5.3.11**.

The section has proved remarkably flexible and has been used more than any other provision in current or former food law. It is by no means limited to the context, in which it was enacted, of ensuring that the composition of food is as described. Where unfitness for human consumption in contravention of what is now section 8 could not clearly be established, it has been used for cases of chemical contamination, for cases of bacterial contamination by mould or microorganisms and their toxins and for cases of contamination by extraneous matter (ie foreign bodies)[2].

However, section 14 is not without limitation. By its very nature it is unavailable in respect of food in possession or offered or exposed for sale. There must be a sale to constitute an offence. This was perceived as a significant shortcoming particularly in relation to contamination cases and, on the enactment of FSA 1990, the opportunity was taken to fill the gap. This was achieved by creating a third limb to the concept of 'food safety requirements' in section 8(2)[3].

It should also be noted that, in cases concerning a seller's description, there can be an overlap between section 14 and section 1 of the Trade Descriptions Act 1968 (TDA 1968) which prohibits false trade descriptions (including oral statements[4]) applied to goods.

1 FSA 1990, s 14.
2 See further paras **5.3.5–5.3.8**.
3 See further para **9.2.2**.
4 Scc TDA 1968, s 4(2).

Sell

5.3.2 For the commission of an offence contrary to section 14 of the FSA 1990 there must have been a sale for human consumption[1], taking into account the extended meaning of 'sale'[2] — see para **4.6.1** above. In self-service stores a sale does not take place until the cash is accepted at the check-out[3]. This is of importance to authorised officers of enforcement authorities in purchasing samples for analysis or examination[4] and undertaking the subsequent procedures prescribed for these purposes[5].

1 *Thompson v Ball* (1948) 92 Sol Jo 272.
2 FSA 1990, s 2.
3 *Pharmaceutical Society of Great Britain v Boots Cash Chemists (Southern) Ltd* [1952] 2 QB 795, [1952] 2 All ER 456.
4 See para **17.4.2** below.
5 See paras **17.4.3** and **17.4.4** respectively below.

Prejudice of the purchaser

5.3.3 For an offence to arise under this section the purchaser must have been prejudiced[1]. The word 'prejudice' does not imply actual damage to the purchaser. As early as 1879, it was decided[2] that the prejudice contemplated by the legislation is paying for one thing but getting something inferior. Without the words 'to the prejudice of the purchaser', an offence would be committed if the purchaser received a product superior to what was demanded. Moreover, had the section been construed as meaning that the purchaser must suffer pecuniary prejudice, much of the beneficial effect of the legislation would have been nullified. An enforcement officer making a test purchase uses not his own, but public money. On this point, later that same year an amending provision (now to be found in section 14(2) of the FSA 1990) expressly excluded the defence that a purchaser buying for analysis or examination is not prejudiced.

1 *TW Lawrence & Sons Ltd v Burleigh* (1981) 146 JP 134.
2 *Hoyle v Hitchman* (1879) 4 QBD 233.

5.3.4 The predecessors to the current Act contained provision for notices by which the true nature, substance and quality of the food in question could be declared thus avoiding prejudice to the purchaser and liability under the section. There was much judicial consideration of the sufficiency or otherwise of notices given to purchasers[1]. Although the FSA 1990 dropped specific provision of this kind in favour of a general due diligence defence[2], it evidently remains the case that a person cannot be prejudiced if given positive information as to the true nature, substance and quality of the food. However, such information, no matter how accurate, is no defence where a compositional standard has been laid down by law for the food. Thus, a purchaser would be prejudiced by the sale to him of pork sausages containing only 50% of meat notwithstanding a notice to that effect, because such products are required by regulations[3] to contain not less than 65% of meat. In such a case there would be an offence of 'quality' under this section and one of deficiency of meat content under the Regulations.

1 See, for example, *Sandys v Small* (1878) 3 QBD 449; and *Goldup v John Manson Ltd* [1982] QB 161, [1981] 3 All ER 257.
2 See section **19.3** below.
3 Meat Products and Spreadable Fish Products Regulations 1984.

Nature, substance, quality

5.3.5 Since 1928 these terms have been alternatives[1]. For the purposes of proceedings only one of them must be selected, otherwise the information will be bad for duplicity[2].

However, it is important to bear in mind, when considering what is said of them below, that they are by no means mutually exclusive categories and where a case falls within more than one, it is open to the prosecutor to choose whichever is considered the most appropriate[3]. See, for example, paras **5.3.7** and **5.3.8** below on the substance and quality of mouldy food.

1 Until the Food and Drugs (Adulteration) Act 1928, the provision read 'nature, substance *and* quality'.
2 Magistrates' Courts Rules 1981, r 12; *Bastin v Davies* [1950] 2 KB 579, [1950] 1 All ER 1095. See further para **18.2.7** below.
3 *Preston v Greenclose Ltd* (1975) 139 JP Jo 245; *Shearer v Rowe* (1985) 149 JP 698.

Nature

5.3.6 This term is evidently appropriate where a different sort of food is sold from that demanded by the purchaser. Thus, fruit or fish not of the variety or species asked for would not be of the 'nature' demanded. It has, for example, been held to cover savin sold for saffron[1], reformed white fish sold as scampi[2], minced beef containing quantities of pork and lamb meat[3] and, in one startling case, caustic soda mistakenly sold as lemonade[4].

It should also be noted that where the food sold is of a different sort from that described there might also be contraventions of regulation 5(a) of the Food Labelling Regulations 1996, section 15 of the FSA 1990 or section 1 of the TDA 1968.

1 *Knight v Bowers* (1885) 14 QBD 845.
2 *Preston v Greenclose Ltd* (1975) 139 JP Jo 245.
3 *Shearer v Rowe* (1985) 149 JP 698.
4 *Meah v Roberts* [1978] 1 All ER 97, [1977] 1 WLR 1187.

Substance

5.3.7 This term is usually applied to circumstances in which the composition of the food is incompatible with what was demanded, as in cases where the food contains improper ingredients or adulterants. Until the 1990 Act, it would also have been the most obvious head for dealing with foreign bodies[1] and contaminants[2] in food, but section 8(2)(c) of the Act, referred to in para **9.2.2** below, now affords a more specific basis.

Even though a foreign body is not of the substance demanded, an offence may not necessarily be committed. A distinction was drawn in two milk cases. There was a good defence where the foreign body was a sterile and harmless milk cap[3], but a conviction where it was a dangerous sliver of glass[4]. In a more recent case, however, a bottle of milk containing a green straw was held not to be of the quality demanded[5].

Mould has also been regarded as contamination of food and a matter affecting its substance[6].

1 *Smedleys Ltd v Breed* [1974] AC 839, [1974] 2 All ER 21 (caterpillar in a tin of peas).
2 *Hall v Owen-Jones and Jones (t/a Central Dairies)* [1967] 1 WLR 1362 (excess penicillin in milk).
3 *Edwards v Llaethdy Meirion Ltd* [1957] Crim LR 402.
4 *Southworth v Whitewell Dairies Ltd* (1958) 122 JP 322.
5 *Barber v Co-operative Wholesale Society Ltd* (1983) 147 JP 296.
6 See further paras **5.3.8** and **9.2.2** below.

Quality

5.3.8 In *Anness v Grivell* [1915] 3 KB 685, it was held that 'quality' means 'commercial quality' and not merely description. The appellant sold as 'a very good mixture of butter and margarine' food containing 80% margarine, 15.5% water, salt etc and only 4.5% butter. The magistrates considered that such a small quantity of butter prevented the mixture being of the quality claimed for it. Because at that time the legislation prohibited sale of margarine containing more than 10% butter fat, the Divisional Court felt compelled to hold that no offence had been committed, but intimated that their decision might well have been otherwise had it not been for the limit on butter content. As indicated in para **5.3.1**, where there is neither statutory standard for the food nor special demand by the purchaser, the courts must decide what quality of food an ordinary purchaser would expect to receive. Other instances of food quality which have been considered by the courts have concerned deficient extract of meat and malt wine[1], alleged sugar deficiency in orange citric flavoured cordial[2], excess fat in minced beef[3] and excess sugar in diet cola[4].

Additionally, action under the quality head has been taken against mouldy, bad and decomposed food[5].

1 *Bowker v Woodroffe* [1928] 1 KB 217, [1927] All ER Rep 415.
2 *Collins Arden Products Ltd v Barking Corpn* [1943] KB 419, [1943] 2 All ER 249.
3 *TW Lawrence & Sons Ltd v Burleigh* (1981) 146 JP 134.
4 *McDonald's Hamburgers Ltd v Windle* (1986) 151 JP 333.
5 *Watford Corpn v Maypole Ltd* [1970] 1 QB 573, [1970] 1 All ER 554; *Swain v Old Kentucky Restaurants* (1973) 138 JP 84; *Tesco Stores Ltd v Roberts* [1974] 3 All ER 74, [1974] 1 WLR 1253. As to mouldy food, see also paras **5.3.7** and **9.2.2**.

The food demanded

5.3.9 As indicated in para **5.3.1** above, the nature, substance and quality of the food for the purposes of section 14 is defined in terms of the purchaser's demand.

5.3.10 Where there is a statutory standard, as indicated in para **5.3.4**, the purchaser will be deemed to have demanded a food of that standard. The logic of this proposition is that if a buyer demands a food for which there is a statutory standard but receives an inferior product, he is prejudiced and the offence is committed.

A purchaser who insisted on a product inferior to the statutory standard would evidently be guilty of a secondary party offence such as procuring the illegal sale.

5.3.11 Paragraphs **5.3.1** and **5.3.8** above have already noted that where there is no statutory standard the justices must determine the nature, substance and quality of the food demanded by the purchaser as a question of fact on the basis of the evidence[1]. There may have been an express contract term[2], but for the most part what was demanded must be ascertained from the surrounding circumstances of the case. In many cases, it has been concluded that the purchaser demanded food which corresponds in nature, substance or quality with that normally sold in the trade[3]. In some cases, the quality of the food impliedly demanded may depend on whether different qualities were available at different prices[4]. The public analyst's opinion about the normal standard for the food has always been an important contribution to the magistrates' deliberations. It cannot be substituted for the standard demanded by the purchaser[5], but has often been accepted as that standard where the defence has elected to call no evidence of its own on the point[6].

Non-statutory recommendations, such as those of the Food Advisory Committee[7], may afford influential evidence of what purchasers normally demand. For this reason the Government has, since the lifting of emergency controls after the Second World War, been wary of responding to requests to put out codes of practice and similar guidance containing specific recommendations about food composition. For the Government to define the citizen's obligations under section 14 by this backdoor method would potentially obfuscate criminal liability and sidestep the safeguards of parliamentary scrutiny and publicity attendant on standards set by the authorised process of regulations under sections 16 or 17 of the Act.

1 *Roberts v Leeming* (1905) 69 JP 417 (margarine); *Wilson and McPhee v Wilson* (1903) 68 JP 175 (brandy); *Preston v Jackson* (1928) 73 Sol Jo 712 (vinegar); *Hunt v Richardson* [1916] 2 KB 446 (milk).
2 *Hunt v Richardson* [1916] 2 KB 446.
3 See, for example, *Sandys v Rhodes* (1903) 67 JP 352 (variety of tapioca sold as sago); *Webb v Jackson Wyness Ltd* [1948] 2 All ER 1054 (non-brewed vinegar); *Hughes v Traynor* [1916] 2 IR 275 (maize meal with husk and germ removed sold as white meal).
4 *Morton v Green* (1881) 8 R (Ct of Sess) 36, 18 Sc LR 570; *Goldup v John Manson Ltd* [1982] QB 161, [1981] 3 All ER 257.
5 *Goldup v John Manson Ltd* [1982] QB 161, [1981] 3 All ER 257.
6 *Bowker v Woodroffe* [1928] 1 KB 217, [1927] All ER Rep 415; *Broughton v Whittaker* [1944] 2 All ER 544, [1944] KB 269; *Webb v Jackson Wyness Ltd* [1948] 2 All ER 1054; *Mills (AJ) & Co Ltd v Williams* [1964] Crim L R 533, DC.
7 *Mills (AJ) & Co Ltd v Williams* [1964] Crim L R 533, DC.

The future

5.3.12 The deliberate withdrawal of the Government and the European Community in recent years from the wholesale fixing of food standards[1] could result in increased recourse to section 14. In any event, this venerable provision continues to stand as the principal protection for the consumer against the sale of unsatisfactory food.

1 See in particular section **1.3** above and paras **7.1.1** and **7.5.1** below.

Chapter 6

Food labelling, presentation and advertising

6.1 INTRODUCTION

6.1.1 Rules for the protection of consumers through the control of labelling, presentation and advertising of food either restrict or require what is displayed. Labelling restrictions and requirements have long been employed in British food law which thus needed only adaptation in order to comply with the same two pronged approach adopted by Community law.

6.1.2 The basic Community provision restricting what may appear on food labels is Article 2(1) of the general labelling Directive 79/112/EEC, as amended. Labelling and methods used are prohibited if they could mislead the purchaser to a material degree. This restriction is applied by Article 2(3)(a) and (b) of the Directive respectively to presentation and to advertising of foodstuffs[1].

1 For the British implementing law, see sections **6.2** and **6.3** below.

6.1.3 The basic Community provision requiring what is to appear on food labels is Article 3 of the general labelling Directive 79/112/EEC, as amended. In particular the name and the list of ingredients are compulsory in the labelling of foodstuffs[1]. These provisions assumed a special importance after the landmark European Court *Cassis de Dijon* judgment[2]. Since then, national measures have been permitted to restrict import of products lawfully marketed in other Member States only if they aim to protect an important public interest and are proportionate to that objective. For consumer protection and the defence of fair trading, the European Court has regarded compulsory labelling in compliance with the Directive 79/112/EEC as adequate. Even a national requirement that bearnais sauce made from vegetable fat (rather than butter and eggs) be designated accordingly was held to be an illegal hindrance to imports from other Member States, if the substance was already included in the list of ingredients in accordance with Directive 79/112/EEC[3].

As noted in its White Paper on Food Safety[4], the Commission is currently pursuing a proposal to consolidate Directive 79/112/EEC.

1 For the British implementing law, see section **6.5** below.
2 See section **1.3** above.
3 Case C-51/94 *EC Commission v Germany* [1995] ECR I-3599. As to the requirement to list ingredients, see para **6.5.7** below.
4 COM (1999) 719 final.

6.2 FALSE OR MISLEADING LABELS AND ADVERTISEMENTS

6.2.1 In Great Britain Article 2(1) of Directive 79/112/EEC is primarily[1] implemented by the Food Safety Act 1990 (FSA 1990), section 15(1) whereby it is an offence to give with any food sold, or to display with any food offered or exposed for sale, or in possession for sale, a label, whether or not attached to or printed on the wrapper or container, which falsely describes the food or which is likely to mislead as to the nature or substance or quality of the food. The comprehensiveness of the prohibition imposed by section 15(1) is confirmed by Article 2(1)(a) of the Directive which governs its interpretation[2]. Thus, labelling must not mislead to a material degree as to the characteristics of the foodstuff and, in particular, as to its nature, identity, properties, composition, quantity, durability, origin or provenance, method of manufacture or production[3]. Additionally, misleading food claims are prohibited[4].

1 See also Trade Descriptions Act 1968 (TDA 1968), s 1. As to the implementation of Article 2(1)(b) by the Food Labelling Regulations 1996, Sch 6, Pt I, para 2, see para **8.2.2** below.
2 See para **1.2.1** above.
3 Directive 79/112/EEC, Art 2(1)(a)(i).
4 Directive 79/112/EEC, Art 2(1)(a)(ii) and (iii), as to which see para **8.1.1** below.

6.2.2 Article 2(1) of Directive 79/112/EEC, as applied to advertising by Article 2(3)(b), is implemented by the FSA 1990, section 15(2). This provides that it is an offence to publish, or to be a party to the publication of, an advertisement which falsely describes any food or which is likely to mislead as to the nature or substance or quality of any food.

A label or advertisement

6.2.3 These offences are basic to the prevention of false or misleading labels and advertisements and are very wide in their application. 'Labelling' is defined by Article 1(3)(a) of Directive 79/112/EEC as 'any words, particulars, trade marks, brand name, pictorial matter or symbol relating to a foodstuff and placed on any packaging, document, notice, label, ring or collar accompanying or referring to such foodstuff'. That definition is not reproduced in the Act but the use of the words 'whether or not attached to or printed on the wrapper or container' suggests that information given visually by words or illustrations could give rise to an offence. A label would not include a verbal statement but the definition of 'advertisement' in the Act[1] includes any notice, circular, label, wrapper, invoice or other document, and any public announcement made orally or by any means of producing or transmitting light or sound. It should also be borne in mind that a verbal statement can be a false trade description under the TDA 1968[2] which, in appropriate cases, is often employed by enforcement authorities instead of or in addition to proceedings under the FSA 1990[3]. For all practical purposes it may be assumed that any false or misleading statement as to food for human consumption, however given, is an offence.

1 FSA 1990, s 53(1).
2 TDA 1968, ss 1 and 4(2).
3 See, however, TDA 1968, s 2(5)(a) noted at para **7.1.2**(1) below.

Falsely describes the food

6.2.4 Prosecuting authorities have not employed this offence as frequently as the alternative 'likely to mislead . . .' because the term 'false' is stronger and more difficult to prove. It is necessary to prove that a label or advertisement is explicitly false, that is, wholly untrue. However, a court is not precluded from finding that a label or advertisement is false or misleading even if it contains an accurate statement of the composition of the food[1]. The numerous occasions on which the concept of falseness of food labels has been considered by the courts in civil litigation or with regard to offences against the trade descriptions law should be treated with some caution bearing in mind that the burden of proof of falseness in civil proceedings is different from that in criminal law and that 'a false trade description' includes a misleading statement[2].

As regards civil law, examples have already been given, in para **3.1.1** above, of cases in which the public has been held to have been deceived into believing that one producer's food is in fact that of another (that is, where the tort of passing off has been committed). Examples of false trade descriptions are—

(a) the use of the word 'port' for a product not from Portugal[3];
(b) the labelling as 'Fine British Tarragona Wine', a mixture of British and Tarragona wine which was nothing like Tarragona wine[4];
(c) the description of a solution of acetic acid and caramel as 'vinegar'[5].

Under a forerunner of section 15 of the FSA 1990, a fruit juice was held not to have been falsely described as 'natural' even though it had been reconstituted in part from concentrated juice and had been pasteurised[6].

1 FSA 1990, s 15(4).
2 TDA 1968, s 3(2).
3 *Sandeman v Gold* [1924] 1 KB 107.
4 *Holmes v Pipers Ltd* [1914] 1 KB 57.
5 *Kat v Diment* [1951] 1 KB 34, [1950] 2 All ER 657.
6 *Amos v Britvic Ltd* (1984) 149 JP 13.

Likely to mislead

6.2.5 Although representations may be literally true but practically false because of what is omitted[1], it would no doubt in general be prudent for a prosecutor under section 15 of the FSA 1990 to employ a charge of 'likely to mislead' unless there is a misstatement of fact which is sufficiently clear to sustain the allegation of the 'falseness' of the description in question.

As indicated above, a label or advertisement may be misleading even where it contains a factually correct statement of the composition of the food. Notwithstanding that a label bears an accurate list of ingredients in compliance with labelling requirements[2], it may be misleading by virtue of the product name, instructions for use, background illustrations, processes or treatments. A label which stated 'fully prepared, sliced, selected tinned apples (unsweetened)' was held to be misleading because the fruit had lost about 25% of its original solids through the addition of water[3].

Attempts to prevent supposed misuses of traditional food names and terms have not proved an unqualified success. A label which stated '2 Chicken Breast Steaks — Flaked and formed chicken in a crispy crumb' was held by the Crown Court on appeal not be to be misleading, even though the product was not comprised of solid muscle meat[4]. Similarly, in proceedings under the TDA 1968 and the Food Labelling Regulations, a product labelled 'Pura Vegetable Lard' with a subsidiary statement '100% vegetable oils' was held not to be misleading despite the fact that lard is a product wholly of pig fat[5]. On the other hand, labels stating 'Elmlea Single' and 'Elmlea Whipping', with the additional words 'the real alternative to cream', were held by the Crown Court on appeal to be misleading when used on products made from vegetable oil and packed in cartons resembling those usually used for cream[6]. The information given on the labels was factually correct but the average customer was likely to be misled.

1 *R v Lord Kylsant* [1932] 1 KB 442; *R v Bishirgian* [1936] 1 All ER 586; *Curtis v Chemical Cleaning and Dyeing Co Ltd* [1951] 1 KB 805, [1951] 1 All ER 631, CA.
2 Food Labelling Regulations 1996, regs 5(b) and 12–18.
3 *Arlidge v Blue Cap Foods (Kent) Ltd* (1965) 63 LGR 167.
4 *GW Padley (Poultry) Ltd v Elkington* (1986) unreported.
5 *Wolkind and Northcott v Pura Foods Ltd* (1987) 151 JP 492.
6 *Burleigh v Van Den Berghs & Jurgens Ltd* [1987] BTLC 337.

6.3 PRESENTATION

6.3.1 The Community restriction on misleading presentation of foodstuffs imposed by Article 2(1) and 2(3)(a) of General Labelling Directive 79/112/EEC was a novel one to British law. In implementation of these provisions the FSA 1990, section 15(3) now makes it unlawful to sell, offer or expose for sale, or have in possession for the purpose of sale, any food the presentation of which is likely to mislead as to the nature or substance or quality of the food.

Definition of presentation

6.3.2 Presentation is defined[1] as including the shape, appearance and packaging of the food, the way in which the food is arranged when it is exposed for sale and the setting in which the food is displayed with a view to sale, but does not include any form of labelling or advertising. Truthful labelling may mitigate or negate any misleading presentation.

1 FSA 1990, s 53(1).

Examples of food presentation

6.3.3 Prosecutions for misleading presentation have included cases on fatty mince displayed under red lighting to give a misleading impression as to its fat content; meat containing novel protein displayed together with whole meat; analogue dairy products being displayed with genuine milk-based products; and artificially-flavoured fruit products being packed in fruit-shaped containers.

6.4 CONTROL OF MISLEADING AND COMPARATIVE ADVERTISING

6.4.1 In addition to the prohibition on misleading food advertising imposed by Article 2 of Directive 79/112/EEC but in no way affecting it, the Community has made provision, by Council Directive 84/450/EEC, in respect of misleading advertising and, by amending Directive 97/55/EC, in respect of comparative advertising. A further amendment to Directive 84/450/EEC is proposed by the Commission's White Paper on Food Safety[1] to clarify its scope with regard to claims concerning food, health and the environment.

Directive 84/450/EEC is primarily implemented by the Control of Misleading Advertisements Regulations 1988, as amended. These Regulations are to be amended again as from 23 April 2000 to take account of the provisions of Directive 97/55/EC.

Directive 84/450/EEC requires Member States to ensure that adequate and effective means exist to combat misleading advertising and for compliance with the provisions on comparative advertising in the interests of consumers as well as competitors and the general public.

In the United Kingdom, the Director General of Fair Trading is required to consider complaints other than those covered by the Broadcasting Act 1990. Before doing so, the Director may require the complainant to satisfy him that appropriate means of dealing with the complaint have been tried and that, despite being given reasonable opportunity to do so, those means have not adequately dealt with the complaint. The Director determines what means he considers appropriate in any particular case. He might, for example, expect the matter to be referred to the relevant food authority or, as described in para **6.4.2**, to the self-regulatory Advertising Standards Authority. The Director can bring proceedings for an injunction to prevent illegal advertisements.

Needless to say, frivolous and vexatious complaints are expressly excluded from consideration.

In implementation of Directive 97/55/EC, the duties and powers of the Director in respect of misleading advertising are to be extended to apply in relation to comparative advertising.

Complaints about broadcast advertising are to be referred to the Independent Television Commission, the Radio Authority or the Welsh Fourth Channel Authority as described in para **6.4.3**.

1 COM (1999) 719 final.

6.4.2 Non-broadcast advertising is subject to the self-regulatory system of the advertising industry. The British Code of Advertising and Sales Promotion[1] contains specific rules for alcoholic drinks, vitamins, minerals and other food supplements and slimming aids. The Code is administered by the Advertising Standards Authority from whom copies of the code can be obtained[2].

1 British Code of Advertising and Sales Promotion (October 1999).
2 Advertising Standards Authority, Brook House, 2–16, Torrington Place, London, WC1E 7HW; Tel: 020 7580 5555.

6.4.3 Broadcast food advertisements are subject to control under the Broadcasting Act 1990 (BA 1990). For commercial television services and for independent radio services the responsible bodies are the Independent Television Commission[1] and the Radio Authority[2] respectively, in each case in relation to the services which they license. They are each charged with drawing up and securing observance of Codes for these purposes[3]. The Codes contain provisions on health claims and dietary supplements. The Commission and Authority are also required to consider complaints about misleading advertisements in licensed services[4] and in certain circumstances may give directions to exclude advertisements[5]. Sianel Pedawr Cymru (SC4) is regulated by the Welsh Fourth Channel Authority, which is also responsible for dealing with complaints about misleading advertisements[6].

In implementation of Directive 97/55/EC, the duties of the Commission, the Radio Authority and the Welsh Authority in relation to misleading advertisements are to be extended to apply to comparative advertisements.

1 BA 1990, s 9.
2 BA 1990, s 93.
3 Copies of the Codes can be obtained from the Independent Television Commission, 31 Foley Street, London W1; Tel: 020 7255 3000 and the Radio Authority, Holbrook House, Great Queen Street, London WC2; Tel: 020 7430 2724.
4 Control of Misleading Advertisements Regulations 1988, reg 8
5 Control of Misleading Advertisements Regulations 1988, reg 9.
6 Control of Misleading Advertisements Regulations 1988, regs 10 and 11.

6.5 FOOD LABELLING REQUIREMENTS

6.5.1 The principal Community food labelling requirements are prescribed by the general food labelling Directive 79/112/EEC[1] and implemented in Great Britain by the Food Labelling Regulations 1996 as amended. The major part of this section is devoted to these implementing provisions. Paragraph **6.5.22** summarises the implementation of Regulations 1139/98/EC and 50/2000/EC concerning indications on food produced from genetically modified organisms (gmos). Paragraph **6.5.24** summarises the Food (Lot Marking) Regulations 1996 which implement Directive 89/396/EEC (on indications or marks the lot to which a foodstuff belongs).

1 See para **6.1.3** above.

The Food Labelling Regulations 1996 generally

6.5.2 The Food Labelling Regulations 1996 are arranged into the following five parts—

- Part I (Preliminary)
- Part II (Food to be delivered as such to the ultimate consumer or to caterers)
- Part III (Claims, nutrition labelling and misleading descriptions)
- Part IV (Offences and legal proceedings)
- Part V (Revocations, amendments and transitional provisions).

The provisions of Part II are considered in this section together with the requirement for indications on food produced from genetically modified organisms and for lot marking, while the provisions of Part III are explained in section **7.6** (on misleading descriptions), section **8.2** (on claims) and sections **8.3** and **8.4** (on nutrition labelling).

These substantive requirements are supported by the provisions of Parts I and IV. Besides containing essential definitions, Part I sets out the general exemptions. These include a mutual recognition clause[1] the general effect of which is to permit the import of food coming from a Member State and complying with the rules laid down by that State[2], as well as of food to which the EEA Agreement applies brought into Great Britain from an EEA State in which it was lawfully produced and sold[3]. Except insofar as they relate to advertising, the Regulations also do not apply to food which is not intended for sale for human consumption[4].

1 Food Labelling Regulations 1996, reg 3(1). See *Hackney London Borough Council v Cedar Trading Ltd* (1999) 163 JP 749.
2 As to mutual recognition and mutual recognition clauses, see para **1.3.2** above.
3 As to the EEA Agreement and EEA States, see para **1.9.1** above.
4 Food Labelling Regulations 1996, reg 3(3)(a).

The Food Labelling Regulations 1996 Part II

6.5.3 As indicated above, Part II of the Food Labelling Regulations 1996 generally implements food labelling Directive 79/112/EEC and applies to food which is ready for delivery to the ultimate consumer or to a catering establishment. However, for some foods specific labelling provision is made. As a result, except for the provisions relating to packaging gases and foods containing sweeteners, added sugar and sweeteners, aspartame or more than 10% added polyols[1], Part II does not apply to the following products so far as their labelling is controlled by other Regulations—

(a) specified sugar products;
(b) cocoa and chocolate products;
(c) honey;
(d) condensed milk products and dried milk products;
(e) coffee, coffee mixture, coffee extract product, chicory extract product or other such designated product which is ready for delivery to a catering establishment;
(f) hen eggs;
(g) spreadable fats;
(h) wine and grape musts;
(i) sparkling wines and aerated sparkling wines;
(j) liqueur wines, semi-sparkling wines and aerated semi-sparkling wines;
(k) spirit drinks;
(l) fresh fruit and vegetables;
(m) preserved sardines;
(n) preserved tuna and bonito;
(o) additives sold as such[2].

Part II also does not apply to certain alcoholic drinks bottled before 1 January 1993, to food prepared on domestic premises for sale for the benefit of the person preparing it by a society registered under the Industrial and Provident Societies Act 1965 and to food prepared otherwise than in the course of a business[3].

1 See para **6.5.24** below.
2 Food Labelling Regulations 1996, reg 4(2). For the additive labelling rules, see para **10.2.2** below.
3 Food Labelling Regulations 1996, reg 4(3).

General labelling requirement

6.5.4 Subject to the provisions of Part II of the Food Labelling Regulations 1996, all non-exempted food must be marked or labelled with[1]—

(a) the name of the food;
(b) a list of ingredients; and (added in 1998 to implement Directive 97/4/EC) the quantities of certain ingredients or categories of ingredients;
(c) the appropriate durability indication;
(d) any special storage conditions or conditions of use;
(e) the name or business name and an address or registered office of the manufacturer or packer, or of a seller established within the European Community[2];
(f) particulars of the place of origin or provenance of the food if failure to give such particulars might mislead a purchaser to a material degree as to the true origin of the food; and

(g) instructions for use if it would be difficult to make appropriate use of the food in the absence of such instructions.

These requirements are considered in detail below. The separate requirements of the Community gmo labelling Regulations and the Food (Lot Marking) Regulations 1996 must not be overlooked. They are considered in paras **6.5.22** and **6.5.24** respectively.

1 Food Labelling Regulations 1996, reg 5.
2 The words 'established within the Community' refer only to the seller. See case C-83/96 *Provincia Autonoma di Trento v Dega di Depretto Gino Snc* [1998] All ER (EC) 252.

Food names

6.5.5 A food must be labelled or marked with (i) a name prescribed by law, or if there is none, (ii) a customary name or (iii) a name which indicates the true nature of the food. These categories are explained below.

(i) Names prescribed by law[1]

Where there is a name prescribed by law that name must be used as the name of the food. Such a name may be qualified by other words which make it more precise unless such qualification is prohibited.

Foods for which names have been prescribed by Schedule 1 to the 1996 Regulations are fish, melons (the species must be given), potatoes (the variety must be given) and vitamins. With regard to the prescribed fish names, Council Regulation 104/2000/EC (on the common organisation of the markets in fishery and aquaculture products) considered in para **7.3.14** below will, as from 1 January 2002, require Member States to draw up and publish a list of the commercial designations of specified fish, crustaceans and molluscs accepted within their territory for the purpose of retail labelling.

As will be seen from chapter 7, many other names are prescribed by legislation on specific products. Names are prescribed in implementation of Community Directives for sugar products, cocoa and chocolate products, coffee products, honey, fruit juices and fruit nectars, condensed milk and dried milk, jam and similar products, natural mineral waters and caseins and caseinates. Names are also prescribed by Community common agricultural policy Regulations for drinking milk, spreadable fats, poultrymeat, still wine, sparkling wine, aromatised wine, spirit drinks and olive oil. Finally, it might be noted that names are in part prescribed for certain meat products by regulation 5 of the national Meat Products and Spreadable Fish Products Regulations 1984.

The difference between prescribed and reserved names is explained in para **7.1.2** below. Even where the law does not prescribe but only reserves a name, it will in practice be very difficult to devise an alternative designation for the product which would satisfy the requirements as to 'true nature' etc discussed at (iii) below.

(ii) Customary names[2]

Where there is no name prescribed by law a customary name may be used. A customary name is one which has come to be accepted in the United Kingdom or in the area where the food is sold. Examples are 'fish fingers', 'Bakewell tart', 'Cornish Pasty', 'Welsh Rarebit', 'Lancashire Hot Pot' and so on. Some food names of foreign origin have become common in the United Kingdom over the years and may qualify as customary names. Examples are 'muesli', 'lasagne', 'macaroni' and 'petit fours'.

Whether a food name is customary in a given area is a question of fact. Some food manufacturers are tempted to apply geographical words to a common product or to search out old-fashioned and seldom used names which have a marketing appeal in the belief that they will qualify as customary names. And a name which is customary in a particular area (eg 'clutie dumpling') may not be understood on its own when sold outside that area. In such cases it will be wise to add an accompanying description satisfying the requirements as to indication of true nature discussed below. In time such a name or a fancy name (eg 'Mississipi Mud Pie') may possibly become acceptable as a customary name without the necessity of an accompanying description.

The Food Advisory Committee has recommended that the option to use a customary name should be abolished. Note also that a trade mark, brand name or fancy name may not be used as a substitute for the name of the food[3].

(iii) Indication of the true nature of the food[4]

If there is no name prescribed by law and if there is no customary name or if the customary name is not used, the name used for the food must be sufficiently precise to inform the purchaser of the true nature of the food and to enable the food to be distinguished from products with which it could be confused[5] and, if necessary, must include a description of its use.

'True nature' means a clear and accurate description of the characteristics of the food but it does not require a detailed description including all the main ingredients. The name should be easy to understand and should not be confused by superfluous adjectives.

As indicated above, a trade mark, brand name or fancy name may not be used as a substitute for a name satisfying the requirements of this regulation. However, it is acceptable to print a trade mark, brand name or fancy name in large type followed by a name which meets these requirements, provided always that the provisions as to intelligibility in regulation 38 are met[6].

Following the judgments of the European Court of Justice in the *Smanor*[7] and *Deserbais*[8] cases, the Commission published an interpretive Communication[9] on the conditions under which a name different from that used in the producing Member State may be required to avoid confusing consumers in the importing Member State. The Commission offered opinions as to the use of the names 'vinegar', 'caviar' and 'yoghurt'. Only the courts can give an authoritative interpretation of the law and the opinion on 'yoghurt' was particularly controversial since the Commission expressed the questionable view that an importing Member State was legitimately entitled to refuse to allow this description to be used where the product has undergone treatment and no longer contains live bacteria.

1 Food Labelling Regulations 1996, reg 6. See also MAFF Guidance notes on the 1996 Regulations.

2 Food Labelling Regulations 1996, reg 7. See also MAFF Guidance notes on the 1996 Regulations of which this passage takes account.

3 Food Labelling Regulations 1996, reg 10. See *Hackney London Borough Council v Cedar Trading Ltd* (1999) 163 JP 749; Times, 30 April.

4 Food Labelling Regulations 1996, reg 8.

5 As to the requirement that the name should enable the food to be distinguished from products with which it could be confused, see, in relation to the use of textured vegetable protein in meat products, *Bird's Eye Wall's Ltd v Shropshire County Council* (1994) 158 JP 961. See also *Wolkind and Northcott v Pura Foods Ltd* (1987) 151 JP 492.

6 See para **6.5.25** below.

7 Case 298/87 *Smanor* [1988] ECR 4489.
8 Case 286/86 *Ministère Public v Déserbais* [1988] ECR 4907.
9 Commission interpretative Communication (91/C 270/02) on the names under which foodstuffs are sold. See also para **1.3.3** above.

Physical condition or treatment[1]

6.5.6 Where a food is powdered or is in any other physical condition or if it has been dried, freeze dried, frozen, concentrated, smoked or subjected to any other treatment, and the omission of an indication of such condition or treatment would be misleading to a purchaser, then the name of the food must be accompanied by such an indication. The following particular requirements apply[2]—

(a) Where meat has been treated with proteolytic enzymes or is derived from an animal which has been so treated, it must include or be accompanied by the word 'tenderised'.
(b) Where food has been irradiated, it must include or be accompanied by the word 'irradiated' or the words 'treated with ionising radiation'.

Apart from these two special cases, whether or not a condition or treatment must be disclosed is a matter of common sense. It must not be assumed that a purchaser has special culinary skills which would render the statement unnecessary. The test is whether the ordinary consumer would be misled by its omission. Ministry of Agriculture, Fisheries and Food guidance notes on the 1996 Regulations contain recommendations in relation to milk treatment, thawed meat and offal, fish products incorporating minced fish, sliced or diced vegetables and roasted, smoked and filleted foods. The Advisory Committee on the Microbiological Safety of Food has made recommendations relating to the provision of information on cheeses made from raw milk from cows and other species.

1 Food Labelling Regulations 1996, reg 11.
2 Food Labelling Regulations 1996, Sch 2.

List of ingredients[1]

6.5.7 Food must normally[2] be labelled with a list of ingredients which is headed by the word 'ingredients' and sets out all the ingredients in descending order by weight as determined at the time of use in the preparation of the food.

The order of ingredients in the list is determined at the 'mixing bowl' stage of production and not as they may be when a sample is taken of the finished product. It is sometimes the case that the order of ingredients determined by analysis of the finished product is different from that of the recipe because of chemical changes and the leaching of ingredients. Provided the manufacturer can prove that the ingredients were introduced to the product in accordance with the recipe, subsequent changes in the order may be disregarded. Enforcement officers have the power to examine recipes to verify the correctness of lists of ingredients.

If an ingredient is used in the making of the food in a concentrated or dehydrated form and is reconstituted during the preparation of the food, its position in the list of ingredients may be that based on the weight before concentration or dehydration. Where the food itself is in concentrated or dehydrated form and is intended to be re-constituted before use by the addition of water, the ingredients may be listed according to their weight when reconstituted provided the list of ingredients is accompanied by the words 'ingredients of the reconstituted product' or 'ingredients of the ready to use product' or by similar words[3].

Where a product contains mixed fruit, nuts, vegetables, spices or herbs and no particular fruit, nut, vegetable etc predominates they may be listed other than in descending order by weight as follows—

(a) if the food consists entirely of such a mixture, the list of ingredients should be accompanied by the words 'in variable proportion' or similar words;
(b) if the food consists of such a mixture with other ingredients, that part of the list of ingredients which refers to the mixture should bear words similar to those in (a) above[4].

Added water must appear in the list of ingredients in its correct position unless it has been used in the preparation of the food solely for the re-constitution or partial reconstitution of an ingredient used in concentrated or dehydrated form, or it is used as a medium not normally consumed, or it does not exceed 5% of the finished product[5].

The Commission White Paper on Food Safety[6] confirms that consideration is being given to requiring specific indications of the presence of allergens (that is, ingredients known to cause hypersensitivity) for which currently, as noted below, only the category need be given.

1 Food Labelling Regulations 1996, regs 5(a), 12 and 13.
2 Food Labelling Regulations 1996, reg 18.
3 Food Labelling Regulations 1996, regs 13(2) and 16.
4 Food Labelling Regulations 1996, reg 13(5).
5 Food Labelling Regulations 1996, reg 16. See the European Court judgment of 9 February 1999 in case C-383/97 *Staatsanwaltschaft Osnabrück v Arnoldus van der Laan* (9 February 1999, unreported).
6 COM (1999) 719 final.

The names of ingredients[1]

6.5.8 The name used for an ingredient in the list of ingredients must be a name which could be lawfully used if the ingredient was being sold as a food in its own right including appropriate indication of physical condition or treatment (see para **6.5.6** above) which it has undergone where omission of such indication could mislead. Listed names of ingredients which have been irradiated must include or be accompanied by the word 'irradiated' or the words 'treated with ionising radiation'.

In most cases the name used for an ingredient must be a specific name satisfying the requirements discussed in para **6.5.5** above. However, certain generic names may be used as prescribed in the regulations[2] subject to certain conditions. They are—

Column 1	Column 2	Column 3
Generic name	*Ingredients*	*Conditions of use of generic name*
Cheese	Any type of cheese or mixture of cheese	The labelling of the food of which the cheese is an ingredient must not refer to a specific type of cheese
Cocoa butter	Press, expeller or refined cocoa butter	
Crumbs *or* rusks, *as is appropriate*	Any type of crumbled, baked cereal product	
Crystallised fruit not	Any crystallised fruit	The proportion of crystallised fruit in the food of which it is an ingredient must exceed 10 per cent
Dextrose	Anhydrous dextrose or dextrose monohydrate	
Fat	Any refined fat	The generic name must be accompanied by either— (a) the description 'animal' or 'vegetable', as is appropriate, or (b) an indication of the specific animal origin or the specific vegetable origin of the fat, as is appropriate. In the case of a hydrogenated fat, the generic name must also be accompanied by the description 'hydrogenated'.
Fish	Any species of fish	The labelling of the food of which the fish is an ingredient must not refer to a specific species of fish
Flour	Any mixture of flour derived from two or more cereal species	The generic name shall be followed by a list of the cereals from which the flour is derived in descending order of weight
Glucose syrup	Glucose syrup or anhydrous glucose syrup	

Gum base	Any type of gum preparation used in the preparation of chewing gum	
Herb, herbs *or* mixed herbs	Any herb or parts of a herb or combination of two or more herbs or parts of herbs	The proportion of herb or herbs in the food of which it or they are an ingredient must not exceed 2 per cent by weight of the food
Milk proteins	Any caseins, caseinates or whey proteins, or any mixture of these	
Oil	Any refined oil, other than olive oil	The generic name must be accompanied by either— (a) the description 'animal' or 'vegetable', as is appropriate, or (b) an indication of the specific animal origin or the specific vegetable origin of the oil, as is appropriate. In the case of a hydrogenated oil, the generic name must also be accompanied by the description 'hydrogenated'.
Spice, spices *or* mixed spices	Any spice or any combination of two or more spices	The proportion of spice or spices in the food of which it or they are an ingredient must not exceed 2 per cent by weight of the food
Starch	Any unmodified starch or any starch which has been modified either by physical means or by enzymes	In the case of a starch which may contain gluten, the generic name must be accompanied by an indication of the specific vegetable origin of the starch
Sugar	Any type of sucrose	
Vegetables	Any mixture of vegetables	The proportion of vegetables in the food of which they are an ingredient must not exceed 10 per cent by weight of the food
Wine	Any type of wine defined in Council Regulation 822/87/EEC	

The Ministry of Agriculture, Fisheries and Food guidance notes on the 1996 Regulations advise that combinations of generic terms are acceptable if their intention is made clear to the consumer (eg vegetable and animal oils, vegetable oils and fats, or vegetable and animal oils in varying proportions).

1 Food Labelling Regulations 1996, reg 14 and Sch 3.
2 Food Labelling Regulations 1996, Sch 3.

Designation of flavourings in the list of ingredients[1]

6.5.9 Special rules have been enacted for ingredient listing of flavourings. They must be designated by the word 'flavouring(s)' or a more specific description. The use of the word 'natural' and any word of substantially the same meaning are restricted to specified flavouring ingredients in which the flavouring component consists exclusively of specified flavouring substances and/or flavouring preparations[2]. If the name of a flavouring ingredient refers to the vegetable or animal nature or origin of the incorporated material, the word 'natural' and any word of substantially the same meaning are restricted to such ingredients in which the flavouring component has been isolated by physical, enzymatic or microbiological processes, or by a process normally used in preparing food for human consumption, solely or almost solely from that vegetable or animal source[3].

1 Food Labelling Regulations 1996, reg 14(5)–(8).
2 As to 'flavouring substances' and 'flavouring preparations', see para **10.3.4** below.
3 As to 'physical process' and 'process normally used in preparing food for human consumption', see Food Labelling Regulations 1996, reg 14(8).

Identification of additives[1]

6.5.10 Additives must be declared in the list of ingredients in the same way as any other ingredient, but any additive serving the function of any of the following categories must be identified by the category name (or by the category name of the principal function) followed by its specific name and/or serial number (if any)—

Acid *	Flour treatment agent
Acidity regulator	Gelling agent
Anti-caking agent	Glazing agent
Anti-foaming agent	Humectant
Antioxidant	Modified starch**
Bulking agent	Preservative
Colour	Propellant gas
Emulsifier	Raising agent
Emulsifying Salts	Stabiliser
Firming agent	Sweetener
Flavour enhancer	Thickener

* In the case of an additive which is added to or used in food to serve the function of an acid and whose specific name includes the word 'acid', it is not necessary to use the category name.
** Neither the specific name nor the serial number need be indicated. In the case of modified starch which may contain gluten, the category name must be accompanied by an indication of the specific vegetable origin of the starch.

Any additive which is required to be named in the list of ingredients and is neither a flavouring nor serves a function of one of these categories must be declared in the list of ingredients by its specific name.

For a discussion of the regulations on additives see chapter 10. For lists of permitted food additives, see Appendix F.

1 Food Labelling Regulations 1996, reg 14(9), (10), (11) and Sch 4.

Compound ingredients[1]

6.5.11 Food ingredients which themselves consist of two or more ingredients are known as compound ingredients. Mayonnaise, custard and seasoning mixes are given as examples by the Ministry of Agriculture, Fisheries and Food guidance notes. The names of ingredients of compound ingredients must appear in ingredients list either instead of or in addition to the name of the compound ingredient. If the name of the compound ingredient is given, the names of its ingredients must follow that name immediately in such a way as to make it clear that they are ingredients of the compound ingredient. It is not necessary to give the names of the ingredients of a compound ingredient—

(a) where the compound ingredient would not be required to be marked or labelled with a list of ingredients if it were itself being sold prepacked as a food (see regulation 18 of the 1996 Regulations);
(b) where the compound ingredient is identified in the list of ingredients by a generic name (see para **6.5.8**);
(c) generally where the compound ingredient constitutes less than 25% of the finished product.

After consultations with Member States, the Commission White Paper on Food Safety[2] indicates that an amendment will be proposed to remove the exemption at (c).

1 Food Labelling Regulations 1996, reg 15.
2 COM (1999) 719 final.

Ingredients which need not be named[1]

6.5.12 Ingredients need not be named in the list of ingredients in the following circumstances—

(a) where the constituents of an ingredient have become separated during a manufacturing process and are later re-introduced in their original proportions;
(b) where an additive is used in an ingredient but serves no significant technological function in the finished product[2];
(c) where an additive is used solely as a processing aid;
(d) any substance other than water which is used as a solvent or carrier for an additive and is used in an amount no greater than that which is strictly necessary for the purpose.

1 Food Labelling Regulations 1996, reg 17.
2 As to an ingredient which serves no technological function in the finished product, see case c-144/93 *Pfanni Werke Otto Eckart KG v Landeshaupstadt München* [1994] ECR I-4605.

Foods which need not bear a list of ingredients[1]

6.5.13 The following foods are not required to bear a list of ingredients—

(a) fresh fruit and vegetables, including potatoes, which have not been peeled or cut into pieces;
(b) carbonated water, to which no ingredient other than carbon dioxide has been added, and whose name indicates that it has been carbonated;
(c) vinegar which is derived by fermentation exclusively from a single basic product and to which no other ingredient has been added;*
(d) cheese, butter, fermented milk and fermented cream to which no ingredient has been added other than lactic products, enzymes and micro-organism cultures essential to manufacture or, in the case of cheese other than fresh curd cheese and processed cheese, such amount of salt as is needed for its manufacture;*
(e) flour, to which no substances have been added other than those which are required to be added;
(f) any drink with an alcoholic strength by volume of more than 1.2%**;
(g) any food consisting of a single ingredient, where—
  (i) the name of the food is identical with the name of the ingredients; or
  (ii) the name of the food enables the nature of the food to be clearly identified.

* In these cases only other added ingredients need be listed but the list must be headed by the words 'added ingredients'.
** Proposals are currently under discussion within the Community for amendment of Directive 79/112/EEC to provide for the introduction of ingredient listing of alcoholic drinks.

If a list of ingredients is given in respect of any exempted food it must be a complete list in accordance with the Food Labelling Regulations.

1 Food Labelling Regulations 1996, reg 18.

Indication of quantities of certain ingredients or categories of ingredients[1]

6.5.14 The previous provisions regarding ingredients given special emphasis have been replaced[2] in implementation of new Community rules on quantitative ingredient declarations for foodstuffs (QUID)[3]. The quantity of an ingredient or category of ingredients used in the preparation of a food must be indicated where—

(a) that ingredient or category of ingredients appears in the name of the food or is usually associated with that name by the consumer;
(b) that ingredient or category of ingredients is emphasised on the labelling in words, pictures or graphics; or
(c) that ingredient or category of ingredients is essential to characterise a food and to distinguish it from products with which it might be confused because of its name or appearance[4].

MAFF has issued Guidance Notes on QUID which were used as a starting point and issued in parallel with Guidelines drawn up by mutual agreement between the Commission and Member States. These guides confirm that, subject to some exemptions, the requirement to give QUID declarations will in principle apply to all food, including drink, with more than one ingredient. They offer illustrations of how the rules might apply. Thus, under the first part of (a) above, the QUID declaration would be required for the underlined ingredients in the example 'ham and mushroom pizza' ('ingredient included in the name of the food'); but only in respect of the total vegetable content of 'vegetable pasty' (the 'category of ingredient in the name of the food'). It is thought that the last part of (a) is likely to apply where products are described using customary names[5] without additional descriptive words. For the purposes of deciding in such cases which ingredient or category of ingredients is usually associated by the consumer with the product's name, it might prove helpful to consider what the appropriate descriptive name of the product might be. For example, 'Lancashire hot pot' is mutton and potatoes with onions, carrots and gravy and would, it is suggested, need a QUID declaration for the mutton content.

A requirement to make a declaration under (b) above (ingredients or categories of ingredients emphasised on the labelling in words, pictures or graphics), is said to be likely to be triggered when a particular ingredient is given emphasis on the label otherwise than in the name of the food (eg 'made with butter') and when pictorial representation is used to emphasise selectively one or a few of the ingredients.

A requirement to make a declaration under (c) above (ingredients or categories of ingredients essential to characterise a food and to distinguish it from products with which it might be confused because of its name or appearance) is said to be designed to cover products whose composition can differ markedly from one Member State to another but which are usually marketed under the same name[6]. The range of foods affected is likely to be very narrow: only mayonnaise and marzipan were identified during discussion on amending Directive 94/7/EC. In respect of products made in the United Kingdom, QUID declarations under this provision are unlikely to be necessary for home market sales, but may be required for marketing in some other Member States.

QUID declarations are not required in respect of an ingredient or category of ingredients—

(i) the drained net weight of which is indicated in accordance with Article 8(4) of Directive 79/112/EEC;
(ii) the quantities of which are already required to be given on the labelling by the Community fruit juice Directive 75/726/EEC, jam Directive 79/693/EEC or spreadable fats Regulation 2991/94/EC;
(iii) which is used in small quantities for the purposes of flavouring;
(iv) which, though it appears in the name of the food, is not such as to govern the choice of the consumer because the variation in quantity is not essential to characterise the food or does not distinguish it from similar foods;
(v) for which the quantity is stipulated precisely by specific Community provisions without providing for the indication thereof on the labelling; or
(vi) covered by the provisions for mixtures of fruit or vegetables or nuts, or mixtures of spices or herbs described in para **6.5.7** above.

The MAFF and Commission guides comment on each of these exemptions. Some of the salient points are as follows. As to (i) above, Article 8(4) of Directive 79/112/EEC requires foods presented in a liquid medium (ie vinegar, fruit and vegetable juices or aqueous solutions of salts, food acids, sugars or other sweetening substances) to declare on the label the drained net weight as well as the net weight. As a result of the discussions in Brussels on Directive 94/7/EC, the exemption at (iv) above is understood at least to cover alcoholic drinks (such as malt whisky/whiskey and wheat beer); liqueurs and fruit based spirits which include an ingredient in their name; rye bread and other breads (including rolls and flour confectionery), and single cereal breakfast cereals, which include mention a seed or cereal ingredient in their name (eg 'sesame seed bun'; 'corn flakes'; 'puffed rice'); products which mention several minor ingredients in their name (eg 'chicken platter, including potatoes, peas and carrots', where the exemption would apply to the vegetable ingredients); dried pasta which mentions more than one type of wheat on its label; products, such as pickles and sauces, which are highly processed and in which it is only the spices and/or flavourings which are likely to distinguish one product from another; products such as cake, bread, and dessert mixes, which are essentially mixtures of flour, oil/fat, sugar/salt and flavouring/seasonings; seasonings which are generally named using a combination of characterising ingredients and end-usage description, for example 'chicken seasoning – a blend of salt, paprika, parsley and other spices'. As to (v) above, the Commission and Member States profess themselves unaware of any Community provisions which stipulate precise quantities of ingredients without providing for indication on the labelling.

A QUID declaration is not required in the case of indications of sweeteners(s) and sugar(s) as required by Directive 94/54/EEC[7] or particulars of vitamins and minerals indicated in nutrition labelling[8].

The QUID indication of quantity of an ingredient or a category of ingredients must, subject to some derogations, be expressed as a percentage determined as at the time of use of the ingredient or category in the preparation of the food. The indication must appear in or next to the food name, or in the list of ingredients in connection with the ingredient or category in question.

1 Food Labelling Regulations 1996, reg 19.
2 The new regulation 19 was substituted by SI 1998/1398 and amended by SI 1999/1483.
3 General labelling Directive 79/112/EEC, Art 7 was replaced by Directive 94/7/EC, derogations to which were provided by Directive 1999/10/EC.
4 Directive 79/112/EEC, Art 7 makes provision for QUID labelling to be required in further cases prescribed by the Commission through the Standing Committee on Foodstuffs procedure. As to such procedures generally, see para **1.7.5** above.
5 See para **6.5.5**(ii) above.
6 See further para **6.5.5**(iii) above.
7 See para **6.5.24** below.
8 See sections **8.3** and **8.4** below.

Appropriate durability indication

6.5.15 Two kinds of food date marking are encapsulated in the term 'appropriate durability indication'. This term is defined by the Food Labelling Regulations 1996 as follows—

(a) in the case of a food other than one specified in subparagraph (b) of this definition, an indication of minimum durability; and
(b) in the case of a food which, from the microbiological point of view, is highly perishable and in consequence likely after a short period to constitute an immediate danger to health, a 'use by' date[1].

The 'use by' date is thus for highly perishable foods which could become a food safety risk, such as some meat products or ready-prepared products, while most food that can safely be kept longer carries an indication of minimum durability (or 'best before' date) indicating the period for which it can reasonably be expected to retain its optimum condition and will not be stale.

The difference between the two kinds of food date marking is reflected in the remedies for contravention of the rules. It is an offence for any person other than the manufacturer, packer or seller originally responsible for marking the food to alter either kind of appropriate durability indication[2], but only in the case of 'use by' dates is it an offence to sell the food after the date shown[3]. Although not an offence in the case of 'best before' dates, if the food is not of the substance or quality demanded (see ch 5) or if it fails the food safety requirement (see ch 9), the fact that the date had expired could be damaging to the defendant. It might also be significant in any civil proceedings which may be brought by an aggrieved purchaser (see ch 3).

Additional forms of date marking, such as 'display until', are sometimes used by retailers as instructions to shop staff. As noted by the Food Advisory Committee, consumers are unlikely to be confused or mislead by this practice.

The detailed rules for the two kinds of compulsory food date marking are summarised in paras **6.5.16** and **6.5.17** respectively. Foods which need not bear an appropriate durability indication are noted in para **6.5.18**.

1 Food Labelling Regulations 1996, reg 2(1).
2 Food Labelling Regulations 1996, reg 44(1)(e).
3 Food Labelling Regulations 1996, reg 44(1)(d). See *Lincolnshire County Council v Safeway Stores plc* (1999) unreported.

Form of indication of minimum durability[1]

6.5.16 Subject to what is said below, the minimum durability of a food must be indicated by the words 'best before' followed by the date up to and including which the food can reasonably be expected to retain its specific properties if properly stored, and by any storage conditions which need to be observed if the food is to retain its specific properties until that date.

The date in the indication of minimum durability must be expressed in terms of a day, month and year (in that order), except that, in the case of a food which can reasonably be expected to retain its specific properties—

(a) for three months or less, the date may be expressed in terms of a day and month only (eg 'Best before 15 October');
(b) for more than three months but not more than 18 months, the date may be expressed in terms of a month and year only (eg 'Best before end October 2000');
(c) for more than 18 months, the date may be expressed either in terms of a month and year only or in terms of a year, but only if the formula 'best before end' is used (eg 'Best before end December 2000' or 'Best before end 2000').

The date and any storage conditions may appear on the labelling separately from the words 'best before' or 'best before end' if followed by a reference to the place where they appear (eg 'best before end – see top of can').

The Food Advisory Committee has suggested that where strict storage temperatures are required to maintain food safety and quality the appropriate temperatures should be given on the label.

1 Food Labelling Regulations 1996, reg 20.

Form of indication of 'use by' date[1]

6.5.17 Subject to what is said below, a 'use by' date must be indicated by the words 'use by . . .' followed by the date up to and including which the food, if properly stored, is recommended for use, and any storage conditions which need to be observed[2].

The 'use by date' must be expressed in terms either of a day and month (in that order) or of a day, a month and a year (in that order). The date and any storage conditions may appear separately from the words 'use by' provided that those words are followed by a reference to the place where they appear (eg 'see lid').

The decision as to whether a particular food requires a 'use by' date is one for the manufacturer or packer who originally marks it. However, the Ministry of Agriculture, Fisheries and Food has issued Guidance Notes on 'What foods should carry a 'use by' date'. These suggest that in particular those foods which under the Food Safety (Temperature Control) Regulations 1995 are likely to support the growth of pathogenic micro-organisms or the formation of toxins and which, according to Department of Health Guidance, must in consequence be held at or below 8°C will generally need a use by date[3]. The Notes also suggest that a 'use by' date is not required on bread and cakes which deteriorate quickly but do not pose a danger to health, or on foods which would normally need a 'use by' date but are sold to the consumer frozen.

1 Food Labelling Regulations 1996, reg 21.
2 As to the Food Advisory Committee's views on labelling with strict storage temperatures required to maintain food safety and quality, see para **6.5.16**.
3 See paras **14.2.1** and **14.2.2** below. As to fresh poultrymeat, see para **7.3.7** below.

Foods which need not bear an appropriate durability indication[1]

6.5.18 The following foods need not be labelled or marked with an indication of minimum durability or a 'use by' date—

(a) fresh fruit and vegetables (including potatoes but not including sprouting seeds, legume sprouts and similar products) which have not been peeled or cut into pieces;
(b) wine, liqueur wine, sparkling wine, aromatised wine and any similar drink obtained from fruit other than grapes;
(c) any drink made from grapes or grape musts and coming within codes 2206 00 39, 2206 00 59 and 2206 00 89 of the Combined Nomenclature[2];
(d) any drink with an alcoholic strength by volume of 10% or more;
(e) any soft drink, fruit juice or fruit nectar or alcoholic drink, sold in a container containing more than five litres and intended for supply to catering establishments;
(f) any flour confectionery and bread which, given the nature of its content, is normally consumed within 24 hours of its preparation;
(g) vinegar;
(h) cooking and table salt;
(i) solid sugar and products consisting almost solely of flavoured or coloured sugars;
(j) chewing gum and similar products;
(k) edible ices in individual portions.

1 Food Labelling Regulations 1996, reg 22.
2 Council Regulation 2658/87/EEC (OJ No L 259 16.9.91, p 1) as amended.

Special storage conditions and conditions of and instructions for use

6.5.19 The requirement to label with special storage conditions and conditions of use[1] must be distinguished from the storage condition required as part of the date mark to ensure that the consumer knows how to store the food if it is to last as long as the date indicates while unopened[2]. According to the Ministry Guidance Notes, special storage conditions and conditions of use should be given—

- if the consumer needs to observe certain practices once the packaging of a food has been opened (eg *once opened keep refrigerated and consume within 3 days*);
- if various options are available (eg *suitable for home freezing*);
- if foods are not appropriate or suitable for use in certain circumstances (eg *not suitable for frying or shake well before use*).

Instructions for use[3] must be given if it would be difficult to make appropriate use of the food without them and must be sufficiently detailed to enable appropriate preparation or use to be made of the food. Advice from the Advisory Committee on the Microbiological Safety of Food on the appropriate instructions for raw minced beef, minced beef products, beefburgers and raw, flash-fried poultry products is annexed to the Ministry Guidance Notes. The Ministry publication *The new microwave labels* gives guidance on the voluntary labelling scheme for ovens and food packs developed by MAFF in partnership with oven and food manufacturers, retailers and consumer organisations.

1 Food Labelling Regulations 1996, reg 5(d).
2 See paras **6.5.15** and **6.5.16** above.
3 Food Labelling Regulations 1996, reg 5(g).

Origin or provenance of the food[1]

6.5.20 Origin marking is required if the consumer might be misled to a material degree as to the true place of origin of the food. The text of regulation 5(f) is derived from general labelling Directive 79/112/EEC, Article 3(1)(7). The Ministry Guidance Notes on place of origin were revised in January 2000 in view of concerns that the main source of ingredients and the country of final processing might be confused[2]. The following comments on regulation 5(f) draw on the Ministry Notes.

It should be recalled that there is other legislation of relevance to origin marking in Article 2 of general labelling Directive 79/112/EEC, the FSA 1990, sections 14 and 15, the TDA 1968, section 1[3], and the protected names Regulations 2081/92/EEC and 2082/92/EEC[4].

As to 'the place of origin', section 36 of the TDA 1968 is considered to be a reasonable working guide for the purposes of the Food Labelling Regulations 1996. This provides, for the purposes of the TDA 1968, that goods are deemed to have been manufactured or produced in the country in which they last underwent a treatment or process resulting in a substantial change. Interpretation of this is a matter for the courts. By way of example, it is suggested that whilst the transformation of pork into bacon, ham or pies may be regarded as a treatment or process resulting in a substantial change, this is less likely to be the case with the simple slicing, cutting and/or packing of meat.

The true place of origin should always be given if the label as a whole would otherwise imply that the food comes from, or has been made in, a different place or area. Consumers are, however, unlikely to expect products such as Chelsea buns, Madras curry or Frankfurters to come from those areas in the absence of other material on the label suggesting that they do.

A specific place of origin on the label will clearly lead consumers to attribute a particular place of origin to a food. The use of country or place names in the name of the food, its trade name, brand name, or fancy name may also do so, as may other written or illustrative material appearing on the label (including maps, flags or famous landmarks). Care must be taken to ensure that health marks applied to meet the requirements of Community hygiene legislation[5] do not by reason of their size, prominence or position, contributing to a misleading impression of the origin of the food.

Place of origin indications should be provided when consumers may otherwise incorrectly attribute a particular place of origin to a food because of the way it has been labelled, described or presented. To avoid possible contravention of the FSA 1990 or the TDA 1968, care should be taken to avoid misleading consumers when giving place of origin information particularly where the labelling or presentation of the food might lead consumers to assume incorrectly that the source of the ingredients and the country of final processing are the same. If the place of origin of the food is not the same as place of origin of its ingredients it may be necessary to provide information on the origin of the ingredients. For example—

- bacon or ham made in Britain using Danish pork should not be described as 'British bacon' or 'British ham' but could be described as '[imported] [Danish] pork [cured] [baked] [roasted] in Britain';
- pork sausages made in Britain using pork from countries outside the UK should not be described as 'British pork sausages' but could be described as 'made in Britain from [imported] [country of origin] pork [from more than one country]';
- butter churned in England from milk brought in from outside the UK (eg Belgium) should not be labelled as 'English' or 'produced in England' but could be labelled as 'produced in England from [imported][Belgian] milk'.

It may be better to use terms like 'bottled', 'packed', 'sliced and packed' or 'processed' instead of rather broader terms like 'produced'.

While regulation 5(f) of the Food Labelling Regulations 1996 does not generally apply to non-prepacked foods, care should be taken to ensure that display material does not convey messages about places of origin which may conflict with the FSA 1990 or the TDA 1968.

1 Food Labelling Regulations 1996, reg 5(f).
2 The Department of Trade and Industry has issued separate guidance on implied origin marking which is annexed to the Ministry Notes.
3 See para **6.2.1** above.
4 See paras **7.4.2** and **7.4.3** below.
5 See para **13.1.3** below.
6 See para **7.4.2** below.
7 See para **6.5.5**(ii) above.

Indication of irradiation[1]

6.5.21 Food which has been irradiated or which contains irradiated ingredients must, subject to certain exemptions, be marked 'irradiated' or 'treated with ionising irradiation'. Non pre-packed food, food prepacked for direct sale, certain flour confectionery and fancy confectionery products need not be so marked if they are not exposed for sale.

1 Food Labelling Regulations 1996, regs 11(2), 14(2) and 25.

Indications on food produced from genetically modified organisms

6.5.22 Council Regulation 1139/98/EC makes provision for the compulsory indication, on the labelling of certain foodstuffs produced from genetically modified organisms (GMOs), of particulars other than those provided for in general labelling Directive 79/112/EEC[1]. As amended by Regulation 49/2000/EC, Regulation 1139/98/EC applies to foods and food ingredients which are to be delivered as such to the final consumer or mass caterers and have been produced, in whole or in part, from genetically modified soya beans covered by Decision 96/281/EC or genetically modified maize covered by Decision 97/98/EC. It does not apply to food additives, flavourings for use in foodstuffs or extraction solvents used in the production of foodstuffs as referred to in Article 2(1) of Novel Foods Regulation 258/97/EC[2]. As genetically modified soya and maize were used for human consumption to a significant degree before the entry into force of Regulation 258/97/EC, they were not regarded as novel and were not subject to the additional specific labelling requirements which it lays down.

For food consisting of more than one ingredient, the words 'produced from genetically modified soya' or 'produced from genetically modified maize' must appear in the list of ingredients[3] immediately after the name of the ingredient concerned. Alternatively, these words may appear in a prominently displayed footnote to the list of ingredients, related by means of an asterisk to the ingredient concerned. Particular requirements are prescribed for ingredients already listed as being produced from soya or maize, for the typeface used in footnotes, for products bearing no list of ingredients[4], for ingredients identified by generic names[5] and for compound ingredients[6].

Foods in which neither protein nor DNA resulting from genetic modification is present are exempt from these additional specific labelling requirements; so also are foods in which GMO material is adventitiously present in the ingredients in a proportion no higher than 1%. To establish that the presence is adventitious, operators must be in a position to demonstrate that they have taken appropriate steps to avoid using GMOs.

Commission Regulation 50/2000/EC makes provision for the additional labelling of foods which are intended for the final consumer or mass caterers and which contain additives[7] and flavourings[8] that have been genetically modified or have been produced from genetically modified organisms and that are in consequence not equivalent to their traditional counterparts. The words 'produced from genetically modified . . .' or 'genetically modified', as appropriate, are required to appear in the list of ingredients[3] immediately after the additive or flavouring in question. Provision is made for this information to be given alternatively by footnote and for foodstuffs bearing no list of ingredients[4].

The Genetically Modified and Novel Foods (Labelling) (England) Regulations 2000 provide for the enforcement of Regulation 1139/98/EC, as amended by Regulation 49/2000/EC, and of Regulation 50/2000/EC. Pursuant to general labelling Directive 79/112/EC, provision is made for the manner of marking or labelling, which allows exemptions for small packages and certain indelibly marked bottles[9] as well as alternative arrangements for sales to the ultimate consumer at appropriate premises of food which is not prepacked or is prepacked for direct sale. At appropriate premises the staff on request provide the information having themselves been kept informed through an established procedure.

The Commission is understood to be preparing proposals on the use of 'GM-free' labelling, on a negative list of ingredients containing neither protein nor DNA and on a de mimimis exemption in respect of foods containing GM additives and flavourings. Obligatory labelling for additives and flavourings sold as such also remain to be introduced.

1 Guidance Notes on 'Labelling of food containing genetically modified soya and maize, food containing additives/flavourings from GM sources and novel foods' have been prepared by the Ministry of Agriculture, Fisheries and Food and the Department of Health.
2 See para **7.2.12** below.
3 See para **6.5.7**.
4 See para **6.5.13**.
5 See para **6.5.8**.
6 See para **6.5.11**.
7 See para **10.2.1** below
8 See para **10.3.1** below.
9 Compare para **6.5.25** below.

Omission of particulars from non-prepacked and other foods[1]

6.5.23 Certain foods are exempt from labelling with most of the statutory information described in this chapter, including the additional declarations about packaging gases, sweeteners and skimmed milk with non-milk fat required by regulations 32, 33 and 34[2]. These foods are principally—

(a) food which is not prepacked (eg food sold loose from a delicatessen);
(b) food which is prepacked for direct sale (ie broadly, food packed by a retailer or dairy farmer for sale from his premises);
(c) specified flour confectionery;
(d) specified fancy confectionery products.

They are required only to bear—

(i) (except for non-irradiated white bread and flour confectionery) the name of the food, and, in the case of milk, particulars of the place of origin[3] as well as, for raw milk, the name and address of the producer or packer;
(ii) a specified indication in respect of additives used to serve the function of an antioxidant, colour, flavouring, flavour enhancer, preservative or sweetener;
(iii) a specified indication in respect of irradiated ingredients;
(iv) the additional specific labelling required in respect of genetically modified ingredients[4].

Subject to provision for particular cases, prepacked foods in reusable indelibly marked glass bottles or in packaging of specified maximum dimensions, which are not caught by the above provisions or those below relating to catering establishments, need not be labelled with—

- the general labelling particulars specified in para **6.5.4** above except the name of the food and, where required, the appropriate durability indication; or
- indications of the use of packaging gas and sweeteners as described in para **6.5.24** below.

Exemptions are also provided for foods sold as an accompaniment to another food or service.

Labelling requirements for foods sold at catering establishments, which are not prepacked or are prepacked for direct sale, are confined to limited provisions in respect of milk prepacked for direct sale, irradiated food and genetically modified ingredients[4].

Seasonal selection packs do not need to be labelled if the individual items which they contain are correctly labelled.

1 Food Labelling Regulations 1996, regs 23, 24, 25, 26, 27, and 28. For the definitions of 'prepacked', 'prepacked for direct sale', 'flour confectionery', 'fancy confectionery product', 'catering establishment' and 'seasonal selection pack', see Food Labelling Regulations 1996, reg 2.
2 See para **6.5.24**.
3 See para **6.5.20**.
4 See para **6.5.22**.

Additional labelling requirements for certain categories of food[1]

6.5.24 Additional labelling requirements are imposed by Part II of the Food Labelling Regulations 1996 for certain categories of food[2].

Vending machines must show on the front of the machine the name of the food sold (unless easily and clearly visible through the outside), together, for non-prepacked products, with abbreviated nutrition labelling information and, in appropriate cases, with reheating instructions. These requirements do not apply to natural mineral water, except water that has been artificially carbonated[3].

In implementation of Commission Directive 87/250/EEC, prepacked alcoholic drinks with an alcoholic strength by volume of more than 1.2%, other than Community-controlled wine, must be marked or labelled with an indication of the alcoholic strength by volume in the form of a figure to not more than one decimal place in one of the following forms, eg—

'10.5% vol', or 'alcohol 10.5% vol' or 'alc 10.5% vol'.

Positive and negative tolerances for the indication are prescribed[4]. The alcoholic strength must be determined at 20°C.

A health warning in prescribed form must appear on the containers of raw milk, other than from buffaloes, and in catering establishments where the product is sold non-prepacked[5].

The container of any product consisting of skimmed milk together with non-milk fat, which is capable of being used as a substitute for milk and which is neither an infant formula or follow-on formula[6] nor a product specially for infants or young children for medical purposes, must bear a warning about its unsuitability as food for babies.

Finally, two regulations impose requirements in implementation of Commission Directive 94/54/EC. First, a food the durability of which has been extended by a packaging gas authorised pursuant to Council Directive 89/107/EEC (concerning food additives for use in foodstuffs for human consumption) must be labelled 'packaged in a protective atmosphere'. Secondly, a food containing any of the following ingredients must bear the indication specified in relation to it—

- authorised sweetener – 'with sweetener(s)'*;
- added sugar and authorised sweetener – 'with sugar(s) and sweetener(s)'*;
- aspartame – 'contains a source of phenylalanine';
- more than 10% added polyols – 'excessive consumption may produce laxative effects'.

* These indications must accompany the name of the food.

---

1 Food Labelling Regulations 1996, regs 29, 30, 32, 33 and 34.
2 Other regulations (eg on lot marking, spreadable fat, meat products and fish products) also contain specific labelling requirements.
3 Food Labelling Regulations 1996, reg 3(4).
4 Food Labelling Regulations 1996, Sch 5.
5 In Scotland, the sale of raw cows' drinking milk is banned.
6 See para **8.6.2** below.

Manner of marking or labelling[1]

6.5.25 All the information required to be marked or labelled on food must generally appear on the packaging; on a label attached to the packaging; on a label that is clearly visible through the packaging; or, where the sale is otherwise than to the ultimate consumer, in relevant trade documents.

For non-prepacked and similar food, fancy confectionery products and certain food sold at catering establishments in each case when sold to the ultimate consumer, the required particulars shall be on a label attached to the food or on a readily discernible menu, notice, ticket or label at the place where the food is chosen.

Special provision is made for irradiated food and, as explained in para **6.5.22**, for genetically modified soya or maize ingredients.

In the case of bottled milk, the required particulars, except the raw milk health warning, may appear on the bottle cap.

All information required by the Regulations must be easy to understand[2], clearly legible and indelible.

Subject to exceptions for small packages and indelibly marked glass bottles, the name of the food, the appropriate durability indication, the alcoholic strength indication, the warnings in respect of raw milk and of skimmed milk with non-milk fat, and the indication of net quantity, as required, must appear in the same field of vision.

The term 'same field of vision' is undefined, but might reasonably be expected to mean simultaneously visible under normal conditions of purchase.

1 Food Labelling Regulations 1996, regs 35, 36, 37, 38 and 39.

2 As to language easily understood by consumers in a State or region and the use of other measures such as designs, symbols or pictograms, see case C-85/94 *Groupement des producteurs, importeurs et agents généraux d'eaux minérales étrangères, VZW (Piageme) and Others v Peeters NV* [1995] ECR I-2955; and in case C-385/96 *Herman Josef Goerres* [1998] ECR I-4431 and *Hackney London Borough Council v Cedar Trading Ltd* (199) 163 JP 749.

Lot marking

6.5.26 Council Directive 89/396/EEC (on indications or marks identifying the lot to which a foodstuff belongs), as amended, aims at the establishment of a framework for a common 'lot' or 'batch' identification system throughout the European Community in order to facilitate the tracing and identification of products along the food chain where, for example, a product constitutes a health risk to consumers. The Directive is implemented in Great Britain by the Food (Lot Marking) Regulations 1996.

Subject to exceptions noted below, the Regulations prohibit the sale of food which forms part of a lot unless it is accompanied by a lot marking indication. A 'lot' is defined as a batch of sales units of food produced, manufactured or packaged under similar conditions. A 'lot marking indication' is defined as an indication which allows identification of the lot to which the sales unit belongs.

MAFF Guidance Notes point out that the requirements are very flexible. They leave the producer, manufacturer or first seller established within the Community to determine the appropriate size of a lot and the form the lot marking indication should take. However, the Regulations require it to be preceded by the letter 'L' except in cases where it is clearly distinguishable from other indications on the label. It must appear on the prepackaging or on a label attached to the prepackaging or, if the food is not prepacked, on the container or on an accompanying commercial document. The indication must also be easily visible, clearly legible and indelible.

These requirements do not apply to—

- sales of agricultural products (ie the products of the soil, of stockfarming and of fisheries)[1] which are either sold or delivered to temporary storage, preparation or packing stations or to producers' organisations; or which are collected for immediate use in an operational preparation or processing system;
- sales to the ultimate consumer of food which is not prepacked, is packed at the request of the purchaser or is prepacked for immediate sale;
- sales units of food of specified maximum dimensions;
- prepacked sales units of food intended as a minor accompaniment to another food or service;
- sales units of individual portions of edible ice supplied to the seller in bulk packaging bearing the lot marking indication;
- sales units marked or labelled before 1 July 1992 or, in the case of indelibly marked glass bottles for reuse, before 1 July 1997;
- sales units of food bearing an indication of minimum durability or 'use by' date.

1 Despite the definition of in Article 32 (ex 38) EC, MAFF Guidance Notes reasonably advise that the term 'agricultural products' used in this context does not include products of first stage processing.

Chapter 7

Food standards and descriptions

7.1 FOOD STANDARDS

Introduction

7.1.1 Section **5.3** above explained how magistrates' courts have used section 14 of the Food Safety Act 1990 (FSA 1990) and its predecessors since 1875 to establish (in the absence of bespoke or legislative requirements) what standard of food a purchaser must be deemed to have demanded of the seller. In fact one of the main ways of protecting the public from unhealthy or fraudulent food is by imposing specific standards with which it must comply. During the twentieth century, subordinate legislation was increasingly used by the Government to do this. The highpoint was probably reached in the years after the Second World War. Since then, Community free trade law[1] and the UK deregulation initiative has caused a movement away from this method of food control towards greater use of compulsory labelling with information about the product sold in the way described in section **6.5** above. However, food standards are still much employed in the areas noted in para **7.1.3** below.

1 See section **1.3** and para **6.1.3** above.

What are food standards?

7.1.2 Before considering the food standards imposed in various sectors of control, it is important to clarify what is meant here by the expression. Essentially it is used to cover any provision which, with regard to the composition of a specified food, prescribes a quantity or quality level or imposes a total ban. It includes such provisions when they are part of some wider emergency prohibition[1] and notwithstanding that they may also prescribe a microbiological standard[2]. Paragraph **7.1.3** explains the specific sectors in which food standards are imposed. However, the expression is not intended to include—

(a) provisions of a general nature like sections 7, 8, 14 and 15 of the FSA 1990;
(b) provisions which require food to be labelled without setting a standard for it (see sections **6.5** and **8.4**);
(c) preparation[3] and, except as mentioned in para **7.1.3**, hygiene requirements in respect of specific foods (see section **12.4**, chapter 13 and relevant parts of chapter 14); and
(d) quantity and price marking provisions (see chapter 15).

It will be observed that elsewhere 'food standards' has wider meanings. In statutory Code of Practice no 8 (Food Standards Inspections) it is defined in a way which covers the work of Trading Standards Officers, rather than that of Environmental Health Officers dealt with in statutory Code of Practice no 9 (Food Hygiene Inspections). In the title of the 'Food Standards Agency', the expression is obviously intended also to include food hygiene and much more.

Within the limits explained, this chapter is certainly intended to embrace food standards imposed by different methods. Provisions establishing them appear in a bewildering variety of guises, but there are really only the three types described below.

(1) Reserved name or description

This is the basic and least onerous method of imposing a standard. The use of a name or designation is reserved to food of the prescribed standard. For example, regulation 4 of the Jam and Similar Products Regulations 1981 reserves the name 'marmalade' to food which in particular has a fruit content standard of 20% with at least 7½% obtained from the endocarp. The provision imposes no obligation to use the reserved name, but if it is used, the food to which it is applied must comply with the standard. Put another way, there is a commercial sanction against selling sub-standard food: you cannot call it by the name that the consumer expects. Setting standards by reserving names is a widely used device.

Decisions of the European Court on the Community free trade rules have often concerned the lawfulness of national food standards[4] and many of these have related to reserved names[5].

Some British provisions protect a 'word' or 'description'[6] rather than a 'name'. Nonetheless, these too are setting food standards: the use of the term is forbidden unless the standard is observed.

All such provisions reserving names and descriptions under the FSA 1990 are evidently caught by section 2(5)(a) of the Trade Descriptions Act 1968 so that the terms they protect are deemed not to be trade descriptions.

(2) Prescribed name

Less frequently, the use of a specified name is made compulsory on the sale of food of a defined standard. These are the names 'prescribed by law' referred to in relation to food labelling in para **6.5.5**(i). In the 'marmalade' example above, regulation 5 of the Jam and Similar Products Regulations 1981 requires use of the name by prescribing it for the food. In fact a requirement to use a prescribed name can work only if that name is also reserved to food which meets the standard. Without this, there is nothing to prevent the use of the name on non-compliant food. National provisions declared by the European Court to be contrary to Community free movement rules include examples of prescribed name requirements[7].

(3) Prohibited product

The last and most severe way of prescribing a standard is the total prohibition on the marketing of food which fails to comply. For a time after the Second World War this form was used in the United Kingdom to prevent misleading labelling. Since then, more sensibly and in line with Community philosophy, total prohibition on sale has been confined to cases where health is at risk. Given their oppressive character, it is not surprising that various national standards of this kind have been held by the European Court to be contrary to the free movement of goods principle[8].

As indicated above, the term 'composition' is often applied to any three categories in the sense that they all set standards for food. However, in the terminology of the powers in section 16 of the FSA 1990, only category (3) provisions directly regulate the 'composition' of food (see section 16(1)(a)). Strictly speaking, categories (1) and (2) regulate the 'labelling' of food defined according to its composition (see section 16(1)(e)).

1 See orders under Pt I of the Food and Emergency Protection Act 1985 considered in section **11.7** below.
2 See, for example, the Natural Mineral Water, Spring Water and Bottled Drinking Water Regulations 1999 considered in para **7.2.10** below.
3 As to food preparation, see FSA 1990, s 53(1) and section **12.4** below.
4 See section **1.3** above.
5 See for example case 281/83 *EC Commission v Italy* [1985] ECR 3397 (vinegar); case 178/84 *EC Commission v Germany* [1987] ECR 1227 (beer); case 286/86 *Minister Public v Déserbais* [1988] ECR 4907 (cheese).
6 See in particular section **7.6** below.
7 See for example case 27/80 *Fietje* [1980] ECR 3839 (liqueur); case 407/85 *Drei Glocken* [1988] ECR 4233 (pasta made from durum wheat).
8 See for example case 193/80 *EC Commission v Italy* [1981] ECR 3019 (vinegar); case 407/85 *Drei Glocken* [1988] ECR 4233 (dry pasta); Case C17/93 *Van der Veldt* [1994] ECR I-3537, [1991] CMLR 621 (bread).

Specific food standards and descriptions

7.1.3 As indicated above, specific standards are imposed in England and Wales to control various food sectors. The most obvious ones are explained in the rest of this chapter. Others of equal importance but applied for special purposes are dealt with elsewhere in the book. Thus, food claims are explained in section **8.2**; foods for particular nutritional purposes in section **8.6**; additives, flavourings, contaminants, contact materials, residues and other substances in chapter 10; emergency control orders and emergency orders in sections **11.6** and **11.7**; and the anomalous BSE provisions in section **13.8**.

For completeness, mention should be made of the Agricultural Produce (Grading and Marking) Acts 1928 and 1931 which provide for the prescription and use of grade designations and marks for agricultural produce. The legislation has fallen into disuse because the voluntary trade quality schemes which it supported have evidently not been operated since the Second World War. Special provision in respect of preserved eggs also still subsists in the 1928 Act and the Eggs (Marketing and Storage) Regulations 1965, although cold and chemical storage of eggs seems no longer to be practised.

Considered in turn below are the following areas in which control is imposed by food standards—

(a) Community internal market instruments;
(b) Community common agricultural policy regulations;
(c) Community regulations on quality marks or labels;
(d) National regulations on specific foods;
(e) Regulations to prevent misleading descriptions.

7.2 COMMUNITY INTERNAL MARKET INSTRUMENTS

7.2.1 The *Cassis de Dijon* judgment[1] significantly reduced the scope for national food standards restricting Community imports. In consequence, from 1985 the Commission decided[2] to concentrate its harmonisation policy on more informative labelling and on the public interest areas which potentially remained within Member States' competence.

Before that, the Commission's harmonisation programme had, in particular, involved the enactment of a series of vertical Directives laying down detailed specifications for particular foodstuffs. Summarised below are the regulations implementing these Directives, together with those on bottled waters and the 1997 Regulations on novel foods. In considering more modern provisions implementing specific Community food standards, it is important not to overlook the special set of provisions implementing Community Directives on foods for particular nutritional purposes. These have been grouped in chapter 8 with other nutrition oriented provisions. Mention should also be made of the anomalous quick-frozen foodstuffs Directive 89/108/EEC, implementation of which is explained in para **14.5** below.

On 17 April 1996, the Commission adopted a package of seven proposals to simplify the main group of pre-1985 directives (that is, those concerning honey, sugars, coffee extracts, fruit juices, jams and cocoa and chocolate products). At the time of writing the coffee Directive has been made and that for chocolate essentially agreed. For most if not all of others, it would appear that the legislative procedures are likely to be completed in 2000.

1 See paras **1.3.1** and **1.3.2** above.
2 See para **1.3.3** above.

7.2.2 The main group of foods for which standards are prescribed by Community internal market instruments are considered below.

Sugar products

7.2.3 The Specified Sugar Products Regulations 1976, as amended, implement Council Directive 73/437/EEC, as amended.

The Regulations reserve descriptions to specified sugar products and require the use of those descriptions and specified declarations. They also impose restrictions on labelling sugar solution, invert solution and invert sugar syrup with the word 'white'. Methods of analysis are prescribed for the specified sugar product definitions.

On 30 May 1996 the Commission submitted a proposal for a Council Directive to repeal and replace Council Directive 73/437/EEC and simplify the law relating to certain sugars intended for human consumption[1]. At the time of writing some technical points still have to be considered by the European Parliament.

1 See OJ C 231 9.8.86, p 6.

Cocoa and chocolate products

7.2.4 The Cocoa and Chocolate Products Regulations 1976, as amended, implement Council Directive 73/241/EEC, as amended.

The Regulations reserve descriptions to defined cocoa and chocolate products and require the use of those descriptions and specified declarations as to cocoa and milk solids content and other matters. They also impose restrictions on—

(a) labelling of specified chocolate products with descriptions of fillings and ingredients, the description 'dark couverture chocolate' and descriptions as to quality; and
(b) labelling and advertising of cocoa and chocolate products with references to natural sources of flavouring substances.

Compositional requirements are specified for cocoa beans used as ingredients and limits are prescribed for other permitted ingredients.

The Regulations are especially complex because the standards are not all mutually exclusive.

On 30 May 1996 the Commission submitted a proposal for a European Parliament and Council Directive to repeal and replace Council Directive 73/241/EEC and simplify the law relating to cocoa and chocolate products intended for human consumption. At the time of writing, only final approval by the Council is necessary to enactment of the new Directive. This will resolve the long-standing problem of Continental resistance to British style milk chocolate containing up to 5% vegetable fat. Under the new provisions, it will be possible to trade the product freely from the United Kingdom and Ireland to other Member States under the designation 'family milk chocolate'.

Coffee products

7.2.5 Coffee and Coffee Products Regulations 1978, as amended, implement Council Directive 77/436/EEC, as amended.

The Regulations reserve descriptions for coffee, coffee mixtures, coffee extracts, chicory extracts and extracts of blends of coffee and chicory and require the use of those descriptions and specified declarations as to decaffeination and other matters. Compositional requirements are specified for raw materials and limits are prescribed for permitted ingredients.

With effect from 13 September 2000, Directive 77/436/EEC is repealed and replaced by Directive 1999/4/EC so as to simplify the provisions relating to coffee extracts and chicory extracts. Regulations are expected to be enacted by that date which will authorise the marketing of products conforming to Directive 1999/4/EC and prohibit the marketing of those that do not.

Honey

7.2.6 The Honey Regulations 1976, as amended, implement Council Directive 74/409/EEC, as amended.

The Regulations specify requirements for the composition of honey, prescribe the method of determining diastase activity and impose a restriction on the use of honey as an ingredient in the preparation of food. The word 'honey' is reserved to products complying with the compositional requirements and, for honey sold in containers, the use of that description is required, preceded by in specified cases by the word 'comb' or the word 'chunk' or by the word 'baker's' or 'industrial', as the case may be. Restrictions are also imposed on the labelling and advertisement of honey with reference to origin.

On 30 May 1996 the Commission submitted a proposal for a Council Directive to repeal and replace Council Directive 74/409/EEC and simplify the law relating to honey[1]. At the time of writing the draft Directive has still to be considered by the internal market Council.

1 See OJ C 231 9.8.86, p 10.

Fruit juices and fruit nectars

7.2.7 The Fruit Juices and Fruit Nectars Regulations 1977, as amended, implement Council Directive 93/77/EEC, as amended.

The Regulations define fruit juice, concentrated fruit juice, dried fruit juice and fruit nectar names prescribe names for the purposes of the Food Labelling Regulations 1996[1], to be accompanied in each case by an indication of the type of fruit from which the food is prepared. They reserve the names to the foods and require the use of specified declarations as to fruit content, sweetening and concentration. Limits are also prescribed for permitted ingredients.

On 30 May 1996 the Commission submitted a proposal for a Council Directive to repeal and replace Council Directive 93/77/EEC and simplify the law relating to fruit juices and certain similar products intended for human consumption[1]. At the time of writing some technical points still have to be considered by the European Parliament.

1 See OJ C 231 9.8.86, p 14.

Condensed milk and dried milk

7.2.8 The Condensed Milk and Dried Milk Regulations 1977, as amended, implement Council Directive 76/118/EEC, as amended.

The Regulations reserve descriptions for condensed milk and dried milk products and, for those products sold in containers, require the use of those descriptions and, in the case of retail sales, specified declarations. They also require the milk ingredients used in the preparation of any condensed milk or dried milk product to have been subjected to a heat treatment at least equivalent to pasteurisation if the product itself is not so treated. Limits are also prescribed for permitted ingredients.

On 30 May 1996 the Commission submitted a proposal for a Council Directive to repeal and replace Council Directive 76/118/EEC and simplify the law relating to certain partly or wholly dehydrated preserved milk for human consumption[1]. At the time of writing some technical points still have to be considered by the European Parliament.

1 See OJ C 231 9.8.86, p 20.

Jam and similar products

7.2.9 Jam and Similar Products Regulations 1981, as amended, implement Council Directive 79/693/EEC, as amended.

In respect of defined foods, the Regulations prescribe for the purposes of the Food Labelling Regulations 1996[1], and reserve the names 'extra jam', 'jam', 'extra jelly', 'jelly', 'marmalade', 'sweetened chestnut puree', 'reduced sugar jam', 'reduced sugar jelly', 'reduced sugar marmalade', 'UK standard jelly', '"X" curd', 'lemon cheese', '"Y" flavour curd' and 'mincemeat'. Also reserved are the names 'conserve' and 'preserve'. Additional requirements are imposed for labelling and for the fruit, sweetening agents, sulphur dioxide and additional ingredients in the foods.

On 30 May 1996 the Commission submitted a proposal for a Council Directive to repeal and replace Council Directive 79/693/EEC and simplify the law relating to fruit jams, jellies and marmalades and chestnut purée intended for human consumption[2].

At the time of writing some technical points still have to be considered by the European Parliament.

1 See para **6.5.5**(i) above.
2 See OJ C 231 9.8.86, p 27.

Natural mineral water, spring water and bottled drinking water

7.2.10 Provision for the approximation of Member States' laws relating to the exploitation and marketing of natural mineral waters was made by Council Directive 80/777/EEC. This Directive has, in particular, been amended by Council Directive 96/70/EC so as to extend to spring waters some of the requirements that apply to natural mineral waters, such as bottling at source, certain microbiological criteria and restrictions on the treatment of water. The amendment also permits the treatment of natural mineral water and spring water with ozone-enriched air in prescribed circumstances.

The standards for other bottled drinking water are prescribed by Council Directive 80/778/EEC on the quality of water for human consumption, as to which see further below.

The provisions are implemented in Great Britain by the Natural Mineral Water, Spring Water and Bottled Drinking Water Regulations 1999. The Regulations—

(a) prescribe the conditions for recognition of natural mineral waters[1];
(b) prohibit the sale, as natural mineral water, of water which is not natural mineral water;
(c) prohibit the sale of water from natural mineral water springs which fails to comply with prescribed exploitation and bottling conditions;
(d) regulate the treatment of natural mineral waters;
(e) prohibit the bottling and sale of natural mineral water which fails to comply with specified colony count requirements or contains any organoleptic defect;
(f) prohibit the bottling and sale of natural mineral water in other than a specified type of container;
(g) prescribe labelling requirements for natural mineral water;
(h) prohibit the labelling of water as spring water, or sale of water so labelled, unless specified conditions are met;
(i) prohibit the bottling or sale of bottled drinking water which fails to satisfy specified requirements and prohibit the use of specified labelling;
(j) make provision for enforcement and analysis.

A *Guide to Good Bottled Water Standards* has been produced by the Packaged Water and Natural Mineral Water members of the British Soft Drinks Association (BSDA).

In relation to the quality of bottled drinking water for human consumption, the 1999 Regulations are due to be amended before the end of 2000 to implement Council Directive 98/83/EC which is replacing Directive 80/778/EEC.

1 Member States are precluded from making recognition of natural mineral water dependent on the water possessing properties favourable to health; see case C-17/96 *Badische Erfrischungs-Getränke GmbH & Co KG v Land Baden Württemburg* [1998] 1 CMLR 341.

Caseins and caseinates

7.2.11 The Caseins and Caseinates Regulations 1985, as amended, implement Council Directive 83/417/EEC as amended.

The Regulations reserve descriptions for defined casein products and require the use of those descriptions and other specified indications. The use of any casein or caseinate in casein products is forbidden unless it has been subjected to heat treatment at least equivalent to pasteurisation.

Novel foods and novel food ingredients

7.2.12 Except as explained below, Council Regulation 258/97/EC concerning novel foods and novel food ingredients is supplemented in Great Britain by the Novel Foods and Novel Food Ingredients Regulations 1997, as amended[1]. The Novel Foods and Novel Food Ingredients (Fees) Regulations 1997 prescribes fees to be paid for the processing of requests to assess novel foods and novel food ingredients.

Before they may be placed on the market, novel foods and novel food ingredients must be subjected to a safety assessment procedure. This applies to foods and ingredients which have not hitherto been used for human consumption to a significant degree within the Community and which fall under the following categories in respect of which the Ministry *Guidance Notes* give the examples cited below—

(a) foods and food ingredients containing or consisting of genetically modified organisms within the meaning of Directive 90/220/EEC (eg a genetically modified tomato);
(b) foods and food ingredients produced from, but not containing, genetically modified organisms (a highly refined oil produced from a genetically modified oil seed rape);
(c) foods and food ingredients with a new or intentionally modified primary molecular structure (eg a fat replacer);
(d) foods and food ingredients consisting of or isolated from microorganisms, fungi or algae (eg a new non-genetically modified organism used as a yoghurt starter culture);
(e) foods and food ingredients consisting of or isolated from plants and food ingredients isolated from animals, except for foods and food ingredients obtained by traditional propagating or breeding practices and having a history of safe food use (a new plant oil);
(f) foods and food ingredients to which has been applied a production process not currently used, where that process gives rise to significant changes in the composition or structure of the foods or food ingredients which affect their nutritional value, metabolism or level of undesirable substances.

Regulation 258/97/EC does not affect the obligation, in the case of a genetically modified organism, to obtain consent under the Genetically Modified Organisms (Deliberate Release) Regulations 1992, as amended.

Provided the safety level of Regulation 258/97/EC is met, it does not apply to food additives[2], flavourings[3] or extraction solvents[4].

Foods and food ingredients falling within the scope of the Regulation must not—

- present a danger for the consumer;
- mislead the consumer;
- differ from foods and food ingredients which they are intended to replace to such an extent that their normal consumption would be nutritionally disadvantageous for the consumer.

Subject to certain exceptions, for the purpose of placing such a food or food ingredient on the market, a request containing all necessary information[5] and copied to the Commission must be submitted to the competent authority in the Member State in which the product is to be marketed for the first time. Responsibility as competent authority for assessments is to be assumed, in England, by the Food Standards Agency and, in Wales, by the National Assembly acting in the light of the Agency's advice[6]. The

Advisory Committee on Novel Foods and Processes (ACNFP), in consultation with any other relevant expert advisory committee, will continue to carry out the assessments for them. It also appraises assessments carried out by other Member States[7]. As explained in para **2.4.4** above, pending the coming into force of the Agency's power under section 19 of the Food Standards Act 1999 (FSA 1999) to publish non-confidential information provided in support of novel food applications, the Novel Foods and Novel Food Ingredients (Amendment) (England) Regulations 1999 will permit routine disclosure by the ACNFP.

The competent authority has three months to carry out the initial safety assessment after which the Commission and other Member States have 60 days in which to comment. If the initial assessment was favourable and there are no objections, the product may be marketed. If the Member State's initial assessment decided that an additional assessment is required or if objections are raised, an 'authorisation decision' must be taken. The application must be referred to the EC Standing Committee on Foodstuffs (consulting the EC Scientific Committee as necessary) under a regulatory committee procedure. If the Commission does not follow the Standing Committee's opinion or if no opinion is given, the matter must be referred to the Council acting by qualified majority. If the Council has not acted within three months, the Commission may adopt its proposal[8].

A less rigorous procedure is prescribed for novel foods and food ingredients that are recognised as substantially equivalent to existing foods or ingredients as regards their composition, nutritional value, metabolism, intended use and level of undesirable substances. Where this is true of a food or ingredient referred to in (b), (d) or (e) above, an applicant, who supplies prescribed evidence of the substantial equivalence, may notify the Commission when first marketing the product.

In every case, additional labelling requirements must be complied with to ensure that the final consumer is informed of any characteristic or food property which renders the novel food or ingredient no longer equivalent to an existing food or ingredient; of the presence in the food or ingredient of material which is not present in an existing equivalent foodstuff and which may have implications for the health of certain sections of the population or gives rise to ethical concerns; or of the presence of genetically modified organisms[9]. These labelling requirements are enforced by the Genetically Modified and Novel Foods (Labelling) (England) Regulations 2000.

Provision is made for temporary restriction or suspension of trade in and use of a food or ingredient where, as a result of new information or a reassessment of existing information, a Member State has grounds for considering that the use of the food or ingredient endangers human health or the environment.

In its White Paper on Food Safety of 12 January 2000[10], the Commission stated its intention to adopt an implementing Regulation to clarify and make more transparent the procedures under Regulation 258/97/EC.

1 *Guidance Notes on Novel Foods and Novel Food Ingredients Legislation* have been issued by the Ministry of Agriculture, Fisheries and Food and the Department of Health.

2 See Directive 89/107/EEC and para **10.2.1** below.

3 See Directive 88/388/EEC and para **10.3.1** below.

4 See Directive 88/344/EEC and para **10.4.6** below.

5 Commission Recommendation 97/618/EC concerning the scientific aspects and the presentation of information necessary to support applications for placing on the market of novel foods and novel food ingredients and the preparation of initial assessment reports was published at OJ L, 253 16.9.97 p 1.

6 Novel Foods and Novel Food Ingredients Regulations 1997 as amended by the Food Standards Act 1999 (Transitional and Consequential Provisions and Savings) (England and Wales) Regulations 2000.

7 On expert advisory committees generally, see section **2.4** and, on the ANCFP in particular, see para **2.4.4** above.

8 See para **1.7.5**.

9 As to the labelling of genetically modified food, see para **6.5.22** and the Genetically Modified and Novel Foods (Labelling) (England) Regulations 2000.
10 COM (1999) 719 final.

7.3 COMMUNITY COMMON AGRICULTURAL POLICY REGULATIONS

Introduction

7.3.1 Marketing standards have been a feature of common market organisations from the early days of the common agricultural policy. They have been used to define agricultural products eligible for support and to facilitate sales. They are in practice enacted by Regulation and so have required national legislation only to provide enforcement mechanisms and penalties. Since the products in question are mostly also foodstuffs, British legislation for this purpose has often been made in whole or in part under the Food Safety Act 1990. Even where the Community objectives in question have extended beyond what the 1990 Act comprehends, the concepts and enforcement methods of the Act have, in Regulations under the European Communities Act 1972, been applied to the food standards aspects.

7.3.2 The foods for which standards are prescribed in Community common agricultural policy regulations are considered below.

Drinking milk

7.3.3 Council Regulation 2597/97/EC laying down additional rules on the common organisation of the market in milk and milk products for drinking milk, as amended, is supplemented by the Drinking Milk Regulations 1998.

Only milk complying with the requirements laid down for drinking milk may be delivered or sold without processing to the final consumer. The sales descriptions given below must be used for those products.

The following products are considered as drinking milk—

(a) raw milk: milk which has not been heated above 40°C or subjected to treatment having equivalent effect;
(b) whole milk: heat-treated milk which, with respect to fat content, meets one of the following requirements—
- standardised whole milk: milk with a fat content of at least 3.5% (m/m);
- non-standardised whole milk: milk with a fat content that has not been altered since the milking stage either by the addition or removal of milk fats or by mixture the fat content may not be less that 3.5% (m/m);

(c) semi-skimmed milk: heat-treated milk whose fat content has been reduced to at least 1.5% (m/m) and at most 1.80% (m/m);
(d) skimmed milk: heat-treated milk whose fat content has been reduced to not more than 0.50% (m/m).

Modification of milk is authorised in particular to meet the fat content standards and to provide for enrichment with milk proteins, mineral salts or vitamins.

Milk and milk product designations

7.3.4 Council Regulation 1898/87/EEC, as amended, and the detailed rules in Commission Regulation 577/97 EC, as amended, are supplemented by the Milk and Milk Products (Protection of Designations) Regulations 1990.

Regulation 1898/87/EEC caused such difficulty when enacted that the Ministry of Agriculture, Fisheries and Food produced a guidance note on its interpretation. This recalls that the Regulation was introduced largely to meet concerns about the marketing of so-called 'imitation products' ie those non-dairy or partly non-dairy products (for example fat spreads and 'imitation' cream and cheese) which compete directly with dairy products and which can, by trading on the dairy image, mislead the consumer and thus compete unfairly with dairy products.

In particular the Regulation reserves to dairy products the term 'milk' and the designations 'whey', 'cream', 'butter', 'buttermilk', 'butteroil', 'caseins', 'anhydrous milkfat', 'cheese', 'yoghurt', 'kephir', 'koumiss', 'viili/fil', 'smetana' and 'fil' and generally prohibits any label, commercial document, publicity material, advertising or presentation which claims, implies or suggests that a non-dairy product is a dairy product. Under these provisions, the United Kingdom felt constrained to agree with the Commission that the term 'soya milk' should no longer be used. Moreover, the European Court recently decided that a milk product in which the milk fat has been replaced by vegetable fat for dietetic reasons may not be designated as 'cheese'[1].

However, there are exemptions from the Regulation—

- listed in Commission Decision 88/566/EEC (see further spreadable fats – para **7.3.5** below), for the names of traditional products (such as 'cream sherry' 'butter beans' and 'peanut butter') which, although containing a 'dairy' reference, are clearly understood not to imply a dairy product; and/or – where the 'dairy' reference is to describe a characteristic quality of the product (eg 'creamed potatoes'); and
- for the use of a protected name to describe the 'basic raw materials' of a product to meet the requirements of the Food Labelling Directive 79/112/EEC[2].

Provision is made for the use of the term 'milk' and the other milk product designations (supplemented in the case of the designation 'butter' by Regulation 577/97/EC) to designate composite products (such as 'strawberry yoghurt', 'cheesecake' and 'brandy butter') if the milk product elements have not been replaced by non-dairy fats (see further spreadable fats, para **7.3.5** below).

1 See judgment of the European Court of 16 December 1999 in case C-101/98 *Union Deutsche Lebensmittelwerke GmbH v Schutzverband gegen Unwesen* (16 December 1999, unreported).
2 See para **6.5.5**(iii) above.

Spreadable fats

7.3.5 Council Regulation 2991/94/EC laying down standards for spreadable fats and the detailed rules in Commission Regulation 577/97/EC, as amended, are supplemented by the Spreadable Fats (Marketing Standards) (England) Regulations 1999. Similar but separate regulations are to be made for Wales.

Regulation 2991/94/EC sets standards for spreadable fats with a fat content of at least 10% but less than 90% by weight intended for human consumption. The Regulation—

- restricts supply to the ultimate consumer to specified milk fats, fats and fats composed of plant and/or animal to products complying with prescribed requirements;

- specifies, in relation to those products, the sales descriptions 'butter', 'three-quarter fat butter', 'half-fat butter', 'dairy spread X', 'margarine', 'three-quarter fat margarine', 'half-fat margarine', 'fat spreads X', 'blend', 'three-quarter fat blend', 'half-fat blend' and 'blended spread X'; and
- reserves those descriptions for those products.

Exempt from these provisions are concentrated products (butter, margarine, blends) with a fat content of 90% or more.

As with Council Regulation 1898/87/EEC, exemptions are also provided for designations of products the exact nature of which is clear from traditional usage and/or when the designations are clearly used to describe a characteristic quality of the product. These designations are specified in Commission Regulation 577/97/EC and are in addition to those containing the word 'butter' listed in Decision 88/566/EEC (see milk and milk products designations, para **7.3.4** above).

Further provision is made by Regulation 577/97/EC for the use of the designation 'butter' in respect of composite products of which the essential part is butter.

In addition to the rules laid down in general labelling Directive 79/112/EEC[1], requirements are specified by Regulation 2991/94/EC as to the labelling and presentation of spreadable fats. In particular, the sales description, the total percentage fat content by weight, the vegetable, milk or other animal fat content and the percentage salt content must be indicated. Terms which suggest fat content for the specified products other than those prescribed are prohibited, but derogations are provided for the terms 'reduced-fat', 'low-fat' and 'light'.

As well as providing for the enforcement of these Community standards, the national Marketing Standards Regulations lay down compulsory vitamin content requirements for margarine sold by retail.

1 See para **6.5.4** above.

Eggs

7.3.6 Council Regulation 1907/90/EEC on certain marketing standards for eggs, as amended, and Commission Regulation 1274/91/EEC introducing detailed rules, as amended, are supplemented by the Eggs (Marketing Standards) Regulations 1995, as amended.

Marketing of hen eggs by way of business within the Community is prohibited unless they satisfy the marketing standards set by Council Regulation 1907/90/EEC and Commission Regulation 1274/91/EEC.

The quality grades for eggs are—

- Class A or 'fresh eggs',
- Class B or 'second quality or preserved eggs',
- Class C or 'down graded eggs intended for food industry undertakings approved in accordance with Directive 89/437/EEC[1] and the non-food industry'.

The quality standards for Grade A and B eggs relate to the condition of the shell and cuticle; the air space; the clarity and consistency of the white; the visibility on candling of the yolk and its freedom from extraneous matter; the absence of germ cell; and freedom from odour. Grade C eggs are those which do not meet the requirements for Grade A or B eggs.

Additionally, weight grades are laid down for Class A eggs. They are—

- XL—very large: 73 g and more;
- L—large: from 63 g up to 73 g;
- M—medium: from 53 g up to 63 g;
- S—small: under 53 g.

Comprehensive provision is made in respect of the marking of eggs, of large packs and of small packs[2].

In labelling large and small packs of eggs, the following information is mandatory—

- the name or business name and address of the undertaking who packed the eggs or had them packed; the name, business name or trade mark used by that undertaking, which may be a trade mark used collectively by a number of undertakings, may be shown if it contains no statement or symbol incompatible with the Regulation as to the quality or freshness of the eggs, the type of farming used, or the origin of the eggs;
- the distinguishing number of the packing centre in its prescribed form;
- the quality and weight gradings. Grade A eggs may be identified either by the words 'Class A' or the letter 'A' whether alone or in combination with the word 'fresh';
- the number of eggs packed;
- the date of minimum durability ('best-before date')[3] followed by appropriate storage recommendations for grade A eggs, and the packing date for eggs of other grades;
- particulars as to refrigeration or to the method of preservation, in uncoded form, in respect of refrigerated or preserved eggs.

The following additional information is permitted on large and small packs—

- the selling price;
- the retail management and/or stock control codes;
- one or more further dates aimed at providing the consumer with additional information;
- particulars as to special storage conditions;
- statements or symbols designed to promote sales of eggs or other items, provided that such statements or symbols and the manner in which they are made are not likely to mislead the purchaser.

The words 'extra' or 'extra fresh' may also be used in relation to small packs containing class A eggs. They must be printed on a band or label which must be removed not later than the seventh day after packing or the ninth day after laying.

The use on grade A eggs and small packs containing them of statements to indicate the type of farming, other than organic or biological farming, is limited to particular terms. The terms, which for small packs are 'Free range eggs'; 'Semi-intensive eggs'; 'Deep litter eggs' and 'Perchery eggs (Barn eggs)', are respectively restricted to eggs complying with specified criteria.

Regulation 7 of the Eggs (Marketing Standards) Regulations 1995 prescribes a United Kingdom official mark for the purpose of indicating the origin of grade A eggs and small packs containing them.

Eggs from third countries must be labelled with—

- the country of origin;
- the name of the packing undertaking in the third country;
- the quality and weight grading;

- for large packs, the weight in kilograms of the packed eggs and their number, and, for small packs, the number;
- the date of packing and the date of minimum durability followed by appropriate storage recommendations, for Grade A eggs, and the packing date for eggs of other grades.

The element of discretion left to Member States in organising supervision of the Community Regulations has the effect of authorising them to entrust exclusively to appointed agencies the taking of necessary implementing measures and services. In respect of such measures and services Member States may require payment provided that it is not in excess of the real costs involved[4].

Regulation 1907/90/EEC does not apply to eggs sold directly to the consumer for his own use, by the producer on his own farm, in a local public market with the exception of auction markets, or by door-to-door selling. Its predecessor, Regulation 2772/75/EEC, exempted similar circumstances, in respect of which the Ungraded Eggs (Hygiene) Regulations 1990, as amended, prohibit the sale by retail of any egg which contains a crack visible without candling to the naked eye[5].

As a result of the provision made by Council Directive 1999/74/EC[6] for improvement of minimum battery cage standards for laying hens, changes are understood to be in contemplation to make compulsory declaration of the system employed in egg production and to amend the criteria for 'free range' and other systems.

1 As to Directive 89/437/EEC, see para **13.10.1** below.
2 As to marking egg packs, see case C-210/96 *Gut Springenheide GmbH and Rudolf Tusky v Oberkreisdirektor des Kreises Steinfurt-Amt für Lebensmittelüberwachtung* [1998] ECR I-4657, [1999] 1 CMLR 1383; case C-203/90 *Erzeugergemeinschaft Gutshof-Ei GmbH v Stadt Bühl Ordnungs und Socialamt* [1992] ECR I-1003, [1994] 1 CMLR 397; case C-372/89 *Gold-Ei Erzeugerverbund GmbH v Überwachungsstelle für Milcherzeugnisse und Handelsklassen* [1991] ECR I-43; case C-204/88 *Ministère Public v Jean-Jacques Paris* [1989] ECR 4361, [1991] 1 CMLR 841, ECJ; case 91/87 *Erzeugergemeinschaft Gutshof-Ei GmbH v Land Rheinland-Pfalz* [1988] ECR 2541, [1990] 1 CMLR 96, ECJ; case 130/85 *Groothandel in Im-En Export van Eieren en Eirprodukten Wulro BV v Tuchtgerecht van de Stichting Scharreleiren-Controle* [1986] ECR 2035, [1988] 1 CMLR 496, ECJ. See also *Ministry of Agriculture, Fisheries and Food v Porter* [1987] 3 CMLR 57, QBD.
3 See further para **6.5.16** above.
4 See case 31/78 *Bussone v Italian Ministry for Agriculture and Forestry* [1978] ECR 2429, [1979] 3 CMLR 18, ECJ.
5 See also para **13.10.3** below.
6 OJ L 203 3.8.99, p 53.

Poultrymeat

7.3.7 Marketing standards for poultrymeat are laid down by Council Regulation 1906/90/EEC, as amended, and by Commission Regulation 1538/91/EEC, as amended, which sets out detailed rules[1].

The Community Regulations are expected shortly to be supplemented in this country by Poultrymeat (Marketing Standards) Regulations. These Regulations will in particular supersede the Poultrymeat (Water Content) Regulations 1984, as amended, which have been obsolete since the replacement of Council Regulation 2967/76/EEC (on the maximum water content of frozen poultry carcases) by Regulations 1906/90/EEC and 1538/91/EEC. The national Regulations have in part been delayed by the need to take account of further Community provisions in respect of the water content in poultry cuts.

Council Regulation 1906/90/EEC and Commission Regulation 1538/91/EEC lay down marketing standards for certain types and presentations of poultrymeat of the following species: domestic fowl, ducks, geese, turkeys and guinea fowl. The marketing of poultrymeat by way of business within the Community is prohibited unless these standards are satisfied.

The poultry carcases, the poultry cuts and foie gras to which the Regulations apply are defined and the names under which carcases and poultry cuts must be sold[2] are prescribed. Products other than those defined may be marketed in the Community only under names which do not mislead the consumer to a material degree through confusion with the prescribed names or with indications of the type of farming referred to below.

Poultry carcases and poultry cuts must be graded Class 'A' or Class 'B', in respect of each of which minimum requirements are specified as to conformation and appearance.

Poultry carcases must be presented for marketing as partially eviscerated ('effilé', 'roped'), with giblets or without giblets. Poultrymeat also must be marketed in one of the respectively defined conditions of 'fresh', 'frozen'[3] or 'quick-frozen'[4], provision being made for the optional classification of the prepackaged frozen and quick-frozen products according to specified weight categories.

In addition to the general rules for the labelling of foodstuffs[5], poultrymeat must comply with specifically prescribed requirements. With exceptions in the case of poultrymeat cut and boned at the place of sale[6], the following additional particulars must appear—

- the poultrymeat class;
- for retail sales of fresh poultrymeat, the total price and the price per weight unit;
- the condition in which the poultrymeat is marketed and the recommended storage temperature;
- the registered number of the slaughterhouse or cutting plant;
- for third country imports, the country of origin.

For fresh poultrymeat, a 'use by' date must be applied[7].

An indication of 'air chilling', 'air-spray chilling' or 'immersion chilling', as defined, may appear on the labelling as the method used for chilling poultry carcases.

Indications (sometimes referred to as special marketing terms) of the type of farming, other than organic or biological farming, are limited to the terms 'Fed with . . . % . . .'; 'Extensive indoor' ('Barn reared'); 'Free range'; 'Traditional free range' and 'Free range – total freedom' which are respectively restricted to products complying with specified criteria.

The Regulations also prescribe the percentages of technically unavoidable water absorption which must not be exceeded during preparation of fresh, frozen and quick frozen carcases and cuts thereof.

1 An *Enforcement Guide to EC Poultrymeat Marketing Standards Regulations* has been produced by the Ministry of Agriculture, Fisheries and Food.
2 See generally para **6.5.5**(i) above.
3 As to fresh and frozen poultrymeat, see also para **14.3.2**(b) below.
4 As to quick-frozen poultrymeat, see also para **14.5.2** below.
5 See para **6.5.4** above.
6 See para **13.3.1** below.
7 See para **6.5.17** above.

Description and presentation of wine

7.3.8 Under the Common Agricultural Policy (Wine) Regulations 1996[1], Regulations within the common organisation of the market in wine are enforced in the United

Kingdom at importation by Customs and Excise, at subsequent stages by the Wine Standards Board of the Vintners' Company[2] except retail level, where food authorities act. The Community wine Regulations include extensive rules governing description and presentation. These are briefly considered in paras **7.3.9–7.3.11** below according to the different types of wine. For this purpose, it should be noted that Council Regulation 822/87/EEC on common organisation of the market in wine, as amended, contains definitions of wine, table wine, liqueur wine, sparkling wine, aerated sparkling wine, semi-sparkling wine and aerated semi-sparkling wine. The definition of quality wines produced in specified regions (psr) is to be found in Council Regulation 823/87/EEC which lays down special provisions for these products.

From 1 August 2000—

(a) these Community provisions on description and presentation of wine are replaced by Title V, Chapter II of and Annexes VII and VIII to consolidating Council Regulation 1493/1999/EC on common organisation of the market in wine; and
(b) detailed rules for the protection of the additional traditional terms used to designate certain types of quality wines (psr) are prescribed by Commission Regulation 881/98/EC, as amended.

To provide for enforcement of the new Community provisions, the Common Agricultural Policy (Wine) Regulations 1996 may also be expected to be replaced during 2000.

Paragraph **7.3.12** below summarises the rules on aromatised wines, aromatised wine-based drinks and aromatised wine product cocktails.

For British legislation on the use of the word 'wine' in composite names for foods or drinks which are not wine, see para **7.6.18** below.

Restrictions on the sulphur dioxide levels in wine laid down by Council Regulation 822/87/EEC, as amended, Council Regulation 4252/88/EEC, as amended, Council Regulation 2332/92/EEC, as amended, and Council Regulation 1873/84/EEC, as amended, are enforced by the Miscellaneous Food Additive Regulations 1995 in implementation of European Parliament and Council Directive 95/2/EC[3].

1 See *Hurley v Martinez & Co Ltd* (1990) 154 JP 821.
2 The Wine Standards Board, Five Kings House, 1 Queen Street Place, London EC4R 1QS; tel: 020 7236 9512.
3 See para **10.2.6** and Appendix F, Part III.2B. As from 1 August 2000, these Community Regulations are replaced by Council Regulation 1493/1999/EC.

Still wines and grape musts

7.3.9 Council Regulation 2392/89/EEC, as amended, lays down general rules for the description and presentation of wines and grape musts. Subject to exceptions[1], detailed rules are laid down by Commission Regulation 3201/90/EEC, as amended. The definition of 'labelling' in Regulation 2392/89/EEC covers decoration or advertising which is unconnected with the wine concerned[2]. In labelling table wines originating within the Community, the mandatory information is—

(a) the words 'table wine';
(b) the nominal volume;
(c) for containers of not more than 60 litres, the name or business name of the bottler, the local administrative area and the Member State; for other containers, the name

or business name of the consignor, the local administrative area and the Member State;

(d) in the case of—
 (i) a consignment to another Member State or export, the name of the Member State in whose territory the grapes were harvested and turned into wine, provided both operations took place in the same Member State;
 (ii) a table wine made in a Member State other than that in which the grapes were harvested, the words 'wine made in . . . from grapes harvested in . . .';
 (iii) table wine resulting from a mixture of grapes or from coupage or products originating in more than one Member State, the words 'blend of wines from different countries of the EC';

(e) for certain designated wines the word 'Retsina';

(f) in the case of wines obtained in Spain by mixing red wines with white wines, the words 'vino tinto mezela' in Spanish territory;

(g) the actual alcoholic strength, the natural or technical conditions, and the ageing of the wine.

The following information is permitted in labelling table wine—

(a) a statement of whether the wine is red, rosé or white or, in the case of Spain, a mixture thereof;
(b) a brand name;
(c) a distributor's name and address and their local administrative area;
(d) any distinction awarded;
(e) where the wine is not exported or consigned to another Member State or exported, the name of the Member State where the grapes were harvested and turned into wine;
(f) certain analytical data;
(g) recommendations to the consumer as to use;
(h) details as to the type of product or the particular colour of the table wine;
(i) the 'e' mark[3].

In the case of geographical ascriptions authorised for table wine by Member States, the descriptions may be further supplemented by the following information—

(a) the name of a geographical unit which is smaller than a Member State[4];
(b) the name of one or two vine varieties;
(c) the vintage year;
(d) details regarding the method of production of the table wine;
(e) any award granted by an official body;
(f) a statement that the wine was bottled at the vineyard, in a group of vineyards or in an undertaking in the specified region;
(g) the name of the vineyard or group of vineyards where the table wine was made;
(h) information concerning the history of wine, the bottler or the distributor of the wine or any other factor, particularly of an organoleptic nature, which is characteristic of the product;
(i) where the producer Member State has laid down appropriate rules, the term 'regional wine' for table wines originating in the United Kingdom or similar terms for other Member States[5].

Similar information, mutatis mutandis, is required and permitted in the labelling of—

- quality wines produced in specified regions (psr) (that is, 'appellation contrôlée' and similar wines) originating within the Community[6];

- products other than table wines and quality wines psr (that is, other wines and grape musts) originating within the Community; and
- products originating in third countries.

Provision is also made for presentation of the products and to prevent incorrect, confusing or misleading description, presentation or advertising[7].

1 As to exemptions in the United Kingdom from the labelling requirements, see the Common Agricultural Policy (Wine) Regulations 1996, reg 6.
2 European Court judgment of 5 July 1995 in case C-46/94 *Michèle Voisine* [1995] ECR I-1859.
3 See para **15.6.2** below.
4 As to United Kingdom geographical ascriptions, see the Common Agricultural Policy (Wine) Regulations 1996, reg 5.
5 As to the United Kingdom rules governing the use of the term 'regional wine', see the Common Agricultural Policy (Wine) Regulations 1996, reg 5A and Sch 3A.
6 See case 56/80 *Weigand v Schutzverband Deutscher Wein* [1981] ECR 583, [1983] 1 CMLR 146.
7 See *Taittinger v Allbev Ltd* [1994] 4 All ER 75, [1993] 2 CMLR 741 (the Elderflower champagne case).

Sparkling wines and aerated sparkling wines

7.3.10 For the description and presentation of sparkling wines and aerated sparkling wines, general and detailed rules are respectively laid down by Council Regulation 2333/92/EEC, as amended and Commission Regulation 554/95/EEC, as amended. The mandatory information prescribed is similar to that noted in para **7.3.9** in respect of table wine, with separate requirements according to circumstances for Community wines, third country wines, products produced from third country wines, quality sparkling wines psr and quality sparkling wines of the aromatic type.

The description on the labelling may be supplemented by other particulars, provided that they are not liable to mislead. Requirements are laid down for the presentation of these wines and provision made for presentation of the products and to prevent incorrect, confusing or misleading description, presentation or advertising[1].

1 See judgment of 28 January 1999 in case C-303/97 *Verbraucherschutzverein v Sektkellerei G C Kessler* [1997] 1 CMLR 756.

Liqueur wines, semi-sparkling wines and aerated semi-sparkling wines

7.3.11 Council Regulation No 3895/91/EEC, as amended, and Commission Regulation 3901/91/EEC, as amended, lay down rules for the description and presentation of liqueur wines, semi-sparkling wines and aerated semi-sparkling wines. The alcoholic strength must be indicated on the labelling and lead-based closing devices are prohibited.

Aromatised wines, aromatised wine-based drinks and aromatised wine product cocktails

7.3.12 Council Regulation No 1601/91/EEC, as amended, lays down general rules on the definition, description and presentation of aromatised wines (such as 'vermouth'), aromatised wine-based drinks (such as 'sangria' and 'glühwein') and aromatised wine product cocktails.

The use of the descriptions specified in the Regulation is restricted to the products defined in it. The descriptions are prescribed for these products and other requirements laid down in addition to the general labelling rules[1].

1 See para **6.5.4** above.

Spirit drinks

7.3.13 Council Regulation No 1576/89/EEC laying down general rules on the definition, description and presentation of spirit drinks, as amended, and Commission Regulation 1014/90/EEC introducing detailed rules, as amended, are supplemented by the Spirits Drinks Regulations 1990, as amended.

Definitions and requirements are specified for the following spirit drinks: rum, whisky/whiskey[1], grain spirit, wine spirit, brandy/Weinbrand, grape marc spirit/grape marc, fruit marc spirit, raisin spirit/raisin brandy, fruit spirits, cider spirit/cider brandy/perry spirit, gentian spirit, fruit spirit drinks, juniper-flavoured spirit drinks, caraway-flavoured spirit drinks, aniseed-flavoured spirit drinks, bitter-tasting spirit drinks/bitter, vodka, liqueur, egg liqueur/advocaat/avocat/Advokat, liqueur with egg and Väkevä glögi/Spritglögg.

These names are reserved to spirit drinks for human consumption complying with the definitions and requirements in particular as to minimum alcoholic strength and permitted additions. Provision is made for the reserved names to be supplemented with geographical designations. Other spirit drinks must be described simply as spirit drinks or spirits[2].

In addition to the general rules for the labelling of foodstuffs[3], defined spirit drinks for the final consumer must comply with the following requirements—

- the reserved name must be used;
- where the labelling indicates the raw material used to produce the ethyl alcohol of agricultural origin, each agricultural alcohol must be mentioned in descending order of quantity used;
- where appropriate, the name may be supplemented by the term 'blend';
- saving exceptions, a maturation period may be specified only where it refers to the youngest alcoholic component;
- lead based closing devices may not be used.

As to British legislation on Scotch whisky, see para **7.5.4** below.

1 See *Scotch Whisky Association v Glen Kella Distillers* [1997] 16 LS Gaz R 29; *Matthew Gloag and Son Ltd and Another v Welsh Distillers Ltd and Others* (1998) Times, 27 February [1998] 2 CMLR 203.
2 European Court judgment of 16 July 1998 in case C-136/96 *Scotch Whisky Association v Compagnie Financière Européenne de Prises de Participation (COFEPP)* [1998] ECR I-4571.
3 See para **6.5.4** above.

Olive oil

7.3.13A Article 35 of Council Regulation 136/66/EEC on the establishment of a common organisation of the market in oils and fats, as amended, makes compulsory, for the purposes of marketing, the use of descriptions and definitions of olive oil and olive-pomace oil prescribed in the Annex to that Regulation. It also prohibits the marketing at the retail stage of oil other than extra virgin olive oil, virgin olive oil, olive oil and olive pomace oil.

Commission Regulation 2568/91/EEC, as amended, lays down the characteristics of olive oil and olive-residue oil for the purpose of differentiating between the various types and specifies relevant methods of analysis.

These provisions are supplemented in Great Britain by the Olive Oil (Marketing Standards) Regulations 1987, as amended.

As to tetrachloroethylene in olive oil, see para **10.5.1** below.

Commission Regulation 2815/98/EC, as amended, authorises designations of origin on consumer sales of extra virgin and virgin olive oil, including blends of more than 75%. These designations may mention only a geographical area whose name has been registered as protected designation of origin or protected geographical indication[1] and/or a Member State, the European Community or a third country. Designations must also comply with the Food Labelling Regulations 1996[2] and identify blends for consumers. Provision for the enforcement and execution of Regulation 2815/98/EC in Great Britain is made by the Olive Oil (Designations of Origin) Regulations 1999.

1 See para **7.4.2** below.
2 See in particular para **6.5.20** above.

Fishery and aquaculture products

7.3.14 Council Regulation 3759/92/EEC on the common organisation of the market in fishery and aquaculture products, as amended, includes power to determine marketing standards for these products in particular covering classification by quality, size or weight, packing, presentation and labelling.

When standards have been adopted, products to which they apply may not be displayed for sale, offered for sale or sold or otherwise marketed unless they conform to these standards, subject to special rules which may be adopted for trade with third countries. The standards which have been adopted are briefly considered in paras **7.3.15–7.3.17** below according to the different types of products.

The framework provisions on the common organisation of the market in fishery and aquaculture products have now been amended by replacement of Regulation 3759/92/EEC. New Council Regulation 104/2000/EC aims to improve transparency and knowledge of the products among consumers and, except as noted below, applies from 1 January 2001. Title I is of significance to food law. The existing powers in respect of marketing standards are re-enacted. To these are added provision for consumer information which applies from 1 January 2002. Without prejudice to the provisions of general labelling Directive 79/112/EEC[1], specified fish, crustaceans and molluscs offered for retail sale to the final consumer must from that date be labelled with the commercial name, production method and place where caught. For these purposes, Member States are required to draw up and publish a list of the commercial designations accepted within their territory[2].

In consequence of the enactment of Regulation 104/2000/EC, the provisions made by the Sea Fish (Marketing Standards) Regulations 1986, as amended, for the enforcement in the United Kingdom of Community rules in and under Regulation 3759/92/EEC, may be expected to be amended during 2000.

1 See in particular para **6.5.4** above.
2 See para **6.5.5**(i) above.

Specified fishery products

7.3.15 For specified saltwater fish, crustaceans (shrimps, edible crabs and Norway lobsters) and cephalopods (cuttlefish), common marketing standards have been laid down by Council Regulation 2406/96/EC, as amended, and as augmented by Commission Regulation 3703/85/EEC (laying down detailed rules for applying common marketing standards for certain fresh or chilled fish) and by Commission Regulation 3863/91/EEC (determining a minimum marketing size for crabs applicable in certain United Kingdom coastal areas).

Fishery products admitted as fit for human consumption must be classified by lot in defined freshness categories. These are E in the case of live Norway lobsters; Extra, A or B in the case of fish, selachii, cephalopods and other Norway lobsters; and Extra or A in the case of shrimps. Crabs are not subject to specific freshness standards. Products must also be sized by weight or by number per kilogram.

Products imported from third countries must comply with requirements as to packaging and labelling, while products landed from third country vessels are subject to the same provisions as Community catches.

Fishery products may be marketed only if they comply with Regulation 2406/96/EC, for the purpose of which 'marketing' means the first offer for sale and/or the first sale on Community territory, for human consumption. Since local authority enforcement was traditionally targeted at retail level, powers to enforce the Community legislation that Regulation 2406/96/EC replaced were conferred on fisheries ministers rather than on local authorities. At the time of writing, the United Kingdom legislation that supplements Community fishery products common marketing standards (that is, the Sea Fish (Marketing Standards) Regulations 1986, as amended) has yet to be updated so as to apply to Regulation 2406/96/EC.

Preserved sardines

7.3.16 For preserved sardines, common marketing standards have been laid down by Council Regulation 2136/89/EEC which is supplemented in England and Wales by the Preserved Sardines (Marketing Standards) Regulations 1990, as amended. Requirements are prescribed as to the presentation, covering media, quality after sterilisation and labelling and marketing is restricted to compliant products.

Preserved tuna and bonito

7.3.17 For preserved tuna and bonito, common marketing standards have been laid down by Council Regulation 1536/92/EEC which is supplemented in Great Britain by the Preserved Tuna and Bonito (Marketing Standards) Regulations 1994, as amended. Requirements are prescribed as to the presentation, covering media and labelling of preserved tuna and bonito and the use of that description is reserved to defined products.

Fruit and vegetables

7.3.18 The classification, by reference to a set of standards, of products to be delivered fresh to the consumer has long been part of the common organisation of the market in fruit and vegetables. The enabling powers are currently to be found in Council

Regulation 2200/96/EC, as amended[1]. Marketing standards have been adopted for dessert apples and pears; apricots; artichokes; asparagus; aubergines; avocados; beans; Brussels sprouts; cabbages; carrots; cauliflowers; ribbed celery; cherries; citrus fruit; courgettes; cucumbers; garlic; kiwifruit; leeks; lettuces, curled-leaved endives and broad-leaved (Batavian) endives; melons; onions; peaches and nectarines; peas for shelling; plums; spinach; strawberries; sweet peppers; table grapes; tomatoes; water melons; and witloof chicory. Council Regulation 2200/96/EC also contemplates standards for almonds, hazelnuts and walnuts and confers power on the Commission to extend the list of products to which standards are applied.

Marketing within the Community of products covered by the quality standards otherwise than in conformity with the standards is prohibited[2]. However, there are exemptions for products, within a given production area, transported to preparation and packaging stations or storage facilities, or from storage facilities to preparation and packaging stations. Also exempt from compliance with the quality standards are (a) products consigned to processing plants, unless quality criteria have been set for products for industrial processing; and (b) products transferred by the producer on his holding to consumers for their personal use.

The marketing standards for the various products are similar in that each set lays down criteria as to quality (such as colour, cleanliness, shape), size, packaging, presentation and marking.

The standards for each product generally specify three quality classifications. These are Extra Class, which must be of superior quality; Class I, which must be of good quality; and Class II, which must meet the prescribed minimum requirements. Very occasionally, a Class III classification has been used for a particular product where justified economically and to satisfy consumer demand.

Packaging is required to be legibly and indelibly marked, in letters grouped on the same side and visible from the outside, with (a) the identification of the packer and/or dispatcher; (b) the nature of the produce, if the contents are not visible from the outside; (c) the origin of the produce (that is, the country and sometimes the district, of origin); and (d) the commercial specifications (as to quality class and size and/or count).

Commission Regulation 2251/92/EEC, as amended, provides for quality inspection of fresh fruit and vegetables.

In Great Britain, the Grading of Horticultural Produce (Amendment) Regulations 1973, as amended, provide for the application, subject to modifications, of the Agriculture and Horticulture Act 1964 in relation to Community grading rules and standards. Further provision is made by the Grading of Horticultural Produce (Forms of Labels) Regulations 1982 and the Horticultural Produce Act 1986. Enforcement of the Community standards in England and Wales is the responsibility of the Ministry of Agriculture, Fisheries and Food Horticultural Marketing Inspectorate.

It should be noted that any description or mark applied in pursuance of the Agriculture and Horticulture Act 1964 or any Community grading rules within the meaning of Part III of that Act is deemed not to be a trade description[3].

1 See Council Regulation 2200/96/EC, as amended, Art 2.
2 *Antonio Muñoz Y Cia v Frumar Ltd* (1999) Times, April 2
3 Trade Descriptions Act 1968, s 2(4)(d).

Bananas

7.3.19 Council Regulation 404/93/EEC on the common organisation of the market in bananas, as amended, makes provision for common quality standards for bananas intended for consumption fresh, not including plantains. The standards are laid down by Commission Regulation 2257/94/EEC, as amended.

Like most products subject to the fresh fruit and vegetables regime, bananas are classified into three classes. These are Extra Class, which must be of superior quality; Class I, which must be of good quality; and Class II, which must meet the specified minimum requirements. Criteria are also similarly prescribed as to size, packaging, presentation and marking with the identification of the packer and/or dispatcher; the nature of the produce; the origin of the produce; and the commercial specifications.

Commission Regulation 2898/95/EEC, as amended, provides for verification of compliance with the standards.

The enforcement legislation and responsibilities in Great Britain for the Community grading rules and standards for bananas are the same as those described for fruit and vegetables in para **7.3.18**.

7.4 COMMUNITY REGULATIONS ON QUALITY MARKS AND LABELS

Introduction

7.4.1 Generally speaking the Commission has pursued a different quality promotion policy for agricultural products from that for products controlled within the internal market[1].

Within the framework of the common agricultural policy, we have already noted in section **7.3** above, the provision made for origin marking of wine, spirit drinks and olive oil. Community quality marking provisions have also been made (1) by Regulation 2081/92/EEC, for products which originate in areas known for their traditional production; (2) by Regulation 2082/92/EEC, for products which are subject to special production quality requirements; and (3) by Regulation 2092/91/EEC, for products produced using organic methods. These provisions are considered in paras **7.4.2–7.4.4** below.

The Commission regards the third item as but the main example of a wider class of foods which should have special status on account of their production methods. Thus, only eggs and poultrymeat complying with specified criteria have since 1991 been permitted to bear the term 'Free range' and similar expressions concerning the type of specialist farming employed in their production[2].

Although the provisions on the origin marking of beef and beef products are arguably concerned more with traceability than with laying down quality standards, it might usefully be noted here that they are summarised in para **13.8.6** below and that consideration is being given to measures to improve the traceability of other animal products.

The Commission's general approach to the quality of foodstuffs controlled within the internal market sector was formulated in 1985. Following the *Cassis de Dijon* judgment[3], the Commission decided normally to leave the question of quality standards and certification within the internal market to the initiative of operators. In establishing trade codes of practice, operators are encouraged to adhere to the standards recognised at international and European level, in particular the ISO 9000 and EN 29 000 series on quality management and quality assurance standards[4].

1 Commission Green Paper COM (97) 176 on 'the General Principles of Food Law in the European Union' Part III.7.3.

2 See respectively paras **7.3.6** and **7.3.7** above.

3 See paras **1.3.1–1.3.3** above.
4 See further Council Resolution of 7 May 1985 on a new approach to technical harmonisation and standards (85/C 136/01), OJ C 136 4.6.85, and Council Resolution of 21 December 1989 on a global approach to conformity assessment (90/C 10/01) OJ C 10 16.1.90, p1.

Protection of geographical indications and designations of origin

7.4.2 Provision for registration to protect geographical indications and designations of origin for agricultural products and foodstuffs is made by Council Regulation 2081/92/EEC, as amended, with detailed rules in Commission Regulation 2037/93/EEC, as amended[1]. Subordinate legislation is planned in the United Kingdom to make provision as soon as possible for enforcement of the Community Regulations.

Regulation 2081/92/EEC generally applies to agricultural products listed in the EC Treaty[2] and in the Regulation[3] and to foodstuffs listed in the Regulation. In particular, meat and meat products, milk and dairy products, eggs, honey, fruit, vegetable and food plants, animal and vegetable fats, fish, shell fish and molluscs, spices, bread, pastries, cakes, beer and beverages made from plant extracts are covered. However, wine products and spirits are excluded since provision is already made to protect their geographical descriptions[4].

Diversity in Member States' previous practices made it appropriate to allow for the protection of two different types of geographical description—namely, the designation of origin and the geographical indication. Each signifies the name of a region, a specific place or, exceptionally, a country, used to describe an agricultural product or a foodstuff originating in that region, place or country. In the case of a 'designation of origin', the quality or characteristics of the product must essentially or exclusively be due to a particular geographical environment with its inherent natural and human factors, and the production, processing and preparation of which take place in the defined geographical area. The term is thus used to describe foodstuffs which are produced, processed and prepared in a given geographical area using recognised know-how. By contrast, in the case of a 'geographical indication', the product must possess a specific quality, reputation or other characteristics attributable to that geographical origin and the production and/or processing and/or preparation of which takes place in the geographical area. In this case, therefore, the geographical link must occur in at least one of the stages of production, processing or preparation. In exceptional cases the definition of designation of origin is extended to certain traditional geographical or non-geographical names and to products the raw materials of which come from outside the processing area.

Geographical descriptions have been protected by the Community in respect of products such as meat, meat products, cheese, eggs, honey, milk products, olive oil, fruit, vegetables, cereals, natural mineral and spring waters, bread, pastry, cakes, confectionery, biscuits, baker's wares, natural gums and resins and shell fish. Among United Kingdom descriptions, 'Orkney beef', 'White Stilton cheese'and 'Jersey Royal potatoes' have been protected as designations of origin; and 'Exmoor blue cheese', 'Scotch beef', 'Herefordshire cider', 'Kentish Ale' and 'Whitstable oysters' as geographical indications.

A name may not be registered if it has become generic (taking account of the existing situation in the originating and other Member States and national and Community law) or where it conflicts with the name of a plant variety or animal breed and is likely to mislead the public as to the true nature of the product.

A name may also not be registered if this is likely to mislead the consumer as to the true identity of the product due to the reputation, renown and long usage of an existing trade mark.

To be eligible to use a protected designation of origin (PDO) or a protected geographical indication (PGI) an agricultural product or foodstuff must comply with a specification, which must at least include—

(a) the name of the agricultural product or foodstuff, including the designation of origin or geographical indication;
(b) a description of the agricultural product or foodstuff including the raw materials, if appropriate, and principal physical, chemical, microbiological and/or organoleptic characteristics of the product or foodstuff;
(c) the definition or the geographical area;
(d) evidence that the agricultural product or foodstuff originates in the geographical area;
(e) a description of the method of obtaining the agricultural product or foodstuff;
(f) the details bearing out the link with the geographical environment or geographical origin;
(g) details of the inspection structures;
(h) the specific labelling details relating to the permitted designation of origin or permitted geographical indication or traditional national indication;
(i) any requirement laid down by Community and/or national provisions.

Provision is made for applications for registration of designations of origin or geographical indications, for temporary protection by the Member State, for registration objections by other Member States and for registration and publication of entries in the 'Register of protected designations of origin and protected geographical indications'.

By Article 17 of Regulation 2081/92/EEC, following entry into force of the Regulation[5], Member States were allowed six months in which to forward to the Commission their legally protected names or, where there was no protection system, those of the names protected by usage that they wished to register. The prescribed objection procedure did not apply to these applications. The names registered as PDOs or PGIs as a result of this initial simplified procedure were published in Commission Regulation 1107/96/EC, as amended. On 16 March 1999 in joined cases C-289/96, C-293/96 and C-299/96 *Denmark, Germany and France v Commission*[6], the European Court annulled Regulation 1107/96/EEC to the extent that it registered 'Feta' as a protected designation for cheese. As noted above, a name may not be registered if it has become generic and, in rejecting this possibility and making the registration, the Commission had failed to take account of the fact that it had been used for a considerable time for cheese produced and marketed in Member States other than Greece. Following this judgment, the Commission Regulation 1070/99/EC deleted 'Feta' from the Register, declaring that, in accordance with Article 17(3) of Regulation 2081/92/EEC, the name 'Feta' remains protected at national level until such time as a decision is taken in this regard.

Names registered under the normal procedure are published in Commission Regulation 2400/96/EC, as amended and supplemented.

A scientific committee, set up by Commission Decision 93/53/EEC, as amended, assists the Commission with technical problems relating to the application of Regulation 2081/92/EEC with regard to the registration of names of agricultural products and foodstuffs and cases of conflict between Member States.

The indications PDO and PGI, equivalent traditional indications and the prescribed Community symbol may appear only on products which comply with Regulation 2081/92/EEC.

The registered name of the product is protected from any direct or indirect commercial use by an unregistered producer. This includes expressions such as 'style', 'type', 'method', 'as produced in', 'imitation' or similar words. False or misleading indications as to the provenance, origin, nature or essential qualities of the product on the packaging and any other practice liable to mislead the public as to the true origin of the product are also prohibited. In particular, applications for registration of a trade mark corresponding to one of these situations in relation to a registered PDO or PGI must be refused, although the use of such a trade mark registered in good faith before the application of the PDO or PGI may continue provided there are no grounds for invalidity or revocation under Council Directive 89/104/EEC to approximate the laws of Member States relating to trade marks[7]. The question of whether a constituent part of a 'compound' protected designation of origin is itself protected is a matter for determination by the national court on the basis of a detailed analysis of the facts[8].

Amendment of a PDO or PGI specification may be requested by the Member State concerned, in particular to take account of developments in scientific and technical knowledge to redefine the geographical area. A Member State may not, by adopting provisions of national law, alter a designation of origin for which it has requested registration.

Member States are obliged to have in place inspection structures to ensure that products bearing a protected name meet the requirements in the specifications. Compliance with each specification must be checked by a designated inspection authority or a private body approved for the purpose. They must offer adequate guarantees of objectivity and impartiality and must fulfil the requirements laid down in standard EN45011 of 26 June 1989 on general requirements for bodies operating product certification systems. At the time of writing, the inspection bodies for particular products in respect of which the United Kingdom is responsible are States of Jersey Department of Agriculture and Fisheries; Forest of Dean District Council; Product Authentication Inspectorate; Herefordshire Council Environmental, Health and Trading Standards Service; Cornwall County Council; Dorset County Council Trading Standards Services; and Scottish Food Quality Certification Limited.

1 The Ministry, of Agriculture, Fisheries and Food has produced a guidance booklet 'Protecting Food Names'. See also *Consorzio del Prosciutto di Parma v Asda* [1999] ETMR 319 in which the Court of Appeal held that Regulation 2081/92/EEC did not have direct effect or prevent the slicing and packaging of Parma ham in England.
2 See EC Treaty, Annex I (ex-Annex II).
3 By Art 32 (ex-Art 38) EC, products of first-stage processing directly related to products of the soil, of stockfarming and of fisheries are themselves 'agricultural products'.
4 As to wine products, see paras **7.3.8–7.3.12**. As to spirits, see para **7.3.13**.
5 Regulation 2081/92/EEC entered into force 12 months after its date of publication in the Official Journal which was 24 July 1992.
6 See European Court judgment of 16 March 1999 in joined cases C-289/96, C-293/96 and C-299/96 *Denmark, Germany and France v EC Commission* (1999) Times, 17 April.
7 See European Court judgment of 4 March 1999 in case C-87/97 *Conzorzio per la tutela del formaggio Gorgonzola v Käserei Champignon Hofmeister GmbH & Co KG and Eduard Bracharz GmbH* [1999] 1 CMLR 1203 (legality of 'Cambozola' trade mark). As to Directive 89/104/EEC and the registration of geographical names as trade marks, see European judgment of 4 May 1999 in joined cases C-108/97 and C-109/97 *Windsurfing Chiemsee Produktions- und Vertriebs GmbH v Boots- Segelzubehör Walter Huber*.
8 See European Court judgment of 9 June 1998 in joined cases C-129/97 and C-130/97 *Chiciak and Fol* [1998] ECR I-3315.

Certificates of specific character

7.4.3 Rules under which certificates of specific character may be obtained for agricultural products are laid down by Council Regulation 2082/92/EEC, as amended, with detailed rules in Commission Regulation 1848/93/EEC, as amended[1]. Subordinate legislation is planned in the United Kingdom to make provision as soon as possible for enforcement of the Community Regulations.

Regulation 2082/92/EEC applies to agricultural products listed in the EC Treaty[2] and to foodstuffs listed in the Regulation. More products are included than is the case for geographical indications and designations of origin. In addition to covering meat and meat products, milk and dairy products, eggs, honey, fruit, vegetable and food plants, animal and vegetable fats, fish, shell fish and molluscs, spices, bread, pastries, cakes, beer and beverages made from plant extracts, the Regulation 2082/92/EEC list extends to chocolate, pasta, prepared dishes, sauces and seasoning, soups, ice cream and sorbets, wine and vinegar. However, the Regulation applies without prejudice to other specific Community provisions.

As defined in the Regulation, a 'certificate of specific character' means recognition by the Community of the specific character of a product by means of its registration in accordance with the Regulation, 'specific character' being the feature or set of features which distinguishes an agricultural product or a foodstuff clearly from other similar products or foodstuffs belonging to the same category. A product covered by the certificate of specific character can claim to be a 'Traditional Speciality Guaranteed'. By contrast with protected geographical indications and designations of origin, this does not refer to the origin, but emphasises traditional character, either in composition or means of production. A product bearing a certificate of specific character can thus be produced anywhere in the European Community. Examples of products in respect of which certificates of specific character are appropriate are Belgian-style beers and mozarella cheese, which have already been registered, and traditional farm fresh turkeys, for which application has been made.

The Commission is required to administer the 'Register of certificates of specific character' which must distinguish those products which may use the registered name as well as the Community symbol and indication from those which may use only the registered name.

As indicated, to appear in the Register, a product must either be produced using traditional raw materials or be characterised by a traditional composition or a mode of production and/or processing reflecting a traditional type of production and/or processing.

To be registered, the name must—

- be specific in itself (eg pumpernickel, haggis), traditional and comply with national provisions or be established by custom; or
- express the specific character of the product (eg corn-fed chicken) and not be misleading.

In order to qualify for a certificate of specific character, a product must comply with a product specification, which must at least include—

(a) the name of the product in one or more languages;
(b) a description of the method of production, including the nature and characteristics of the raw material and/or ingredients used and/or the method of preparation of the product, referring to its specific character;
(c) aspects allowing appraisal of its traditional character;
(d) a description of the characteristics of the product giving its main physical, chemical, microbiological and/or organoleptic characteristics which relate to the specific character;
(e) the minimum requirements and inspection procedures to which the specific character is subject.

Provision is made for applications for registration of the specific character of products, for objections and for registration and publication of entries in the Register.

Names entered in the Register are published in Commission Regulation 2301/97/EC, as amended.

The scientific committee, set up by Commission Decision 93/53/EEC, as amended, assists the Commission with technical problems relating to the application of Regulation 2082/92/EC with regard to the registration of names of agricultural products and foodstuffs and cases of conflict between Member States.

Any Member States may submit that a criterion laid down in the specification for a product is no longer met, while amendments to a specification may be requested by a Member State at the request of a group established in its territory.

The registered name, a prescribed Community indication and a Community symbol, are reserved to products corresponding to the relevant published specification. Registered names must be protected against any practice liable to mislead the public including false suggestions that a product is covered by a certificate of specific character.

Member States are obliged to have in place inspection structures to ensure that products bearing a certificate of specific character meet the requirements in the specifications. Compliance with each specification must be checked by a designated inspection authority or a private body approved for the purpose. They must offer adequate guarantees of objectivity and impartiality and must fulfil the requirements laid down in standard EN45011 of 26 June 1989 on general requirements for bodies operating product certification systems.

1 The Ministry of Agriculture, Fisheries and Food have produced a guidance booklet 'Protecting Food Names'.
2 See EC Treaty, Annex I (ex-Annex II).

Organic products

7.4.4 Council Regulation 2092/91/EEC, as amended, establishes criteria for the organic production of agricultural products and the indications referring thereto on agricultural products and foodstuffs. To implement the arrangements made by the Regulation for imports from third countries, detailed rules are laid down by Commission Regulation 94/92/EEC, as amended, and, in respect of the inspection certificate for imports, by Commission Regulation 3457/92/EEC, as amended. Arrangements for imports from certain third countries are deferred by Commission Regulation 529/95/EEC, as amended.

With effect from 24 August 2000, Regulation 2092/91 has been amended by Regulation 1804/1999/EC so as to include rules on livestock production. In consequence, Regulation 2092/91/EEC will henceforth apply to the following products bearing indications of organic production methods—

(a) unprocessed agricultural crop products: also animals and unprocessed animal products, to the extent that principles of production and specific inspection rules for them have been introduced by the amendments;
(b) processed agricultural crop and livestock products intended for human consumption prepared essentially from one or more ingredients of plant and/or animal origin; and
(c) feeding stuffs, compound feeding stuffs and feed materials[1] not covered by (a) above, as from the adoption of a further Regulation providing labelling and inspection requirements[2].

Pending the adoption of this further Regulation, national rules in conformity with Community law, or in their absence private standards accepted or recognised by the Member States, are to apply to products specified at (c).

Detailed production rules are laid down by Regulation 2092/91/EEC for livestock and livestock products from the following species: bovine (including bubalus and bison species), porcine, ovine, caprine, equidae and poultry, as well as for beekeeping and beekeeping products. The Community is to introduce production rules as soon as possible for other species besides aquaculture and aquaculture products. Until Community rules are made, national rules, or in their absence private standards accepted or recognised by the Member States, are to apply.

In food labelling and advertising, the term 'organic' and other indications referring to organic production methods are reserved to products which comply with relevant provisions of Regulation 2092/91/EEC. Products specified at (a) must have been produced in accordance with prescribed rules, or imported from a third country under prescribed arrangements, in each case, by an operator who is subject to the specified inspection system. Products specified at (b) must in particular be at least 95% comprised of ingredients of agricultural origin which are, or are derived from, products which comply with the production or import rules and have been prepared or imported by an operator who is subject to the specified inspection system. This strict standard must be met by products specified at (b) where indications referring to organic production methods appear in the sales description. Qualified conditions are prescribed for other cases. In particular, at least 70% of the ingredients of agricultural origin must be, or must be derived from, products complying with the production or import rules under the specified inspection arrangements. However, the indications must appear in lettering identical to the rest of the information and the percentage of organic ingredients must appear in a separate statement in the same visual field as the sales description. Moreover, in every case the product specified at (b) must have been produced without the use of genetically modified organisms or any products derived from them.

The Community Regulations are supplemented in the United Kingdom by the Organic Products Regulations 1992, which will require further amendment to take account of Regulation 1804/1999/EC.

In the United Kingdom, the inspection system under Regulation 2092/91/EEC is administered by the pre-existing United Kingdom Register of Organic Food Standards (UKROFS)[3] and six approved organic sector bodies. UKROFS sets standards for organic food in accordance with the Regulation 2092/91/EEC and certifies conformity with these standards of schemes operated by the sector bodies and of production by independent operators. Operators producing, preparing or importing organic products for the market are required by Regulation 2092/91/EEC to notify the competent authority and submit to the inspection system. Most fulfil these obligations by registering with a sector body or with UKROFS direct.

Labelling is required to include a reference to the code number of the relevant inspection body, and the prescribed indication that products are covered by the inspection system is reserved to products complying with further specified conditions.

Imports from third countries are restricted to products produced and inspected under rules equivalent to those applying in the Community.

1 As to feeding stuffs and compound feeding stuffs, see Directive 79/373/EEC and para **16.3.1** below. As to feed materials, see Directive 96/25/EEC and paras **16.3.1** and **16.3.2** below.
2 The Commission is required to bring forward proposals for the Regulation not later than 24 August 2001.
3 United Kingdom Register of Organic Food Standards, Nobel House, 17 Smith Square, London SW1P 3JR/EEC.

7.5 NATIONAL REGULATIONS ON SPECIFIC FOODS

7.5.1 We have already seen how the scope to enact national food standards has been limited through the occupation of the field by Community provisions[1], the obligation to notify draft technical legislation to the Commission[2] and the European Court's *Cassis de Dijon* doctrine[3]. The exemption from national standards that this doctrine confers on many imports, coupled with the Government's inclination during the 1990s to deregulate business, led it greatly to reduce their numbers[4]. Nevertheless, even in areas which are densely controlled by Community legislation, gaps remain which it is sometimes thought right to fill. As noted in para **7.3.5** above, the Spreadable Fats (Marketing Standards) (England) Regulations 1999 not only supplement the Community standards, but also continue to lay down national compulsory vitamin content requirements for margarine sold by retail. The remaining national food standards are summarised below. It is interesting to observe that the margarine example above and the obligation to fortify wheat flour described in para **7.5.2** below exceptionally promote consumers' health by requiring the incorporation of particular ingredients in staple foods.

1 See para **1.2.1** above.
2 See para **1.4.1** above.
3 See paras **1.3.1** and **1.3.2** above.
4 See in particular the Food (Miscellaneous Revocations and Amendments) Regulations 1995.

Bread and flour

7.5.2 The Bread and Flour Regulations 1998 require, subject to exceptions, that wheat flour be fortified with specified minimum proportions of calcium carbonate, iron, thiamin (vitamin B1) and nicotinic acid or nicotinamide. The use of certain additional ingredients and additives in flour and bread is restricted and, in labelling bread, an indication must be given of the presence of any flour improving agent. The names 'wholemeal' and 'wheat germ' are reserved to bread complying with specified requirements.

Meat products and spreadable fish products

7.5.3 In the labelling and advertising of meat and spreadable fish products, the Meat Products and Spreadable Fish Products Regulations 1984, as amended, restrict the use of specified names to products complying with prescribed meat and fish content requirements.

Requirements are specified for meat products which might be taken to consist purely of meat. The ingredients must, subject to exceptions, be indicated as part of the name and added water declared.

Products must bear a declaration of the minimum meat, fish or corned meat content, of which, in the case of meat products, a specified proportion must be lean meat. Otherwise undeclared fat in meat products must be separately identified in the list of ingredients.

Scotch whisky

7.5.4 The Scotch Whisky Order 1990 defines this product and specifies its minimum alcoholic strength. The enabling statute, the Scotch Whisky Act 1988, makes it unlawful to sell as Scotch whisky any spirits not conforming to these requirements and provides for injunctive action to restrain contraventions.

The Scotland Act 1998 (Modification of Functions) Order 1999, SI 1999/1756, makes provision, in respect of Scotland, for the transfer to Scottish Ministers of the order making powers in the 1988 Act.

As to Community legislation on Scotch whisky and other spirit drinks, see para **7.3.13** above.

7.6 REGULATIONS TO PREVENT MISLEADING DESCRIPTIONS

7.6.1 As indicated in section **6.2** above, any description of a food product which is misleading may contravene the FSA 1990[1]. In each case the court has to decide on the deceptiveness or otherwise of the description in question. In addition to this general restriction, the Food Labelling Regulations 1996 prohibit the use of specified words and descriptions[2] in the labelling or advertising of a food unless certain conditions are satisfied.

The difference between, on the one hand, reserving descriptions (summarised below) to prevent consumers from being misled about the food in question and, on the other hand, reserving descriptions (see para **7.1.2** above) so as to assure consumers of a reliable food standard, is not one of kind. In both cases, low quality food is being denied unfair use of the name that consumers expect. Indeed, the descriptions of 'ice cream', 'dairy ice cream', 'indian tonic water', 'quinine tonic water' and the various types of 'cheese' and 'cream' now protected by the Food Labelling Regulations 1996 were separately reserved to prescribed standards for these respective foods until the relevant sets of Regulations were revoked in the Government's 1995 deregulation exercise[3].

Moreover, the provisions, considered in section **8.2** below, restricting the making of claims in respect of food are likewise akin to those restricting descriptions. Whether or not the legislator aims the restriction at preventing a misleading description or a misleading claim will, it is submitted, depend on the terms in which unscrupulous traders are perceived to practice their deception.

Descriptions subject to conditions imposed by the Food Labelling Regulations 1996 are considered below.

By virtue of regulation 3(4) and (5) of the Food Labelling Regulations 1996 only the provisions described in para **7.6.2** below do not apply to natural mineral water, other than water which has been artificially carbonated.

1 FSA 1990, s 15.
2 Food Labelling Regulations 1996, reg 42, Sch 8.
3 See the former Ice Cream Regulations 1967, SI 1967/1866; Soft Drinks Regulations 1964, SI 1964/760; Cheese Regulations 1970, SI 1970/3240; and Cream Regulations 1970, SI 1970/752.

Dietary or dietetic

7.6.2 In implementation of Article 2 of Council Directive 89/398/EEC (on the approximation of the laws of the Member States relating to foodstuffs intended for particular nutritional uses)[1], the descriptions 'dietary' or 'dietetic' must not be applied to any food unless it is a food for a particular nutritional use (excluding such foods formulated for infants and young children in good health) which (a) has been specially made for a class of persons whose digestive process or metabolism is disturbed or who, by reason of their special physiological condition, obtain special benefit from a controlled consumption of certain substances and (b) is suitable for fulfilling the particular nutritional requirements of that class of persons.

1 See further para **8.6.1** below.

Flavours

7.6.3 Any description incorporating the name of a food in such a way as to imply that the food, or the part of the food, being described has the flavour of the food named in the description may not be applied to any food unless the flavour of the food is derived wholly or mainly from the food named in the description. However, any description incorporating the word 'chocolate' which is such as to imply that the food has a chocolate flavour (eg 'chocolate cake') may be applied to a food which has a chocolate flavour derived wholly or mainly from non-fat cocoa solids where the purchaser would not be misled by the description.

The foregoing does not prevent the use of the word 'flavour' preceded by the name of a food when the flavour of the food is not derived wholly or mainly from the food named in the description. This is to allow the use of artificial flavours and to distinguish them from flavours derived from natural foods.

A pictorial representation of a food which is such as to imply that the food to which the representation is applied has the flavour of the food depicted in the representation must not be applied to any food unless the flavour of the food to which the representation is applied is derived wholly or mainly from the depicted food.

Thus, a flavour of a soft drink may be communicated by a picture of a fruit on the label, if that flavour is derived wholly or mainly from that fruit.

Ice cream

7.6.4 The description 'ice cream' is reserved to a defined frozen product. It must contain not less than 5% fat and not less than 2.5% milk proteins, not necessarily in natural proportions. It must be obtained by subjecting an emulsion of fat, milk solids and sugar (including any sweetener permitted in ice cream by the Sweeteners in Food Regulations 1995[1]), with or without the addition of other substances, to heat treatment and either to subsequent freezing or evaporation, addition of water and subsequent freezing.

The description 'dairy ice cream' is reserved to food which fulfils these conditions and other requirements. The minimum 5% fat content must consist exclusively of milk fat and the food must contain no fat other than milk fat or any fat present by reason of the use as an ingredient of any egg, any flavouring, or any emulsifier or stabiliser.

1 See para **10.2.4** below.

Milk of animals other than cows

7.6.5 The word 'milk' or any other word or description which implies that the food being described contains milk must not be used as part of the name of a food which contains the milk of an animal other than a cow unless—

(a) (i) such milk has all the normal constituents in their natural proportions, and
(ii) the word or description is accompanied by the name of that animal; or
(b) (i) such milk has been subjected to a process or treatment, and
(ii) the word or description is accompanied by the name of that animal and an indication of that process or treatment; or
(c) the word or description is used in accordance with any regulations or order made or continued in force under the Food Safety Act 1990.

The word 'milk' must not be used as the name of an ingredient where the ingredient is the milk of an animal other than a cow unless the word or description is accompanied by the name of that animal and its use complies in all other respects with the Food Labelling Regulations 1996.

Starch-reduced

7.6.6 This description must not be applied to any food unless less than 50% of the food consists of anhydrous carbohydrate calculated by weight on the dry matter of the food, and the starch content of a given quantity of the food is substantially less than that of the same quantity of similar foods to which the description is not applied.

Vitamins

7.6.7 The word 'vitamin' or any other word or description which implies that the food to which the word or description relates is a vitamin must not be used in labelling or advertising unless the food is one of the vitamins specified in column 1 of Table A in Schedule 6 to the 1996 Regulations[1] or is vitamin K.

1 See para **8.2.12** below.

Alcohol-free

7.6.8 The description 'alcohol-free' must not be applied to any alcoholic drink from which the alcohol has been extracted, unless the drink has a strength by volume of not more than 0.05%, and it is marked or labelled with an indication of its maximum alcoholic strength immediately preceded by the words 'not more than' or, in an appropriate case, with an indication that it contains no alcohol.

Dealcoholised

7.6.9 The description 'dealcoholised' must not be applied to any drink unless the drink, being an alcoholic drink from which the alcohol has been extracted, has an alcoholic strength by volume of not more than 0.5%, and is marked or labelled with an indication of its maximum alcoholic strength immediately preceded by words 'not more than' or, in an appropriate case, with an indication that it contains no alcohol.

Low alcohol

7.6.10 The description 'low alcohol' or any other word or description which implies that the drink being described is low in alcohol must not be applied to an alcoholic drink unless the drink has an alcoholic strength of not more than 1.2%, and the drink is marked or labelled with an indication of its maximum alcoholic strength immediately preceded by the words 'not more than'.

Low calorie

7.6.11 The description 'low calorie' or any other word or description which implies that the drink being described is low in calories must not be applied to a soft drink unless the soft drink (where applicable, after subsequent preparation – which may include dilution – in accordance with accompanying instructions) contains not more than 10 kcal per 100 ml and 42 kJ per 100 ml of the drink.

Non-alcoholic

7.6.12 The description 'non-alcoholic' must not be used in conjunction with a name commonly associated with an alcoholic drink, except in the composite name 'non-alcoholic wine' when that composite is used as in para **7.6.18** below.

Liqueur

7.6.13 The name 'liqueur' may be applied only to a drink qualifying under the definition of that term in Council Regulation No 1576/89/EEC[1].

1 See para **7.3.13** above.

Indian tonic water or quinine tonic water

7.6.14 The name 'Indian tonic water' or 'quinine tonic water' must not be applied to any drink unless it contains not less than 57 mg of quinine (calculated as quinine sulphate BP) per litre of the drink.

Tonic wine

7.6.15 The name 'tonic wine' must not be applied to any drink unless there appears in immediate proximity to the words 'tonic wine' the clear statement: 'the name "tonic wine" does not imply health giving or medicinal properties'. No recommendation as to consumption or dosage may appear in the labelling or advertising of the drink.

Cheese

7.6.16 In the labelling or advertising of cheese, the names Cheddar, Blue Stilton, Derby, Leicester, Cheshire, Dunlop, Gloucester, Double Gloucester, Caerphilly, Wensleydale, White Stilton and Lancashire, whether or not qualified by any other words, are reserved to products which comply with maximum percentages of water respectively prescribed and contain not less than 48% milk fat.

Cream

7.6.17 In the labelling or advertising of cream, the names 'clotted cream', 'double cream', 'whipping cream', 'whipped cream', 'sterilised cream', 'cream' or 'single cream', 'sterilised half-cream' and 'half cream', whether or not qualified by any other words, are reserved to products which comply with minimum percentages of milk fat and other requirements respectively prescribed. The requirements as to milk fat content need not be complied with if the name contains qualifying words which indicate that the milk fat content is greater or less than prescribed.

The word 'wine' in composite names for other foods or drinks

7.6.18 The appellation 'wine' is reserved to products conforming to the definition in Annex I to Council Regulation 822/87/EEC[1] by Article 43(1)(a) of Council Regulation 2392/89/EEC[2]. However, on the authority of the derogation in that Article, the word 'wine' may be used in a composite name in the labelling or advertising of food for a drink which is not within that definition[3], unless the composite name is likely to cause confusion with wine or table wine.

Each word in a composite name must appear in lettering of the same type and colour and of such a height that the composite name is clearly distinguishable from other products. The composite name 'non-alcoholic wine' must not be used except for a drink derived from unfermented grape juice which is intended exclusively for sacramental use and is labelled as such.

When the word 'wine' is used in a composite name for a drink which is derived from fruit other than grapes, that drink shall be obtained by an alcoholic fermentation of that fruit.

1 See further para **7.3.8** above.
2 See further para **7.3.9** above.
3 Food Labelling Regulations 1996, reg 43.

Chapter 8

Food claims, nutrition labelling and particular nutritional uses

8.1 INTRODUCTION

8.1.1 Since the enactment of the general labelling Directive 79/112/EEC, national control of claims in respect of food has taken place within a specific Community framework. It will be recalled that Article 2(1)(a) of the Directive, which is implemented by section 15 of the Food Safety Act 1990 (FSA 1990), forbids labelling which could mislead purchasers to a material degree[1]. So far as claims are concerned, this general prohibition is aimed in particular at the prevention of those attributing to a foodstuff effects or properties which it does not possess[2] and those suggesting that it possesses special characteristics when in fact all similar foodstuffs possess such characteristics[3]. Additionally, provision was made by Article 2(2) of the Directive for the Council to draw up a non-exhaustive list of the claims which must be prohibited or restricted. In the event, except for the enactment of certain nutrition provisions, the Commission claims proposals have been shelved, at least for the time being, and work concentrated on reinforcing the provisions of the misleading advertisements Directive 84/450/EEC[4]. As explained later in this chapter, even in respect of nutrition labelling, obvious gaps in Community law still remain and the United Kingdom has been moved to explore the adoption of Codex Alimentarius standards. In its reply to the Commission's Green Paper on European Food Law[4], the UK Government asserted its belief that the Codex Alimentarius Committee on Food Labelling is making satisfactory progress in achieving international consensus on nutrition and health claims. It advocated that the work should be supported and the agreed guidelines eventually adopted by Member States[5]. More recently, the Commission's White Paper on Food Safety of 12 January 2000 [6] has indicated its intention to consider a proposal for amending Directive 79/112/EEC to specify the conditions for making 'functional claims' (eg claims related to beneficial effects of a nutrient on certain normal bodily functions) and 'nutritional claims' (eg claims which describe the presence, absence or level of a nutrient, as the case may be, contained in a foodstuff or its value compared to similar foodstuffs).

1 Para **6.2.1** above.
2 Directive 79/112/EEC, Art 2(1)(a)(ii).
3 Directive 79/112/EEC, Art 2(1)(a)(iii).
4 COM (97)176 on 'the General Principles of Food Law in the European Union', Pt III.8. As to Directive 84/450/EEC, see para **6.4.1** above.
5 Copies of the UK Government response are available from the Food Standards Agency.
6 COM (1999) 719 final.

8.1.2 But some progress has been made with food claim rules through Community legislation and certain non-statutory work. By Council Directive 77/94/EEC, the

Community established a framework for the approximation of Member States' laws in relation to foods claimed to be suitable for particular nutritional uses. Directive 77/94/EEC has since been replaced by Council Directive 89/398/EEC. Moreover, by Council Directive 90/496/EEC nutrition labelling was made compulsory where nutrition claims appear on food and provision laid down as to what this should constitute in such cases and where it is provided voluntarily. The Commission's White Paper on Food Safety of 12 January 2000[1] has indicated that an amendment is proposed to bring the provisions of Directive 89/398/EEC into line with consumer needs and expectations.

Useful guidance is also to be obtained from the proceedings of the Food Advisory Committee and the Codex Alimentarius Commission.

This chapter considers—

(a) claims controlled by the Food Labelling Regulations, in section **8.2**;
(b) prescribed nutrition labelling, in section **8.3**;
(c) requirements for nutrition labelling given voluntarily, in section **8.4**;
(d) other claims, in section **8.5**;

It also summarises, in section **8.6**, the special group of food standards imposed in respect of foodstuffs for particular nutritional uses.

1 COM (1999) 719 final.

8.2 CLAIMS CONTROLLED BY THE FOOD LABELLING REGULATIONS

8.2.1 The core provisions of British law on claims in respect of food are to be found in regulations 40 and 41 of and Schedules 6 and 7 to the Food Labelling Regulations 1996.

This section summarises the restrictions on the making of specific claims. Of particular importance are the conditions imposed in respect of each 'nutrition claim'. This term is defined in the Regulations as meaning 'any statement, suggestion or implication in any labelling, presentation or advertising of a food that that food has particular nutritional properties, but does not include a reference to any quality or quantity of any nutrient where such reference is required by law'. In implementation of Article 2(2) of Council Directive 90/496/EEC (on the nutrition labelling of food), the Regulations require nutrition labelling to be given when a nutrition claim is made. As will be seen below, this is achieved in relation to the various nutrition claims, by requiring the food in question to be marked or labelled with the 'prescribed nutrition labelling'. The detailed provisions imported by the use of this term are explained later in section **8.3**.

It should be noted that the requirements summarised in section **8.2** are subject to qualifications set out in regulation 41(1)–(3) of the Food Labelling Regulations 1996. Thus, nothing in the provisions as to claims should be taken to prevent the dissemination of useful information or recommendations intended exclusively for persons having qualifications in dentistry, medicine, nutrition, dietetics or pharmacy[1].

In implementation of Article 6(2) of Directive 89/398/EEC, this provision is an exception to the prohibition on claims that a food has the property of preventing, treating or curing a human disease noted in para **8.2.2** below. Moreover, a reference to a substance in a list of ingredients or in any nutrition labelling does not of itself constitute a claim of a type considered below[2].

Finally, any condition that a food shall be labelled with the prescribed nutrition labelling shall not apply in the case of—

(a) a food (other than sold from a vending machine) which is not prepacked and which is sold to the ultimate consumer at a catering establishment, or
(b) a claim contained within generic advertising.

For food described at (a), elements of the prescribed nutrition labelling may nevertheless be given subject, mutatis mutandis, to compliance with relevant provisions described in section **8.3**[3].

By virtue of regulation 3(4) and (5) of the Food Labelling Regulations 1996, of the claims provisions described in sections **8.2** and **8.3**, only those described in para **8.2.4** applies to natural mineral water (other than such water which has been artificially carbonated).

1 Food Labelling Regulations 1996, reg 41(1).
2 Food Labelling Regulations 1996, reg 41(2).
3 Food Labelling Regulations 1996, reg 41(3).

Prohibited claims[1]

8.2.2 The Regulations wholly forbid the making, either expressly or by implication, of two kinds of claims in the labelling or advertising of food. The first of these is any claim that a food has tonic properties. However, the use of the word 'tonic' in the description 'Indian tonic water' or 'quinine tonic water' does not of itself constitute such a claim.

Secondly, in implementation of Article 2(1)(b) of the general food labelling Directive 79/112/EEC and Article 6(1) of the particular nutritional uses Directive 89/398/EEC, a claim that a food has the property of preventing, treating or curing a human disease or any reference to such a property is prohibited[2]. An exception is noted in para **8.2.1** above.

1 Food Labelling Regulations 1996, reg 40(1) and Pt I of Sch 6.
2 Compare *Cheshire County County Council Fair Trading and Advice Service v Mornflakes Oats Ltd* (1993) 157 JP 1011.

Restricted claims: generally[1]

8.2.3 A claim of a type describe in paras **8.2.4–8.2.11** below shall not be made, either expressly or by implication, in the labelling or advertising of a food except in accordance with the stated appropriate conditions. Where a claim of two or more of these types is made, the conditions appropriate to each must be observed.

1 Food Labelling Regulations 1996, reg 40(2) and (3) and Pt II of Sch 6.

Claims relating to foods for particular nutritional uses

8.2.4 In implementation of Council Directive 89/398/EEC[1], claims that a food is suitable, or has been specially made for a particular nutritional purpose are subject to the conditions set out below. 'Particular nutritional purpose' is defined as the fulfilment of the particular nutritional requirements of—

(a) a person whose digestive processes are, or whose metabolism is disturbed, or

(b) a person whose physiological condition renders him able to obtain a special benefit from the controlled consumption of any substance in food, or
(c) infants or young children[2] in good health.

Conditions

1. The food must be capable of fulfilling the claim.
2. The food must be marked or labelled with an indication of the particular aspects of its composition or manufacturing process that give the food its particular nutritional characteristics.
3. The food—

(a) must be marked or labelled with the prescribed nutrition labelling[3] and may be marked or labelled with further information in respect of either or both of—
  (i) any nutrient or component of a nutrient (whether or not a claim is made in respect of such nutrient or component), or
  (ii) any other component or characteristic which is essential to the food's suitability for its particular nutritional use, and
(b) when sold to the ultimate consumer, must be prepacked and completely enclosed by its packaging.

1 See further para **8.6.1** below.
2 By the Food Labelling Regulations 1996, reg 2(1), 'infants' is defined as children under the age of twelve months and 'young children' as children between one and three years.
3 See para **8.2.1** and section **8.3**.

Reduced or low energy value claims

8.2.5 Claims that a food has a reduced or low energy value are subject to the conditions set out below. There are two qualifications to this. First, the appearance of the words 'low calorie' on a container of soft drink in accordance with the conditions in Schedule 8 to the Food Labelling Regulations 1996[1] does not of itself constitute a claim. Secondly, where a food is in concentrated or dehydrated form and is intended to be reconstituted by the addition of water or other substances, condition 2 below applies to the food when reconstituted as directed.

Conditions

1. If the claim is that the food has a reduced energy value, the energy value of a given weight of the food, or of a given volume in the case of a liquid food, must not be more than three quarters of that of the equivalent weight, or volume, of a similar food in relation to which no such claim is made, unless the food is—

(a) an intense sweetener, or
(b) a product which consists of a mixture of an intense sweetener with other substances and which, when compared on a weight for weight basis, is significantly sweeter than sucrose.

2. If the claim is that the food has a low energy value—

(a) the energy value of the food must not be more than 167 kJ (40 kcal) per 100 g or 100 ml, as appropriate, unless the food is—
  (i) an intense sweetener, or
  (ii) a product which consists of a mixture of an intense sweetener with other

substances and which, when compared on a weight for weight basis, is significantly sweeter than sucrose,

(b) the energy value of a normal serving of the food must not be more than 167 kJ (40 kcal), and

(c) in the case of an uncooked food which naturally has a low energy value, the claim must be in the form 'a low energy food' or 'a low calorie food' or 'a low joule food'.

3. The food must be marked or labelled with the prescribed nutritional labelling[2].

1 See para **7.6.11** above.
2 See para **8.2.1** and section **8.3**.

Protein claims

8.2.6 Claims that a food, other than a food intended for babies or young children[1] which satisfies the conditions of the item described in para **8.2.4** above, is a source of protein are subject to the conditions set out below.

Conditions

1. The quantity of the food that can reasonably be expected to be consumed in one day must contribute at least 12 g of protein.

2.—(1) If the claim is that the food is a rich or excellent source of protein, at least 20% of the energy value of the food must be provided by protein.
(2) In any other case at least 12% of the energy value of the food must be provided by protein.

3. The food must be marked or labelled with the prescribed nutritional labelling[2].

1 By the Food Labelling Regulations 1996, reg 2(1), 'young children' is defined as children between one and three years.
2 See para **8.2.1** and section **8.3**.

Vitamin claims

8.2.7 Claims that a food other than a food intended for babies or young children[1] which satisfies the conditions of the item described in para **8.2.4** above, is a source of vitamins are subject to the conditions set out below. Table A referred to in this paragraph is in para **8.2.12**.

A reference to a vitamin in the name of a food does not of itself constitute a claim of a type to which this item applies if the food consists solely of—

(i) vitamins, or
(ii) a mixture of vitamins and minerals, or
(iii) a mixture of vitamins, or vitamins and minerals, and a carrying agent, or
(iv) a mixture of vitamins, or of vitamins and minerals, and other substances sold in tablet, capsule or elixir form.

Conditions

1.—(1) If the claim is not confined to named vitamins, every vitamin named in the claim must be a vitamin specified in column 1 of Table A below, and—

(a) where the claim is that the food is a rich or excellent source of vitamins, the quantity of the food that can reasonably be expected to be consumed in one day must contain at least one half of the recommended daily allowance of two or more of the vitamins specified in column 1 of Table A below, and

(b) in any other case, the quantity of the food that can reasonably be expected to be consumed in one day must contain at least one sixth of the recommended daily allowance of two or more of the vitamins specified in column 1 of Table A below.

(2) If the claim is confined to named vitamins, every vitamin named in the claim must be a vitamin specified in column 1 of Table A below, and—

(a) where the claim is that the food is a rich or excellent source of vitamins, the quantity of the food that can reasonably be expected to be consumed in one day must contain at least one half of the recommended daily allowance of every vitamin named in the claim, and

(b) in any other case, the quantity of the food that can reasonably be expected to be consumed in one day must contain at least one sixth of the recommended daily allowance of every vitamin named in the claim.

2. The food must be marked or labelled—

(a) in the case of a food to which nutrition labelling[2] relates—

(i) where the claim is in respect of unnamed vitamins (whether alone or together with named vitamins), then in respect of any of those unnamed vitamins which are listed in Table A, with the prescribed nutrition labelling[3] and, in addition, with a statement of the percentage of the recommended daily allowance for such vitamins as are contained in either a quantified serving of the food or, provided that the total number of portions contained in the sales unit of the food is stated, in one such portion of the food, and

(ii) where the claim is in respect of a named vitamin or of named vitamins (whether alone or together with unnamed vitamins), then in respect of that named vitamin or those named vitamins, with the prescribed nutrition labelling[3] and, in addition, with a statement of the percentage of the recommended daily allowance for such vitamins as are contained in either a quantified serving of the food or, provided that the total number of portions contained in the sales unit of the food is stated, in one such portion of the food, and

(b) in the case of food supplements or waters other than natural mineral waters, in respect of any vitamins, whether unnamed, named or both—

(i) with a statement of the percentage of the recommended daily allowance of those vitamins contained in either a quantified serving of the food or (provided that the food is prepacked) a portion of the food, and

(ii) where the food is prepacked, of the number of portions contained in the package,

and the name used in any such marking or labelling for any such vitamin shall be the name specified for that vitamin in column 1 of Table A below.

1 By the Food Labelling Regulations 1996, reg 2(1), 'young children' is defined as children between one and three years.
2 As to the meaning of 'nutrition labelling', see para **8.4.1** below.
3 See para **8.2.1** and section **8.3**.

Mineral claims

8.2.8 Claims that a food other than a food intended for babies or young children[1] which satisfies the conditions of the item described in para **8.2.4** above, is a source of minerals are subject to the conditions specified below.

A claim that a food has a low or reduced level of minerals shall not be regarded as a claim of a type described in this item.

The note on the item summarised in para **8.2.7** above applies equally to this item with the substitution of the word 'mineral(s)' for 'vitamin(s)' and vice versa as appropriate. Table B referred to in this paragraph is in para **8.2.12**.

Conditions

The conditions are the same as those set out in the item described in para **8.2.7** above with appropriate substitution of the word 'mineral' for 'vitamin' and 'Table B' for 'Table A'.

1 By the Food Labelling Regulations 1996, reg 2(1), 'young children' is defined as children between one and three years.

Cholesterol claims

8.2.9 Claims relating to the presence or absence of cholesterol[1] in a food are subject to the conditions set out below.

Conditions

1. Subject to condition 3, the food must contain no more than 0.005% of cholesterol.
2. The claim must not be accompanied by a suggestion, whether express or implied, that the food is beneficial to human health because of its level of cholesterol.
3. If the claim relates to the removal of cholesterol from, or its reduction in, the food and condition 1 is not met, such claims shall only be made—

(a) as part of an indication of the true nature of the food,
(b) as part of an indication of the treatment of the food,
(c) within the list of ingredients, or
(d) as a footnote in respect of a prescribed nutrition labelling[2].

4. The food must be marked or labelled with the prescribed nutritional labelling[2].

1 *Cheshire County County Council Fair Trading and Advice Service v Mornflakes Oats Ltd* (1993) 157 JP 1011.
2 See para **8.2.1** and section **8.3**.

Other nutrition claims

8.2.10 Nutrition claims not dealt with under any of the items described in paras **8.2.4–8.2.9** above[1] are subject to the conditions specified below.

Conditions

1. The food must be capable of fulfilling the claim.
2. The food must be marked or labelled with the prescribed nutritional labelling[2].

1 As to other nutrition claims, see para **8.5.3** below.
2 See para **8.2.1** and section **8.3**.

Claims which depend on another food

8.2.11 In the case of claims that a food has a particular value or conveys a particular benefit, the value or benefit must not be derived wholly or partly from another food that is intended to be consumed with the food in relation to which the claim is made.

Vitamins and minerals

8.2.12 The Tables referred to in paras **8.2.7** and **8.2.8** above in relation to vitamins and minerals respectively are as follows—

Table A – Vitamins in respect of which claims may be made

Vitamin	*Recommended daily allowance*
Vitamin A	800 micro g
Vitamin D	5 micro g
Vitamin E	10 mg
Vitamin C	60 mg
Thiamin	1.4 mg
Riboflavin	0.16 mg
Niacin	18 mg
Vitamin B6	2 mg
Folacin	200 micro g
Vitamin B12	1 micro g
Biotin	0.15 mg
Pantothenic acid	6 mg

Table B – Minerals in respect of which claims may be made

Mineral	*Recommended daily allowance*
Calcium	800 mg
Phosphorus	800 mg
Iron	14 mg
Magnesium	300 mg
Zinc	15 mg
Iodine	150 micro g

Note

As a rule, a significant amount means 15% of the recommended daily allowance listed in respect of each vitamin and mineral specified in Table A and B above that is supplied by 100 g or 100 ml of a food, or per package of a food if the package contains only a single portion.

8.3 PRESCRIBED NUTRITION LABELLING

8.3.1 As noted in section **8.2**, the Community requirement that nutrition labelling must be given where a nutrition claim appears is imposed by the condition that the food must be marked or labelled with the 'prescribed nutritional labelling'. Parts I and II of Schedule 7 to the Food Labelling Regulations 1996 respectively set out the requirements for the presentation and the contents of prescribed nutritional labelling[1].

These provisions are summarised below.

1 In relation to the requirements of the 1996 Regulations which implement nutrition labelling Directive 90/496/EEC, Guidance Notes on Nutrition Labelling were issued by the Ministry of Agriculture, Fisheries and Food in May 1999.

Contents of prescribed nutrition labelling

8.3.2 For the purposes of explanation, it will be clearer to deal first with the contents of prescribed nutritional labelling.

Subject to exceptions mentioned below for non-prepacked foods, prescribed nutrition labelling must consist one of the two following groups of information—

(a) by the first alternative called 'group 1' by Directive 90/496/EEC, the information given must be the energy and the amounts of protein, carbohydrate and fat;

(b) by the second alternative called 'group 2' by Directive 90/496/EEC, the information given must be the energy and the amounts of protein, carbohydrate, sugars, fat, saturates, fibre and sodium.

Where a nutrition claim is made for sugars, saturates, fibre or sodium, the information given must be in accordance with (b).

The amounts of any polyols, starch, mono-unsaturates, polyunsaturates, cholesterol and, if present in significant amounts, minerals or vitamins may also be included in the nutrition labelling and must be included where such is the subject of a nutrition claim. As a rule, 'a significant amount', in relation to vitamins or minerals, means 15% of the recommended daily allowance listed in respect of each vitamin or mineral specified in Table A or B in para **8.2.12** that is supplied by 100 g or 100 ml of a food, or per package of a food if the package contains only a single portion.

Where the amount of any mono-unsaturates, polyunsaturates or cholesterol is given with labelling in accordance with (a) above, the amount of saturates must also be included.

Where such is the subject of a nutrition claim, the prescribed nutrition labelling must also include the name and amount of any substance which belongs to, or is a component of, one of the nutrients already required or permitted to be included. As examples of components, the MAFF Guidance notes give fructose as a component of sugars and trans fatty acids as a component of fat.

In exercise of the derogation in Article 8 of Directive 90/496/EEC, the prescribed nutritional labelling that must be borne by non-prepacked food sold to ultimate consumers, other than at catering establishments, from vending machines and to catering establishments, is restricted to information about any nutrition claim, but information may be given voluntarily for any or all of the energy or nutrients listed in the Regulations.

Presentation of prescribed nutrition labelling

8.3.3 The rules on the presentation of prescribed nutrition labelling are in Part I of Schedule 7 to the Food Labelling Regulations 1996. Subject to the further provisions below, the order and manner of prescribed nutrition labelling must, where appropriate, be as follows—

energy value	[x] kJ and [x] kcal
protein	[x] g
carbohydrate	[x] g
of which:	
— sugars	[x] g
— polyols	[x] g
— starch	[x] g
fat	[x] g
of which:	
— saturates	[x] g
— mono-unsaturates	[x] g
— polyunsaturates	[x] g
— cholesterol	[x] mg
fibre	[x] g
sodium	[x] g
[vitamins]	[x units]
[minerals]	[x units].

If there is also an obligation to give the name and amount of any substance which belongs to, or is a component of, an item already given, the substance or component must be listed immediately after the item to which it relates, thus—

[item]	[x] g or mg
of which:	
— [substance or component]	[x] g or mg.

For [vitamins] and [minerals] there shall be substituted, as appropriate, the names of any vitamin or mineral listed in Table A or B listed in para **8.2.12** above.

For [item] there shall be substituted the name of the relevant item [from the above list].

For [substance or component] there shall be substituted the name of the substance or component.

For [x] there shall be substituted the appropriate amount in each case and, in respect of vitamins and minerals, such amounts—

(i) shall be expressed in the units of measurement specified in relation to the respective vitamins and minerals given in Table A or B listed in para **8.2.12** above, and
(ii) shall also be expressed as a percentage of the recommended daily allowance specified for such vitamins and minerals in those Tables.

In implementation of Article 6 of Directive 90/496/EEC, all amounts are required to be given per 100 g or 100 ml, as appropriate. In addition, this information may be given per serving as quantified on the label or per portion, provided that the number of portions contained in the package is stated. The amounts shall be as contained in the food sold to the ultimate consumer or to a catering establishment, or they may (if expressly said to be so) be such amounts as are contained in the food after the completion of such preparation in accordance with detailed instructions given for the preparation for consumption of the food.

The amounts shall be averages based, either alone or in any combination, on—

(i) the manufacturer's analysis of the food;
(ii) a calculation from the known or actual values of the ingredients used;
(iii) a calculation from generally established and accepted data,

and 'averages' means the figures which best represent the respective amounts of the nutrients which a given food contains, there having been taken into account seasonal variability, patterns of consumption and any other factor which may cause the actual amount to vary.

In implementation of Article 5 of Directive 90/496/EEC, the following conversion factors are required to be used for the purposes of calculating the energy value—

- 1 g of carbohydrate (excluding polyols) shall be deemed to contribute 17 kJg (4 kcal)
- 1 g of polyols shall be deemed to contribute 10 kJg (2.4 kcal)
- 1 g of protein shall be deemed to contribute 17 kJg (4 kcal)
- 1 g of fat shall be deemed to contribute 37 kJg (9 kcal)
- 1 g of ethanol shall be deemed to contribute 29 kJg (7 kcal)
- 1 g of organic acid shall be deemed to contribute 13 kJg (3 kcal).

In implementation of Article 7 of Directive 90/496/EEC, any prescribed nutrition labelling is required to be printed together in one conspicuous place—

(a) in tabular form, with any numbers aligned, or
(b) if there is insufficient space to permit tabular listing, in linear form.

8.4 REQUIREMENTS FOR NUTRITION LABELLING GIVEN VOLUNTARILY

8.4.1 Paragraph **8.1.2** referred to the Community requirement that nutrition labelling, if given, must be given in accordance with specified rules. This requirement is to be found in Articles 2(1) and 4 of the nutrition labelling Directive 90/496/EEC and is implemented in Great Britain by regulation 41(4) of and Schedule 7 to the Food Labelling Regulations 1996.

As defined by the Food Labelling Regulations 1996, 'nutrition labelling', in relation to a food (other than a natural mineral water or other water intended for human consumption or any food supplement), means any information appearing on labelling (other than where it appears solely as part of a list of ingredients) and relating to energy value or any nutrient or to energy value and any nutrient, including any information relating to any substance which belongs to, or is a component of, a nutrient.

Where food is labelled voluntarily with nutrition labelling, the requirements for prescribed nutrition labelling[1] apply except in two express particulars. These are the requirements[2]—

(a) that the Group 2 information must be given where a nutrition claim is made for sugars, saturates, fibre or sodium; and
(b) that the labelling must include the name and amount of any substance which belongs to, or is a component of, one of the nutrients required or permitted to be included, where such is the subject of a nutrition claim.

1 See section **8.3**.
2 See para **8.3.2**.

8.5 OTHER CLAIMS

8.5.1 In addition to statutory requirements regarding claims in the Food Labelling Regulations 1996, mention should be made of certain non-statutory material which can constitute a guide to good practice and might be relevant in proceedings, for example, under section 15 of the FSA 1990[1].

Useful general sources are to be found in the reports of the Food Advisory Committee (FAC)[2] and standards drawn up by the Codex Alimentarius Commission[3].

Notable FAC contributions on the subject of claims are to be found in their 1980 Second Report on Claims and Misleading Descriptions; their 1988 Report on Nutrition Claims in Food Labelling and Advertising; their 1990 Report on their Review of Food Labelling and Advertising; and their 1993 Recommendations on the use of the term 'Natural' in Food Labelling and Advertising.

As noted in para **1.10.2**, the work of the Codex Alimentarius Commission continues to contribute to the development of international food standards, not least in relation to labelling and nutrition claims.

This section specifically considers non-statutory material on—

(a) general principles in respect of claims;
(b) claims about fat, saturates, sugar, sodium and fibre;
(c) claims that food is 'natural'.

1 See paras **6.2.1** and **8.1.1** above.
2 See para **2.4.2** above.
3 See para **1.10.2** above.

General principles in respect of claims

8.5.2 In order to provide a more consistent and readily understandable framework for legislation, in the 1990 Report on their Review of Food Labelling and Advertising, the Food Advisory Committee recommended that food claims should be controlled by the following general principles—

(a) a food must be able to fulfil the claim being made for it and adequate labelling information should be given to show consumers that the claim is justified;
(b) where the claim is potentially ambiguous or imprecise (for example 'light') it should be clearly explained and justified on the label and be capable of substantiation;
(c) a claim that a food is 'free from' a substance or treatment should not be made if all the same class or category of foods are similarly free;

(d) words or phrases which imply that a food is free from any specific characteristic ingredient or substance should not be used if the food contains other ingredients or substances with the same characteristic;
(e) meaningless descriptions should not be used;
(f) comparative claims should be justified against relative and generally acceptable criteria;
(g) the label should give a sufficiently full description of the food in relation to the area for which the claim is made to ensure that selective claims, even if true, do not mislead;
(h) absolute claims should be justified against absolute criteria set for a given nutrient and applying to all foods;
(i) where a food is naturally 'low' or 'high' in a substance the claim should be 'a low/high X food'.

They further recommended that health claims should be controlled by the following additional general principles—

(a) the claim should relate to the food as eaten rather than to generic properties of any of the ingredients;
(b) the food when consumed in normal dietary quantities should be able to fulfil the claim being made for it and adequate labelling information should be given to show consumers that the claim is justified;
(c) the label should give a full description of the food to ensure that selective claims, even if true, do not mislead and any claim should trigger full nutritional labelling;
(d) the role of the specific food should be explained in relation to the overall diet and other factors.

Fat, saturates, sugar, sodium and fibre

8.5.3 In relation to fat, saturates, sugar(s), salt/sodium and fibre in food, the Ministry of Agriculture, Fisheries and Food has also issued guidelines for the use of the following nutrition claims – Low; No added; Free/without; Source; Increased; Reduced; More/less; and High/rich[1]. They are based on recommendations made by the Food Advisory Committee and take account of Guidelines for Nutrition Claims adopted by the 22nd Session of the Codex Alimentarius Commission[2].

The Ministry guidelines are additional to the legislative provisions described in this chapter and are advisory only.

1 The latest version of the guidance (dated November 1999) is obtainable from the Food Standards Agency.
2 See para **1.10.2**.

'Natural' claims

8.5.4 The latest version of the Food Advisory Committee's recommendations on the use of the term 'natural' and similar terms in food labelling and advertising were issued in 1993 to take account of recent legislative changes. The guidelines do not have the force of law, but Government has expressed itself willing to consider legislation if they are disregarded.

The guidelines suggest six principles on which such labelling should be based—

1.1 The term 'natural' without qualification should be used only in the following cases—

(a) To describe single foods, of a traditional nature to which nothing has been added and which have been subjected only to such processing as to render them suitable for human consumption.
   - Freezing, concentration, fermentation, pasteurisation[1], sterilisation, smoking (without chemicals) and traditional cooking processes such as baking, roasting and blanching are processes which would be acceptable.
   - Bleaching, oxidation, smoking (with chemicals), tenderising (with chemicals), hydrogenation and similar processes clearly fall outside.
   - As a general rule for single ingredient foods such as cheese, yoghurt and butter, acceptable processing is that which is strictly necessary to produce the final product.
   - The restriction to 'foods of a traditional nature' is intended to exclude novel foods, which may technically be products of natural sources but which do not accord with the public perception of 'natural'.

(b) To describe food ingredients obtained from recognised food sources and which meet the criteria in (a).

(c) To describe permitted food additives obtained from recognised food sources by appropriate physical processing (including distillation and solvent extraction) or traditional food preparation processes.

(d) To describe flavourings when in conformity with the UK Flavourings in Food Regulations and EC Directives 91/71/EEC and 91/72/EEC.

(e) To describe preserved tuna and bonito when in conformity with Regulation 1536/92/EEC.

1.2 Compound foods should not therefore be described directly or by implication as 'natural', but it may be acceptable to describe such foods as made from natural ingredients if all the ingredients meet the criteria in 1.1(b) or (c).
1.3 A food which does not meet the criteria in 1.1(a) or 1.2 should not be claimed to have a 'natural' taste, flavour or colour.
1.4 'Natural' or its derivatives, should not be included in brand or fancy names nor in coined or meaningless phrases in such a way as to imply that a food which does not meet the criteria in 1.1(a) is natural or made from natural ingredients.
1.5 Claims such as 'natural goodness', 'naturally better' or 'nature's way' are largely meaningless and should not be used.
1.6 'Natural' meaning no more than plain or unflavoured should not be used except where the food in question meets the criteria in 1.1(a) or 1.2.

2. The principles above also apply when other words similar to 'natural', such as 'real', 'genuine', 'pure' which have separate and distinctive meanings of their own, are used in place of 'natural' in such a way as to imply similar benefits for consumers.

3. Other claims (which might be termed 'negative claims') which do not use the term 'natural' or its derivatives, but the effect of which is to imply 'naturalness' to the consumer are potentially misleading and confusing. At least the following should not be used—

(1) a claim that a food is 'free from X' if all foods in the same class or category are free from 'X';

(2) statements or implications which give undue emphasis to the fact that a product is free from certain non-natural additives when the product contains other non-natural additives;

(3) a claim that a food is 'free from' one category of additive when an additive of another category, or an ingredient having broadly similar effect is used.

The conditions do not affect 'negative claims' which do not imply 'naturalness' to the consumer, (such as 'free from "X"', where X is a particular additive), and which may provide them with accurate and beneficial information.

1 See *Amos v Britvic Ltd* (1984) 149 JP 13.

8.6 FOODSTUFFS FOR PARTICULAR NUTRITIONAL USES

8.6.1 Council Directive 89/398/EEC provides a Community framework for provisions relating to foodstuffs intended for particular nutritional uses, often colloquially designated 'PARNUTS'. These products are foodstuffs which, owing to their special composition or manufacturing process, are clearly distinguishable from foodstuffs for normal consumption, which are suitable for their claimed nutritional purposes and which are marketed in such a way as to indicate such suitability[1]. As indicated in para **8.2.4**[2], a particular nutritional use must fulfil the particular nutritional requirements of persons falling within one of three defined categories. Subject to any changes necessary to meet these criteria, the products must comply with mandatory provisions applicable to foodstuffs for normal consumption[3] as well as bearing the prescribed nutrition labelling.

A few substantive provisions in Directive 89/398/EEC have called for implementation by the Food Labelling Regulations 1996[4]. A key element is Article 4 which, as recently amended by Directive 1999/4/EC, confers on the Commission power to draw up specific implementing provisions for six groups of foods for particular nutritional uses[5]. A final decision will be made on whether diabetic food should continue to be included after the advice of the Scientific Committee for Food has been obtained.

Specific Directives have been enacted for the following groups—

(a) infant formulae and follow-on formulae,
(b) processed cereal-based foods and baby foods for infants and young children,
(c) foods intended for use in energy-restricted diets for weight reduction, and
(d) dietary foods for special medical purposes.

In the context of Britain implementing Regulations so far made, the requirements of these Directives are respectively summarised in paras **8.6.2–8.6.5** below. A Directive has yet to be made for foods intended to meet the expenditure of intense muscular effort, especially for sportsmen.

Additionally, Article 4a of Directive 89/398/EEC provides for the adoption of rules governing the use of terms concerning low-sodium foods and gluten-free foods.

Article 4(2) of Directive 89/398/EEC provides for the establishment of a list of substances that may be used in the manufacture of foods for particular nutritional uses. Lists were included in the specific Directives on infant formulae and follow-on formulae and on processed cereal-based foods and baby foods for infants and young children: proposals are under active consideration for the adoption of a list in respect of the other foods.

For foodstuffs for particular nutritional uses which do not belong to one of the specified groups, Article 9 of Directive 89/398/EEC requires the national competent authority to be notified when a product is first placed on the market. Pending British Regulations on the point, the provision is implemented administratively by notification to the producer's local food authority.

The Commission's White Paper on Food Safety of 12 January 2000[6] confirms that, in addition to pursuing the outstanding matters mentioned above, it will submit proposals for Directives on food supplements (ie concentrated sources of nutrients such as vitamins and minerals) and fortified foods (ie foods to which nutrients have been added).

1 See the Advocate-General's opinion of 22 October 1998 in case C-107/97 *Ministère Public v Max Rombi* (22 October 1998, unreported), ECJ.
2 The term considered in para **8.2.4** is 'particular nutritional purpose' used in the Food Labelling Regulations 1996, Sch 6, Pt II item 1. However that provision implements the definition of 'foodstuffs for particular nutritional uses' in Directive 89/398/EEC and the three categories of persons are in substance the same.
3 See European Court judgment of 16 December 1999 in case C-101/98 *Union Deutsche Lebensmittelwerke GmbH v Schutzverband gegen Unwesen* (16 December 1999, unreported).
4 See paras **7.6.2**, **8.2.2** and **8.2.4**.
5 Regulation of additives permitted in foodstuffs intended for particular nutritional uses is reserved to the Council.
6 COM (1999) 719 final.

Infant formula and follow-on formula

8.6.2 The Infant Formula and Follow-on Formula Regulations 1995, as amended, implement Commission Directive 91/321/EEC (on infant formulae and follow-on formulae), as amended, and Council Directive 92/52/EEC (on infant formulae and follow-on formulae intended for export to third countries).

For the purposes of the Regulations, 'infant formula' is defined as a food intended for particular nutritional use by infants in good health during the first four to six months of life, and satisfying by itself the nutritional requirements of such infants and 'follow-on formula' is defined as a food intended for particular nutritional use by infants in good health who are aged over four months, and constituting the principal liquid element in a progressively diversified diet.

The sale of food represented as infant formulae or follow-on formulae is prohibited unless it complies with specified requirements as to composition, labelling, appearance and packaging. Similar compositional restrictions are imposed on exports to third countries, except where an importing country permits, together with appropriate labelling requirements. Advertising of infant formulae and follow-on formulae is restricted and specified promotion of infant formulae prohibited. Requirements are also laid down about the provision of information and education regarding infant and child feeding.

Infant Formula and Follow-on Formula (Amendment) (England) Regulations will shortly implement Commission Regulation 1999/50/EC which sets a maximum limit of 0.01 mg/kg for individual pesticides in infant formula and follow-on formula.

Processed cereal-based foods and baby foods for infants and young children

8.6.3 The Processed Cereal-based Foods and Baby Foods for Infants and Young Children Regulations 1997, as amended, implement Commission Directive 96/5/EEC (on processed cereal-based foods and baby foods for infants and young children), as amended.

For the purposes of the Regulations, 'processed cereal-based foods' are foods for particular nutritional use within specified categories of cereal products fulfilling the particular requirements of infants and young children in good health and intended for use by infants while they are being weaned, and by young children as a supplement to their diet or for their progressive adaptation to ordinary food and 'baby foods' are other foods for particular nutritional use fulfilling the same particular requirements. The Regulations do not, however, apply to baby food which is milk intended for young children.

The sale of processed cereal-based foods and baby foods is prohibited unless it is labelled and complies with specified requirements as to manufacture and composition. For specified processed cereal-based foods or baby foods manufactured with a view to sale after 31 December 1999 maximum limits for added nutrients are prescribed.

Processed Cereal-based Foods and Baby Foods for Infants and Young Children (Amendment) (England) Regulations will shortly implement Commission Regulation 1999/39/EC which sets a maximum limit of 0.01 mg/kg for individual pesticides in processed cereal-based foods or baby foods.

Foods intended for use in energy-restricted diets for weight reduction

8.6.4 The Foods Intended for Use in Energy Restricted Diets for Weight Reduction Regulations 1997 implement Commission Directive 96/8/EEC (on foods intended for use in energy-restricted diets for weight reduction).

The Regulations control specially formulated food intended for use in energy restricted diets for weight reduction, being food which complies with specified compositional requirements and which, when used as instructed by the manufacturer, replaces—

(a) the whole of the total diet; or
(b) one or more meals of the daily diet.

The controlled food must be sold under the name 'total diet replacement for weight control' or 'meal replacement for weight control', as appropriate, the use of those names being reserved to such food. The sale of the food is prohibited if it is not labelled with specified particulars, if reference is made to the rate or amount of weight loss which may result from its use or to a reduction in the sense of hunger or an increase in the sense of satiety and, in the case of food intended as a replacement for the whole daily diet, if all the components are not contained in the same package.

Dietary foods for special medical purposes

8.6.5 The most recent specific Directive in respect of foods for particular nutritional uses is Commission Directive 99/21/EC (on foods for special medical purposes). It is implemented by the Medical Food (England) Regulations 2000.

'Dietary foods for special medical purposes' are defined as a category of foods for particular nutritional uses specially processed or formulated and intended for dietary management of patients and intended to be used under medical supervision. They are intended for the exclusive or partial feeding of patients with a limited, impaired or disturbed capacity to take, digest, absorb, metabolise or excrete ordinary foodstuffs or certain nutrients contained therein or metabolites, or with other medically-determined nutrient requirements, whose dietary management cannot be achieved only by modification of the normal diet, by other foods for particular nutritional uses, or by a combination of the two. Foods for special medical purposes are classified into categories for (i) nutritionally complete foods with a standard formulation, (ii) nutritionally complete foods specific for a disease, disorder or medical condition and (iii) nutritionally incomplete foods. The Commission has confirmed that the definition is not intended to catch freely available products which are not aimed at patients with specific problems, other foods for particular nutritional uses and low birth weight formulae.

The implementing Regulations prohibit the marketing of dietary foods for special medical purposes unless they comply with specified compositional criteria, are sold under the prescribed name 'Food(s) for special medical purposes' and are labelled with mandatory particulars.

Chapter 9

The food safety requirements and inspection and seizure of suspected food

9.1 INTRODUCTION

9.1.1 It will be recalled from chapter 1 that the prohibition on selling unfit food and the powers for its inspection, seizure and condemnation which form the core of sections 8 and 9 of the Food Safety Act 1990 (FSA 1990) were introduced by the Public Heath Act 1875 to provide basic safeguards against biological (bacterial) contamination of food[1]. We have also briefly observed that the FSA 1990 integrated with these provisions first the prohibition on selling etc food rendered injurious to health (derived from what is now section 7) and secondly, to fill a gap in the previous law, an additional prohibition on selling etc contaminated food[2]. These three elements are contained in a new concept of 'food safety requirements' considered in section **9.2** below. This concept is additionally the basis for the re-enacted and extended provisions for the inspection, seizure and condemnation of suspected food explained in section **9.3**.

Time will tell whether these general food safety provisions of the FSA 1990 will require further amendment in response to the Community proposal for a general food law embodying prescribed principles of food safety[3].

1 See para **1.1.1** above.
2 See paras **5.1.1** and **5.3.1** respectively above.
3 See paras **1.2.1** and **1.8.1** above.

9.1.2 Mention should be made here of the general safety requirement enacted by the General Product Safety Regulations 1994, as amended, whereby, in implementation of Council Directive 92/59/EEC, producers are forbidden to place a product on the market unless the product is a safe product[1]. Where a product conforms to the specific rules of the law of the United Kingdom laying down the health and safety requirements which the product must satisfy in order to be marketed, there is a presumption that the product is a safe product[2]. Paragraph 48 of Department of Trade and Industry Guidance for Businesses, Consumer and Enforcement Authorities on these Regulations gives some assistance about their application in relation to food. It says—

> 'Where the safety of a product is covered by national legislation (ie an Act or specific regulations) that legislation will continue to provide the means for assessing the safety and, accordingly, should be considered to be the appropriate vehicle for any necessary enforcement action. An example is food where the Food Safety Act 1990 (and regulations made under that Act) is recognised as dealing with the significant safety issues relating to food (and is enforced by Food Authorities). Thus the 1990 Act (and regulations made under that Act) will prevail in the case of food safety and food satisfying those requirements should be presumed to satisfy the requirements of the Regulations. Relevant enforcement action should be taken under the provisions of the 1990 Act (or regulations made under that Act as appropriate) and businesses should not be placed under double jeopardy by parallel action for the same matter also being taken under the Regulations.'

Moreover, the Ministry of Agriculture, Fisheries and Food has expressed the view[3] that if a foodstuff meets a 'specific rule of national law' such as the food safety requirements[4] an enforcement authority would have to demonstrate to a court that the food in some way did not meet the 'different' standard set in the General Product Safety Regulations. The Ministry suggests this would apply only to foodstuffs which might meet the food safety requirements yet may also be considered unsafe under the General Product Safety Regulations. The Ministry believes that this would only apply to such items as 'extra large' gob stoppers (which could cause suffocation) and 'freeze pop' lollipops (where the plastic can have sharp edges).

1 General Product Safety Regulations 1994, reg 7.
2 General Product Safety Regulations 1994, reg 10.
3 MAFF 'Explanatory note on the UK statutory and guideline limits and EC legislation relating to chemical contaminants in food'.
4 See para **9.2.1**.

9.2 THE FOOD SAFETY REQUIREMENTS

9.2.1 It is unlawful to sell for human consumption, or offer, expose or advertise for sale for such consumption, or have in possession for the purpose of such sale or preparation for such sale, or to deposit with, or consign to, any other person for the purpose of such sale or preparation for such sale, any food[1] which fails to comply with the food safety requirements[2]. Unlike the overlapping offence under section 14 of the FSA 1990 which applies only at the point of sale[3], an offence under section 8 may arise at any point of manufacture or distribution.

1 As to the supply of caustic soda pursuant to an agreement to sell food, see *Meah v Roberts*; *Lansley v Roberts* [1978] 1 All ER 97, [1977] 1 WLR 1187.
2 FSA 1990, s 8(1).
3 See para **5.3.1** above.

9.2.2 Food fails to comply with the food safety requirements if—

(a) it has been rendered injurious to health by means of—
- adding any article or substance to the food;
- using any article or substance as an ingredient in the preparation of the food;
- abstracting any constituent from food; or
- subjecting the food to any other process or treatment with the intention that it shall be sold for human consumption[1];

(b) it is unfit for human consumption; or
(c) it is so contaminated (whether by extraneous matter or otherwise) that it would not be reasonable to expect it to be used for human consumption in that state[2].

Of the three elements comprising the concept of food safety requirements, paragraph (a) (the rendering of food injurious to health) has already been considered in section **5.2**.

The main element of the concept is in paragraph (b). As explained above, the safety requirement that the food shall not be unfit for human consumption long predated the FSA 1990 and is, therefore, by no means unfamiliar to the courts. But they have not always found it easy to state what is meant by the expression 'unfit for human consumption'. In 1961, in upholding a conviction for sale of a pork pie bearing mould of the penicillin type, Lord Parker CJ said the phrase meant more than unsuitable. A stale loaf would be unsuitable but not unfit. He was not prepared to say that in all cases the prosecution must prove the food injurious or dangerous. The phrase must be looked at in a broad sense. When an article of food is admittedly going mouldy, it is prima facie unfit for human consumption whether or not there is evidence as to whether there would be any injury to health if it were eaten. It is a matter of degree in every case[3].

Extraneous objects, which have often formed the subject of proceedings, do not necessarily render food unfit for human consumption. Offences were found to have been committed where there was potential toxicity such as from a dirty bandage in a loaf of bread[4], or a dead mouse in a bottle of milk[5]. However, cases in which a piece of metal was found in a cream bun[6] and a piece of string in a loaf of bread[7] did not cause the food to be unfit.

As indicated in para **5.3.1**, the uncertainty of being able to establish the unfitness of contaminated food in all but the most serious cases, caused some difficulty before the FSA 1990. Enforcement authorities often played safe and took proceedings under the predecessor of section 14. But they were thereby denied the possibility of prosecuting in respect of food in possession, or offered or exposed for sale and section 8(2)(c) of the FSA 1990 added a third limb to the food safety requirements. Following the change, Government advice is that cases involving contamination (whether by microorganisms and their toxins, chemicals, mould or foreign matter) and cases involving the microbiological quality of food should be taken under sections 7 or 8 whenever possible[8].

How far paragraph (c) has extended the food safety requirements beyond the obligation of fitness for human consumption has yet to be thoroughly tested. In one of two cases before superior courts in 1995, the prosecution decision to proceed under section 8(1)(c) rather than under 8(1)(b) in respect of a nut brittle sweet containing a Stanley knife blade, might well be regarded as over-cautious and not having carried matters further forward[9]. The second, however, is of a kind which, before 1990, would probably have been taken under the predecessor of section 14. Mould spots found on crumpets at 2.30 pm were held to be sufficient evidence that they must have been so contaminated at 9.30 am (the time of purchase) and that it would not be reasonable to expect them to be used for human consumption in that state[10]. It is to be hoped that the use in section 8(2)(c) of the words 'whether by extraneous matter or otherwise' when read with 'would not be reasonable to expect it to be used for human consumption in that state' will catch most occurrences which might deter the ordinary consumer from eating a food.

Due regard must be had to the words 'in that state' because there would appear to be no offence if the food is to be subjected to further processing or treatment[11].

1 FSA 1990, s 7(1).
2 FSA 1990, s 8(2).
3 *David Greig Ltd v Goldfinch* (1961) 105 Sol Jo 367, LGR 304, DC. Applied in *Guild v Gateway Foodmarkets Ltd* 1990 SLT 578. See also *Kyle v Laird* 1951 JC 65.
4 *Chibnall's Bakeries v Cope Brown* [1956] Crim LR 263.
5 *Barton v Unigate Dairies Ltd* [1987] Crim LR 121, DC.
6 *J Miller Ltd v Battersea Borough Council* [1956] 1 QB 43, [1955] 3 All ER 279.
7 *Turner & Son Ltd v Owen* [1956] 1 QB 48, [1955] 3 All ER 565n.
8 Statutory Code of Practice no 1: Responsibility for Enforcement of the FSA 1990, para 18.
9 *R v F & M Dobson* (1995) 16 Cr App Rep (S) 957, CA.
10 *Kwik Save Group plc v Blaenau Gwent* (1995) Unreported (ref CO/2246/95), DC.
11 *R v Archer, ex p Barrow, Lane & Ballard Ltd* (1983) 147 JP 503, CA.

Treatment of batches, lots or consignments of food

9.2.3 Where any food which fails to comply with the food safety requirements is part of a batch or lot or consignment of food of the same class or description, it is presumed, until the contrary is proved, that all the food in that batch, lot or consignment fails to comply with those requirements[1]. The burden of proof that the whole of a batch, lot or consignment of food does not fail to satisfy the food safety requirements is on the owner of the food and not the investigating officer. In circumstances where a part of such batch, lot or consignment is obviously in breach of the requirements, that would be a difficult burden to discharge.

This provision applies also for the purposes of section 9, so that the seizure powers which it confers are not restricted to samples of suspected food[2].

1 FSA 1990, s 8(3).
2 See section **9.3** below.

Meat from knacker's yards

9.2.4 The FSA 1990 creates a further presumption that any product or part of a product derived wholly or partly from an animal which has been slaughtered in a knacker's yard, or of which the carcase has been brought into a knacker's yard (in Scotland, otherwise than in a slaughterhouse), is unfit for human consumption[1]. A knacker's yard is defined as 'any premises used in connection with the business of slaughtering, flaying or cutting up animals the flesh of which is not intended for human consumption'[2].

1 FSA 1990, s 8(4).
2 FSA 1990, s 53(1).

Consumer complaints

9.2.5 Offences against the food safety requirements are most likely to arise from consumer complaints to local environmental health departments. Central Government guidance to food authorities on the handling of consumer complaints[1] includes the following important points—

(a) *Notification of complaints* As a general rule any person who may be prosecuted as a result of a consumer complaint should be notified that the complaint has been made as soon as reasonably practicable. Normally, as soon as preliminary investigations suggest that the complaint may be well-founded, the food authority should notify the supplier, manufacturer or importer. The initial notification may be oral and should be followed by notification in writing. The written notification should describe the date and nature of the complaint. Other potential defendants should be notified as they emerge. Exceptionally there may be circumstances in which notification could impede the progress of further investigations. In these circumstances, notification should take place as soon as can be achieved without prejudicing further investigations.

(b) *Involvement of other food authorities* If an investigation of a complaint brings to light a problem or potential problem outside the area of the enforcing authority, the other appropriate authorities directly affected (for example the authority where the food was manufactured and/or the authority where a company's decision-making base is located) should be informed as soon as possible. If there is a public health problem which may affect a wide geographical area, central government (that is, now the Food Standards Agency) should be informed, as a hazard warning or emergency order may be needed[2].

(c) *Investigation of complaint samples* The authorised officer will need to consider whether any scientific investigation is to be undertaken. If the authorised officer is in any doubt he should consult the public analyst and/or food examiner who will advise on the form of scientific investigation which may be appropriate for that complaint sample, particularly since some will require a combination of analysis and examination. If the authorised officer considers that a complaint sample should be analysed, he should send it to a public analyst. If he considers it should be microbiologically examined, he should send it to a food examiner. If he considers any other investigation is necessary, he should ensure that the person to whom he sends the complaint sample is suitably qualified and able to give evidence in the event of a prosecution.

(d) *When samples can be surrendered* The food authority should try to comply with any reasonable request by the person under investigation provided that it does not impede the proper storage, analysis, examination or evidential value of the samples. However, as explained in para **18.4.11** below, this guidance has now been overtaken and rendered inadequate by the Criminal Procedure and Investigations Act 1996.

(e) *Taking legal proceedings* Prosecutions should be brought without unnecessary delay. (In Scotland, the decision on referral to the Prosecutor Fiscal should be taken without unnecessary delay.)

In addition to this guidance, when dealing with consumer complaints enforcement authorities should have in mind that prospective defendants are entitled to know the identity of those who have complained about them. Judgments to this effect were given by the Divisional Court in *Daventry District Council v Olins*[3] (which concerned the sale of pork alleged to be unfit for human consumption) and subsequently confirmed by the Court of Appeal in *R v Taylor*[4]. A defendant in a criminal trial has a fundamental right to see and to know the identity of his accusers, including witnesses for the prosecution. That right should only be denied in rare and exceptional circumstances: whether such circumstances exist is pre-eminently a matter for the exercise of the trial judge's discretion.

1 Code of Practice no 2: Legal Matters.
2 As to hazard warnings, emergency control orders and emergency orders, see sections **11.5**, **11.6** and **11.7** below.
3 (1990) 154 JP 478, DC.
4 (1994) Times, 17 August, CA.

9.3 INSPECTION, DETENTION AND SEIZURE OF SUSPECTED FOOD

9.3.1 The FSA 1990 re-enacted the provisions of the Food Act 1984 and its predecessors as to the power of authorised officers to seize and detain suspect food and, on the order of a justice of the peace, have it destroyed or disposed of to prevent it being used for human consumption[1]. However, the powers were considerably extended and improved so that they are based on the food safety requirements discussed above and in addition apply to foods likely to cause food poisoning or any communicable disease.

Guidance on inspection, detention and seizure of suspected food is given by statutory Code of Practice no 4.

1 FSA 1990, s 9(1), (2) and (3).

The powers

9.3.2 An authorised officer of a food authority may at all reasonable times inspect any food intended for human consumption which has been sold or is offered or exposed for sale or is in the possession of, or has been deposited with or consigned to, any person for the purpose of sale or preparation for sale. Where it appears to the officer on such an inspection that the food fails to comply with the food safety requirements or in other circumstances that food is likely to cause food poisoning or any disease communicable to human beings, he may either give notice to the person in charge of the food that, until the notice is withdrawn, the food or any specified portion of it is not to be used for human consumption and either is not to be removed or is not to be removed except to some place specified in the notice, or he may seize the food and remove it in order to have it dealt with by a justice of the peace.

The form of notice is prescribed[1] and it is an offence knowingly to contravene the requirements of a notice. The inclusion of the word 'knowingly' in this offence requires proof by the prosecution of criminal intention; that is, that the defendant knew of the existence of the notice and its contents[2]. Since the notice must be given to the person in charge of the food, it is submitted that proof of service of the notice in accordance with the FSA 1990[3] should normally be sufficient in the case of an inspection since the recipient would find it difficult to claim ignorance of its contents.

Ordinarily, 'reasonable times' for inspection will be when premises are open for business purposes[4]. However, in the case of a serious danger to public health, it may be reasonable to inspect at other times.

1 Detention of Food (Prescribed Forms) Regulations 1990.
2 See further para **19.1.1** below.
3 FSA 1990, s 50.
4 *Small v Bickley* (1875) 40 JP 119.

Termination of notice

9.3.3 Where an authorised officer has issued a notice he must, as soon as is reasonably practicable and in any event within 21 days, determine whether or not he is satisfied that the food complies with the food safety requirements. If he is so satisfied he must forthwith withdraw the notice. If he is not so satisfied, he must seize the food and remove it to have it dealt with by a justice of the peace[1]. A notice withdrawing a detention notice should, notwithstanding the above, be served as soon as possible to avoid further deterioration of the food[2].

1 FSA 1990, s 9(4).
2 Code of Practice no 4: Inspection, Detention and Seizure of Suspect Food, para 28.

Referral to a justice of the peace

9.3.4 Where the authorised officer exercises his powers to refer the matter to a justice of the peace he must inform the person in charge of the food of his intention so to do. A person who might be liable for prosecution in respect of the food concerned must be given an opportunity to attend before the justice of the peace, to give evidence and to call witnesses[1].

If it appears to the justice of the peace, on the basis of such evidence as he considers appropriate in the circumstances, that the food fails to comply with the food safety requirement he must condemn the food and order the food to be destroyed or to be so disposed of as to prevent it from being used for human consumption; and any expenses reasonably incurred in connection with the destruction or disposal must be defrayed by the owner of the food[2].

Referral to a justice of the peace should normally be within two days of seizure and in the case of perishable food such referral should be as soon as possible[3].

Although, in condemning food, a justice is acting in administrative capacity[4], the powers must be exercised in accordance with natural justice which would be denied by a refusal to allow evidence to be tested by crossexamination[5].

As to the limitation of the section 9 powers of a justice of the peace by orders under section 13 of the FSA 1990, see para **11.6.4** below.

1 FSA 1990, s 9(5).
2 FSA 1990, s 9(6).
3 Code of Practice no 4: Inspection, Detention and Seizure of Suspect Food, para 11.
4 *R v Cornwall Quarter Sessions, ex p Kerley* [1956] 2 All ER 872, [1956] 1 WLR 906.
5 *Errington v Wilson* 1995 SC 550, 1995 SLT 1193.

Compensation

9.3.5 If a notice issued by an authorised officer is withdrawn or if a justice of the peace refuses to condemn the food the food authority must compensate the owner of the food for any depreciation in its value resulting from the action taken by the authorised officer. Any dispute as to the amount of compensation must be settled by arbitration[1]. As to the exclusion of compensation in particular circumstances by orders under section 13 of the FSA 1990, see para **11.6.4** below.

1 Arbitration Act 1996—see 2 Halsbury's Statutes (4th Edn).

Prosecution

9.3.6 Action by an authorised officer under the above provisions does not preclude a subsequent prosecution by the food authority in respect of the failure of the food safety requirements or the food having been rendered injurious to health.

Action in cases of food poisoning

9.3.7 In the event of a food poisoning outbreak[1], the authorised officer should seek expert advice from the consultant in communicable disease control (CCDC) and may also need to contact the local public health laboratory service (PHLS) or the public analyst. (In Scotland advice should be sought, for example, from the consultant in public health medicine or the microbiologist in charge of the laboratory investigating the outbreak.) Whenever possible and appropriate there should be full and open discussions with the owner or person in charge of the food and with the manufacturer[2].

1 Powers in respect of persons suffering from food poisoning are provided by the Public Health (Control of Disease) Act 1984—see 35 Halsbury's Statutes (4th Edn).
2 Code of Practice no 4: Inspection, Detention and Seizure of Suspect Food, para 14.

Destruction or disposal of food

9.3.8 Where destruction or disposal of food is necessary the food authority is responsible for the necessary arrangements. The food should be fully supervised until it can be dealt with in the appropriate manner. If possible, and if there is likely to be considerable delay before destruction, the food should be disfigured in some way to prevent any possibility of it being returned to the market place illegally or accidentally.

If food is to be destroyed, the food authority should arrange for total destruction of the food, for example by incineration. If this is not possible the authority should arrange for such a degree of disfigurement that the food could never again enter the food chain, for example by flattening tin cans for disposal in a suitably licensed land-fill site[1].

1 Code of Practice no 4: Inspection, Detention and Seizure of Suspect Food, paras 52, 53.

Wider implications

9.3.9 The provisions discussed above are intended and suitable for dealing with individual batches, lots or consignments of dangerous food discovered and dealt with within the area of a food authority. For cases with wider implications, the powers in relation to emergency prohibition notices[1] and emergency control orders[2] should be borne in mind (see chapter 11).

1 FSA 1990, s 12.
2 FSA 1990, s 13.

Chapter 10

Food safety: additives, contaminants, flavourings, contact materials, residues and other substances in food

10.1 INTRODUCTION

10.1.1 The general food safety requirements laid down by the Food Safety Act 1990 (FSA 1990) are described in chapter 9. We deal here with the Regulations which make provision for the chemical safety of food by controlling the presence in or on food of specific classes of substances. These classes are summarised below as follows—

(a) additives, in section **10.2**;
(b) flavourings, in section **10.3**;
(c) other added substances, in section **10.4**;
(d) contaminants, in section **10.5**;
(e) food contact materials, in section **10.6**;
(f) pesticide residues, in section **10.7**; and
(g) veterinary residues, in section **10.8**.

10.2 ADDITIVES

The food additive framework Directive

10.2.1 Council Directive 89/107/EEC, as amended, established the framework for food additives authorised for use in foodstuffs for human consumption.

The Directive applies to food additives the various categories of which are set out in Annex I and which are used or intended to be used as ingredients during the manufacture or preparation of a foodstuff and are still present in the final product, even if in altered form.

The categories of food additives are—

- Colour
- Preservative
- Antioxidant
- Emulsifier
- Emulsifying salt
- Thickener
- Gelling agent
- Stabiliser (including foam stabilisers)
- Flavour enhancer
- Acid
- Acidity regulator (can act as two-way acidity regulators)

- Anti-caking agent
- Modified starch
- Sweetener
- Raising agent
- Anti-foaming agent
- Glazing agent (including lubricants)
- Flour treatment agent
- Firming agent
- Humectant
- Sequestrant (without prejudice to any further decision or mention thereof in the labelling of foodstuffs)
- Enzyme (without prejudice to any further decision or mention thereof in the labelling of foodstuffs; only those used as additives)
- Bulking agent
- Propellant gas and packaging gas.

For the purposes of the Directive, 'food additive' is defined as any substance not normally consumed as a food in itself and not normally used as a characteristic ingredient of food whether or not it has nutritive value, the intentional addition of which to food for a technological purpose in the manufacture, processing, preparation, treatment, packaging, transport or storage of such food results, or may be reasonably expected to result, in it or its by-products becoming directly or indirectly a component of such foods.

The Directive does not apply to—

(a) processing aids;
(b) substances used in the protection of plants and plant products in conformity with plant health;
(c) flavourings for use in foodstuffs, falling within the scope of Council Directive 88/388/EEC[1];
(d) substances added to foodstuffs as nutrients (for example minerals, trace elements or vitamins).

By way of derogation from the general rules on additives permitted under Directive 89/107/EEC, the maintenance of certain national restrictions on the use of additives in particular traditional foodstuffs is authorised by Decision of the European Parliament and Council 292/97/EC.

1 See para **10.3.1**.

Food additives labelling

10.2.2 Articles 7 and 8 of the food additive framework Directive 89/107/EEC lay down requirements for the labelling of food additives respectively not intended and intended for sale to the ultimate consumer. These requirements are implemented in Great Britain by the Food Additives Labelling Regulations 1992, as amended.

The specific food additive Directives

10.2.3 On the basis of general criteria laid down in Annex II to the food additive framework Directive (which, in particular, limit approved food additives to those which perform a useful purpose, are safe and do not mislead the consumer), specific Directives

94/35/EC, 94/36/EC and 95/2/EC have prescribed lists of sweeteners, colours and other additives respectively[1]. Like the previous national provisions, the Community food additive framework Directive operates on the 'positive list principle': only those food additives included in the lists may be used in the manufacture or preparation of foodstuffs and only under the conditions of use specified therein. The inclusion of a food additive in a category is on the basis of the principal function normally associated with it. However, by contrast with previous British additive legislation, the allocation of an additive to a particular category does not exclude the possibility of its authorisation for other functions. For example, although when sorbitol is used for its commonly known sweetening properties it is subject to the sweeteners Directives 94/35/EC and implementing Regulations[2], it may also be used as a humectant within the scope of the miscellaneous additives Directive 95/2/EC and the Regulations which implement it[3].

The specific Directives manifest further common features—

(a) foodstuffs to which permitted additives may be added are specified, together with the conditions which apply;
(b) for this purpose, each specific Directive lists a number of food categories. These were left undefined to accommodate food product differences between Member States. In cases of difficulty, some assistance may be obtained from Guidance Notes on food additives legislation produced by the Ministry of Agriculture, Fisheries and Food or from food authority enforcement officers. Ultimately, decisions on the appropriate category for a food are taken by Commission management committee procedure[4];
(c) for many additives in food, a 'maximum level' or, in the case of sweeteners Directive 94/35/EC, 'maximum usable dose' is prescribed by the Directives. This refers, in the sweeteners and colours Directives 94/35/EC and 94/36/EC, to ready-to-eat foodstuffs prepared according to the instructions, and, in the other additives Directive 95/2/EC, except where otherwise stated, to foodstuffs as marketed;
(d) where there is no need on safety grounds to set a maximum level for particular additive use, a *quantum satis* level is specified. In these cases, the additive is to be used in accordance with good manufacturing practice, at a level no higher than is necessary to achieve the intended purpose and provided such use does not mislead the purchaser;
(e) additives are permitted in most compound foods to the extent permitted in an ingredient, and in foods intended as such ingredients, to the extent permitted for their destined compound foods.

Under powers in the food additive framework Directive, the Commission has also laid down specific purity criteria for sweeteners, colours and other additives in Directives 95/31/EC, 95/45/EC and 96/77/EC respectively[5].

In its White Paper of 12 January 2000 on Food Safety[6], the Commission notes amendments which it believes to be necessary to Community additive provisions. They are: conferring power on the Commission to maintain the lists of permitted additives; clarification of the status of enzymes; updating the purity criteria for sweeteners, colours and other additives; and laying down criteria for additives made from novel sources[7].

1 As to these Directives and their implementation, see further paras **10.2.4**, **10.2.5** and **10.2.6** respectively. General Guidance Notes on the New Food Additives legislation which implemented them have been produced by the Ministry of Agriculture, Fisheries and Food.
2 See para **10.2.4** and Appendix F, Part I.
3 See para **10.2.6** and Appendix F, Part III. 3.
4 See Directives 94/35/EC, Art 4, 94/36/EC, Art 4 and 95/2/EC, Art 6.
5 See n 1 above.

6 COM (1999) 719 final.
7 See para **7.2.12** above.

Sweeteners

10.2.4 European Parliament and Council Directive 94/35/EC, as amended (on sweeteners for use in foodstuffs), and Commission Directive 95/31/EC (laying down specific purity criteria concerning sweeteners for use in foodstuffs) are implemented in Great Britain by the Sweeteners in Food Regulations 1995[1], as amended.

The main provisions of the Regulations—

(a) define permitted sweetener in terms of a list of sweeteners[2] which satisfy the specific purity criteria for those sweeteners in Directive 95/31/EC;
(b) prohibit the sale of any sweetener intended either for sale to the ultimate consumer or for use in or on any food, other than a permitted sweetener;
(c) prohibit the use of any sweetener in or on any food, other than for certain foods in which only specified permitted sweeteners may be used in accordance with conditions contained in the Regulations;
(d) prohibit the use of any sweetener in or on foods for infants and young children specified in Council Directive 89/398/EEC (on the approximation of the laws of the Member States relating to foodstuffs intended for particular nutritional uses)[3];
(d) prohibit the sale of table top sweeteners unless they contain no sweetener other than a permitted sweetener and are labelled in accordance with the Regulations;
(f) prohibit the sale of any food containing added sweetener other than a permitted sweetener used in or on it in accordance with the Regulations;
(g) make provision in relation to compound foods.

1 Guidance Notes on the Regulations have been produced by the Ministry of Agriculture, Fisheries and Food.
2 See Appendix F, Pt I.
3 As to Directive 89/398/EEC, see para **8.6.1** above.

Colours

10.2.5 European Parliament and Council Directive 94/36/EC (on colours for use in foodstuffs) and Commission Directive 95/45/EC (laying down specific purity criteria concerning colours for use in foodstuffs), as amended, are implemented in Great Britain by the Colours in Food Regulations 1995, as amended[1].

The main provisions of the Regulations—

(a) define permitted colour in terms of a list of colours[2] which satisfy the specific purity criteria for those colours in Directive 95/45/EC;
(b) prohibit the use in or on any food of any colour other than a permitted colour;
(c) prohibit the use of any permitted colour in or on food, otherwise than in accordance with the Regulations;
(d) prohibit the use of any colour other than certain permitted colours for the health marking etc of certain meat and meat products[3];
(e) prohibit the use of any colour on eggshells other than a permitted colour[4];
(f) make provision in relation to compound foods;
(g) prohibit the sale for use in or on any food of any colour other than a permitted colour, of which only some may be sold directly to consumers;

(h) prohibit the sale of any food containing any added colour other than a permitted colour used in or on it in accordance with the Regulations.

1 Guidance Notes on the Regulations have been produced by the Ministry of Agriculture, Fisheries and Food.
2 See Appendix F, Pt II.
3 See paras **13.1.3** and **13.1.4** below.
4 See Regulation 1274/91/EC considered at para **7.3.6** above.

Miscellaneous additives

10.2.6 European Parliament and Council Directive 95/2/EC (on food additives other than colours and sweeteners) and Commission Directive 96/77/EC (laying down specific purity criteria on food additives other than colours and sweeteners) are implemented in Great Britain by the Miscellaneous Food Additives Regulations 1995[1], as amended.

The Regulations define 'miscellaneous additive' as any food additive which is used or intended to be used primarily as an acid, acidity regulator, anti-caking agent, anti-foaming agent, antioxidant, bulking agent, carrier, carrier solvent, emulsifier, emulsifying salt, firming agent, flavour enhancer, flour treatment agent, foaming agent, gelling agent, glazing agent, humectant, modified starch, packaging gas, preservative, propellant, raising agent, sequestrant, stabiliser or thickener, but does not include any processing aid or any enzyme except invertase or lysozyme.

The Regulations define 'carrier' and 'carrier solvent' as any substance, other than a substance generally considered as food, used to dissolve, dilute, disperse or otherwise physically modify a miscellaneous additive, colour or sweetener, or an enzyme which is not acting as a processing aid, without its technological function (and without exerting any technological effect itself) in order to facilitate its handling, application or use.

A 'processing aid' means any substance not consumed as a food by itself, intentionally used in the processing of raw materials, foods or their ingredients to fulfil a certain technological purpose during treatment or processing, and which may result in the unintentional but technically unavoidable presence of residues of the substance or its derivatives in the final product, provided that these residues do not present any health risk and do not have any technological effect on the finished product.

The main provisions of the Regulations—

(a) define permitted miscellaneous additive in terms of lists of miscellaneous additives[2] which satisfy any purity criteria for those miscellaneous additives set out in Directive 96/77/EC or specified or referred to in Schedule 5 to the Regulations;
(b) prohibit the use in or on any food of any miscellaneous additive other than a permitted miscellaneous additive;
(c) prohibit the use of any permitted miscellaneous additive in or on food, otherwise than in accordance with the Regulations;
(d) restrict the use of miscellaneous additives primarily as a carrier or carrier solvent[3] and the presence of such additives in certain foods;
(e) make provision in relation to compound foods;
(f) prohibit the sale for use in or on food, or the sale direct to the consumer, of any miscellaneous additive other than a permitted miscellaneous additive;
(g) restrict the sale of miscellaneous additives primarily as a carrier or carrier solvent[3] and the sale of food additives in combination with miscellaneous additives which have been so used;

(h) prohibit the sale of food containing any added miscellaneous additive other than a permitted miscellaneous additive used or present in accordance with (b) and (c) above.

1 Guidance Notes on the Regulations have been produced by the Ministry of Agriculture, Fisheries and Food.
2 See Appendix F, Pt III.
3 The permitted miscellaneous additives which may be used primarily as carriers and carrier solvents are listed in Appendix F, Pt III:4.

10.3 FLAVOURINGS

Flavourings framework Directive

10.3.1 Council Directive 88/388/EEC, as amended ('the flavourings framework Directive'), established a framework for Community control of flavourings used or intended for use in or on foodstuffs to impart odour and/or taste, and of source materials used in the production of flavourings. Given the complexity of the subject, the flavourings framework Directive mainly sets up the mechanisms by which appropriate provisions will be prescribed—

- for individual categories of flavourings and source materials and for their use and production methods (see further para **10.3.2**); and
- for specified detailed Commission rules (see further para **10.3.3**).

But substantive provisions were prescribed by the flavourings framework Directive on definitions, general purity criteria and labelling (see further paras **10.3.4** and **10.3.5**).

Proposals for amendment of the flavourings framework Directive are summarised in para **10.3.6**.

Flavouring sources and substances

10.3.2 For seven specified classes of flavouring sources and substances used in the preparation of flavourings—

(a) Council Decision 88/389/EEC requires the Commission to draw up an inventory of those sources and substances; and
(b) Article 5 of the flavourings framework Directive requires the Council to adopt appropriate provisions, as well as any provisions generally necessary for the production of flavourings, the use of additives and the maximum limits for contaminants and undesirable substances.

The seven specified classes of flavouring sources and substances are—

(1) flavouring sources composed of foodstuffs, and of herbs and spices normally considered as foods;
(2) flavouring sources composed of vegetable or animal raw materials not normally considered as foods;
(3) flavouring substances obtained by appropriate physical processes or by enzymatic or microbiological processes from vegetable or animal raw materials;

(4) chemically synthesised or chemically isolated flavouring substances chemically identical to flavouring substances naturally present in foodstuffs or in herbs and spices normally considered as foods;
(5) chemically synthesised or chemically isolated flavouring substances chemically identical to flavouring substances naturally present in vegetable or animal raw materials not normally considered as foods;
(6) chemically synthesised or chemically isolated flavouring substances other than those referred to above;
(7) source materials used for the production of smoke flavourings or process flavourings, and the reaction conditions under which they are prepared.

For flavouring substances (ie classes (3), (4), (5) and (6)), Council Regulation 2232/96/EC has prescribed general use criteria (as to safety and not misleading the consumer) and laid down a Community procedure for the establishment of a positive list (ie a list of substances the use of which is to be permitted to the exclusion of all others). A register has been adopted of flavouring substances the use of which in one Member State must be recognised by the others[1]. The substances are now to be evaluated and the positive list drawn up. Until the list is enacted, the use at national level of substances not included on the register is not prohibited.

1 See Commission Decision 1999/217/EC.

Detailed Commission flavouring rules

10.3.3 Article 6 of the flavourings framework Directive provides for the adoption, by a management procedure, of lists of additives, diluents and processing aids, analysis and sampling methods, purity and microbiological criteria and, for flavourings intended for sale to the final consumer, labelling rules. By amendment to the flavourings framework Directive, Commission Directive 91/71/EEC prescribed these labelling rules.

A proposal by the Commission would restrict the use of additives in flavourings to some of those permitted by Directive 95/2/EC on food additives other than colours and sweeteners[1].

1 See para **10.2.6**.

'Flavouring'

10.3.4 The complexity of flavouring control is further demonstrated by the definition of the term in the flavourings framework Directive. 'Flavouring' is defined as—

> 'flavouring substances, flavouring preparations, process flavourings, smoke flavourings or mixtures thereof.'

These subsidiary concepts are themselves defined as follows—

- 'flavouring substance' means a defined chemical substance with flavouring properties which is obtained—
  (i) by appropriate physical process (including distillation and solvent extraction) or enzymatic or microbiological processes from material of vegetable or animal origin either in the raw state or after processing for human consumption by traditional food preparation processes (including drying, torrefaction and fermentation);

(ii) by chemical synthesis or isolated by chemical processes and which is chemically identical to a substance naturally present in material of vegetable or animal origin as described in (i) above;
(iii) by chemical synthesis but which is not chemically identical to a substance naturally present in material of vegetable or animal origin as described in (i) above;

- 'flavouring preparation' means a product, other than the substances defined in sub-paragraph (i) of the definition of 'flavouring substance', whether concentrated or not, with flavouring properties, which is obtained by appropriate physical processes (including distillation and solvent extraction) or by enzymatic or microbiological processes from material of animal or vegetable origin, either in the raw state or after processing for human consumption by traditional food preparation processes (including drying, torrefaction and fermentation);
- 'process flavouring' means a product which is obtained according to good manufacturing practices by heating to a temperature not exceeding 180°C for a period not exceeding 15 minutes a mixture of ingredients, not necessarily themselves having flavouring properties, of which at least one contains nitrogen (amino) and another is a reducing sugar;
- 'smoke flavouring' means a smoke extract used in traditional foodstuffs smoking processes.

The flavourings framework Directive does not apply to—

- edible substances and products intended to be consumed as such, with or without reconstitution;
- substances which have exclusively a sweet, sour or salt taste;
- material of vegetable or animal origin, having inherent flavouring properties, where they are not used as flavouring sources.

Flavourings in Food Regulations

10.3.5 The substantive provisions of the flavourings framework Directive are implemented by the Flavourings in Food Regulations 1992, as amended. The Regulations—

(a) restrict, to flavourings complying with general purity criteria, the added flavourings permitted in or on food;
(b) set a maximum limit for 3,4 benzopyrene in food by virtue of the presence of a flavouring as an ingredient;
(c) define agaric acid, aloin, beta asarone, berberine, coumarin, hydrocyanic acid, hypericine, pulegone, quassine, safrole and isosafrole, santonin or thuyone (alpha and beta) as 'specified substances';
(d) prohibit the presence in food containing flavourings, of specified substances added as such;
(e) prohibit the presence in food containing flavourings, of specified substances other than substances present naturally or as a result of flavourings prepared from natural raw materials;
(f) prohibit the presence, in food generally and in particular specified foods containing flavourings, of more than permitted proportions of specified substances;
(g) prohibit the sale of food which does not comply with these provisions.

The sale and advertisement for sale of flavourings for use as ingredients in the preparation of food is restricted to flavourings complying with general purity criteria.

The Regulations also prescribe labelling requirements for business and consumer sales of flavourings. Restrictions are imposed on the use of the word 'natural' and similar expressions.

Proposed amendments to the flavourings framework Directive

10.3.6 Amendments of the flavourings framework Directive are under consideration including proposals for a revised definition of 'process flavouring' and a reduction in the permitted general level for coumarin. The procedures for technical amendment of the Directive are also expected to be relaxed and the labelling requirements for genetically modified food[1] extended to genetically modified flavourings.

The Commission's White Paper on Food Safety[2] also confirms its plans in particular to set maximum limits for toxic substances and to lay down a list of additives authorised for use in flavourings.

1 See para **6.5.22**.
2 COM (1999) 719 final.

10.4 OTHER ADDED SUBSTANCES

10.4.1 Besides additives and flavourings as defined by Community law, there are various other substances for which the quantity added to food is controlled by Community or national legislation. The relevant provisions are summarised in paras **10.4.2–10.4.5** below.

10.4.2 *Mineral hydrocarbons* in the composition or preparation of food are generally prohibited by the Mineral Hydrocarbons in Food Regulations 1966, as amended. Limited exceptions are prescribed for lubricants, chewing compounds, the rind of cheese and permitted miscellaneous additives[1].

1 See para **10.2.6**.

10.4.3 *Erucic acid* is a normal constituent of colza oil and other edible oils and fats. Due to undesirable effects which it was found to cause in experimental animals, a maximum level was fixed for it by Council Directive 76/621/EEC, as amended, in oils and fats and in foodstuffs containing added oils and fats sold for human consumption. The Directive is implemented for England and Wales by the Erucic Acid in Food Regulations 1977, as amended. The Regulations also implement Commission Directive 80/891/EEC which prescribes the method of analysis for determining erucic acid content.

10.4.4 *Chloroform* added to food sold in or imported into England and Wales is prohibited by the Chloroform in Food Regulations 1980, as amended, except in medicinal products to which the Medicines (Chloroform Prohibition) Regulations 1979, SI 1979/382, apply.

10.4.5 *Tryptophan* is an amino acid, formerly used in certain food supplements, which was perceived in 1990 to be the cause of unusual but serious clinical symptoms known as eosinophilia myalgia syndrome. The addition of tryptophan to food and the exposure for sale of food containing it was consequently prohibited by the Tryptophan in Food Regulations 1990, as amended, except for persons needing the food on medical grounds.

10.4.6 *Extraction solvents* are used for the extraction from food of ingredients or components, including contaminants, or for the extraction of food from other articles or substances. The Extraction Solvents in Food Regulations 1993, as amended, implement Council Directive 88/344/EEC, as amended, to prohibit the sale or importation into Great Britain of extraction solvents other than permitted extraction solvents and, subject to specified conditions, of food having in it or on it any extraction solvent other than a permitted extraction solvent. Labelling requirements for permitted extraction solvents are also prescribed.

10.5 CONTAMINANTS

Introduction

10.5.1 Community procedures for contaminants in food have been laid down by Council Regulation 315/93/EEC. This defines 'contaminant' as any substance not intentionally added to food which is present in such food as a result of the production (including operations carried out in crop husbandry, animal husbandry and veterinary medicine), manufacture, processing, preparation, treatment, packing, packaging, transport or holding of such food, or as a result of environmental contamination. Extraneous matter, such as, for example, insect fragments, animal hair, etc, is not covered by this definition.

The Regulation does not apply to contaminants which are the subject of more specific Community rules[1]. The Community provisions on contact materials and pesticide and veterinary residues are explained in sections **10.6–10.8** below and various other specific Community provisions have prescribed contaminant levels. For example, Council Directives 91/492/EEC and 91/493/EEC, which lay down health conditions for live bivalve molluscs and fishery products respectively, prohibit the presence of contaminants in quantities exceeding acceptable levels[2]. Commission Decision 93/351/EEC specifies average limits for mercury in fish. Maximum levels for various contaminants have also been specified as purity criteria for sweeteners (by Commission Directive 95/31/EC), for colours (by Commission Directive 95/45/EC), for other additives (by Commission Directive 96/77/EC) and for flavourings (by Article 4 of Council Directive 88/388/EEC).

Commission Regulation 1860/88/EEC, which formerly prohibited the retail sale of olive oils and olive-pomace oils with a tetrachloroethylene content of more than 0.1 milligram per kilogram, was repealed by Commission Regulation 3009/91/EEC (OJ L 286 16.10.91 p 19). As a result of this repeal, the Tetrachloroethylene in Olive Oil Regulations 1989, which were made to enforce Regulation 1860/88/EEC, would now appear to be spent.

Council Regulation 315/93/EEC prohibits the placing on the market of food containing contaminants in amounts unacceptable from the public health viewpoint. No specific offence has been created to enforce this prohibition in England and Wales, but contravention might reasonably be expected to be a breach of section 8 or 14 of the FSA 1990[3].

1 Provision is made by Art 1(2) of Regulation 315/93/EEC for the Commission to publish a list of contaminants which are the subject of more specific rules, but this has not yet been done.

2 Directives 91/492/EEC and 91/493/EEC are implemented in Great Britain by the Food Safety (Fishery Products and Live Shellfish) (Hygiene) Regulations 1998. See further, section **13.11** below.
3 See paras **9.2.1** and **5.3.1** above respectively.

Maximum Community contaminant levels

10.5.2 In exercise of powers in Council Regulation 315/93/EEC, Commission Regulation 194/97/EC, as amended, was made to set maximum levels for certain contaminants in food. At the time of writing, levels have been set for nitrate in lettuce and spinach and in respect of a group of mycotoxins known as aflatoxins. Aflatoxins are naturally occurring toxicants produced by moulds in improperly stored produce. Maximum limits are set for nuts, cereals, milk, dried fruits (the most commonly affected foods) and for products derived from them. For nuts and dried fruits there are separate limits for aflatoxin B_1 and total aflatoxins, with higher limits for products for further treatment. Currently the same aflatoxin B_1 and total aflatoxins limits for cereals apply whether or not they are to be treated further. A limit is set for aflatoxin M_1 in milk.

The sampling method established by Commission Directive 79/700/EEC is prescribed in respect of nitrate levels in lettuce and spinach and Commission Directive 98/53/EC laid down sampling and analysis methods for aflatoxins.

For Great Britain, the Contaminants in Food Regulations 1997, as amended, enforce these Community provisions and revoke and supersede the Aflatoxins in Nuts, Nut Products, Dried Figs and Dried Fig Products Regulations 1992.

According to the Commission's White Paper on Food Safety[1], the Belgian dioxin crisis[2] has drawn attention to the need to define contaminant standards throughout the chain from feed to food. It proposes setting maximum limits for several contaminants. Proposals for limits in respect of lead and cadmium in fish, molluscs and milk as raw materials have been under consideration for some time[3].

1 COM (1999) 719 final.
2 See further paras **11.6.2** and **11.6.4** below.
3 Commission document III/5125/95.

Maximum national contaminant levels

10.5.3 Where Community provisions concerning maximum tolerances have not been adopted, Council Regulation 315/93/EEC provides that, subject to compliance with the EC Treaty, the relevant national provisions shall be applicable. These provisions are summarised in paras **10.5.4–10.5.6** below.

10.5.4 *Arsenic* in food is, subject to certain exceptions, generally limited to 1.0 milligram per kilogram. Lower limits are prescribed for drinks; and higher ones for certain other foods including onions, hops, liquorice, gelatine, yeast, chicory, herbs, spices, finings and clearing agents and specified chemicals[1].

1 Arsenic in Food Regulations 1959, as amended.

10.5.5 *Lead* in food is also generally limited to 1.0 milligram per kilogram, but lower limits are prescribed in particular for drinks and infant food and higher ones allowed for specified other foods[1].

1 Lead in Food Regulations 1979, as amended.

10.5.6 *Tin* in food sold or imported into Great Britain must not exceed 200 milligrams per kilogram[1].

1 Tin in Food Regulations 1992, as amended.

10.6 FOOD CONTACT MATERIALS

Materials and articles in contact with food

10.6.1 Control of food contact materials and articles is another dynamic area of Community law. Its foundation is Council Directive 89/109/EEC, as amended, a framework Directive which replaced Council Directive 76/893/EEC. It applies to all materials and articles in their finished state (for example, printing inks and adhesive labels) which are intended to be brought into contact with food. It does not, however, apply to covering or coating substances, like cheese rinds, nor to water supply equipment or antiques.

In Great Britain, the Materials and Articles in Contact with Food Regulations 1987, as amended, implement the framework Directive, and those specific Directives made under it or its predecessor which are referred to below. The sale, importation or commercial use of materials and articles which fail to comply with the Regulations is prohibited. Materials and articles must not, under normal or foreseeable conditions of use, transfer their constituents to food in quantities which could endanger human health or bring about an unacceptable change in the nature, substance or quality of the food.

In implementation of Council Directive 78/142/EEC and Commission Directives 80/766/EEC and 81/432/EEC, for materials and articles manufactured with vinyl chloride polymers or co-polymers, limits are prescribed for the quantity of vinyl chloride monomer which they may contain and to the quantity of vinyl chloride which they may transfer to the food.

In implementation of Commission Directive 93/10/EEC, as amended, for materials and articles made of regenerated cellulose film, the substances from which they may be manufactured are prescribed together with conditions and restrictions on use. At marketing stages other than retail, these materials and articles must be accompanied by a written declaration of compliance with the applicable legislation.

Further provisions implemented by the Regulations are those, in particular of the framework Directive and of Commission Directive 80/590/EEC, which prescribe requirements for the labelling of materials and articles sold by retail and otherwise than by retail and restrict to compliant materials and articles, descriptions and symbols indicating suitability for food use.

Commission Directive 90/128/EEC, as amended, on plastic materials and articles intended to come in contact with food, is an important specific Directive made under the framework Directive. Together with the Council Directives mentioned below, it is implemented in Great Britain by the Plastic Materials and Articles in Contact with Food Regulations 1998. Directive 90/128/EEC applies to materials and articles made exclusively of plastic, which in their finished state, are intended for use in contact with food. It also applies to materials and articles made of bonded layers of plastic, but not if one or more of the layers are non-plastic. This excludes, for example, plastic coatings on paper or metal cans, which must meet the general requirements of the framework Directive. 'Plastics' are defined broadly as organic polymers. Silicones are specifically included. However, regenerated cellulose film, elastomers and rubber, paper and board, surface coatings containing paraffin or micro-crystalline waxes and ion-exchange resins are excluded: for them, specific Directives have been or will be enacted. Directive 90/128/EEC sets overall limits on the quantities of constituents of plastic materials and articles permitted to transfer into food. The 1998 Regulations impose restrictions on manufacture with monomers and additives and, in implementation of Council Directives 82/711/EEC and 85/572/EEC, lay down rules for testing migration of the constituents of plastic materials and articles. At marketing stages other than retail, plastic materials and articles must be accompanied by a written declaration of compliance with the applicable legislation.

Two materials and articles Directives are implemented by Regulations under the Consumer Protection Act 1987. Council Directive 84/500/EEC is implemented by the Ceramic Ware (Safety) Regulations 1988 to set limits for the migration of lead and cadmium from glazes on ceramic tableware and cookware. Commission Directive 93/11/EEC is implemented by the N-nitrosamines and N-nitrosatable Substances in Elastomer or Rubber Teats and Dummies (Safety) Regulations 1995 to restrict the amount of release of those substances in the rubber of babies' teats and dummies.

The Commission White Paper on food safety[1] contemplates amendments to provide for the updating of Directives 89/109/EEC and 90/128/EEC.

1 COM (1999) 719 final.

Other food contact materials and food imitations

10.6.2 The Community has yet to make specific legislation for food contact metals, but the Cooking Utensils (Safety) Regulations 1972, having effect under the Consumer Protection Act 1987, restrict the lead content of tin or other metallic coatings for kitchen utensils.

The Food Imitations (Safety) Regulations 1989 have also been made under the 1987 Act to implement Council Directive 87/357/EEC concerning products which, appearing to be other than they are, endanger the health or safety of consumers.

10.7 PESTICIDE RESIDUES

10.7.1 Approval and use of pesticides in Great Britain is controlled under Part III of the Food and Environment Protection Act 1985 (F&EPA 1985) and the Control of Pesticides Regulations 1986, as amended, and, in implementation of Council Directive 91/414/EEC (concerning the placing of plant protection products on the market), as amended, under the Plant Protection Products Regulations 1995[1], as amended, and the Plant Protection Products (Basic Conditions) Regulations 1997. Further provision is shortly to be made to implement European Parliament and Council Directive 98/8/EC, for the approval and placing on the market of biocidal products which are not controlled as veterinary medicinal products, food additives, food flavourings, food contact materials and articles, plant protection products or other specified products.

By way of additional measures to protect consumers from harmful effects, maximum residue levels for particular pesticides in specified foods are prescribed by three substantially amended Directives ('the principal residue Directives'). They are—

- Council Directive 86/362/EEC on the fixing of maximum levels for pesticide residues in and on cereals;

- Council Directive 86/363/EEC on the fixing of maximum levels for pesticide residues in and on foodstuffs of animal origin (namely meat and milk and derived products);
- Council Directive 90/642/EEC on the fixing of maximum levels for pesticide residues in and on certain products of plant origin, including fruit and vegetables[2].

For fruit and vegetables, Commission Directive 79/700/EEC also establishes Community methods of sampling for the official control of pesticide residues.

The principal residue Directives are implemented by the Pesticides (Maximum Residue Levels in Crops, Food and Feeding Stuffs) (England and Wales) Regulations 1999. In respect of fruit and vegetables, the Regulations prescribe certain further maximum residues levels authorised, under Council Directive 76/895/EEC, for application within a Member State's own territory, until mandatory maximum Community levels have been determined for the purposes of Directive 90/642/EEC.

For the purpose of implementing the principal residue Directives, the Regulations invoke the powers in the European Communities Act 1972, section 2(2). For crops, food and feeding stuffs which are not subject to the Directives, similar provision is made under the powers in the F&EPA 1985, section 16(1)(k) and (l). It is to be noted that for the future the possibility exists of regulating food sources and feedingstuffs in the specific context of food legislation[3].

The 1999 Regulations—

(a) specify the maximum levels of pesticide residues which may be left in crops, food and feeding stuffs which are not the subject of the principal residue Directives. Since this provision is made under the F&EPA 1985, the offences and penalties prescribed by that Act apply[4];
(b) prohibit the putting into circulation of crops, food and feeding stuffs which are the subject of the principal residue Directives where the specified maximum levels of pesticide residues are exceeded. Offences, penalties and enforcement powers similar to those in the F&EPA 1985 are also prescribed, together with a defence for products exported to third countries or used in manufacture or as seed for planting;
(c) confer powers to seize and dispose of any crops, food and feeding stuffs containing excess residues;
(d) prescribe how much of a particular product is to be taken into account in determining whether a maximum residue level has been exceeded in accordance with Directive 90/642/EEC and make provision with regard to the manner for determining whether maximum residue levels have been exceeded when found in dried or processed products or composite foods, so far as these are subject to the principal residue Directives.

As to maximum levels for pesticide residues in foods for babies and young children, see paras **8.6.2** and **8.6.3** above.

A new Regulation to improve co-ordination and quality of monitoring pesticide residues in food is proposed by the Commission White Paper on food safety[5].

1 See also the Plant Protection Products (Fees) Regulations 1995.
2 See joined cases C-54/94 and C-74/94 *Ulderico Cacchiarelli and Stranghellini* [1995] ECR I-391.
3 See in particular, as explained at para **4.1.4** above, FSA 1990, ss 16(1)(a) and 17(1) and, as explained at para **2.3.8***(e)* above, Food Standards Act 1999, s 30.
4 See F&EPA 1985, ss 16(12) and 21(3) respectively.
5 COM (1999) 719 final.

10.8 VETERINARY RESIDUES

10.8.1 The British rules on veterinary residues in food are wholly derived from Community law. Council Regulation 2377/90/EEC, as amended, establishes, under a Community procedure, maximum residue limits for veterinary medicinal products authorised in foodstuffs of animal origin and prohibits the administration to animals of specified hazardous and unlicensed substances[1]. Council Directive 96/22/EC (which repealed Directives 81/602/EEC, 88/146/EEC and 88/299/EEC) prohibits the use in stockfarming of certain substances having a hormonal or thyrostatic action and of beta-agonists and Council Directive 96/23/EC (which repealed Directives 85/358/EEC and 86/469/EEC and Decisions 89/187/EEC and 91/664/EEC) lays down measures to monitor certain substances and residues thereof in live animals and animal products.

In Great Britain, Regulation 2377/90/EEC and Directives 96/22/EC and 96/23/EC are implemented by the Animals and Animal Products (Examination for Residues and Maximum Residue Limits) Regulations 1997, as amended[2].

The Regulations—

(a) prohibit the sale, possession or administration to animals of beta-agonists or hormonal substances;
(b) prohibit the administration to animals of unlicensed[3] or hazardous substances in contravention of Council Regulation 2377/90/EEC;
(c) prohibit the possession, slaughter or processing the meat of, animals intended for human consumption which contain, or which have been administered with, beta-agonists or hormonal substances;
(d) prohibit the sale or supply for slaughter of animals if the appropriate withdrawal period has not expired and prohibit supply for slaughter or, subject to exceptions, the sale, of animals or the sale of animal products which contain unauthorised products or an excess of authorised substances;
(e) prohibit, subject to an exception, the disposal for human or animal consumption of slaughtered animals containing specified unauthorised substances.

The Regulations also provide for sampling and analysis, offences, penalties and defences and record keeping.

Charges to cover the cost of residue surveillance under Directive 96/23/EC are made by the Charges for Inspections and Controls Regulations 1997, as amended, in part implementation of Council Directive 85/73/EC[4].

1 See judgments of the European Court of First Instance of 25 June 1998 in case T-120/96 *Lilly Industries Ltd v EC Commission* [1998] ECR II-2571 of 22 April 1999 case T-112/97 *Monsanto v EC Commission* (22 April 1999, unreported); and of 1 December 1999 in joined cases T-125/96 and T-152/96 *Boehringer Ingelheim Vetmedica GmbH and CH Boehinger Sohn v EU Council* case T-125, 152/96 [2000] 1 CMLR 97, CFI.
2 As to future veterinary residue Regulations under the FSA 1990, see para **2.2.5** above.
3 The prohibition on administration of 'unlicensed products', gives effect to the European Court judgment of 21 March 1996 in case C-297/94 *Dominique Bruyère v Belgium* [1996] ECR I-1551, in so far as the judgment relates to the administration of veterinary medicinal products to animals within the meaning of 96/22/EC and 96/23/EC.
4 See further para **13.1.6** below.

Chapter 11

Food safety: unhygienic food businesses and emergencies

11.1 INTRODUCTION

11.1.1 The general statutory prohibitions on unsafe food discussed in chapter 9 are supplemented by stringent powers to act locally in respect of particular defective food businesses[1] and centrally by way of coordination and in respect of general emergencies.

Locally, food businesses are not only registered (and in some cases, licensed) as explained in chapter 12: those which are unhygienic are also subject to administrative controls by enforcement authorities and magistrates' courts. These controls (which recall certain provisions of the Health and Safety at Work Act 1974 (H&SWA 1974)[2]) are in the form of the improvement notices, prohibition orders, emergency prohibition notices and orders considered in sections **11.2–11.4** below. It should noted that these notices and orders (which are all subject to appeal or confirmation[3] on their merits) must be objectively justifiable notwithstanding the apparent subjective form of the powers under which they are made[4].

Central government coordination through the food hazard warning system and powers to act by emergency control orders and emergency orders are explained in sections **11.5–11.7**.

1 As to action which may also be taken against persons, see para **11.3.3**.
2 See H&SWA 1974, ss 21–26.
3 See para **11.4.2** on emergency prohibition notices.
4 For example, as to the decision maker's reasonable grounds for belief, see *Nakkuda Ali v Jayaratne* [1951] AC 66; and as to the decision maker's satisfaction as to specified circumstances, see *Secretary of State for Education and Science v Tameside Metropolitan Borough Council* [1977] AC 1014, [1976] 3 All ER 665.

11.2 IMPROVEMENT NOTICES

The power to issue an improvement notice

11.2.1 Section 10 of the Food Safety Act 1990 (FSA 1990) introduced new provisions as to the issue of improvement notices by authorised officers. An 'improvement notice' may be served on the proprietor of a food business by an enforcement authority's authorised officer who has reasonable grounds for believing that the proprietor is failing to comply with any hygiene regulations, or any regulations controlling the processing or treatment of food[1]. Failure to comply with an improvement notice is an offence.

The notice must (a) state the officer's grounds for believing that the proprietor is failing to comply with the regulations; (b) specify the matters which constitute the proprietor's failure so to comply; (c) specify the steps which, in the officer's opinion, the proprietor must take in order to secure compliance; and (d) require the proprietor to take those measures, or measures which are at least equivalent to them, within such period (not less than 14 days) as may be specified in the notice.

These are four separate requirements each of which must be observed to constitute a valid notice[2].

1 FSA 1990, s 10(1).
2 *Bexley London Borough Council v Gardiner Merchant* [1993] COD 383.

The relevant regulations

11.2.2 The regulations to which section 10 (and also section 11[1]) apply are defined, not listed, in the legislation. The test is whether the regulations make provision for requiring, prohibiting or regulating the use of any process or treatment in the preparation of food; or for securing the observance of hygienic conditions and practices in connection with the carrying out of commercial operations with respect to food or food sources[2]. It would appear that most of the Regulations considered in chapters 12 and 13 concern the preparation[3] or hygiene of food and are caught by section 10(3)[4]. However, section 10(3) does not include reference to regulations made under section 2(2) of the European Communities Act 1972 (ECA 1972) and these powers are sometimes invoked to supplement those in Part II of the FSA 1990[5]. It is submitted that the regulations to which sections 10 and 11 apply are not intended to be restricted to those made *exclusively* for the purposes specified in section 10(3)(a) and (b) of the FSA 1990. Such a reading of the subsection would evidently confine its extent to regulations made respectively under section 16(1)(c) and (d) and, since other FSA 1990 powers are also customarily and necessarily cited in these regulations[6], render sections 10 and 11 unworkable even where section 2(2) of the ECA 1972 is not invoked.

1 See section **11.3** below.
2 FSA 1990, s 10(3).
3 As to 'preparation', see FSA 1990, s 53(1) and also para **12.4.1** below.
4 But each must be carefully considered. For example, the Regulations at para **13.8.5** are made under ECA 1972 and fall outside FSA 1990, 510(3).
5 See regulations considered in section 13.2, 13.3 and 13.11 below.
6 For example, FSA 1990, ss 16(1)(b), (e) and (f) and 17(1).

The use of improvement notices

11.2.3 To coordinate, guide and direct the work of local enforcement officers a statutory Code of Practice on the use of improvement notices[1] has been issued. This recommends authorised officers to act by advice and informal letters as long as they believe that these will secure compliance with the food hygiene or food processing regulations within a timescale that is reasonable in the circumstances. The use of the improvement notice is not advised as the first option where breaches are found on inspection. The Code states that their use may be appropriate in any of the following circumstances, or combination thereof—

(a) where formal action is proportionate to the risk to public health;
(b) where there is a record of non-compliance with breaches of food hygiene or food processing regulations;

(c) where the authorised officer has reason to believe that an informal approach will not be successful.

The improvement notice procedure is *not* considered appropriate in the following circumstances—

(i) where the contravention might be a continuing one, for example personal cleanliness of staff, and a notice would only secure an improvement at one point in time;
(ii) in transient situations, where breaches exist which pose a potential and imminent risk of injury to health and it is considered that swift enforcement action is needed, for example a one day festival or sporting event. An emergency prohibition notice[2] would be the only formal remedy which would have immediate effect;
(iii) where there is a breach of a recommendation of good hygiene practice an improvement notice cannot be issued if there is no failure to comply with an appropriate regulation.

Improvement notices might thus be seen as dealing with situations where there have been breaches of the relevant regulations, which are not sufficiently serious to justify emergency action (see section **11.4** below) but too immediate in their impact to await a prosecution. Issue of an improvement notice does not, of course, preclude a prosecution in relation to the same incident.

As explained in para **2.5.3** above, at the time of writing amendment of Code of Practice no 5 is under consideration. Amongst other things, the proposals revise the explanation of circumstances in which the use of improvement notices may be appropriate, in particular, to add (d) in the case of new businesses or new requirements, where the authorised officer assesses that the proprietor is unwilling to comply or is unlikely to do so, for whatever reason; and (e) where there is a breakdown in procedural controls, including hygiene practices falling within that category, which are *critical* for food safety or, where no such controls exist.

1 Code of Practice no 5 on the use of improvement notices (revised 1994).
2 See section **11.4** below.

Proprietor's representations

11.2.4 In response to concerns about over-assiduous enforcement activity and in implementation of the Government policy of reducing burdens on business, the Deregulation (Improvement of Enforcement Procedures) (Food Safety Act 1990) Order 1996, made under section 5 of the Deregulation and Contracting Out Act 1994 (D&COA 1994), required the authorised officer to afford the proprietor the opportunity to make representations before the issue of an improvement notice.

The pendulum then swung back. Consultations by the new Government showed that local authority enforcers felt that 'minded to' provisions of this kind were excessively bureaucratic and could be manipulated by illegitimate businesses. It therefore decided not to pursue section 5 procedures, but instead in 1998 issued the non-statutory Enforcement Concordat described at para **17.3.1** below. Moreover, in September 1999 the Government Regulation Impact Unit circulated a consultative document proposing the repeal of section 5 of the D&COA 1994 (and hence the 1996 Order), and substitution of a power to set out a code of good enforcement practice in subordinate legislation. Its stated plan is to use this power only if it proves impossible to achieve widespread adoption of the Enforcement Concordat on a voluntary basis.

Formalities

11.2.5 An improvement notice must be in the prescribed form[1] and should contain all necessary information, with references as to the regulations which are allegedly contravened; as to the matters which do not comply; and how such compliance can be achieved. In the event of non-compliance with an improvement notice a prosecution may follow and a notice which was wrongly drafted would be fatal to the proceedings. Service of the notice should comply with statutory requirements[2]. The minimum time which may be specified in an improvement notice is 14 days. The period of time given for remedial work to be carried out should be realistic in the light of the amount of work and the mischief to be corrected. Although there is no provision in the Act for extensions of time, in certain circumstances it may be reasonable to defer enforcement of an improvement notice until a further period of time has elapsed.

Hygiene regulations are of necessity broadly drafted and enforcement officers should take care to ensure that their reasons for issuing an improvement notice are based on sound hygiene practice[3].

An improvement notice must be served on the proprietor of the food business. If that proprietor is a body corporate, the notice should be addressed to the company secretary at the company's registered office. It would not be sufficient to address it to or leave it with, for example, a store manager.

In the event of a prosecution for failure to comply with an improvement notice, the summons alleges a single offence and is not bad for duplicity notwithstanding that the notice requires more than one measure to be taken[4].

Moreover, in a prosecution for failure to comply with Food Hygiene Regulations and with an improvement notice, it was held the evidence of the environmental health officer was admissible notwithstanding that she was not an expert witness. She gave evidence of what she saw in the kitchens and indicated that there was a risk of contamination. In context the evidence was fairly put to the jury. There had been no obligation to quantify the risk of contamination in terms of indicating a chance that someone would be harmed[5].

1 Food Safety (Improvement and Prohibition – Prescribed Forms) Regulations 1991, Form 1.
2 As to service of documents, see FSA 1990, s 50.
3 The notice must be objectively justifiable. See para **11.1.1** above.
4 *Sabz Ali Khan v Rhondda Borough Council* (1995) unreported.
5 *R v Tang* [1995] Crim LR 813.

Appeals

11.2.6 A person who is aggrieved by a decision of an authorised officer to serve an improvement notice may appeal to a magistrates' court[1] and, if that appeal is dismissed, to the Crown Court[2]. The effect of an appeal is to stop time running on the notice[3].

On an appeal against an improvement notice, the court may either cancel or affirm the notice and, if it affirms it, may do so either in its original form or with such modifications as the court may in the circumstances think fit[4]. However, the power of modification cannot be used to remedy a failure to comply with all four separate requirements for an improvement notice specified by section 10(1)[5] or so as to rewrite the regulations in question[6].

1 FSA 1990, s 37(1)(a).
2 FSA 1990, s 38(a).
3 FSA 1990, s 39(2) and (3).

4 FSA 1990, s 39(1).
5 *Bexley London Borough Council v Gardiner Merchant* [1993] COD 383.
6 See *Salford City Council v Abbeyfield (Worsley) Society Ltd* [1993] COD 384.

Enforcement authority liability

11.2.7 Unlike section 12 in relation to emergency prohibition notices[1], section 10 does not provide compensation for the proprietor where the enforcement authority fails to obtain confirmation of an improvement notice by a magistrates' court. However, where an authorised officer negligently required the owner of food premises to undertake works which were unnecessary to secure compliance with the FSA 1990 and regulations made thereunder and the owner, in reliance on the officer's oral requirements, closure threat and close supervision, incurred substantial and unnecessary expenditure in executing the works, the local food authority was under a common law duty of care to the owner and liable in damages for the economic loss sustained[2]. On the other hand, no duty of care or liability was owed to a business by a health and safety inspector in giving advice that led to the issue of an improvement and prohibition notices under the H&SWA 1974[3]. It was held to be implicit in the H&SWA 1974 that such notices might cause economic loss and the Act itself provided remedies against errors or excesses on the part of inspectors and enforcing authorities.

1 See para **11.4.5**.
2 *Welton v North Cornwall District Council* [1997] 1 WLR 570.
3 *Harris v Evans* [1998] 3 All ER 522, [1998] 1 WLR 1285.

11.3 PROHIBITION ORDERS

11.3.1 Section 11 of the FSA 1990 provide for two classes of administrative action by magistrates' courts, both of which are within the concept of a 'prohibition order'. First, courts have a duty, consequent on the conviction of the proprietor of a food business for a contravention of hygiene or processing regulations, to impose prohibitions on processes, treatment, premises and equipment used for the purposes of the business. Secondly, courts are empowered to ban proprietors or managers convicted of a contravention of hygiene regulations, from participating in the management of food businesses. Before 1990, it was not possible to prevent a person, the closure of whose business had been ordered, from perpetuating dangerous practices in another business. These prohibition orders are described in paras **11.3.2** and **11.3.3**.

Statutory Code of Practice no 6 gives guidance on prohibition procedures under the FSA 1990, sections 11 and 12 concentrating, however, on the latter, no doubt because in that case, as will be seen in section **11.4**, the enforcement authority not the court imposes the prohibition. Amendment of Code of Practice no 6 is under consideration at the time of writing.

Mandatory prohibition orders on processes, treatment, premises or equipment

11.3.2 The first class of prohibition order applies where a food business proprietor is convicted of an offence under any hygiene regulations, or any regulations controlling the processing or treatment of food[1] and the court by or before which he is so convicted is satisfied that the 'health risk condition' is fulfilled with respect to that business. In such a case, the court is required to impose the 'appropriate prohibition'[2].

The health risk condition is fulfilled if any of the following involves risk of injury to health—

(a) the use for the purposes of the business of any process or treatment;
(b) the construction of any premises used for the purposes of the business, or the use for those purposes of any equipment; and
(c) the state or condition of any premises or equipment used for the purposes of the business[3].

The appropriate prohibition is—

- in a case within (a), a prohibition on the use of the process or treatment for the purposes of the business;
- in a case within (b), a prohibition on the use of the premises or equipment for the purposes of the business or any other food business of the same class or description;
- in a case within (c), a prohibition on the use of the premises or equipment for the purposes of any food business[4].

Thus, the imposition of prohibition orders in relation to the use of processes or treatment, or to the construction of premises or equipment or to their condition is mandatory in the prescribed circumstances. It will be noted that each appropriate prohibition is broadly tailored to the related category of health risk. The use of a risky process or treatment (category (a)) (eg one which fails to achieve the correct cooking temperature or pH level) is forbidden simply to the food business in question, but for risky premises or equipment more extensive prohibitions are laid down. If the risk relates to construction (category (b)) (eg flooding caused by drainage defects), the premises are, or the equipment is, regarded as unsuitable for all food businesses of the kind in question; and if the risk relates to condition (category (c)) (eg vermin infestation), the premises are, or the equipment is, regarded as unsuitable for any food business at all.

1 See para **11.2.2** above.
2 FSA 1990, s 11(1).
3 FSA 1990, s 11(2).
4 FSA 1990, s 11(3).

Discretionary prohibition orders on persons

11.3.3 The second class of prohibition order differs from the first: it is discretionary and is in the nature of a penalty, since it relates to persons rather than processes, treatment, premises or equipment. It applies where a food business proprietor or a manager of a food business is convicted of an offence under those of the regulations in para **11.2.2**, which are for securing the observance of hygienic conditions and practices in connection with the carrying out of commercial operations with respect to food or food sources. If the court by which or before which the proprietor or a manager is so convicted thinks it proper to do so in all the circumstances of the case, it may by an order prohibit him from participating in the management of any food business, or any food business of a class or description specified in the order[1].

1 FSA 1990, s 11(4) and (10).

Managers

11.3.4 For the purposes of the power under para **11.3.3** above, a manager in relation to a food business means any person who is entrusted by the proprietor with the day to day running of the business, or any part of the business[1]. Before a manager can be the subject of a prohibition order he must himself have been convicted of a relevant offence. A manager by whose act or default an offence by the proprietor is alleged to have been committed[2] cannot, on the conviction of the proprietor, be the subject of a prohibition order. It is, of course, open to a prosecuting food authority, knowing that the proprietor will plead a defence of act or default of his manager, to bring proceedings against that manager in addition to or instead of the proprietor, thus enabling the court, if it thinks fit, to issue a prohibition order against the manager.

1 FSA 1990, s 11(11).
2 FSA 1990, s 20.

Action before and at the hearing

11.3.5 So that the court's attention may, in appropriate cases, be drawn to the need to consider a prohibition order under section 11(1)[1] in appropriate cases where the proprietor is convicted, paragraph 53 of Code of Practice no 6 on prohibition procedures recommends food authorities to inspect the premises subject to a prosecution prior to the hearing. If the defect in question has not been removed or, having been removed, has re-occurred, a prohibition order would prevent a health risk pending remedial action.

Consistent with natural justice, the officer should inform the proprietor of his intention to draw the attention of the court to provisions relating to prohibition and any evidence available to the food authority should be made available to the proprietor or his solicitors prior to the hearing.

Paragraph 57 of Code of Practice no 6 also advises the prosecution to draw the court's attention to the power contained in section 11(4)[2] and to provide any information which might assist it in making a decision.

1 See para **11.3.2** above.
2 See para **11.3.3** above.

Service of prohibition orders

11.3.6 As soon as practicable after the making of a prohibition order the enforcement authority must serve[1] a copy of the order on the proprietor of the business (and/or the manager as appropriate), and, in a case described in para **11.3.2** above, affix a copy of the order in a conspicuous position on such premises used for the purposes of the business as they consider appropriate[2]. Any person knowingly[3] contravening an order is guilty of an offence.

The FSA 1990 makes no specific reference to unauthorised removal or defacement of notices or orders and paragraphs 71–74 of Code of Practice no 6 make recommendations for action in this event. First, it is suggested that proceedings might be considered under section 1 of the Criminal Damage Act 1971. Second (and probably better given the need to prove guilty knowledge or recklessness in proceedings for criminal damage) the food authority should consider the desirability of asking the court to exercise its power[4] to make ancillary provision and provide in the prohibition order that it must not be defaced or removed. If the problem is thus anticipated, defacement or removal would constitute an offence.

1 As to service of documents, see FSA 1990, s 50.
2 FSA 1990, s 11(5) and (10).
3 As to 'knowingly' contravening the order, see para **19.1.1** below.
4 Magistrates' Courts Act 1980, s 63.

Appeals

11.3.7 Any person who is aggrieved by a decision of a magistrates' court to make a prohibition order may appeal to the Crown Court[1].

1 FSA 1990, s 38(b).

Termination of prohibition orders

11.3.8 By section 11(6) of the FSA 1990, a prohibition order ceases to have effect, (a) in a case described in para **11.3.2** above, on the issue by an enforcement authority of a certificate to the effect that they are satisfied that the proprietor has taken sufficient measures to secure that the health risk condition is no longer fulfilled with respect to the business, and, (b) in a case described in para **11.3.3** above, on the giving by the court of a direction to that effect.

A certificate under section 11(6)(a)[1] must be issued within three days of the enforcement authority being satisfied as mentioned above. On an application by the proprietor for such a certificate, the authority must determine, as soon as it is reasonably practical and in any event within 14 days, whether or not they are so satisfied. If they determine that they are not so satisfied, they must give notice[2] to the proprietor of the reasons for that determination[3].

Any person aggrieved by an enforcement authority decision to refuse to issue a certificate may appeal to a magistrates' court and, if that appeal is dismissed, to the Crown Court[4].

A direction under section 11(6)(b) is to be given by the court if, on application by the proprietor (or manager), the court thinks it proper to do so, having regard to all the circumstances, including in particular the conduct of the proprietor or manager since the making of the order. However, no such application can be entertained if made within six months after the making of the prohibition order, or within three months after the making by the proprietor (or manager) of a previous application for such a direction[5].

1 See Food Safety (Improvement and Prohibition—Prescribed Forms) Regulations 1991, Form 4.
2 See Food Safety (Improvement and Prohibition—Prescribed Forms) Regulations 1991, Form 5.
3 FSA 1990, s 11(7).
4 FSA 1990, ss 37(1)(b) and 38(a).
5 FSA 1990, s 11(8) and (10).

11.4 EMERGENCY PROHIBITION NOTICES AND ORDERS

11.4.1 Section 12 of the FSA 1990 introduced further powers to enable urgent action to be taken with respect to food businesses in emergency situations. Where an authorised officer is satisfied that there is an imminent health risk (ie that the 'health risk condition'[1] is fulfilled), he may act administratively to impose 'the appropriate prohibition'[2] by serving an emergency prohibition notice. Within three days of service, this notice must be confirmed by an emergency prohibition order from a magistrates' court if the appropriate prohibition on the food business is not to lapse.

For the purposes of emergency prohibition notices and orders, the health risk condition and the appropriate prohibition are as explained in para **11.3.2** above, except that, in the health risk condition, the risk of injury to health must be 'imminent'[3]. This term is manifestly intended to identify the urgent nature of the risk addressed by section 12. The legislation contains no definition but is evidently not restricted to risks which are immediate. For 'imminent' the *Oxford English Dictionary* gives—

> 'impending threateningly, hanging over one's head; ready to befall or overtake one; close at hand in its incidence; coming on shortly.'

Code of Practice no 6 on prohibition procedures suggests that an authorised officer should consider imposing an emergency prohibition notice if the condition of premises appears to carry an imminent risk of causing food poisoning.

Although also concerned with prohibition procedures under section 11, Code of Practice no 6 is, as noted above, mainly directed to advising food authorities and their authorised enforcement officers on their power to serve emergency prohibition notices under section 12. In particular advice is given on the conditions for closure of premises or prohibition of a process, treatment or piece of equipment.

The detailed provisions of section 12 are explained below.

1 See para **11.3.2** above.
2 See para **11.3.2** above.
3 FSA 1990, s 12(4).

Emergency prohibition notices[1]

11.4.2 If an authorised officer is satisfied that the health risk condition is fulfilled with respect to a food business, he may by an emergency prohibition notice[2] served[3] on the proprietor of the business, impose the appropriate prohibition.

As soon as practicable after the service of an emergency prohibition notice, the enforcement authority must affix a copy of the notice in a conspicuous position on such premises used for the purpose of the business as they consider appropriate[4]; and any person who knowingly contravenes the notice is guilty of an offence[5].

An emergency prohibition notice ceases to have effect if no application is made to a court for an emergency prohibition order within a period of three days beginning with the service of the notice; or, if such an application is so made, on the determination or abandonment of the application[6].

1 FSA 1990, s 12(1).
2 See Food Safety (Improvement and Prohibition – Prescribed Forms) Regulations 1991, Form 2.
3 As to service of documents, see FSA 1990, s 50.
4 As to unauthorised removal or defacement of notices, see para **11.3.6** above.
5 FSA 1990, s 12(5). As to 'knowingly' contravening the notice, see para **19.1.1** below.
6 FSA 1990, s 12(7).

Emergency prohibition orders[1]

11.4.3 If a magistrates' court, on the application of an authorised officer, is satisfied that the health risk condition is fulfilled with respect to any food business, it is required by an emergency prohibition order to impose the appropriate prohibition. But an officer is precluded from making an application unless, at least one day before the application, notice[2] of intention to apply has been served[3] on the proprietor of the business[4].

As soon as practicable after the making of an emergency prohibition order, the enforcement authority must serve[3] a copy of the order on the proprietor of the business and affix a copy of the order in a conspicuous position on such premises used for the purposes of that business as they consider appropriate; and any person who knowingly contravenes the order is guilty of an offence[5].

Any person who is aggrieved by a decision of a magistrates' court to make an emergency prohibition order may appeal to the Crown Court[6].

1 FSA 1990, s 12(2).
2 See Food Safety (Improvement and Prohibition – Prescribed Forms) Regulations 1991, Form 3.
3 As to service of documents, see FSA 1990, s 50.
4 FSA 1990, s 12(3).
5 FSA 1990, s 12(6). As to 'knowingly' contravening the order, see para **19.1.1** below.
6 FSA 1990, s 38(b).

Termination of emergency prohibition notices and orders

11.4.4 An emergency prohibition notice or order ceases to have effect on the issue by the enforcement authority of a certificate[1] to the effect that they are satisfied that the proprietor has taken sufficient measures to secure that the health risk condition is no longer fulfilled with respect to the business[2].

The certificate must be issued within three days of the authority being so satisfied. If an application for a certificate is made by the proprietor of the business the authority must determine as soon as is reasonably practicable, and in any event within 14 days, whether or not they are so satisfied and, if they determine that they are not so satisfied, give notice[3] to the proprietor of the reasons for that determination[4].

Any person aggrieved by an enforcement authority decision to refuse to issue a certificate may appeal to a magistrates' court and, if that appeal is dismissed, to the Crown Court[5].

1 See Food Safety (Improvement and Prohibition – Prescribed Forms) Regulations 1991, Form 4.
2 FSA 1990, s 12(8).
3 See Food Safety (Improvement and Prohibition – Prescribed Forms) Regulations 1991, Form 5.
4 FSA 1990, s 12(9).
5 FSA 1990, s 37(1)(b) and 38(a).

Compensation

11.4.5 Paragraph **11.2.7** above commented on enforcement authority liability in respect of improvement notices. By section 12(10) of the FSA 1990, where an emergency prohibition notice has been served on the proprietor of a business, the enforcement authority must compensate him in respect of any loss suffered by reason of his complying with the notice unless an application for an emergency prohibition order is made within three days beginning with the service of the notice and the court declares itself satisfied, on the hearing of the application, that the health risk condition was fulfilled with respect to the business at the time when the notice was served.

It has been held that an 'application' within the meaning of section 12(10) is the process whereby an application is made to the court and not the hearing of the application[1]. Any dispute as to compensation must be determined by arbitration[2].

1 *Farrand v Tse* (1992) Times, 10 December.
2 As to statutory arbitrations, see Arbitration Act 1996, ss 94–98.

11.5 FOOD HAZARD WARNING SYSTEM

11.5.1 As explained by Code of Practice no 16[1], the Department of Health in conjunction with other central Government departments has operated a system to alert the public and food authorities to serious problems concerning food which does not meet food safety requirements, and food which is inadequately labelled, some of the constituents of which are allergenic. As indicated in paras **2.3.2***(b)* and **2.3.6***(e)* above, the Food Standards Agency will take on responsibility for this 'food hazard warning system'. The system relies mainly on the cooperation of food companies in voluntarily withdrawing contaminated food from the market. Only exceptionally is it necessary to resort to compulsion to protect public health. The Code advises on the action to be taken by a food authority if a problem arises in their area; it describes the action to be taken by central Government departments; and it provides guidance on the action to be taken by food authorities on receipt of a food hazard warning or emergency control order. The Agency is expected as a matter of priority to seek to improve and clarify these arrangements[2].

Before looking at the detail of the current national system, mention should also be made of Community Rapid Alert System for Food (RASFF). The Commission's White Paper on Food Safety[3] considers that in general this functions well for foodstuffs intended for the final consumer, but proposes its extension to cover all feed and food emergencies, as well as to third countries on the basis of reciprocity. The number of food products notified to Member States via the RASFF is growing each year. In 1998 there were 240 notifications to the United Kingdom, an almost three-fold increase on 1997.

1 Code of Practice no 16 (Revised) on the enforcement of the Food Safety Act 1990 in relation to the Food Hazard Warning System.
2 See, for example, Consumer Panel paper CP(99)38/3 'Planning the FSA response to a major food emergency'.
3 COM (1999) 719 final.

11.5.2 The Code reminds food authorities of the ways in which information received locally may indicate a wider problem. These include examination and analysis of food, complaints from the public, information from traders or foreign enforcement agencies and notification of a communicable disease. Authorities are in particular enjoined to make arrangements for prompt notification of problems by their analysts and examiners and for liaison with other authorities over consequent action.

An authority becoming aware of a food hazard is required, with other interested authorities and experts as appropriate—

(a) to consider whether immediate action is necessary (eg under section 9 or 12 of the FSA 1990);
(b) to undertake a detailed initial assessment of the scale, extent and severity of the hazard;

(c) to decide the likely scale, extent and severity of the risk to health and whether the problem constitutes an (i) outbreak of foodborne illness, (ii) a food hazard, (iii) both an outbreak of foodborne illness and a food hazard, or (iv) none of these;
(d) if the problem is an outbreak of foodborne illness, to invoke local authority and health authority/board joint plans to establish an Outbreak Control Group;
(e) if the problem is a food hazard or both an outbreak of foodborne illness and a food hazard to determine whether the hazard is (i) a localised incident, (ii) a serious localised incident or (iii) a wider problem;
(g) in the event of a localised incident, to decide on action to be taken locally;
(h) in the event of a serious localised incident or a wider problem, immediately to notify the appropriate central government Department providing specified details of the case. Arrangements are required for out of hours action.

11.5.3 On being informed of a serious localised incident or a wider problem, the central Government coordinates the investigation in liaison with food authorities and the trade. In England, the Department of Health Food Incident Team has been responsible for action on incidents reported by food authorities and food businesses, by external agencies elsewhere in the United Kingdom and by the European Commission. Responsibility for coordination of action on incidents concerning chemical contamination of food at a particular location and radioactive contamination of food has also passed to the Food Standards Agency. Hitherto these incidents were the responsibility of the Radiological Safety and Nutrition Division in the Ministry of Agriculture, Fisheries and Food, including where necessary the making of emergency orders under Part I of the Food and Environment Protection Act 1985 (F&EPA 1985)[1].

In the case of a food hazard with serious public health or wider implications, the appropriate central Government department will issue a notification (in England, by electronic mail) to all food authorities or to those concerned, who remain responsible for action at local level. The notifications issued by central Government departments fall into the following four categories—

- category A notifications – for immediate action by the food authority;
- category B notifications – for action by the food authority specified in the notification;
- category C notifications – for action as deemed necessary by the food authority;
- category D notifications – for information only.

Action in response to category A or B notifications may include use of the powers in section 9 of the FSA 1990 if voluntary withdrawal of the food cannot be agreed.

In exceptional circumstances, the Secretary of State may make an emergency control order under section 13 of the FSA 1990 to prohibit commercial operations with respect to specified food, food sources or contact materials[2].

Where a product appears to have been deliberately contaminated, an offence under section 38 of the Public Order Act 1986 may have been committed and the police must be informed. Effective liaison with them is vital to balance the needs of any resulting criminal investigation with the primary imperative of protecting of public health.

Finally, Code of Practice no 16 emphasises the need for liaison with all interested parties and gives guidance on media relations.

1 See section **11.7** below.
2 See section **11.6** below.

11.6 EMERGENCY CONTROL ORDERS

11.6.1 Section 13 of the FSA 1990 empowers the Secretary of State to make emergency control orders where there is an imminent risk of injury to health and to grant consents, give directions and recover expenses. Orders made under section 13 may apply generally or to individual food businesses as appropriate. The powers enable central government to deal with emergencies which extend beyond the scope of particular local enforcement authorities to seize suspect food under section 9[1] and to issue emergency prohibition notices under section 12 of the Act[2].

Except where appropriate in relation to Community obligations as explained in para **2.1.2** above, the Welsh Assembly acts in Wales and the Scottish ministers in Scotland[3]: references to the Secretary of State in paras **11.6.2** and **11.6.3** below should be read accordingly.

1 See section **9.3** above.
2 See section **11.4** above.
3 National Assembly for Wales (Transfer of Functions) Order 1999, art 2 and Sch 1; Scotland Act 1998, ss 29, 53 and Sch 5, s C8.

The enabling powers

11.6.2 If it appears to the Secretary of State that the carrying out of commercial operations with respect to food, food sources or contact materials of any class or description involves, or may involve, imminent risk of injury to health, he may, by an order (an 'emergency control order') prohibit the carrying out of such operations with respect to food, food sources or contact materials of that class or description[1]. It is an offence knowingly to contravene an emergency control order[2].

It is to be noted that whereas section 13 has been used to ban contaminated animals and animal products from Belgium[3], it cannot yet be invoked in respect of feeding stuffs[4]. Action to implement Community Decisions has therefore been taken in this regard by regulations under section 2(2) of the ECA 1972[5].

1 FSA 1990, s 13(1).
2 FSA 1990, s 13(2). As to 'knowingly' contravening the order, see para **19.1.1** below.
3 See, for example, the now repealed Food (Animals and Animal Products from Belgium) (Emergency Control) Regulations 1999, SI 1999/2025.
4 As to the future, see para **2.3.8***(e)* above.
5 See, for example, Animal Feedingstuffs from Belgium (Control) (England and Wales) (No 4) Regulations 1999, SI 1999/3422.

Consents, directions and recovery of expenses

11.6.3 To provide flexibility in the operation of emergency control orders, supplemental powers enable the Secretary of State or the Food Standards Agency—

(a) to consent, conditionally or unconditionally, to the doing of anything in a particular case which is prohibited by an order;
(b) to give directions for the purpose of preventing the carrying out of commercial operations with respect to food, food sources or contact materials to which an order applies; and
(c) to recover expenses reasonably incurred in doing anything in consequence of any person failing to comply with an order[1].

1 FSA 1990, s 13(3)–(7).

Exercise of the powers

11.6.4 As might be expected, these stringent and specialist powers have been used sparingly. In response to the possible link between BSE in cattle and new variant CJD in humans, urgent action was taken in 1996 to prohibit the sale for human consumption of meat from bovine animals more than two years six months old[1]. The order was replaced as soon as possible by regulations made under the customary powers of section 16[2], which, unlike section 13 orders, are subject to the prior duty to consult representative organisations[3].

In 1998, as a result of a case of E-coli 0157 poisoning, an order was made prohibiting the carrying out of any commercial operation in relation to cheese originating from a particular Somerset farm[4]. A major wholesale customer of the farm sought a declaration that the order was disproportionate[5] and invalid on the ground that the draconian powers of section 13 should be exercised only if the powers of food authorities under section 9 of the FSA 1990[6] (which would have afforded him the possibility of compensation) were considered inadequate. Reversing the judgment of the Queen's Bench Division, the Court of Appeal held that if section 9 powers are considered to be equally effective, then it is those powers that should be exercised. However, on the particular facts, the section 13 order was a proportionate response to a perceived imminent threat to the health and life of the public[7]. By reaching this conclusion, the court confirmed that section 13 enables provision to be made confining justices of the peace to considering under section 9 whether food is caught by a particular order, thus excluding compensation for any food so caught even where it is not actually unfit for human consumption. The judgment also established that particular firms may be exempted from section 13 orders provided that unfair discrimination is avoided.

Emergency control orders have also been used to implement urgent Community obligations in relation to imports potentially contaminated by aflatoxins[8] and by dioxins[9].

1 Beef (Emergency Control) Order 1996, SI 1996/961, as amended by SIs 1996/1043, 1996/1091 and 1996/1166 and revoked by SI 1996/1742.
2 See now the Fresh Meat (Beef Controls) (No 2) Regulations 1996, as amended, and para **13.8.3**.
3 See FSA 1990, s 48(4).
4 Food (Cheese) (Emergency Control) Order 1998, SI 1998/1277, as amended by SI 1998/1284 and, so as to disapply the prohibition in respect of cheese manufactured on or after 11 July 1998, by SI 1998/1673.
5 As to the proportionality test applied by Community law to national measures, see further para **1.3.1** above.
6 As to the FSA 1990, s 9, see section **9.3** above.
7 *R v Secretary of State for Health, ex p Eastside Cheese* [1999] 3 CMLR 123.
8 Food (Pistachios from Iran) (Emergency Control) Order 1997, SI 1997/2238, as amended by SI 1997/3046, made in implementation of Commission Decision 97/613/EC; and Food (Peanuts from Egypt) (Emergency Control) Order 1999, SI 1999/1800, made in implementation of Commission Decision 1999/356/EC.
9 See Food (Animal Products from Belgium) (Emergency Control) (England and Wales) Order 1999, SI 1999/3421, made in part implementation of Commission Decision 1999/788/EC (on protective measures with regard to contamination by dioxins of certain products of porcine and poultry origin intended for human or animal consumption).

11.7 EMERGENCY ORDERS UNDER THE FOOD AND ENVIRONMENT PROTECTION ACT 1985

The enabling powers

11.7.1 In relation to food hazards the Secretary of State has power under Part I of the F&EPA 1985, as amended, to make emergency orders and to grant consents, give directions and recover expenses.

This paragraph and para **11.7.2** below concentrate on the Secretary of State's responsibilities in relation to England. However, food hazards are no respecters of boundaries. Paragraph **2.2.2** above has already explained how the legislation has been amended in respect of Scotland and that, in relation to Wales, the functions are transferred to the Welsh Assembly except that the order making power, in particular, is exercisable concurrently with the Secretary of State[1]. Additionally, as explained in para **2.1.2** above, the Secretary of State may make orders alone as regards Community obligations.

The power conferred by section 1 of the F&EPA 1985, as amended, enables the Secretary of State to make an emergency order if in his opinion—

(a) there exist circumstances which are likely to create a hazard to human health through human consumption of food; and
(b) in consequence, food—
  (i) which is, or may be in the future, in an area of the United Kingdom, and/or of sea within British fishery limits, or
  (ii) which is or may be in the future derived from anything in such an area,
  is or may become, unsuitable for human consumption.

The order designates the area in question and imposes 'emergency prohibitions' from a range (specified in Schedule 1) of activities that may be prohibited in a designated area, of movements of food etc that may be prohibited and of activities that may be prohibited throughout the United Kingdom.

Although it refers to 'food'[2] and not to 'food sources', the scope of the power is otherwise extended by section 1(3) which provides that food derived from any creature is to be treated for the purposes of the Act as also derived from any feeding stuff which that creature has eaten; and from anything from which any such feeding stuff was derived.

It is an offence to contravene an emergency prohibition or to cause or permit any other person to do so[3].

1 National Assembly for Wales (Transfer of Functions) Order 1999, art 2 and Sch 1.
2 By F&EPA 1985, s 24, 'food' has the same meaning as in the FSA 1990.
3 F&EPA 1985, s 1(6) and (7).

Consents, directions and recovery of expenses

11.7.2 When an emergency order has been made, the Secretary of State or the Food Standards Agency have power[1]—

(a) to consent, conditionally or unconditionally, to the doing in a particular case of anything prohibited by an order;
(b) to give directions to prevent the consumption of food which is unsuitable for consumption or do anything necessary for that purpose; and
(c) to recover expenses reasonably incurred in doing anything in consequence of any person failing or causing or permitting a failure to comply with an order[1].

1 F&EPA 1985, s 2.

Exercise of the powers

11.7.3 It is apparent from what has been said above that, although there is some overlap in scope between the two provisions, section 1 of the F&EPA 1985 has a different focus from section 13 of the FSA 1990[1]. While orders under the FSA 1990 are probably best suited to preventing commercial operations, including importation, in respect of specified hazardous products, orders under the F&EPA 1985 are well geared to preventing produce (including feeding stuffs) from leaving clearly identified contaminated areas of the United Kingdom.

Thus, F&EPA 1985 orders[2] have been in force since 1987 to prevent the human consumption of food derived from sheep in specified areas which continue to be affected as a result of the escape of radioactive substances from the nuclear reactor at Chernobyl in the former Soviet Union[3]. In those cases and generally with the examples given below, the principal orders have been progressively revoked as the hazard has receded and only exceptionally would they subsist as long as the controls following the Chernobyl accident.

Prior to its amendment by the FSA 1990[4], section 1 of the F&EPA 1985 was confined to circumstances in which there had been an 'escape' of hazardous substances. The removal of this limitation (see the summary of the power at para **11.7.1***(a)* above) has rendered the power additionally suitable for prohibiting the taking of toxic shellfish[5].

Emergency orders have also been made in respect of contaminated feeding stuffs[6] and cattle[7], dioxin and heavy metal contamination on particular farms[8], and marine pollution by oil and chemicals[9] and by nuclear fuel[10].

1 See section **11.6** above.
2 See in particular the Food Protection (Emergency Prohibitions) (Radioactivity in Sheep) (Wales) Order 1991, SI 1991/5, as amended; the Food Protection (Emergency Prohibitions) (Radioactivity in Sheep) (England) Order 1991, SI 1991/6, as amended; and the Food Protection (Emergency Prohibitions) (Radioactivity in Sheep) Order 1991, SI 1991/20, as amended.
3 The European Community has fixed permitted levels of radioactivity in foodstuffs and feeding stuffs. See in particular, Council Regulation/(Euratom)3954/87 and Council Regulation 2219/89/EEC (exports) and Council Regulation (EEC) 737/90 (third country imports).
4 FSA 1990, s 51 (1) and (2).
5 See for example, the Food Protection (Emergency Prohibitions) (Paralytic Shellfish Poisoning) Order 1998, SI 1998/1582; and the Food Protection (Emergency Prohibitions) (Amnesic Shellfish Poisoning) Order 1999, SI 1999/1005.
6 See for example, the Food Protection (Emergency Prohibitions) (Contamination of Feedingstuffs) (England) (No 3) Order 1989, SI 1989/2100.
7 See for example, the Food Protection (Emergency Prohibitions) (Lead in Cattle) (England) Order 1991, SI 1991/498; and the Food Protection (Emergency Prohibitions) (Poisonous Substances in Cattle) (Wales) Order 1991, SI 1991/1863.
8 See for example, the Food Protection (Emergency Prohibitions) (Dioxins) (England) (No 2) Order 1992, SI 1992/1274 and the Food Protection (Emergency Prohibitions) (Lead in Ducks and Geese) (England) Order 1992, SI 1992/2726.
9 See for example, the Food Protection (Emergency Prohibitions) (Oil and Chemical Pollution of Fish and Plants) Order 1996, SI 1996/448; and the Food Protection (Emergency Prohibitions) (Oil and Chemical Pollution of Salmon and Migratory Trout) Order 1996, SI 1996/856.
10 Food Protection (Emergency Prohibitions) (Dounreay Nuclear Establishment) Order 1997, SI 1997/2622.

Chapter 12

Food hygiene and food preparation

12.1 INTRODUCTION

12.1.1 Sections **1** to **4** of chapter 11 explained the administrative controls applicable to unhygienic food businesses, which are provided by the Food Safety Act 1990 (FSA 1990). Under the Act, provision can be made by regulations for securing general hygienic conditions and practices and also for the registration or licensing of food premises. The requirements on these aspects are considered in sections **12.2** and **12.3** respectively below. Section **12.4** describes the part played by the concept of 'preparation' in food hygiene controls in and under the FSA 1990, particularly in regulations on the processing or treatment of specific foods. Section **12.4** deals with two important but anomalous cases of this kind. However, most of them concern hygiene in production of and trade in specific products of animal origin for human consumption and are explained together in chapter 13.

The rules on temperature controls for hygiene and other purposes are summarised in chapter 14.

12.2 THE HYGIENE REGULATIONS

The background

12.2.1 Basic food hygiene in the preparation, processing, manufacturing, packaging, storing, transportation, distribution, handling and offering for sale or supply to the consumer of food for human consumption is controlled by Council Directive 93/43/EEC on the hygiene of foodstuffs[1]. This adopts a different approach from that in our pre-Community regulations. Individual food businesses bear the principal responsibility for ensuring consumer safety. There is now a clear emphasis on identifying risks and the control of practices and procedures and the food industry itself is exhorted to develop voluntary guides to good hygiene practice.

In Great Britain the Directive is implemented principally by the Food Safety (General Food Hygiene) Regulations 1995, as amended. However, the Food Safety (Temperature Control) Regulations 1995 implement the requirements of paragraphs 4 and 5 of Chapter IX of the Annex and, as noted above, are described in chapter 14.

The Regulations do not apply to 'primary production' which is defined as including harvesting, slaughter and milking. Thus farmers, horticultural growers, beekeepers, vine growers and fish farmers will be exempt unless they are carrying out a 'commercial operation', that is, deriving food from any food source for the purpose of sale or for purposes connected with sale[2].

The Regulations also do not generally apply to persons carrying on activities regulated by or under product-specific hygiene regulations described in chapter 13 which, like the General Food Hygiene Regulations, are made in implementation of Community Directives. Given the inconsistency and irregularity of Community hygiene legislation, the Commission White Paper on Food Safety[3] proposes consolidation of all the Directives into a single Regulation which will apply, throughout the supply chain, the common HACCP principles of the general Directive to food of plant, as well as animal, origin[4].

Since there can be no absolute standards of cleanliness, hygiene regulations are necessarily broadly drafted leaving a great deal to the common sense of enforcement officers and the courts. In the past this resulted in widely differing interpretations between food authorities. However, the evenness of enforcement has been improved through better coordination and the issue of guidance in the form of statutory Codes of Practice under the FSA 1990[5]. Hygiene regulations have also acquired a new significance with the enactment of the FSA 1990 because improvement notices and prohibition orders depend in part on alleged and actual breaches of specified provisions[6].

1 As regards the transport by sea of bulk liquid oils and fats and raw sugar, derogations from certain provisions of Directive 93/43/EEC are granted by Directives 96/3/EC and 98/28/EC.
2 As to primary production, see further Code of Practice no 9: Food Hygiene Inspections Annex 2. As to commercial operations, see para **4.5.1** above.
3 COM (1999) 719 final, published on 12 January 2000.
4 As to the HACCP principles, see para **12.2.2** below.
5 See in particular, Code of Practice no 9: Food Hygiene Inspections and Code of Practice no 10: Enforcement of the Temperature Control Requirements of Food Hygiene Regulations.
6 See FSA 1990, s 10(3) considered at paras **11.2.1**, **11.2.2** and **11.3.1** above.

The provisions

12.2.2 Pursuant to the Community food hygiene Directive 93/43/EEC, the proprietors of food businesses[1] are subject to specified obligations[2]. They must ensure that the preparation, processing, manufacturing, packaging, storing, transportation, distribution, handling and offering for sale or supply of food is carried out in a hygienic way and must comply with detailed requirements in respect of food businesses. The requirements relate to—

(a) the cleanliness, adequacy and location of wash basins[3], ventilation, lighting, drainage and changing facilities at food premises, other those specified in (c) below;
(b) the cleanliness of rooms where food is prepared, treated or processed, other than dining areas and premises specified in (c) below;
(c) the cleanliness and avoidance of risk of contamination[4] in moveable and/or temporary premises (such as marquees, market stalls, mobile sales vehicles), premises used primarily as a private dwelling house, premises used occasionally for catering purposes and vending machines; and
(d) the cleanliness and avoidance of contamination as regards transport[5], equipment, food waste, water supply, personal hygiene, and storage and other operations regarding foodstuffs and other substances and the training of food handlers.

Food business proprietors are also subject to a further essential requirement of the Community food hygiene Directive. They must identify steps in the activities of the business which are critical to ensuring food safety and ensure that adequate safety procedures are identified, implemented, maintained and reviewed on the basis of the principles used to develop the Hazard Analysis and Critical Control Points system. Commonly referred to as 'HACCP', this is an internationally recognised 'structured approach to assessing the potential hazards in an operation and deciding which are critical to the safety of the consumer. These critical control points (CCPs) are then monitored *in situ* and specified remedial action is taken if any CCPs deviate from their safe limits'[6]. In the Directive and Regulations, the HACCP principles are articulated on the following lines—

(a) analysis of the potential food hazards in a food business operation;
(b) identification of the points in those operations where food hazards may occur;
(c) deciding which of the points identified are critical to ensuring food safety (ie the CCPs);
(d) identification and implementation of effective control and monitoring procedures at those CCPs; and
(e) review of the analysis of food hazards, the CCPs and the control and monitoring procedures periodically, and whenever the food business's operation changes.

To assist local authority environmental health officers in explaining these hazard analysis requirements to small businesses, the Department of Health produced a presentation pack on *Controlling Food Hazards*.

The 1995 Regulations also require persons working in food handling areas to notify the proprietor of the food business if they are suffering from specified medical conditions and there is any likelihood that they will directly or indirectly contaminate food with pathogenic micro-organisms[7].

New enforcement requirements were introduced by the Regulations[8]. Food authorities must inspect food premises with a frequency which has regard to the risk and must assess the potential food safety hazards associated with those premises. They must pay particular attention to the CCPs identified by food businesses. And they must give due consideration to whether the food business proprietor has acted in accordance with any relevant guide to good hygiene practice developed by a national food industry sector and is complying with Article 3 of the food hygiene Directive or developed by a European food industry sector and published in the EC Official Journal. The Department of Health has produced advice to the food industry on the preparation and development of UK voluntary Industry Guides[9]. The 1998 Report of the Advisory Committee on the Microbiological Safety of Food on Foodborne Viral Infections recommended that guides should be developed for more sectors of the industry.

At the time of writing, *Baking*, *Catering*, *Fresh Produce*, *Flour Milling*, *Markets and Fairs*, *Retail* and *Wholesale Distributors Guides* have been published[10]. *Guides on Bottled Water* and *Vending and Dispensing* are nearing completion and a *Butchers' Supplement to the Retail Guide* and a *Transport Guide* are in the course of development.

Statutory Code of Practice no 9 on food hygiene inspections (which is in course of revision) reiterates the central importance of identifying risks arising from the activities carried on and the effectiveness of food businesses' own assessment of hazards and control of risks, including food hygiene training, as well as of identifying contraventions of the FSA 1990 and the regulations under it. In particular the Code sets out the minimum inspection frequencies for the various categories of food premises classified, according to potential health risk, on the basis of an inspection rating system. Following a recommendation of the Pennington Group Report[11], the rating system was amended to ensure in particular that certain high risk premises are visited more frequently.

In pursuance of a further Pennington recommendation, the Food Hygiene Regulations have recently been amended to provide for the annual licensing in England of retail butchers' shops, mobile shops and market stalls, handling both unwrapped raw meat together with other ready to eat foods from the same premises. Certain large mixed business premises selling a range of goods, such as supermarkets, which have a butchery service outlet, are also required to have a licence. The licensing conditions apply only to those parts of the premises engaged in the butchery service. In order to be licensed, premises will have to satisfy a range of conditions. These include compliance with existing food hygiene legislation, enhanced staff training and payment of an annual licence charge of £100. In particular, the five HACCP principles which must be observed by licensees are augmented by two additional ones. They are—

- verification to confirm that the HACCP procedures are working effectively; and
- documentation of all procedures appropriate to the effective application of the other principles, including documentation which identifies persons who have undertaken prescribed training.

Through the Meat and Livestock Commission, the Government has already been pursuing an initiative to improve hygiene controls in butchers' shops, by advice and training in the setting up and management of HACCP systems.

Administration and enforcement of the scheme is a food authority responsibility and includes power to refuse, suspend or revoke licences for non-compliance with the conditions. A right of appeal lies to a magistrates' court.

It should be noted that offences under food hygiene Regulations are continuing offences, committed afresh each day that the Regulations are not complied with[12].

1 As to 'proprietor', see FSA 1990, s 53. As to 'food business', see (General Food Hygiene) Regulations 1995, reg 2(1).
2 Food Safety (General Food Hygiene) Regulations 1995, reg 4.
3 *Storey v Manning* (1958) unreported; *Adams v Flook and Flook* [1987] BTLC 61.
4 *MacFisheries (Wholesale and Retail) Ltd v Coventry Corpn* [1957] 3 All ER 299, [1957] 1 WLR 1066.
5 Food Safety (General Food Hygiene) Regulations 1995, Sch 1, Ch IV provides derogations in respect of the bulk transport by sea of liquid oils and fats and bulk sugar; see para **12.2.1** nl.
6 Report of the Richmond Committee on Microbiological Safety of Food Part I (1990) HMSO, Appendix 4, para A.4.1.
7 Food Safety (General Food Hygiene) Regulations 1995, reg 5.
8 Food Safety (General Food Hygiene) Regulations 1995, reg 8.
9 'A Template: Industry Guides to Good Hygiene Practice'.
10 Copies of the published guides can be obtained from Chadwick House Group Ltd, Publications Department, Chadwick Court, 15 Hatfields, London SE1 8DJ.
11 The Pennington Group: Report on the circumstances leading to the 1996 outbreak of infection with E coli 0157 in Central Scotland, the implications and the lessons to be learned, April 1997.
12 *R v Thames Metropolitan Stipendiary Magistrate and another, ex p Hackney London Borough Council* (1983) Times, 10 November.

Training of food handlers

12.2.3 In implementation of food hygiene Directive 93/43/EEC, provision is made in the Food Safety (General Food Hygiene) Regulations 1995 requiring food business proprietors to ensure that food handlers engaged in the food business are supervised and instructed and/or trained in food hygiene matters commensurate with their work activities[1].

The Department of Health's advice to the food industry on the preparation and development of UK voluntary Industry Guides to good hygiene practice[2] includes advice on the training of food handlers. The Industry Guides are expected to state how the broad requirement as to training in Chapter X of the Annex to Directive 93/43/EEC should apply to the sectors in question.

12.2.3 *Food hygiene and food preparation*

Food authorities are empowered to provide training courses in food hygiene, whether within or outside their area, for persons who are or intend to become involved in food businesses whether as proprietors or otherwise[3]. A food authority may contribute towards the expenses incurred by any other food authority or towards expenses incurred by any other person in providing such courses.

1 See reg 4(2)(d) and Sch 1, Ch X.
2 See para **12.2.2**.
3 FSA 1990, s 23.

12.3 REGISTRATION AND LICENSING OF FOOD PREMISES

12.3.1 The Secretary of State is empowered by the FSA 1990[1] to make regulations requiring the registration or licensing of food premises. The purpose of registration is to provide information to the enforcement authorities about food businesses in their area so that they can target their resources more effectively[2]. Licensing, by contrast, is an expeditious and stringent way of penalising contraventions of prescribed requirements. Rather than having to await the outcome of criminal proceedings, the enforcement authority can take direct action by exercising its discretion to cancel, suspend or revoke the licence. Because of the severity of this sanction, the capacity to make food business licensing regulations under the FSA 1990 is restricted to specified public health and consumer protection circumstances[3].

By the Food Premises (Registration) Regulations 1991, as amended, it is an offence in Great Britain to operate a food business from unregistered premises. Specified premises which are otherwise controlled or at which the commercial operations pose little health risk are exempt from the requirement to register. These include premises which are used on less than five days in five consecutive weeks, various premises controlled under product specific hygiene regulations considered in chapter 14, premises used by voluntary or charitable organisations where food is not stored and domestic premises where there is limited provision of bed and breakfast accommodation, child minding services or food preparation for WI country market stalls.

Environmental health officers have long pressed for licensing of all food premises but, until recently, the government has regarded registration as adequate, except for food irradiation plants[4] and legislation implementing Community obligations in relation to products of animal origin for human consumption[5]. It has already been noted at para **12.2.2** above that, in response to the Pennington Group Report, provision has now been made in England for the licensing of butchers' shops.

1 FSA 1990, ss 19 and 26(2)(b)–(d).
2 See the guidance given by Code of Practice no 11: Enforcement of the Food Premises (Registration) Regulations.
3 FSA 1990, s 19(2).
4 See para **12.4.3** below.
5 See paras **13.1.3** and **13.1.14** below.

12.4 FOOD PREPARATION

12.4.1 The concept of 'preparation' has been an important element in British food hygiene legislation and the FSA 1990 maintained and strengthened the statutory provisions. In relation to food, preparation 'includes manufacture and any form of processing or treatment', while preparation for sale 'includes packaging, and prepare for sale shall be construed accordingly': treatment is defined as including the subjecting of food to heat or cold[1].

The preparation for sale of food may, if defective, result in an offence of rendering food injurious to health[2] and, via the definition of 'commercial operation', is an important element of the concept of 'food business'[3] and the administrative controls provided by improvement notices[4], prohibition orders[5] and emergency prohibition notices and orders[6].

The concept is also material to important presumptions that food is intended for human consumption[7] and to the standard of proof required to establish a 'due diligence' defence[8].

Particularly important in the control of harmful microorganisms in food are the powers to regulate processing and treatment[9], which are now supplemented by powers in respect of novel foods and food sources and genetically modified food sources and foods derived from them[10]. Under the powers, Regulations have been made to prescribe processing and treatment requirements for a substantial number of foods. Most of these are products of animal origin controlled by a series of related Community instruments which, together with the implementing Regulations, are explained in chapter 13. The provisions on ice cream heat treatment and food irradiation do not fall within that group and are summarised in paras **12.4.2** and **12.4.3** respectively below.

1 As to these definitions, see FSA 1990, s 53(1). As to 'preparation', see also *Leeds City Council v J H Dewhurst Ltd* (1990) Times, 22 March.
2 FSA 1990, s 7.
3 FSA 1990, s 1(3) and see para **4.8.1** above.
4 FSA 1990, s 10 and see section **11.2** above.
5 FSA 1990, s 11 and see section **11.3** above.
6 FSA 1990, s 12 and see section **11.4** above.
7 FSA 1990, s 3(3) and see section **4.3** above.
8 FSA 1990, s 21 and see section **19.3** below.
9 FSA 1990, s 16(1)(c).
10 FSA 1990, s 18(1)(a) and (b).

Ice cream

12.4.2 The Ice-Cream (Heat Treatment etc) Regulations 1959, as amended, require the ingredients used in the manufacture of ice-cream, which is not a milk-based product[1], to be pasteurised by one or other of three specified methods or sterilised and thereafter be kept at a specified low temperature until the freezing process is begun. Products which have a pH value of 4.5 or less (and so are acid enough to make heat treatment unnecessary) are exempt. The sale of ice-cream which has not been treated as required or which has been allowed to reach a temperature exceeding 28°F without again being treated is prohibited. As to the temperature control, see further para **14.4.4** below.

1 See section **13.9** below.

Irradiation

12.4.3 Ionising radiation produces an effect similar to pasteurisation, cooking or other forms of heat treatment and can be used to kill pathogenic organisms in a range of foods. It can also be used to reduce spoilage, to delay ripening in fruit and to prevent sprouting in vegetables such as potatoes and onions.

12.4.3 *Food hygiene and food preparation*

Directive 1999/2/EC of the European Parliament and of the Council provides for the approximation of Member States' laws concerning foods and food ingredients treated with ionising radiation. Member States are required to ensure that irradiated foodstuffs placed on the market are restricted to those which comply with specified provisions. Conditions for authorising food irradiation, the sources of ionising radiation and the method of calculating the overall average absorbed dose are prescribed. Although the maximum radiation dose for a foodstuff may be given in partial doses, it must not be exceeded nor used in combination with any chemical treatment having the same purpose. Different labelling requirements are specified according to whether or not the irradiated food is intended for the ultimate consumer and mass caterers. Irradiation facilities must be approved and records must be kept of foodstuffs treated. Conditions are specified for the importation of irradiated foods from third countries.

The provisions laid down by this framework Directive are completed by Directive 1999/3/EC of the European Parliament and of the Council which will progressively list the irradiated foodstuffs and maximum radiation doses which are permitted in Community trade. Dried aromatic herbs, spices and vegetable seasonings have already been authorised for irradiation treatment, with a maximum radiation dose of 10 kGy.

The Food (Control of Irradiation) Regulations 1990 are broadly in line with the Directives but are likely to be replaced so as to permit the marketing of Community-listed irradiated food by 20 September 2000 and prohibit non-compliant food by 20 March 2001.

The Commission White Paper on Food Safety[1] explains the plans in respect of the irradiation of food. An amendment is proposed to Directive 1999/3/EC to complete the list of foods and food ingredients which may be treated with ionising radiation; and a new Decision will list the Community-approved irradiation facilities in Member States and third countries.

1 COM (1999) 719 final, published on 12 January 2000.

Chapter 13

Food hygiene: production and importation of products of animal origin for human consumption

13.1 INTRODUCTION

The European Community context

13.1.1 Since the United Kingdom's accession to what is now the European Community and especially since the completion of the internal market, national law on the hygienic production and importation of food has progressively been replaced by rules of Community inspiration. The relevant Community legislation is made as part of the common agricultural policy and addresses animal as well as human health issues. On production of and intra-Community trade in foodstuffs of animal origin, such meat and dairy and egg products, a series of product-specific vertical directives establish specific conditions of hygiene[1]. A further series of Community provisions lays down the conditions for importation of such foodstuffs from third countries[2].

In respect of both intra-Community trade in and importation from third countries of animals and of products of animal origin (including those for human consumption), a harmonised Community regime of veterinary checks has been established to ensure that they comply with animal and public health conditions. Inspections are primarily at the place of dispatch for intra-community trade and at entry into the community for third country imports. For animals, the procedures are laid down by veterinary checks Directives 90/425/EEC and 91/496/EEC as regards intra-Community trade in and importation from third countries respectively, the Directives being implemented by the Animals and Animal Products (Import and Export) Regulations 1998. For products of animal origin, the procedures are laid down by veterinary checks Directives 89/662/EEC and 97/78/EC as regards intra-Community trade in and importation from third countries respectively. To ensure that implementation of Directives 89/662/EEC and 97/78/EC is fully up to date, the Products of Animal Origin (Import and Export) Regulations 1996 are due to be revoked and replaced during 2000.

It is within the framework of the veterinary checks Directives that the Community has enacted measures to combat bovine spongiform encephalopathy (BSE) by prohibiting the use of specified risk material and exports of bovines and bovine products[3]. The current measures in respect of food and the national BSE rules which implement and supplement them are summarised in section **13.8** below.

As indicated in para **12.2.1**, the general food hygiene Directive 93/43/EEC applies to foodstuffs and activities not covered by the specific Directives on production, marketing and importation and the Commission's White Paper on Food Safety[4] proposes that the common principles of Directive 93/43/EEC shall be extended to them in a single large consolidating Regulation.

For food from third countries still uncontrolled by Community law, residuary national provision is made by the Imported Food Regulations 1997 which, on the lines of previous law, prohibits imports which fail to comply with the food safety requirements or are unsound or unwholesome[5].

It should further be noted that the Animal By-Products (Identification) Regulations 1995 continue to make provision in Great Britain to protect public health from animal by-products not intended for human consumption. The products, as defined in the Regulations, are required to be stained and sterilised and their movement is controlled. There are a number of exemptions from the Regulations. In particular animal by-products controlled by Directive 90/667/EEC (laying down the veterinary rules for the disposal of animal waste) are generally required, by Part II of the Animal By-Products Order 1999, to be rendered, incinerated or buried. Parts III and IV of that Order made provision for catering waste intended for feeding to pigs and poultry and for swill for use as feedingstuffs[6].

As part of the programme to guard against and eradicate bovine spongiform encephalopathy, the Specified Risk Material Regulations 1997 and Specified Risk Material Order 1997 make separate provision to prohibit the use of defined material from cattle, sheep and goats[7].

1 See para **13.1.2** below.
2 See para **13.1.5** below.
3 The Commission's White Paper on Food Safety proposes future action under Art 152 (ex 129) EC.
4 COM (1999) 719 final, published on 12 January 2000.
5 As to the food safety requirements, see paras **9.2.1** and **9.2.2** above.
6 See para **16.10.1** below.
7 See paras **13.8.2** and **16.9.3** below.

The Directives on hygienic production of specific products of animal origin for human consumption and their implementation

13.1.2 The veterinary checks referred to in para **13.1.1** as being required by Directives 89/662/EEC and 97/78/EC in respect of intra-Community trade and third country imports, concern animal as well as human health. In consequence, the Directives do not separately list those products of animal origin which are for human consumption or the production rules which apply to them. In fact the controls on hygienic production of foodstuffs of animal origin for human consumption have developed piecemeal to cover fresh meat, poultrymeat, meat products, minced meat and meat preparations, rabbit meat, farmed and wild game meat, fish, shellfish, eggs and egg products, milk and milk products and other products such as frogs' legs, snails and honey. As noted above, the Commission White Paper on Food Safety[1] proposes that these piecemeal controls shall be consolidated with the general food hygiene Directive 93/43/EEC into a single Regulation. At present, the Community legislation on hygienic production of major products for intra-Community trade is to be found in the following Council Directives—

- Directive 64/433/EEC problems affecting intra-Community trade in fresh meat;
- Directive 71/118/EEC on health problems affecting trade in fresh poultrymeat;
- Directive 91/495/EEC concerning public health and animal health problems affecting the production and placing on the market of rabbit meat and farmed game meat;
- Directive 92/45/EEC on public health and animal health problems relating to the killing of wild game and the placing on the market of wild game meat;
- Directive 94/65/EEC laying down the requirements for the production and placing on the market of minced meat and meat preparations;
- Directive 77/99/EEC on health problems affecting intra-Community trade in meat products and certain other products of animal origin;

- Directive 92/46/EEC laying down the health rules for the production and placing on the market of raw milk, heat-treated milk and milk-base products;
- Directive 89/437/EEC on hygiene and health problems affecting the production and the placing on the market of egg products;
- Directive 91/493/EEC laying down the health conditions for the production and the placing on the market of fishery products;
- Directive 91/492/EEC laying down the health conditions for the production and the placing on the market of live bivalve molluscs.

In Great Britain these Directives are implemented by the following sets of Regulations which are considered in more detail in this chapter—

- Fresh Meat (Hygiene and Inspection) Regulations 1995;
- Poultrymeat, Farmed Game Bird Meat and Rabbit Meat (Hygiene and Inspection) Regulations 1995;
- Wild Game Meat (Hygiene and Inspection) Regulations 1995;
- Minced Meat and Meat Preparations (Hygiene) Regulations 1995;
- Meat Products (Hygiene) Regulations 1994;
- Dairy Products (Hygiene) Regulations 1995;
- Egg Products Regulations 1993;
- Food Safety (Fishery Products and Live Shellfish) (Hygiene) Regulations 1998.

As part of the establishment of the internal market, Directive 92/118/EEC was enacted to sweep up in a single exercise the provision of health requirements governing trade in and imports into the Community of the outstanding products of animal origin. Under this Directive, specific Community health conditions have been prescribed in respect of the putting on the market of certain types of eggs and are contemplated for egg imports[2]. Rules have also been laid down for the production of gelatine[3] and for trade in and import of snails, frogs' legs and honey[4]. As a result of amending Directive 96/90/EC, further rules are to be prescribed for meat from reptiles and other species not otherwise covered and for milk and milk products otherwise than from cows, ewes, goats or buffaloes[5].

1 COM (1999) 719 final, published on 12 January 2000.
2 See para **13.10.2** below.
3 See para **13.12.1** below.
4 See para **13.13.1** below.
5 See pending case C-200/99 *Commission v United Kingdom* OJ C 226 7.8.99, p 18, alleging UK failure to implement Directive 96/90/EC.

General characteristics of the principal Regulations on hygienic production of products of animal origin for human consumption

13.1.3 Similar basic conditions apply to all products of animal origin placed on the market for human consumption. In general, products must be produced in an approved establishment in accordance with specified hygiene requirements and bear an EC health mark attesting this[1]. For the national market, less stringent conditions may sometimes be prescribed, but in that case the use of the health mark is strictly forbidden.

Establishments are approved only if requirements as to construction, equipment and operation are met. Where this no longer obtains, approval may, subject to appeal, be suspended or withdrawn.

Appropriate provision is in particular made for storage, wrapping and transportation of products and for commercial documents or health certificates and transport documentation.

Requirements applicable to particular products are summarised in relation to those products later in this chapter other than temperature requirements which are described in chapter 14.

1 As to English law implications of official clearance for intra-Community trade, see further para **19.3.7** below.

Special provisions on hygienic production of fresh meat for human consumption

13.1.4 Special provision is made by the Fresh Meat (Hygiene and Inspection) Regulations 1995, the Poultrymeat, Farmed Game Bird Meat and Rabbit Meat (Hygiene and Inspection) Regulations 1995 and the Wild Game Meat (Hygiene and Inspection) Regulations 1995 ('the Fresh Meat Hygiene Regulations') for the implementation of Directives 64/433/EEC (fresh meat), 71/118/EEC (fresh poultrymeat), 91/495/EEC (rabbit meat and farmed game meat) and 92/45/EEC (wild game meat).

First, the requirements in those Directives that production establishments be approved[1] are given effect by provision in the Fresh Meat Hygiene Regulations for their licensing and for appeals to a Meat Hygiene Appeals Tribunal in the event of refusal, grant subject to conditions or revocation of a licence. The Regulations make provision in respect of the constitution, appointment of members, remuneration of members and staffing of a tribunal[2]. The procedural rules in respect of an appeal are prescribed in the Meat Hygiene Appeals Tribunal (Procedure) Regulations 1992. A review of the Meat Hygiene Appeals Tribunal for England and Wales is currently under way to ensure that it is still needed and that it is run in a responsive and effective way.

Second, special provision is made in respect of the competent authority charged with enforcement. In accordance with the overall policy on responsibilities of food authorities (see para **2.5.2**), district councils are charged with enforcement of most regulations aimed at the biological safety of food[3]. But with regard to meat, problems over unsatisfactory slaughterhouse standards led to the establishment in April 1995 of a centralised Meat Hygiene Service (MHS) aimed at making relevant enforcement more consistent and effective. As a result, the MHS now has responsibility for meat plant licensing and enforcement under the Fresh Meat Hygiene Regulations. Additionally, the MHS enforces hygiene controls in combined premises subject to the Minced Meat and Meat Preparations (Hygiene) Regulations 1995[4] and the Meat Products (Hygiene) Regulations 1994[5], as well as undertaking enforcement, in licensed slaughterhouses, of rules on welfare at slaughter[6] and, in licensed fresh meat premises, of controls over specified risk material[7] and other animal by-products[8]. As a result of continuing concerns about contamination of carcases, MHS enforcement practices were tightened in 1997. Monthly reports are published of MHS enforcement activity and of the scores of individual abattoirs and cutting plants under the objective, risk-based Hygiene Assessment System (HAS) used by the MHS to assess hygiene standards. Originally an executive agency of the Ministry of Agriculture, Fisheries and Food, the MHS and its functions in respect of England and Wales have been transferred to the Food Standards Agency under the Food Standards Act 1999[9].

Third, premises licensed under the Fresh Meat Hygiene Regulations are supervised by Official Veterinary Surgeons (OVSs)[10] henceforth designated by the Food Standards Agency. An OVS is empowered, subject to appeal by an aggrieved person, to prohibit the use of equipment or the use of part of the premises or reduce the rate of operations. They are also responsible for application of the health mark to meat fit for human consumption produced in the licensed premises. The designation of an OVS deemed unfit to perform the duties may be revoked or suspended.

In March 1999 the Government announced its need, for the purpose of complying fully with fresh meat Directive 64/433/EEC, to increase veterinary supervision particularly in small abattoirs. The MHS introduced a programme of incremental increases in supervision levels as additional veterinary resources became available, priority being given to premises (including low throughput premises with low HAS scores) thought to occasion the greatest risk to public health.

The meat hygiene rules have also recently been strengthened by the Meat (Enhanced Enforcement Powers) (England) Regulations 2000. Similar legislation is expected to be introduced for Wales. The Regulations amend the Fresh Meat (Hygiene and Inspection) Regulations 1995, the Poultrymeat, Farmed Game Bird Meat and Rabbit Meat (Hygiene and Inspection) Regulations 1995, the Meat Products (Hygiene) Regulations 1994, the Minced Meat and Meat Preparations (Hygiene) Regulations 1995, the Meat Hygiene Appeals Tribunal (Procedure) Regulations 1992 and the Products of Animal Origin (Import and Export) Regulations 1996. The main features of the new Regulations in respect of licensed premises are—

- powers to stop an operation or prohibit a process, and to seize meat which has not been produced in accordance with meat hygiene Regulations;
- powers to suspend licences in the event of a serious and immediate threat to public health, or failure to respond to progressive enforcement action;
- the speeding up of the appeals procedure. Operators will have 21 days, instead of 28, to confirm their decision to appeal;
- outside licensed premises, local authority enforcement officers will be able to seize meat which has been illegally produced (for example, from carcases that have not been inspected and health marked) and prosecute those selling or supplying it.

There is also a new requirement for occupiers of licensed premises to identify their key business personnel and notify subsequent changes, as well as clarification of record keeping requirements.

The proceedings of the Government/Industry Working Group on Meat Hygiene set up following the 1997 Pennington Report[11] might usefully be mentioned here. In particular, following the Pennington recommendation that HACCP principles be enshrined in the review and consolidation of the vertical Community Directives[12], the Group has advocated that slaughtering plants producing fresh, poultry and game meat should voluntarily adopt full HACCP plans and that the MHS should publish an annual record of those doing so. The Group is also pursuing initiatives to publicise the Government's clean livestock policy[13], to reduce salmonella and campylobacter in poultry flocks, to investigate the advantages of end-process treatments and to foster training.

1 See para **13.1.3** above.
2 Fresh Meat (Hygiene and Inspection) Regulations 1995, reg 6(2), the Poultrymeat and Rabbit Meat (Hygiene and Inspection) Regulations 1995, reg 6(2) and the Wild Game Meat (Hygiene and Inspection) Regulations 1995, reg 5(2).
3 Enforcement in relation to milk production holdings and raw drinking milk is a central Government function. See para **13.9.1** below.
4 See para **13.5.1** below.
5 See para **13.6.1** below.

6 Welfare of Animals (Slaughter or Killing) Regulations 1995, SI 1995/731, implementing Directive 93/497/EEC.
7 See paras **13.8.2** and **16.9.3** below.
8 See the Animal By-Products (Identification) Regulations 1995 and the Animal By-Products Order 1999; and para **13.1.1** above.
9 See the Food Standards Act 1999 (Transitional and Consequential Provisions and Savings) (England and Wales) Regulations 2000.
10 As to the Community obligation to appoint an 'official veterinarian', see *Ministry of Agriculture, Fisheries and Food v Webbs Country Foods Ltd* [1998] Eu LR 359.
11 See para **12.2.2** above.
12 See paras **12.2.1**, **13.1.1** and **13.1.2** above.
13 See para **13.2.1** below.

Conditions for import of products of animal origin for human consumption and their implemention

13.1.5 In addition to the Directives on hygienic production of products of animal origin for human consumption, other Community instruments specify public and animal health conditions for their importation. From the Community's point of view, 'importation' essentially refers to products from third countries, a major objective of the internal market having been the replacement of veterinary checks at the Community's internal frontiers with checks at the place of dispatch. However, importation into the United Kingdom from elsewhere in the Community still has some significance. For example, outbreaks of animal disease in Member States of origin will call for temporary restrictions on intra-Community trade and Member States of destination are in any event permitted to carry out non-discriminatory spot checks at places of final destination and checks at any point during transit if it is suspected that there has been a breach of the rules for production and placing on the market.

This chapter notes the principal legislation imposing health conditions on import in relation to the respective categories of products of animal origin. Further Community Decisions specify matters such as the third countries and third country establishments from which particular products are imported.

Pending enactment of all necessary specific legislation to implement the import conditions, licences under the Importation of Animal Products and Poultry Products Order 1980 have temporarily been used in Great Britain for the purpose[1]. The Imported Food Regulations 1984 impose health marking and certification requirements for imported meat and meat products[2] and implementing provision has also been made for particular products by the Fresh Meat (Import Conditions) Regulations 1996[3], the Miscellaneous Products of Animal Origin (Import Conditions) Regulations 1999[4] and regulation 22 of the Dairy Products (Hygiene) Regulations 1995[5]. It now seems likely that the opportunity afforded by the revocation and replacement of the Products of Animal Origin (Import and Export) Regulations 1996[6] will be used to replace the licensing arrangements with a direct general requirement that importers must comply with relevant conditions.

1 SI 1980/14 as amended. As to general import licensing systems, see, for example, case C-235/91 *Commission v Ireland* [1992] ECR I-5933.
2 The 1984 Regulations are disapplied in relation to fresh meat. See para **13.2.2** below.
3 See para **13.2.2** below.
4 See para **13.13.1** below.
5 See para **13.9.2** below.
6 See para **13.1.1** above.

Charges for inspections of products of animal origin

13.1.6 As amended and consolidated by Directive 96/43/EC, Directive 85/73/EEC provides for the financing of veterinary inspections covered by veterinary checks Directives 89/662/EEC, 90/425/EEC, 97/78/EC and 91/496EEC[1]. In Great Britain Directive 85/73/EEC is implemented by a series of Regulations providing for charging for inspections.

The Meat (Hygiene and Inspection) (Charges) Regulations 1998 implement the requirement to collect fees for inspections under the Fresh Meat Hygiene Regulations[2]. In pursuance of Article 4 of Directive 85/73/EEC, the Regulations also provide for a charge to be levied in relation to hygiene inspections at the slaughter of other animals and birds for which no standard charge is specified. The charges cover monitoring the welfare of animals slaughtered for human consumption in slaughterhouses under the Welfare of Animals (Slaughter or Killing) Regulations 1995, SI 1995/731.

As amended by the Meat (Hygiene and Inspection) (Charges) (Amendment) (England) Regulations 2000, the 1998 Regulations permit charges to be made for the carrying out of health inspections at repackaging centres and allow MHS inspection services to be withdrawn in the event of non-payment of hygiene inspection charges for which a court judgment has been obtained.

Part VI of the Products of Animal Origin (Import and Export) Regulations 1996, as amended by SI 1997/3023, implements the requirement in Annex A, Chapter II to Directive 85/73/EEC to charge for inspections of imports of products of animal origin from third countries.

The requirement in Annex A, Chapter III, Section II, paragraph 1 to Directive 85/73/EEC to charge for inspections on fishery products landings is implemented by Schedule 4A to the Food Safety (Fishery Products and Live Shellfish) (Hygiene) Regulations 1998, as amended by SI 1999/1585.

Somewhat anomalously, the charging required by Directive 85/73/EEC also extends to inspections for specified veterinary residues under Council Directive 96/23/EC. As noted in para **10.8.1**, the obligation in Article 2 of Directive 85/97/EEC to ensure fees are collected for these inspections is implemented by the Charges for Inspections and Controls Regulations 1997, as amended.

Charges are also made for inspections in respect of certain other products. Provision in respect of England and Wales, is made by the Dairy Products (Hygiene) (Charges) Regulations 1995 for specified charges in respect of sampling dairy farm visits. Charges for general dairy farm visits are to be terminated.

The Specified Risk Material (Inspection Charges) Regulations 1999 now enable inspection charges to be levied on occupiers of slaughterhouses and cutting premises at which specified risk material is removed from the carcases of cattle, sheep and goats[3]. However, a freeze in MHS charges for 1999–2000, announced in December 1999 by the Minister of Agriculture, Fisheries and Food, included postponement of charging in respect of specified risk material controls at least until April 2002[4].

The Bovines and Bovine Products (Trade) Regulations 1999, as amended, authorise the charging of reasonable fees in connection with the issue of health certificates, the application of marks and seals and the registration, approval and supervision of establishments under the Regulations[5].

1 See para **13.1.1** above.

2 See para **13.1.4** above. As to the validity of the obligation under fresh meat Directive 64/433/EEC for the costs of health inspections to be borne by the slaughterhouse at which the animals are slaughtered, see the European Court judgment of 15 April 1997 in case C-27/95 *Woodspring District Council v Bakers of Nailsea Ltd*. See also *Ministry of Agriculture, Fisheries and Food v Webbs Country Foods Ltd* [1998] Eu

LR 359 and European Court judgment of 9 September 1999 in case C-374/97 *Anton Feyrer v Landkreis Rottal-Inn*.
3 See para **13.8.2** below.
4 See MAFF Meat Hygiene Enforcement Report December 1999.
5 See para **13.8.5** below.

13.2 FRESH MEAT

Fresh meat production

13.2.1 Community health rules for the production and placing on the market of fresh meat intended for human consumption from bovine animals (including the species *Bubalus bubalis* and *Bison bison*), swine, sheep and goats, and domestic solipeds are laid down by Directive 64/433/EEC[1]. Sometimes known as the Red Meat Directive, this legislation was re-enacted with substantial modifications by Directive 91/497/EEC so as to apply not only to intra-Community, but also to national trade.

The Directive is implemented in Great Britain by the Fresh Meat (Hygiene and Inspection) Regulations 1995, as amended, which also in part implement Directive 91/495/EEC (concerning public health and animal health problems affecting the production and placing on the market of rabbit meat and farmed game meat)[2] and Directive 92/45/EEC (on public health and animal health problems relating to the killing of wild game and the placing on the market of wild-game meat)[3].

The Fresh Meat Regulations extend to the meat of all parts of animals which are suitable for human consumption, including chilled or frozen meat, which has not undergone any preserving process and includes meat vacuum wrapped or wrapped in a controlled atmosphere.

For the purposes of the Regulations, 'farmed game' is defined as wild land mammals which are reared and slaughtered in captivity, excluding—

(a) mammals of the family *Leporidae*; and
(b) wild land mammals living within an enclosed territory under conditions of freedom similar to those enjoyed by wild game.

Thus, only large farmed game animals such as deer and boar are included in the expression.

Specific provision is made in respect of the dressing, cutting up and storage of wild game meat, the definitions of this expression and of 'wild game', 'wild game meat', 'large wild game', and 'small wild game' being adopted from the Wild Game (Meat Hygiene and Inspection) Regulations 1995[4].

The Regulations do not apply to premises where fresh meat is used only for production of meat products, meat preparations, minced meat or mechanically recovered meat; to premises where fresh meat is cut up or stored for sale to the final consumer from those premises; to premises used for carcase competitions, or to cold stores handling only packaged meat or for sale to the final consumer; or to fresh meat intended for exhibitions, special studies or analysis, for sale to international organisations, or otherwise than for human consumption. Proposals are currently under consideration for Meat Hygiene (Cold Stores) (England) Regulations 2000 that will require cold stores which handle only pre-packaged meat to be licensed.

The sale of fresh meat for human consumption is prohibited unless it has been obtained from licensed premises, has met the hygiene requirements specified in the Schedules, is health marked and is accompanied by a commercial document or health certificate[5]. Extra conditions are specified for meat consigned to EEA States[6] other than Iceland.

Separate provisions concern the admission to and detention in slaughterhouses and farmed game processing facilities of animals and carcases. Important among these provisions is the power to require detention and cleaning of animals which are so dirty as to prevent hygienic dressing operations. In March 1997 following the Scottish E coli outbreak[7], the MHS implemented a policy, specifically endorsed by the Pennington Report, for ensuring the cleanliness of animals presented for slaughter. MHS guidance issued for this purpose defines contamination according to five categories and specifies the action to be taken in each case.

Licences for the operation of slaughterhouses, cutting premises, repackaging centres, cold stores, farmed game handling facilities and farmed game processing facilities are granted by the central Government[8]. Different structural requirements are prescribed for low throughput slaughterhouses, cutting premises and farmed game processing facilities and conditions specified for the slaughter of farmed game at farmed game handling facilities.

Slaughterhouses and farmed game handling facilities may be used for the slaughter of animals not intended for human consumption only in emergency situations or in accordance with a Community slaughter scheme.

Official veterinary surgeons appointed by central Government supervise licensed premises assisted by inspectors. They may, subject to appeal by aggrieved persons, prohibit the use of equipment or the use of part of the premises or reduce the rate of operations. They may also in specified circumstances prohibit the slaughter or the dressing of an animal in a slaughterhouse and permit an animal to be kept in a lairage in exceptional circumstances for more than 72 hours.

1 As to the validity of Directive 64/433/EEC in so far as it requires and/or permits Member States to require health inspections at slaughterhouses to be carried out by official veterinarians and/or in so far as it requires ante mortem inspections to be carried out, see the European Court judgment of 15 April 1997 in case C-27/95 *Woodspring District Council v Bakers of Nailsea Ltd.* See also *Ministry of Agriculture, Fisheries and Food v Webbs Country Foods Ltd* [1998] Eu LR 359.
2 See further section **13.3** below.
3 See further section **13.4** below.
4 See para **13.4.1** below.
5 See para **13.1.3** above.
6 See para **1.9.1** above.
7 See para **12.2.2** above.
8 See para **13.1.4** above.

Fresh meat import conditions

13.2.2 Further provision in pursuance of Community law is made by the Fresh Meat (Import Conditions) Regulations 1996. They implement Directive 72/461/EEC (on health problems affecting intra-Community trade in fresh meat), Directive 72/462/EEC (on health and veterinary inspection problems upon importation of bovine, ovine and caprine animals and swine and fresh meat or meat products from third countries) and Directive 94/59/EEC which amends Directive 77/96/EEC (on the examination for Trichinae upon importation from third countries of fresh meat derived from domestic swine).

The Regulations generally apply to fresh meat from bovine animals, swine, sheep, goats and solipeds for human consumption. They prohibit importation into Great Britain of fresh meat to which a Community non-importation decision applies. Also prohibited are the importation of fresh meat from an EEA State other than Iceland unless, in particular, obtained in accordance with Directive 72/461/EEC and from a listed approved establishment, and of fresh meat from a third country unless, in particular, obtained in accordance with Directive 72/462/EEC and with the Community Decisions relevant to that country.

Specified exceptions are provided in respect of fresh meat for the crew and passengers on board international transport, personal imports, fresh meat imported under authorisation, or for international organisations or visiting forces and provision is made for importation and treatment of samples and their packaging.

Provision is also made for the transhipment through, and storage in, Great Britain, of fresh meat consigned from a third country to an EEA State other than the United Kingdom.

The Importation of Animal Products and Poultry Products Order and the Imported Food Regulations 1984 are disapplied in relation to fresh meat[1].

1 See para **13.1.5** above.

Farmed game meat import conditions

13.2.3 For rabbit meat and farmed game meat, Chapters II and III respectively of Directive 91/495/EEC lay down public and animal health provisions applicable to Community trade. Animal and public health conditions and veterinary certification for imports from third countries are prescribed by Directive 92/118/EEC Annex I, Chapter 11 and by Decision 97/219/EEC.

13.3 POULTRYMEAT, FARMED GAME BIRD MEAT AND RABBIT MEAT

Poultrymeat, farmed game bird meat and rabbit meat production

13.3.1 The Poultrymeat, Farmed Game Bird Meat and Rabbit Meat (Hygiene and Inspection) Regulations 1995, as amended, mainly implement Directive 71/118/EEC (on health problems affecting trade in fresh poultrymeat), as updated by Directive 92/116/EEC. They also in part implement Directive 91/494/EEC (on animal health conditions governing intra-Community trade in and imports from third countries of fresh poultrymeat); Directive 91/495/EEC (concerning public health and animal health problems affecting the production and placing on the market of rabbit meat and farmed game meat); and Directive 92/45/EEC (on public health and animal health problems relating to the killing of wild game and the placing on the market of wild game meat).

The Regulations define—

'poultry' as domestic fowls, turkeys, guinea fowl, ducks and geese;

'farmed game birds' as birds, including ratites, but excluding poultry, which are not generally considered domestic but which are bred, reared and slaughtered in captivity; and

'rabbit' as a domestic rabbit.

'Meat' is to be understood as meaning all parts of these birds or rabbits which are fit for human consumption and 'fresh', as applied to meat, means all meat including chilled or frozen meat, which has not undergone any preserving process and includes meat vacuum wrapped or wrapped in a controlled atmosphere.

Specific provision is made to permit dead small wild game to be brought into a slaughterhouse subject to licensing in accordance with the Wild Game (Meat Hygiene and

Inspection) Regulations 1995 and the definitions of 'small wild game' and 'wild game meat' are adopted from those Regulations[1].

The Regulations do not apply to specified premises preparing fresh meat for sale direct to the final consumer; farmers with an annual production of less than 10,000 birds or farmers or producers with an annual production of less than 10,000 rabbits; cold stores which handle only fresh meat which is packaged; fresh meat intended for exhibitions, special studies or analysis, or for sale to international organisations; or fresh meat not intended for human consumption.

The sale of fresh meat is prohibited unless various conditions are complied with. The meat must be obtained from a licensed slaughterhouse, cutting premises, a cold store or a re-wrapping centre, must have been chilled, prepared, stored, wrapped and transported under specified hygienic conditions, must be health marked and must be accompanied during transportation by a health certificate or commercial document[2].

Extra conditions are specified for meat consigned to EEA States[3] other than Iceland.

Proposals are currently under consideration for Meat Hygiene (Cold Stores) (England) Regulations 2000 that will require cold stores which handle only pre-packaged meat to be licensed.

Central government is responsible for licensing premises and for the designation of OVSs to supervise them with the assistance of inspectors[4]. OVSs may in particular prohibit slaughter in specified circumstances or reduce the rate of operations. OVSs also supervise persons employed at licensed premises who are authorised to act as plant inspection assistants.

Subject to a specified exception, the regulations prohibit the use of a slaughterhouse for slaughtering a bird or rabbit not intended for sale for human consumption.

Further amendments to the Regulations are also expected in 2000—

(a) to restrict the exemption for those producing under 10,000 birds per annum to on-farm production only, and to farmers and producers of under 10,000 rabbits per annum supplying rabbit meat directly to individuals for their own consumption or to local retailers;
(b) to permit the 'hot-skinning' of quail for the domestic market only; and
(c) to make other changes for the better implementation of Directive 71/118/EEC.

1 See para **13.4.1** below.
2 See para **13.1.3** above.
3 See para **1.9.1** above.
4 See para **13.1.4** above.

Fresh poultrymeat import conditions

13.3.2 In respect of fresh poultrymeat, the principal provisions concerning the marketing in the United Kingdom of Community production are prescribed by Chapter II of Directive 71/118/EEC (as amended in particular by Directive 92/116/EEC), to which Chapter II of Directive 91/494/EEC adds further rules governing intra-Community trade. Chapter III of Directives 71/118/EEC and 91/494/EEC respectively lay down conditions for imports from third countries.

Rabbit meat import conditions

13.3.3 Conditions for the import of rabbit meat are prescribed by the Community instruments noted in para **13.2.3** above.

Farmed game bird meat import conditions

13.3.4 Conditions for the import of farmed game bird meat are prescribed by the Community instruments noted in para **13.2.3** above.

13.4 WILD GAME MEAT

Wild game meat production

13.4.1 Directive 92/45/EEC (on public health and animal health problems relating to the killing of wild game and the placing on the market of wild-game meat) is principally implemented by the Wild Game Meat (Hygiene and Inspection) Regulations 1995, as amended[1]. The Regulations define—

'wild game' as (a) wild land mammals which are hunted (including wild mammals within an enclosed area under conditions of freedom similar to those enjoyed by wild game); and (b) wild birds;

'large wild game' as wild ungulates;

'small wild game' as wild mammals of the *Leporidae* family and wild birds intended for human consumption; and

'wild-game meat' as all parts of wild game which are suitable for human consumption and which have not undergone any preserving process other than chilling, freezing, vacuum wrapping or wrapping in a controlled atmosphere.

Provision is made for the control of 'wild game processing facilities' which are establishments used for the purpose of dressing or cutting up wild game, the meat from which is intended for sale for human consumption. Subject to some exceptions, wild game meat consigned to EEA States[2] other than Iceland for human consumption must be obtained from licensed wild game processing facilities, a cold store or re-wrapping centre. Licences are granted by the central Government if the premises comply with prescribed requirements as to structure and operation. Establishments already licensed under the Fresh Meat (Hygiene and Inspection) Regulations 1995[3] or the Poultrymeat, Farmed Game Bird Meat and Rabbit Meat (Hygiene and Inspection) Regulations 1995[4] do not need to comply separately with the requirements as to structure. The wild game meat must be health marked, meet specified hygiene requirements and be accompanied during transportation by a commercial document or health certificate[5]. Further conditions are specified in relation to the fitness of the meat for human consumption. Licensed premises are supervised by OVSs designated by central Government[6]. OVSs are empowered, subject to appeal by an aggrieved person, to prohibit the use of equipment or the use of part of the premises or reduce the rate of operations. They are also responsible for application of the health mark to wild game meat fit for human consumption produced in the licensed premises. The designation of an OVS deemed unfit to perform the duties may be revoked or suspended. Persons employed at the premises may also be authorised to act as plant inspection assistants.

1 The Fresh Meat (Hygiene and Inspection) Regulations 1995 and the Poultrymeat, Farmed Game Bird Meat and Rabbit Meat (Hygiene and Inspection) Regulations 1995 also in part implement Directive 92/45/EEC.

2 See para **1.9.1** above.

3 See para **13.2.1** above.

4 See para **13.3.1** above.
5 See para **13.1.3** above.
6 See para **13.1.4** above.

Wild game meat import conditions

13.4.2 Wild game meat, public and animal health provisions applicable to Community trade and to imports into the Community are laid down by Chapters II and III respectively of Directive 92/45/EEC. Animal and public health conditions and veterinary certification are prescribed by Decision 97/220/EC, for imports from third countries of wild swine meat, and by Decision 97/218/EC, for imports from third countries of other wild game meat.

13.5 MINCED MEAT AND MEAT PREPARATIONS

Minced meat and meat preparations production

13.5.1 Directive 94/65/EC laying down the requirements for the production and placing on the market of minced meat and meat preparations is implemented by the Minced Meat and Meat Preparations (Hygiene) Regulations 1995, as amended[1], which define—

'minced meat' as meat which has been minced into fragments or passed through a spiral screw mincer and includes such meat to which not more than 1 per cent salt has been added; and

'meat preparation' as meat to which foodstuffs, seasonings or additives have been added or which has undergone a treatment insufficient to modify its internal cellular structure and so alter its characteristics.

In the Regulations 'meat' is defined as parts of animals, excluding solipeds, or birds which are suitable for human consumption and have been – (a) produced in establishments licensed under, and given a health mark in accordance with, the Fresh Meat Regulations[2], the Poultrymeat Regulations[3] or the Wild Game Meat Regulations[4]; or (b) imported and examined in accordance with the Products of Animal Origin (Import and Export) Regulations 1996[5].

The central Government Guidance Notes on the enforcement of the Minced Meat and Meat Preparations (Hygiene) Regulations 1995 offer the following advice on the scope of the key definitions. Types of food which fall within the definition of meat preparations include raw sausages, burgers and flash fried products which are not fully cooked (for example chicken *cordon bleu).* Retail 'Barbecue Packs' which may include sausages, burgers, steaks and black puddings (regardless of their individual classification) should also be regarded as meat preparations. Packs which only contain fresh meat do not fall within the scope of the Regulations. Any pastry product which contains meat such as uncooked sausage rolls, or 'ready to cook' meals in which the meat has not been thoroughly heat treated or cooked prior to sale (for example partly cooked 'toad in the hole'), will also be regarded as meat preparations. Minced meat which contains any seasoning, more than 1% salt or other foodstuffs (for example haggis) should be considered to be a meat preparation. Burgers which have been formed from pure minced meat and which contain no other ingredients are also to be regarded as meat preparations. Any product prepared from or with meat which has undergone processing such that the cut surface shows that the product no longer has the characteristics of fresh meat will not fall within the scope of the Regulations (examples include bacon, pork pies, salami, fermented sausages or cooked meat sandwiches). The Meat Products (Hygiene) Regulations 1994[6] may apply to such foods.

The Regulations do not apply to premises producing or storing minced meat or meat preparations for direct sale from those premises to the final consumer, to the production of mechanically recovered meat[7] or to the production or sale of minced meat to be used as a raw material for the production of sausage meat destined for inclusion in a meat product.

The consignment of minced meat for human consumption to EEA States[8] other than Iceland is prohibited unless derived from bovine animals, pigs, sheep or goats, produced in approved premises in accordance with specified hygiene, compositional, treatment, temperature[9], wrapping and transportation requirements. The meat must be health marked and accompanied during transportation by a commercial document and, if from a restricted district or for transport through a third country, also by a health certificate. Provided minced meat is not health marked, the conditions for its sale in Great Britain are less stringent. For example, it may be produced in registered, rather than approved premises.

With relevant changes, parallel provision is made for meat preparations produced for the EEA and national markets respectively. The central Government guidance advises that the Regulations have been drafted on the basis that the requirement in the Directive[10] for meat preparations traded with another EEA State to be accompanied by a health certificate is an error. Traders are recommended to keep in touch with the appropriate Agricultural Departments.

Premises producing minced meat or meat preparations destined for the EEA market must be approved under the Regulations. Specified limited derogations are applicable in approving non-industrial premises, that is, any establishment whose total production of meat products and meat preparations does not exceed 7.5 tonnes per week and which does not produce minced meat.

Except in relation to combined premises, which are a central Government responsibility, food authorities are responsible for approval of premises and enforcement. They are required to provide information regarding the execution of their duties.

1 Guidance notes on the enforcement of the Minced Meat and Meat Preparations (Hygiene) Regulations 1995 have been issued by the Ministry of Agriculture, Fisheries and Food, the Department of Health, the Scottish Office and the Welsh Office.
2 See para **13.2.1** above.
3 See para **13.3.1** above.
4 See para **13.4.1** above.
5 See para **13.1.1** above.
6 See para **13.6.1** below.
7 See para **13.7.1** below.
8 See para **1.9.1** above.
9 See para **14.3.2**(d) below.
10 See Directive 94/65/EEC, Art 5(2)(f).

Minced meat and meat preparations import conditions

13.5.2 For minced meat and meat preparations, Chapters II, III and IV of Directive 94/65/EC lay down rules concerning the marketing of production from other Member States. Provisions for the import from third countries of minced meat and meat preparations are prescribed by Chapter V and by Decision 97/29/EC.

13.6 MEAT PRODUCTS AND OTHER PRODUCTS OF ANIMAL ORIGIN

Meat products and other products of animal origin: production

13.6.1 As part of the completion of the internal market, Directive 92/5/EEC substantially amended and updated Directive 77/99/EEC on health problems affecting intra-Community trade in meat products and certain other products of animal origin. These provisions are generally implemented by the Meat Products (Hygiene) Regulations 1994, as amended[1], although on 26 May 1999 the Commission commenced European Court proceedings against the United Kingdom alleging a failure to have fully implemented amending Directive 95/68/EC[2].

The 1994 Regulations define—

'meat products' as products for human consumption prepared from or with meat which has undergone treatment such that the cut surface shows that the product no longer has the characteristics of fresh meat, but not—

(a) meat which has undergone only cold treatment;

(b) minced meat;

(c) mechanically recovered meat[3];

(d) meat preparations;

'meat-based prepared meal' means a wrapped meat product (excluding sandwiches or products made with pastry, pasta or dough) in which meat has been mixed with other foodstuffs before, during or after cooking and requires refrigeration for preservation;

'other products of animal origin' as the following products intended for human consumption—

(a) meat extracts;

(b) rendered animal fat: fat derived from rendering meat, including bones;

(c) greaves: the protein-containing residue of rendering, after partial separation of fat and water;

(d) meat powder, powdered rind, salted or dried blood, salted or dried blood plasma;

(e) stomachs, bladders and intestines, cleaned, salted or dried, and/or heated.

In the Regulations 'meat' means meat as defined in Directives 64/433/EEC, 72/461/EEC, and 72/462/EEC[4], poultrymeat[5], rabbit meat[6], farmed game meat[7], wild game meat[8] and minced meat and meat preparations[9].

The statutory Code of Practice on enforcement of the Meat Products (Hygiene) Regulations 1994 offers the following advice on the scope of principal definitions. Of 'meat products', it says that products falling within the scope of the Regulations include cooked meats, meat pies, pizza containing meat, sandwiches containing cooked meats and cured products such as bacon. For the purposes of the Regulations, 'meat based prepared meals' are meat products which have been packaged with other foodstuffs (eg vegetables) and which require refrigeration or freezing for preservation. Examples include roast meat dishes with vegetables; and traditional cottage pies (minced meat with potatoes). Meat products made with pastry (eg meat pies), pasta (eg cannelloni, ravioli, lasagna), dough (eg pizza or sandwiches) are not regarded as meat based prepared meals. Similarly meat products such as 'honey roast hams' are not regarded as meat based prepared meals since they are merely glazed with honey. 'Other products of animal origin' only relate to first stage processing of certain materials derived from the slaughtering process and passed fit for human consumption. For example the rendering of animal fats into melted fat is covered, but subsequent processing of the melted fat into margarine is not covered by the Regulations.

The Regulations do not apply to establishments handling or storing meat products or other products of animal origin exclusively for sale from those establishments to the final consumer, or to the staff of such establishments or to the transporting of meat products to the final consumer.

The handling of meat products is prohibited in premises, other than ambient stores, rewrapping centres and cold stores, unless they are approved and comply with specified conditions as to hygienic structure and operation. Proposals are currently under consideration for Meat Hygiene (Cold Stores) (England) Regulations 2000 that will require cold stores which handle only pre-packaged meat products to be approved.

Meat products despatched from premises must comply with the Regulations and despatch to EEA States[10] other than Iceland must be from approved premises.

Approval conditions are prescribed for the handling of meat products which contain a small percentage of meat, for the pasteurisation or sterilisation of meat products in hermetically sealed containers, for the manufacture of meat-based prepared meals and for other handling of meat products.

Specified limited derogations are applicable in approving non-industrial premises, that is, meat products premises whose total production does not exceed 7.5 tonnes of finished meat products per week, or 1 tonne per week in the case of premises producing foie gras, or a lower level of production where a special hygiene direction is given.

Use of ambient stores, rewrapping centres and cold stores and the despatch of meat products to EEA States[10] other than Iceland is also subject to approval.

The Regulations specify conditions to be fulfilled in relation to the sale of meat products for human consumption, lay down requirements as to the wrapping and labelling of meat products and specify requirements as to indications of storage temperatures and durability and as to the storage and transportation of meat products.

Special conditions are prescribed for meat-based prepared meals in respect of which, at the time of writing, an amendment is proposed by Meat Product (Hygiene) (Amendment) (England) Regulations 2000 to specify the alternative cooling option explained in para **14.3.2**(f) below.

Meat products consigned to EEA States other than Iceland must generally carry the British EC health mark, or if imported, the EEA State or third country mark required by Community law. Meat products manufactured or rewrapped and sold in Great Britain must carry the British EC health mark or British national health mark.

The sale for human consumption of prepared food (other than a meat-based prepared meal) is restricted to specified circumstances.

Conditions are specified for the manufacture and sale of other products of animal origin. They must also be accompanied during transport by a commercial document specifying the premises of origin. However, they do not have to be health marked, nor do their production premises have to be approved. They must simply be registered under the Food Premises (Registration) Regulations 1991[11].

Except in relation to combined premises which are a central Government responsibility, food authorities are responsible for approving premises and enforcement. They are required to provide information regarding the execution of their duties.

1 Statutory Code of Practice no 17 and central Government notes to be read in conjunction with it give guidance on Enforcement of the Meat Products (Hygiene) Regulations 1994. This is updated by guidance notes to enforcement authorities on the Meat Products (Hygiene) (Amendment) Regulations 1999.

2 See case C-200/99 *Commission v United Kingdom* OJ C 226 7.8.99, p 18.
3 See section **13.7** below.
4 See Directive 64/433/EEC, Art 2(a), Directive 72/461/EEC, Art 1 and Directive 72/462/EEC, Art 1—section **13.2** above.
5 Directive 71/118/EEC, Art 2—para **13.3.1** above.
6 Directive 91/495/EEC, Art 2(1)—see para **13.3.1** above.
7 Directive 91/495/EEC, Art 2(2)—see paras **13.2.1** and **13.3.1** above.
8 Directive 92/45/EEC, Art 2(1)(d)—see paras **13.2.1** and **13.4.1** above.
9 Directive 94/65/EEC, Art 2—see para **13.5.1** above.
10 See para **1.9.1** above.
11 See para **12.3.1** above.

Meat products and other products of animal origin: import conditions

13.6.2 Directive 77/99/EEC, as amended in particular by Directive 92/5/EC, lays down rules concerning the marketing of meat products and other products of animal origin for human consumption from other Member States, further provision with regard to animal health problems affecting intra-Community trade being made by Directive 80/215/EEC.

With regard to imports from third countries, animal health conditions and model veterinary certificates are laid down by Decision 97/221/EC and, for meat products obtained from poultrymeat, farmed game meat, wild game meat and rabbit meat, public health conditions are prescribed by Directive 92/118/EEC Annex II, Chapter 1 and by Decision 97/41/EC.

13.7 MECHANICALLY RECOVERED MEAT

Mechanically recovered meat production

13.7.1 Article 21 of the minced meat and meat preparations Directive 94/65/EC imposed on the Council the duty to lay down by 1 January 1996 health rules applicable to the production and use of mechanically recovered meat (MRM). No such hygiene Directive having yet been made, it seems likely that the necessary rules will now form part of the proposed consolidation of the hygiene Directives referred to in para **12.2.1**. The Commission's draft for the consolidated Regulation[1] defines 'mechanically separated/recovered meat' as 'the product obtained after recovery or separation by mechanical means of residual meat left on the bones after deboning'.

In advance of full harmonising rules for MRM, some provision is made by Community law. Article 6(1)(c) and (g) of Directive 64/433/EEC require Member States to ensure that MRM undergoes heat treatment in accordance with Directive 77/99/EEC and that the treatment is carried out in the establishment of origin or in any other designated establishment[2]. Article 1(3) of Directive 94/65/EC states that the Directive shall not apply to MRM for industrial use which undergoes heat treatment in establishments approved in accordance with the meat products Directive 77/99/EEC[3], while Article 17 amends the fresh poultrymeat Directive 71/118[4] and the rabbit and farmed game meat Directive 91/495[5] to require that MRM may be traded between Member States only if it has previously undergone heat treatment in accordance with Directive 77/99/EEC in the establishment of origin or any other establishment designated by the competent authority.

In Great Britain regulation 13(1)(k) of the Fresh Meat (Hygiene and Inspection) Regulations 1995 requires MRM to be handled in accordance with Directive 77/99/EEC and, as indicated above, the Minced Meat and Meat Preparations (Hygiene) Regulations 1995[6] provide that the Regulations shall not apply to the production of MRM, which is defined as—

'meat which—

(a) comes from residual meat on the bones apart from
 (i) the bones of the head; and
 (ii) the extremities of the limbs below the carpal and tarsal joints and, in the case of swine, the coccygeal vertebrae;
(b) has been obtained by mechanical means; and
(c) has been passed through a fine mesh such that its cellular structure has been broken down and it flows in puree form.'

It should also be noted that the Specified Risk Material Regulations 1997 control the production of mechanically recovered meat from ruminant animals[7] and that Beef Bones Regulations 1997, as amended[8], prohibit the use of bones and bone-in-beef for manufactured and processed products.

1 Commission working document EN VI/1881/98-Rev 2-partie 0 (III/5227/98-Rev 4).
2 As to heat treatment of MRM in a Member State of importation, see European Court judgment of 15 April 1997 in case C105/95 *Paul Daut GmbH & Co KG v Oberkreisdirektor des Kreises Gütersloh*.
3 See para **13.6.1** above.
4 See para **13.3.1** above.
5 See paras **13.2.1** and **13.3.1** above.
6 See para **13.5.1** above. The central government Guidance notes on the enforcement of the Minced Meat and Meat Preparations (Hygiene) Regulations 1995 comment on the problems of MRM.
7 See para **13.8.2** below.
8 See para **13.8.3** below.

13.8 BOVINE SPONGIFORM ENCEPHALOPATHY

Bovine spongiform encephalopathy: general

13.8.1 BSE is a disease of cattle first identified in 1986. It causes microscopic holes in the brains of infected animals, which become uncoordinated, nervous and eventually die. Since 1988 a series of national and Community measures has been enacted to combat this disease by slaughter of animals, bans on potentially infected material in food, feedingstuffs and fertiliser, processing animal waste, cattle identification, marking and breeding records and trade restrictions. Control activity intensified after the opinion in March 1996 from the Government's Spongiform Encephalopathy Advisory Committee (SEAC) that the most likely cause of a new variant of the human Creutzfeldt-Jakob disease (nvCJD) was exposure to BSE before the 1989 prohibition of the use of specified bovine offals in food. In September 1997 the SEAC concluded that recent research provided compelling evidence that the agent which causes BSE is identical to the agent which causes nvCJD in humans[1]. In response to these serious health imperatives, the United Kingdom has taken a variety of measures. In addition to enacting its own provisions, it has been required to comply with a Community ban on exports of bovine animals, meat and derived products to other Member States and third countries[2] and to introduce other measures to satisfy pre-conditions, agreed at Florence in June 1996 by the European Council, for the lifting of the ban[3].

A full survey of the BSE countermeasures is beyond the scope of this book: the description which follows concentrates on the direct provisions for public health. The controls on feeding stuffs are dealt with in section **16.9** below.

1 See in particular recital (1) to Council Decision 98/256/EC and Commission Decision 98/272/EC.
2 See Commission Decision 96/239/EC and the European Court judgments of 5 May 1998 in case C-80/96 *UK v Commission* and case C-157/96 *Regina v MAFF, ex p NFU and others*. Commission Decision 96/239/EC has now been replaced by Commission Decision 98/256/EC (see para **13.8.5** below).
3 See Decision 96/385/EC approving the plan for the control and eradication of bovine spongiform encephalopathy in the United Kingdom.

Specified risk material

13.8.2 Legislation forbidding the use in food of material which might potentially harbour BSE infectivity has been progressively tightened and extended since specified bovine offals were first banned in 1989. The current provisions are contained in the Specified Risk Material Regulations 1997, as amended, which implement in part—

(a) Decision 94/474/EC concerning certain protection measures relating to BSE; and
(b) the provisions relating to animal waste of Directive 90/667/EEC laying down the veterinary rules for the disposal of animal waste, for its placing on the market and for the prevention of pathogens in feedingstuffs of animal or fish origin.

Together with the Specified Risk Material Order 1997 which relates to feeding stuffs[1], these Regulations were made after Commission Decision 97/534/EC laid down Community-wide controls on specified material in cattle, sheep and goats. Objections from Member States, in the event, meant that the Decision did not come into force. However, the United Kingdom government concluded that, in the interests of public health, the removal of specified risk material from all food and animal feed, including imported products should be required without delay. Unilateral controls were therefore introduced in the 1997 Order and Regulations pending the adoption of Community measures. At the time of writing, Decision 97/534/EC has been deferred by Decision 1999/881/EC for a further period until 30 June 2000. The Commission's White Paper on Food Safety[2] proposes that Decision 97/534 should be replaced.

The Regulations generally prohibit the sale, use and sale for use for human consumption of 'specified risk material'. This broadly comprises—

- in respect of cattle, the head (except the tongue) and the spinal cord, tonsils and spleen from animals over six months old and the thymus and intestines from animals of any age;
- in respect of sheep and goats, the head (except the horns and tongue) and spleen and the tonsils and spinal cord, from animals over 12 months old; and
- specified solid waste.

The prohibition on the sale and use of specified risk material for human consumption does not apply to certain sheep carcases for export or to two categories of food containing specified risk material derived only from animals which were slaughtered or have died outside the United Kingdom. These categories are food not listed in Schedule 1 to the Specified Risk Material Order 1997 and food which, although listed, has been imported in accordance with article 6 of the Order.

The Regulations also prohibit the use of mechanically recovered meat from the vertebral columns of ruminant animals and require premises on which meat is recovered by mechanical means from such animals to be registered.

Requirements are laid down for the initial treatment of specified risk material and the rendering of whole carcases. The Regulations prohibit the removal of the brain and eyes from a bovine animal and the removal of the spinal cord from a ruminant animal.

Particular provision is made for sheep and goats. Requirements are specified as to the marking of young animals with a young lamb stamp, the transport of unmarked carcases of sheep and goats, the presence of OVSs, authorised officers, inspectors and meat technicians at slaughterhouses and the possession of unmarked carcases of sheep and goats. The procedure for bringing in specified risk material from Northern Ireland is prescribed.

The consignment of specified risk material once it has been collected and removed from the carcase is regulated and the approval is required of collection centres, incinerators, rendering plants and other premises that process bovine material. Further provision is made concerning veterinary and laboratory premises, directions, transport, storage and savings of approvals granted in respect of food premises under the Specified Bovine Material Order 1997.

1 See para **16.9.3** below.
2 Com (1999) 719 final.

Meat from cattle over 30 months old

13.8.3 Following the identification of nvCJD in the SEAC report of March 1996, the Government decided, as an extra precautionary measure, henceforth to ban the sale of meat from cattle over the age of 30 months. Enacted at first by emergency control order under section 13 of the Food Safety Act 1990 (FSA 1990)[1], the prohibition is now to be found in the Fresh Meat (Beef Controls) (No 2) Regulations 1996. The Regulations continue to make it an offence to sell for human consumption meat derived from bovine animals slaughtered after 29 March 1996 in which, at the time of slaughter, there were more than two permanent incisors erupted, unless it can be shown by reference to specified documentary evidence that at the time of slaughter the animal was no more than two years and six months. There are exemptions from this prohibition for meat from bovine animals which were born, reared and slaughtered in any of the countries specified in Schedule 2 and for meat from bovine animals which belong to a herd registered under the Beef Assurance Scheme established under the Regulations.

The Government has very recently accepted the SEAC's interim conclusions that there should be no change in the over 30 months rule but that the Committee should continue to keep it under review[2].

1 See para **11.6.4** above.
2 See MAFF/DH Food Safety Information Bulletin February 2000.

Beef on the bone

13.8.4 In December 1997 on-going experimental work by the Ministry of Agriculture, Fisheries and Food detected a risk to public health from BSE infectivity in dorsal root ganglia. Notwithstanding the SEAC's advice that the risk was very small, the Government decided to take further precautionary action in the Beef Bones Regulations 1997 to require all meat from cattle over six months old to be de-boned before sale[1]. The Regulations were amended by the Beef Bones (Amendment) (England) Regulations 1999 and the Beef Bones (Amendment) (Wales) Regulations 1999 so as to confine the ban in England and Wales to the use of bones and bone-in-beef for manufactured and processed products.

As thus amended, the Regulations prohibit the use of bone-in beef in the preparation in the course of a business of food or ingredients for human consumption and the sale of bones removed from beef in Great Britain for such use. The sale of food containing bones removed in Great Britain or their derivatives, or the sale or use of derivatives is also prohibited. The prohibitions do not, however, prevent the retail sale of bone-in-beef or beef bones; their use or (subject to conditions) the use of derived substances in the production of food at catering and take-away premises; or (subject to conditions) catering and take-away sales of food containing beef bones or their derivatives.

The Regulations also provides for separate storage of bones and substances and for record keeping by persons deboning beef at food premises.

1 As to the legality of the 1997 prohibition on use of bone-in-beef in the preparation of food, see the Scottish High Court of Judiciary's judgment of 26 June 1998 in *MacNeill v Sutherland*.

Export of bovine products

13.8.5 The Bovines and Bovine Products (Trade) Regulations 1999, as amended, implement Decision 98/256/EC (in relation to the despatch to third countries and other Member States of bovine animals and embryos and meat, other products and by-products derived from bovine animals) as amended by Decisions 98/564/EC and 98/692/EC.

Despatch abroad is generally prohibited, but the Regulations, together with the equivalent Regulations in Northern Ireland[1], make provision for derogations in respect of—

(a) amino acids, peptides, tallow and tallow products produced in registered establishments from UK-slaughtered animals;
(b) Northern Irish meat and products eligible for the Export Certified Herd Scheme (ECHS)[2]; and
(c) United Kingdom meat and products eligible for the Date Based Export Scheme (DBES)[3].

The Regulations also make provision for the despatch abroad of specified meat and products ('foreign origin export eligible goods') and by-products produced in Great Britain from imported beef.

The ECHS is confined to Northern Ireland produce and outside the scope of this book. However, it might be noted that, by contrast with the DBES, it depends in practice on the Northern Irish official computer database which has been recording the movements of each animal during life.

The DBES relies on the fact that animals born after 1 April 1996 have not been fed mammalian meat and bone meal[4]. Because the only known risk of BSE infection after that date is through maternal transmission, export under the scheme is conditional on the slaughter of offspring of bovine animals in which BSE has been confirmed. That condition was met by the BSE Offspring Slaughter Regulations 1998, SI 1998/3070. By Commission Decision 1999/514/EC, 1 August 1999 was fixed as the date on which despatch under the DBES might commence.

Deboned fresh meat and products derived from bovine animals slaughtered in the United Kingdom may now be dispatched from the United Kingdom when obtained from DBES-eligible animals born after 1 August 1996. To be eligible, each animal must have been clearly identifiable throughout its life by official passport or computerised identification; it must be more than 6 months but no more than 30 months of age; positive official evidence must be obtained that the dam has lived for more than six months after its birth; and the dam must neither have contracted BSE nor be suspected of having done so.

Slaughterhouses for DBES-eligible animals must not be used for ineligible animals and, under the 1999 Regulations, must be approved by the minister. The Regulations also provide for the approval, in particular, of establishments used for the production of DBES goods and foreign origin export eligible goods. Prescribed marks, additional to the Community health mark, must be applied to ECHS and DBES meat and products and foreign origin export eligible goods for despatch abroad.

The provisions authorising charging of reasonable fees are noted at para **13.1.6** above.

At the time of writing, two cases are proceeding in the European Court about the continuing French ban on British beef in defiance of Community law. In case C-514/99, France claims that the Court should annul the Commission decision refusing to modify or cancel Decision 1999/514/EC[5]. In case C-1/00, the Commission is seeking a declaration that France is in breach of the EC Treaty by refusing to adopt the measures necessary to comply with Decisions 98/256/EC, as amended, and 1999/514/EC[6].

The German Bundesrat voted on 17 March 2000 to lift its import ban on UK beef.

1 Bovines and Bovine Products (Trade) Regulations (Northern Ireland) 1998, SR 1998/163.
2 See Decision 98/256/EC, as amended, Art 6 and Annex II.
3 See Decision 98/256/EC, as amended, Art 6 and Annex III.
4 See para **16.9.2** below.
5 See OJ C 63 4.3.2000, p 18.
6 See OJ C 63 4.3.2000, p 19.

Labelling of beef and beef products

13.8.6 In an effort to remedy the fall in consumer confidence and destabilisation of the beef market caused by the BSE crisis, Council Regulation 820/97/EC was enacted to establish a system for the identification and registration of bovine animals. Provisions in and under Title I and the British implementing Cattle Identification Regulations 1998, SI 1998/871, directly concerned the identification and registration of bovine animals and related to food only insofar as they provided the evidential backing for Title II. This made provision for the labelling of beef and beef products. Detailed rules for the application of Title II were laid down by Commission Regulation 1141/97/EC, as amended, and provision for its enforcement in Great Britain was made by the Beef Labelling (Enforcement) Regulations 1998.

Until the end of 1999, the beef labelling scheme operated in Great Britain under Regulation 820/97/EC was wholly voluntary. Operators and organisations wishing to label beef at the point of sale in such a way as to provide information concerning the origin or certain characteristics or production conditions of the labelled meat or the animal from which it derives were required to do so in accordance with Title II. Prior approval had to be obtained for a specification indicating the information to be included on the label, the measures to be taken to ensure the accuracy of the information, the control system to be applied and, in the case of organisations, the measures to be taken in relation to members failing to comply with the specification. A link between the identification of the meat and the animal or animals concerned had to be ensured by the specification and by a reference number or code on the label. Limitations were placed on information that might be given on the label about the animal from which the beef originated.

Meanwhile the Commission, with the support of the European Parliament, sought annulment of Regulation 820/97/EC by the European Court[1]. Because the Regulation had been decided in the context of the BSE crisis, they allege that it concerns public health and should have been founded on Article 95 (ex Article 100A) EC, not on Article 37 (ex 43) EC as part of the common agricultural policy. It will be recalled from paras **1.7.3** and **1.7.4** above that the European Parliament makes legislation jointly with the Council under Article 95, but is entitled only to be consulted on legislation under Article 37. In his Opinion of 18 May 1999 Advocate General Saggio advised the European Court that Regulation 820/97/EC should be annulled for failing to comply with both Articles, but that its legal effects should be maintained until entry into force of a new Regulation made on a proper legal basis.

On 21 December 1999, as required by Article 19 of Regulation 820/97/EC, the Council enacted Regulation 2772/1999/EC to provide for a compulsory beef labelling system from 1 January 2000 onwards. However, it provided for Regulation 2772/1999/EC to apply only on a provisional basis until 31 August 2000 'to enable the European Parliament and the Council to come to a decision on the proposal for a Regulation, establishing a system for the identification and registration of bovine animals and regarding the labelling of beef and beef products, and repealing Regulation 820/97/EC, presented by the Commission on 13 October 1999'.

By Regulation 2772/1999/EC operators and organisations marketing beef are required to label it with the compulsory indications referred to in Article 3(1) of general labelling Directive 79/112/EC[2], with the exception of the particulars of the place of origin or provenance; the indications referred to in Regulations 1208/81/EEC and 1186/90/EEC determining and extending the Community scale for the classification of carcases of adult bovine animals; and the indications relating to the health mark provided for in Directive 64/433/EEC and similar indications provided for in the relevant veterinary legislation[3]. Under Regulation 2772/1999/EC, the pre-2000 voluntary system rules described above continue to apply to any indication of particulars of the place of origin or provenance of beef or beef products.

At the time of writing, it appears that the full compulsory labelling system is likely to be introduced in two stages whereby, as from 1 January 2001, Community slaughterhouse approval numbers will have to be indicated and, as from 1 January 2003, full information on the places of birth, fattening and slaughter will have to be declared.

1 Case C-269/97 *Commission v Council.*
2 See para **6.5.4** above.
3 See paras **13.1.3**, **13.2.1** and **13.8.5** above.

13.9 MILK AND MILK-BASED PRODUCTS

Milk and milk-based products production

13.9.1 The Dairy Products (Hygiene) Regulations 1995[1] in particular implement Directive 92/46/EEC which lays down the health rules for the production and placing on the market of raw milk, heat-treated milk and milk-based products intended for human consumption, as well as Decision 95/165/EC which establishes uniform criteria for the grant of derogations to certain establishments manufacturing milk-based products. The legislation applies not only to cows' milk, but also to the milk of sheep, goats and buffaloes, intended for human consumption.

The following principal definitions are given by the Regulations—

'raw' in relation to milk means milk produced by the secretion of the mammary glands of one or more cows, ewes, goats or buffaloes, which has not been heated beyond 40°C or undergone any treatment which has an equivalent effect;

'heat-treated milk' means milk obtained by heat-treatment;

'heat-treated drinking milk' means either drinking milk intended for sale to the ultimate consumer or to institutions, obtained by heat-treatment and presented as pasteurised, UHT or sterilised milk; or milk treated by pasteurisation, at the request of an individual consumer for sale in bulk to that consumer;

'milk-based product' means—

(a) a milk product exclusively from milk to which other substances necessary for its manufacture may have been added, provided that those substances do not replace in part or in whole any milk constituent; and

(b) a composite milk product of which no part replaces or is intended to replace any milk constituent and of which milk and milk product is an essential part either in terms of quantity or for characterisation of the product, intended for human consumption.

The Regulations do not apply to holdings and establishments producing and handling dairy products for the occupier's consumption, to establishments handling products for supply otherwise than by sale or, subject to specified exemptions, to the handling or sale from catering establishments or shop premises.

The Regulations prohibit the use of any premises as production holdings for the production of raw milk unless they comply with appropriate requirements and are registered. The Food Standards Agency is taking over[2] the minister's functions of granting registrations, allotting registration numbers and listing production holdings.

Standardisation centres, treatment establishments, processing establishments and collection centres must be approved and comply with appropriate requirements. Food authorities grant approvals and list establishments. In implementation of Decision 95/165/EC, dairy establishments processing less than 2 million litres per year into milk-based products may be approved on less stringent terms. Approving authorities may authorise further derogations specified in regulation 19.

The sale for human consumption of raw milk, thermised milk, heat-treated drinking milk, heat-treated milk intended for milk-based products and milk-based products is prohibited unless specified conditions are complied with. Cow's milk sold to catering establishments and thermised cow's milk sold to the ultimate consumer must be heat treated. Ice cream must be pasteurised or sterilised. Cheese matured for at least 60 days is exempt from specified requirements provided the microbiological standards for the finished product are met. Derogations are also provided in relation to milk-based products with traditional characteristics.

The Regulations lay down storage, transport, wrapping and labelling conditions, impose restrictions on the sale of raw cows' milk as drinking milk and prescribe the duties of occupiers of dairy establishments particularly where raw milk is purchased for resale.

The health mark must be applied to milk and milk-based products intended for sale but is restricted to production in accordance with the Regulations.

On the basis of proposals circulated at the beginning of 1999, the 1995 Regulations are expected to be updated and consolidated during 2000. Proposed new provisions include—

(a) the removal of certain derogations for milk-based products with traditional characteristics, to reflect developments in the European Community;

(b) the introduction of new somatic cell count standards for raw buffaloes' milk and a new requirement for purchasers of raw milk and dairy product processors to notify enforcement officers when standards for somatic cell counts and bacterial standards are reached;
(c) the introduction of an extended power so that a production holding's registration may be cancelled when statutory sampling of raw cows' drinking milk is obstructed;
(d) increased frequency of official microbiological sample testing and inspections at raw cows' drinking milk production holdings.

Guidance on the new Regulations is also expected to be issued in the form of a revised version of Statutory Code of Practice no 18 and supporting notes, together with enforcement Guidelines for the Dairy Hygiene Inspectorate.

1 Statutory Code of Practice no 18 and central Government notes to be read in conjunction with it give guidance on Enforcement of the Dairy Products (Hygiene) Regulations 1995. See also the following further MAFF publications: *A Guide to the Dairy Products (Hygiene) Regulations 1995 for Dairy Product Processors*; *A Short Guide to the Dairy Products (Hygiene) Regulations 1995 for Dairy Farmers*; *A Short Guide to the Dairy Products (Hygiene) Regulations 1995 for Farmers Producing and Processing Milk from Goats and Sheep*.
2 See paras **2.1.1** and **2.5.2** above.

Milk and milk-based products intended for human consumption import conditions

13.9.2 For milk and milk-based products, health rules concerning the marketing of production from other Member States and imports from third countries[1] are laid down by Directive 92/46/EEC. Moreover, in respect of importation from third countries, Decision 95/340/EC specifies a provisional list of third countries from which Member States authorise imports of milk and milk-based products, Decision 95/342/EC provides for treatment where there is a risk of foot-and-mouth disease and Decision 95/343/EC prescribes health certificate specimens for heat-treated milk, milk-based products and raw milk intended to be accepted at a collection centre, standardisation centre, treatment establishment or processing establishment.

As indicated in para **13.1.5** above, planned updating of the provision made by regulation 22 of the Dairy Products (Hygiene) Regulations 1995 for implementation of the Community rules now seems likely to be effected in the proposed revocation and replacement of the Products of Animal Origin (Import and Export) Regulations 1996.

1 See European Court judgment of 21 September 1999 in case C-106/97 *Dutch Antillian Dairy Industry v Rijksdienst voor de Keuring van Vee en Vlees*.

Heat treatment orders for infected cows' milk

13.9.3 The Dairy Products (Hygiene) Regulations 1995 replaced most of the Milk and Dairies (General) Regulations 1959 but the powers remain under Part VII (supplemented by Part I) whereby local authorities can issue heat treatment orders in respect of infected milk.

13.10 EGGS AND EGG PRODUCTS

Egg products production

13.10.1 The Egg Products Regulations 1993, as amended, implement in part Directive 89/437/EEC, as amended, on hygiene and health problems affecting the production and the placing on the market of egg products for direct human consumption.

The Regulations define—

'egg' as an egg laid, by a hen, duck, goose, turkey, guinea fowl or quail; and

'egg products' as products obtained from eggs, their various components or mixtures thereof, after removal of the shell and outer membranes, intended for human consumption, and includes such products when partially supplemented by other foodstuffs and additives and such products when liquid, concentrated, crystallised, frozen, quick-frozen, coagulated or dried, but does not include finished foodstuffs.

The Regulations prohibit the sale or use in preparation of food for human consumption of egg products which are mixtures from more than one species, which fail to comply with specified hygiene conditions or which were not prepared in an approved establishment. The preparation conditions include requirements as to the pasteurisation of whole egg and yolk and the heat treatment of albumen and as to microbiological criteria, testing, storage and transport.

The manufacture and heat treatment of egg products is restricted to establishments approved by a food authority. Approval is in particular dependent on the food authority being satisfied that packaging and health marking requirements will be complied with.

Each food authority is responsible for establishments which it has approved. Under the proposed Food Standards Act 1999 (Transitional and Consequential Provisions and Savings) (England and Wales) Regulations 2000, food authorities also took over the minister's power to revoke approvals. This is an exception (albeit a rational one) to the general policy that the Food Standards Agency should take over the minister's former functions[1].

The Regulations prescribe storage and labelling requirements for egg products moved between approved establishments.

1 See paras **2.1.1** and **2.5.2** above.

Eggs production and import of eggs and egg products

13.10.2 Directive 92/118/EEC Annex II, Chapter 2 first indent made provision for the establishment of health conditions applicable to the putting on the market and import of eggs and import of egg products intended for human consumption. Under these powers, in supplementation of—

(a) the general provisions applicable to Community trade in Chapter II of Directive 92/118/EEC, Decision 94/371/EC lays down specific health conditions for the putting on the market of certain types of eggs; and
(b) the general provisions applicable to imports into the Community in Chapter III of Directive 92/118/EEC, Decision 97/38/EC sets specific public health requirements for imports of egg products for human consumption.

Hygiene of ungraded eggs

13.10.3 In addition to these Community measures, for England and Wales the Ungraded Eggs (Hygiene) Regulations 1990[1], as amended, prohibit the retail sale of cracked eggs by producers on their own farms, in local public markets or by door to door selling.

1 See also para **7.3.6** above.

13.11 FISHERY PRODUCTS AND LIVE SHELLFISH

Fishery products and live shellfish production

13.11.1 The Food Safety (Fishery Products and Live Shellfish) (Hygiene) Regulations 1998[1], as amended, implement Directive 91/492/EEC (laying down the health conditions for the production and the placing on the market of live bivalve molluscs) ('the Live Bivalve Molluscs Directive') and Directive 91/493/EEC (laying down the health conditions for the production and the placing on the market of fishery products) ('the Fishery Products Directive').They also in particular implement Directive 92/48/EEC (laying down the minimum hygiene rules applicable to fishery products caught on board certain vessels) ('the Fishing Vessels Directive').

The provisions in Part IV of the Regulations import conditions for fishery products and live shellfish are considered in para **13.11.2**. The provisions of Schedule 4A on inspection charges for fishery products landings made in implementation of the Annex, Chapter III to Directive 85/73/EEC, as amended, are noted at para **13.1.6** above.

The Regulations contain the following significant definitions—

'aquaculture products' means—

(a) all fishery products born and raised in controlled conditions until placed on the market as a foodstuff; and

(b) all seawater fish, freshwater fish or crustaceans caught in their natural environment when juvenile and kept until they reach the desired commercial size for human consumption, other than fish or crustaceans of commercial size caught in their natural environment and kept alive to be sold at a later date, if they are merely kept alive without any attempt being made to increase their size or weight;

'fishery products' means—

(a) all seawater or freshwater animals, including their roes; and

(b) parts of such animals, except in circumstances where they—

    (i) are combined (in whatever way) with other foodstuffs; and

    (ii) comprise less than 10% of the total weight of the combined foodstuffs,

but excluding aquatic mammals, frogs and aquatic animals covered by Community acts other than the Fishery Products Directive, and parts of such mammals, frogs and aquatic animals;

'shellfish' means only bivalve molluscs, echinoderms, tunicates and marine gastropods.

Part II of the Regulations contains provisions relating to the production and placing on the market of live shellfish which, by virtue of the above definition, does not include crustaceans.

The Food Standards Agency has taken over ministers' function of designating production areas for live bivalve molluscs[2]. Relaying areas (where bivalve molluscs may be relaid after harvesting to remove contamination) are designated by food authorities. The Agency has also taken over ministers' power to designate prohibited areas for live shellfish production of various kinds. Food authorities may make temporary prohibition orders concerning production areas. Collecting shellfish from prohibited areas is an offence.

In respect of products intended for placing on the market for human consumption, conditions are prescribed, as regards echinoderms, tunicates and marine gastropods, for their harvesting and transport from production areas and, as regards live bivalve molluscs, for their harvesting and transport from production areas and for their relaying.

Dispatch and purification centres must be approved by the local food authority. Rules are specified for the wrapping, storage, repackaging, storage and transportation of live shellfish intended for placing on the market for human consumption.

Placing on the market of live shellfish for immediate human consumption is prohibited in default of compliance with detailed obligations as to origin, harvesting, keeping, transport, relaying, handling, wrapping, health marking and importation. Local market sales of small quantities of live shellfish are, however, exempt from most of these obligations.

Part III of the Regulations concerns the production and placing on the market of fishery products.

Fishing vessels on board which shrimps and molluscs are cooked must normally be registered with the local food authority. Hygiene rules are prescribed for all fishing vessels with special additional rules for certain longer range vessels. Fishery products establishments and British Islands factory vessels must be approved by the local food authority and their proprietors must comply with specified requirements. Masters of third country factory vessels must give the food authority at their port of arrival at least 24 hours' notice of arrival.

Auction and wholesale markets must be registered by the food authority and those responsible for markets must comply with specified requirements.

For fishery products intended for placing on the market for human consumption, rules are also specified requiring expeditious gutting and relating to the packaging, storage and transportation of fishery products in Great Britain. Placing on the market of fishery products for human consumption is prohibited in default of compliance with detailed obligations where they were handled on board a British Islands fishing vessel or on a British Islands factory vessel or landed in the British Islands. Also prohibited is the placing on the market of unhygienic aquaculture products and of processed shellfish which fail to comply with the prescribed requirements. Fishery products for human consumption which are placed on the market alive must be kept under the most suitable survival conditions. Local market sales of small quantities of products with live shellfish are exempt from these requirements. There is however, an absolute prohibition on the marketing for human consumption of specified poisonous fishery products.

The 1998 Report on Foodborne Viral Infections by the Advisory Committee on the Microbiological Safety of Food makes specific recommendations for the reduction of pollution related illnesses associated with shellfish consumption.

1 Central Government has issued guidance for food authorities on the Food Safety (Fishery Products and Live Shellfish) (Hygiene) Regulations 1998 and on the Food Safety (Fishery Products and Live Shellfish) (Hygiene) Amendment Regulations 1999. Code of Practice no 14: on Enforcement of the Food Safety

(Live Bivalve Molluscs and other Shellfish) Regulations 1992 and Code of Practice no 15: on Enforcement of the Food Safety (Fishery Products) Regulations 1992 will no doubt now be revised. In the meantime, they can probably still provide some assistance with the 1998 Regulations which are mainly a consolidation of previous legislation.

2 See paras **2.1.1** and **2.5.2** above.

Fishery products and live shellfish import conditions

13.11.2 The Food Safety (Fishery Products and Live Shellfish) (Hygiene) Regulations 1998, Part IV implements the Fishery Products Directive, the Fishing Vessels Directive, the Live Bivalve Molluscs Directive and specified Commission decisions in restricting import of fishery products and live shellfish. Additional conditions are prescribed in relation to third country imports. Specified private consignments are exempt from these provisions.

13.12 GELATINE INTENDED FOR HUMAN CONSUMPTION

Gelatine production and importation

13.12.1 As from 1 June 2000, the health conditions applicable to putting on the market and for imports of gelatine intended for human consumption are added as Chapter 4 to Annex II to Council Directive 92/118/EEC by Commission Decision 1999/724/EC. The new Chapter prescribes requirements for establishments producing gelatine; for raw materials and their transport and storage; for manufacture, packaging, storage and transport; for finished products; and for third country imports.

13.13 SNAILS, FROGS' LEGS AND HONEY

Snails, frogs' legs and honey import conditions

13.13.1 In implementation of provisions of Council Directive 92/118/EEC, as amended, the Miscellaneous Products of Animal Origin (Import Conditions) Regulations 1999 prescribe conditions for the import into Great Britain of snails, frogs' legs and honey intended for human consumption[1].

Products from another Member State must (a) originate in a controlled establishment; (b) in the case of snails and frogs' legs, satisfy specified public health requirements[2]; and (c) where the product has passed through a third country, be accompanied by a certificate that it complies with the relevant requirements of Directive 92/118/EEC.

Snails and frogs' legs originating in a third country must (a) comply with the relevant requirements of Directive 92/118/EEC; (b) come from a third country or part of a third country listed in Part XI or XII respectively of the Annex to Commission Decision 94/278/EC drawing up a list of third countries from which Member States authorise imports of certain products subject to Directive 92/118/EEC; and (c) be accompanied by the relevant health certificate. Honey originating in a third country must come from a registered establishment.

1 The provisions implemented concern animal health as well as public health and also impose conditions on the import of agricultural products, which are not intended for human consumption.

2 See Directive 92/118/EEC Annex 2, Ch 3, Pts I and II.

Chapter 14

Food hygiene and quality: temperature controls

14.1 INTRODUCTION

General and specific temperature controls

14.1.1 This chapter summarises the sundry food temperature requirements in relation to food. As noted when the general food hygiene Directive 93/43/EEC was considered in chapter 12, the temperature control requirements in the Annex, Chapter IX, paragraphs 4 and 5 to the Directive are implemented by the Food Safety (Temperature Control) Regulations 1995. These provisions, described in section **14.2**, replace the two-tier chill temperature control system and prescribed list of controlled foods introduced in 1991. Community-inspired temperature controls for the particular products of animal origin described in section **14.3** are to be found in the product-specific hygiene Regulations otherwise described in chapter 13. For other specific foods, further miscellaneous controls—some aimed at quality rather than hygiene—are summarised in section **14.4**. Also in pursuit of food quality, the Quick-frozen Foodstuffs Regulations 1990 enacted the temperature controls summarised at section **14.5** in implementation of Directive 89/108/EEC. The provisions on the international carriage of perishable foodstuffs are briefly noted in section **14.6**.

14.2 GENERAL TEMPERATURE CONTROLS

Chill and hot holding requirements

14.2.1 Besides implementing provisions of Directive 93/43/EEC, the Food Safety (Temperature Control) Regulations 1995 also contain national provisions relating to temperature control. The Regulations apply to all stages of food production except primary production and the activities of food businesses regulated by or under the product-specific Regulations listed in para **13.1.2** above other than the Wild Game Meat (Hygiene and Inspection) Regulations 1995 and, to a specified extent, the Food Safety (Fishery Products and Live Shellfish) (Hygiene) Regulations 1998.

Part II of the Regulations contain the general food temperature controls for England and Wales. Chill holding requirements are prescribed for foods likely to support the growth of pathogenic micro-organisms or the formation of toxins. Department of Health advice[1] indicates that examples of foods likely to fall into this category are dairy products, cooked products, smoked and cured fish, smoked or cured ready-to-eat meat which is not ambient shelf-stable, prepared ready-to-eat foods and uncooked or partly cooked pastry and dough products. Foods of this kind with respect to which a commercial operation is being carried out at or in food premises must not be kept at a temperature above 8°C. Those supplied by mail order must not be kept at a temperature which has given rise to or is likely to give rise to a risk to health. Exemptions from the chill holding requirements are specified for foods such as those which, for the duration of their shelf-life, may be kept at ambient temperatures with no risk to health. A defence is provided where the food business manufacturing, preparing or processing the food has recommended that it be kept at a specified temperature between 8°C and ambient temperatures for a period not exceeding a specified shelf life. Such recommendations must be supported by a well-founded scientific assessment of the safety of the food at the specified temperature. Other defences allow tolerance periods for which food may be held at above the chill holding level of 8°C.

The Regulations additionally prescribe hot holding requirements for foods that need to be kept hot in order to control the growth of pathogenic micro-organisms or the formation of toxins. If, in the course of the activities of a food business, such food has been cooked or reheated and is for service or on display for sale, it must not be kept at a temperature below 63°C. Defences permit lesser temperatures on the basis that a well-founded scientific assessment of the safety of the food has concluded there is no risk and, in any case, for a period of less than two hours.

There is a general prohibition on keeping foodstuffs likely to support the growth of pathogenic micro-organisms or the formation of toxins at temperatures which would result in a risk to health. This is in particular contravened by the keeping of perishable foodstuffs at above a maximum storage temperature recommended in any special storage conditions, notwithstanding they are kept at 8°C or below. The Regulations prescribe a further requirement in relation to the cooling of food and specify the evidential value, in certain circumstances, of guides to good hygiene practice[2].

Part III of the Regulations contain the food temperature control requirements for Scotland.

1 See para **14.2.2** below.
2 See para **12.2.2** above.

Guidance on general temperature controls

14.2.2 Guidance on the above temperature controls is available[1] and advice on the approach to enforcement is to be found in statutory Code of Practice no 10, issued in relation to the 1991 Regulations[2]. The guidance in particular makes clear that the temperature control requirements should be understood in the general context of the hazard analysis requirement contained in the Food Safety (General Food Hygiene) Regulations 1995 and that it is expected to be complementary to UK, and to any EC, Industry Guides to good hygiene practice[3].

1 Department of Health Guidance on the Food Safety (Temperature Control) Regulations 1995.
2 Code of Practice no 10: Enforcement of the Temperature Control Requirements of Food Hygiene Regulations.
3 See para **12.2.2** above.

14.3 TEMPERATURE CONTROLS FOR PRODUCTS OF ANIMAL ORIGIN FOR HUMAN CONSUMPTION

Product-specific hygiene Regulations

14.3.1 Regulations made in implementation of Directives enacted by the Community with the objective of ensuring that major products of animal origin for human consumption are hygienically produced for intra-Community trade[1] lay down certain requirements concerning temperatures to be observed during manufacture. Notably, however, they prescribe maximum temperatures in respect of storage and transport which are summarised in the next paragraph. According to paragraph 2.7 of the introduction to the 1997 second consultation document on the Commission's proposal for consolidation of the product-specific Directives[2], a working group was to consider the health justification for the differences in temperatures for the different commodities.

1 See para **13.1.2** above.
2 See paras **2.2.1** and **13.1.1** above.

Storage and transport temperature controls

14.3.2 Regulations providing for the hygienic production of the major products of animal origin for human consumption intended for intra-Community trade specify the following maximum and other temperature requirements in respect of storage and transport—

(a) *Fresh meat*—
  (i) 7°C for carcases and parts of carcases, 3°C for offals and –12°C for frozen meat;
  (ii) in storage, 4°C for small wild game and 7°C for large wild game;
  (iii) for transport of slaughtered farm game to slaughterhouses or farm game processing facilities, at ambient temperature between 0°C and +4°C[1];

(b) *Poultrymeat, farmed game bird meat and rabbit meat*—
4°C for fresh meat (including small wild game meat) and –12°C for frozen meat (including small wild game meat)[2];

(c) *Wild game meat*—
7°C for large wild game meat, 4°C for small wild game meat and –12°C for frozen wild game meat[3];

(d) *Minced meat and meat preparations*—
  (i) minced meat packaged and presented chilled, subject to a specified exception, 2°C;
  (ii) minced meat packaged and presented deep-frozen, in compliance with paragraph 1 of Schedule 1 to the Quick-frozen Foodstuffs Regulations 1990[4];
  (iii) meat preparations packaged and presented chilled, subject in transport to a specified exception—
    - 2°C where it contains minced meat;
    - 7°C where it contains fresh meat;
    - 4°C where it contains poultrymeat; and
    - 3°C where it contains offal;
  (iv) meat preparations packaged and presented deep-frozen, subject in transport to a specified exception, in compliance with paragraph 1 of Schedule 1 to the Quick-frozen Foodstuffs Regulations 1990[5];

(e) *Meat products*—
meat products which cannot be stored at an ambient temperature, as indicated by the manufacturer[6];

(f) *Meat products in meat-based prepared meals*—
(i) between 10°C and 60°C for no longer than two hours if mixed with the other ingredients before refrigeration;
(ii) refrigerated to 10°C or less before being mixed with the other ingredients; or
(iii) as currently proposed in draft Meat Product (Hygiene) (Amendment) (England) Regulations 2000, between 10°C and 60°C for a minimum time as part of an approved method of cooling and mixing with the other ingredients; and

refrigerated to 10°C or less within a period of not more than two hours[6];

(g) *Other products of animal origin*—
(i) greaves when rendered at a temperature of 70°C or less, at a temperature of less than 7°C for a period not exceeding 24 hours or –18°C or lower;
(ii) greaves when rendered at a temperature of more than 70°C and having a moisture content of 10% (m/m) or more either—
  - at a temperature of less than 7°C for a period not exceeding 48 hours or at a time/temperature ratio offering an equivalent guarantee, or
  - at –18°C or lower;

(iii) greaves when rendered at a temperature of more than 70°C and having a moisture content of less than 10% (m/m): no specific requirement;
(iv) stomachs, bladders and intestines which are not salted or dried, 3°C[7];

(h) *Milk and milk-based products*—
(i) storage of raw milk collected daily, 8°C until collected;
(ii) storage of raw milk not collected daily, 6°C until collected;
(iii) storage of pasteurised milk until it leaves the treatment establishment, 6°C;
(iv) storage of milk at a treatment establishment until treated, 6°C unless treated within four hours;
(v) storage of milk products not intended to be stored at ambient temperature, as established by the manufacturer;
(vi) transport of raw milk, subject to specified exceptions, 10°C;
(vii) transport of pasteurised milk, subject to specified exceptions, 6°C[8];

(i) *Egg products*—
(i) deep frozen products, –18°C;
(ii) other frozen products, –12°C;
(iii) chilled products, 4°C[9];

(j) *Fishery products and live shellfish*—
(i) live shellfish, a temperature which does not adversely affect their quality and viability;
(ii) fresh or thawed fishery products and cooked and chilled crustacean and molluscan shellfish products, a temperature approaching that of melting ice;
(iii) frozen fishery products, except products in brine for manufacture of canned food, –18°C and, during transport, 3°C[10];

(k) *Snails and frogs' legs*—
(i) fresh or thawed products must be kept at the temperature of melting ice;
(ii) frozen products (except those in brine for manufacture of canned food) must be kept at –18°C or less;
(iii) processed products must be kept at the temperature specified by the manufacturer[11].

1 See Fresh Meat (Hygiene and Inspection) Regulations 1995.
2 Poultry Meat, Farmed Game Bird Meat and Rabbit Meat (Hygiene and Inspection) Regulations 1995.
3 Wild Game Meat (Hygiene and Inspection) Regulations 1995.
4 See para **14.5.1** below.
5 Minced Meat and Meat Preparations (Hygiene) Regulations 1995.
6 Meat Products (Hygiene) Regulations 1994.
7 As to the meaning of 'other products of animal origin', see para **13.6.1** above.
8 Dairy Products (Hygiene) Regulations 1995.
9 Egg Products Regulations 1993.
10 Food Safety (Fishery Products and Live Shellfish) (Hygiene) Regulations 1998.
11 Miscellaneous Products of Animal Origin (Import Conditions) 1999 and Directive 92/118/EEC amended by Decision 96/340/EC.

14.4 TEMPERATURE CONTROLS FOR OTHER SPECIFIC FOODS

The nature of the controls

14.4.1 Besides the temperature controls in product specific food hygiene Regulations implementing Community Directives, there are, in respect of certain other specific foods, some miscellaneous controls of Community or national origin with quality or hygiene objectives.

Eggs

14.4.2 Regulation 1274/91/EEC (introducing detailed rules for implementing Regulation 1907/90/EEC on certain marketing standards for eggs)[1] lays down temperature control requirements. If eggs intended for marketing as 'extra' are passed to the packing centre only on every second day, the ambient temperatures at which they are kept on the farm must not exceed 18°C. Moreover, eggs must be maintained during storage and transport at a temperature best suited to assure an optimal conservation of their quality.

Decision 94/371/EC (laying down specific public health conditions for the putting on the market of certain types of eggs)[2] requires that at the producer's premises and until sale to the consumer, eggs must be stored and transported at a constant temperature.

1 See para **7.3.6** above.
2 See para **13.10.2** above.

Poultrymeat

14.4.3 Temperature control is integral to marketing standards for poultrymeat established by Regulation 1906/90/EEC[1]. Poultrymeat may be marketed in one of three conditions: 'fresh', which is generally to be kept at between –2°C and 4°C, 'frozen', which must generally be kept at a temperature no higher than –12°C, and 'quick-frozen', which is to be kept at a temperature no higher than –18°C within tolerances provided for by the quick frozen food Directive 89/108/EEC[2]. These provisions are augmented for frozen poultrymeat by the requirement, in the detailed implementing rules introduced by Directive 1538/91/EEC, that the temperature must be stable and maintained at –12°C or lower, with possible brief upward fluctuations of no more than 3°C. These tolerances in the temperature of the product are permitted in accordance with good storage and distribution practice during local distribution and in retail display cabinets.

1 See para **7.3.7** above.
2 See section **14.5** below.

Ice-cream

14.4.4 Long perceived as a potentially dangerous food, the venerable national Regulations providing for the hygiene of ice cream also contain temperature controls[1]. Offer for sale is prohibited unless the ice-cream has been kept at a temperature not exceeding 28°F since it was frozen or, if its temperature has risen above 28°F at any time since it was frozen, it has again been subjected to the treatment (if any) to which it is required to be subjected by the regulations and, after treatment has been kept at a temperature not exceeding 28°F[1].

1 Ice-cream (Heat Treatment etc) Regulations 1959. See further para **12.4.2** above.

14.5 QUICK-FROZEN FOODS

Definition and description

14.5.1 The Quick-frozen Foodstuffs Regulations 1990, as amended, implement Directive 89/108/EEC and subordinate Directives 92/1/EEC and 92/2/EEC. They define a quick-frozen foodstuff as a product comprising food which has undergone a freezing process known as 'quick-freezing' whereby the zone of maximum crystallisation is crossed as rapidly as possible, depending on the type of product, and which is labelled for the purpose of sale to indicate that it has undergone that process, but does not include ice cream or any other edible ice. The Regulations do not, therefore, apply to a product, even though it may have undergone the quick-freezing process, unless it is labelled as such.

Labelling, packaging and temperature

14.5.2 The description 'quick frozen' and other descriptions listed in Directive 89/108/EEC are reserved to quick-frozen foodstuffs and food which by virtue of that labelling becomes a quick-frozen foodstuff. Where a quick-frozen foodstuff is marked with the description 'quick frozen' it must also be labelled with a sales name and—

(a) an indication of the date of minimum durability[1];
(b) an indication of the maximum period during which it is advisable to store it;
(c) an indication of one or other, or both of—
  (i) the temperature at which, and
  (ii) the equipment in which,
  it is advisable to store it;
(d) a reference allowing identification of the batch to which it belongs[2];
(e) a clear message of the type 'do not refreeze after defrosting'.

It is unlawful to sell to the ultimate consumer any quick-frozen foodstuff unless it has been packed by its manufacturer or packer in such prepackaging as is suitable to protect it from microbial and other forms of external contamination and against dehydration and it has remained in such prepackaging up to the time of sale.

Quick-freezing must result in the temperature of the food after thermal stabilisation being –18°C or colder and it must be maintained, subject to permitted exceptions, at that temperature or below. There are special requirements as to the equipment (including air temperature recording equipment in storage and transport) to be used by the manufacturer, storer, transporter, local distributor and retailer.

The sampling and method of measuring temperatures laid down by Directive 92/2/EEC must be applied by an authorised officer who has reasonable doubt that the prescribed temperature requirements are not being or have not been observed.

1 See paras **6.5.15** and **6.5.16** above.
1 See paras **6.5.15** above.

14.6 INTERNATIONAL CARRIAGE OF PERISHABLE FOODSTUFFS

14.6.1 The International Carriage of Perishable Foodstuffs Act 1976 provided for the United Kingdom's accession to the Agreement on the International Carriage of Perishable Foodstuffs (ATP) which was concluded in Geneva on 1 September 1970[1]. The International Carriage of Perishable Foodstuffs Regulations 1985, as amended, implements the ATP by laying down maximum temperatures at which certain foods may be carried on loading, during carriage and on unloading.

1 Cmnd 6441.

Chapter 15

Quantity and price marking requirements

15.1 INTRODUCTION

15.1.1 The regulatory powers conferred by the Food Safety Act 1990 (FSA 1990)[1] do not extend to the marking of food with statements of quantity by weight or other measurement by number[2]. For food, requirements in respect of quantity marking are imposed by and under Parts IV and V of the Weights and Measures Act 1985 (W&MA 1985). Through these provisions, relevant Community legislation is implemented – in particular, the general food labelling Directive 79/112/EEC[3], the average quantity packaged goods Directives 75/106/EEC and 76/211/EEC and the units of measurement Directive 80/181/EEC. Considered below is the British legislation on general offences relating to deficient quantity etc (section **15.2**), quantity requirements for certain foods (section **15.3**), the average quantity system (section **15.4**), manner of quantity marking and abbreviations of measurement units (section **15.5**) and other manner of marking provisions (section 15.6).

For completeness, it should be noted that, for compound feeding stuffs, quantity marking is required by Council Directive 79/373 as implemented by the Feeding Stuffs Regulations 1995[4], Schedule 1, paragraph 8(a).

It should also be noted that in July 1999 the Department of Trade and Industry (DTI) issued proposals[5] for the repeal of provisions in and under the W&MA 1985, Parts IV and V and their replacement with broad enabling powers in primary legislation supported by detailed provisions in secondary legislation.

The chapter concludes with a summary of the price marking rules. Section **15.7** deals with the prohibition by the Consumer Protection Act 1987 (CPA 1987) of misleading price indications: section **15.8** explains the implementation of Directive 98/6/EEC and other provisions in and under the Prices Act 1974 requiring selling and unit prices to be indicated.

1 FSA 1990, ss 16–18.
2 W&MA 1985, s 93.
3 As to the Food Labelling Directive 79/112/EEC, see in particular section 6.1 above.
4 See para **16.3.1** below.
5 'A Fairer Measure—A Consultation Document on modernising the law on the sale of goods sold by quantity'.

15.2 GENERAL OFFENCES RELATING TO DEFICIENT QUANTITY ETC

15.2.1 Sections 28–31 of the W&MA 1985 prescribe offences in respect of the delivery of short weight or measure in selling goods; the misrepresentation of quantity in selling or purchasing goods; quantities less than stated on sale containers and documents; and materially incorrect statements in documents which are required, by or under Part IV of the Act, to be associated with goods.

Offences are also prescribed by section 25 of the W&MA 1985 for non-compliance with specified requirements as to sales by quantity of non-pre-packed and pre-packed goods[1]. The requirements include those in the Orders described in section **15.3** below.

1 'Pre-packed' means made up in advance ready for retail sale in or on a container. See W&MA 1985, s 94(1).

15.3 QUANTITY REQUIREMENTS FOR CERTAIN FOODS

15.3.1 Detailed provision is made under Part IV of the W&MA 1985 for quantity indications on pre-packed food and sales by quantity of non-pre-packed food. For most pre-packed foodstuffs, requirements are laid down by Community Directives. Quantity indications are prescribed by the general food labelling Directive 79/112/EEC and, for specific foods, by internal market Directives described in section **7.2** above. Additionally, to reduce so far as possible the confusion for consumers arising from the multiplicity of different amounts in which packaged products were made up, Directives 75/106/EEC and 80/232/EEC laid down the 'prescribed quantities' permitted for specific types of drink and food.

The British quantity requirements, the main provisions of which are summarised below in this section, are thus in part of domestic inspiration and in part made in implementation of these Community obligations. The result is complex and difficult to use. The DTI's consultation proposals[1] therefore contemplate a consolidation and simplification based much more closely, where relevant, on the Community provisions.

It should also be noted that marking with indications of quantity is required by directly applicable Community common agricultural policy Regulations[2] in respect of certain poultrymeat[3], fresh fruit and vegetables[4] and wines[5]. In consequence, the DTI consultation document proposes that the substantive British requirements for these products should be replaced by provisions enforcing the Community ones. It will be recalled that Community weight grade marking for eggs is already enforced in this way[6].

At present, the national requirements are to be found in the Weights and Measures Act 1963 (Cheese, Fish, Fresh Fruits and Vegetables, Meat and Poultry) Order 1984 (see para **15.3.2**), the Weights and Measures (Miscellaneous Foods) Order 1988 (see paras **15.3.3–15.3.7**) and the Weights and Measures (Intoxicating Liquor) Order 1988 (see para **15.3.8**).

1 See para **15.1.1** above.
2 See section **7.3** above.
3 Commission Regulation 1538/91/EEC, as amended, Art 8(2) (in relation to prepackaged frozen and quick frozen poultrymeat). Council Regulation 1906/90/EEC, as amended, Art 5(1) confirms that generally the labelling of poultrymeat intended for the final consumer must comply with national legislation adopted in accordance with Directive 79/112/EEC. See further paras **7.3.7** and **15.1.1** above.
4 Council Regulation 2200/96/EEC, as amended, Art 6; and see further para **7.3.18** above.
5 Council Regulation 1493/1999/EEC, Art 47 and Annexes VII A.1 and VIII B.1(b); and see further para **7.3.8** above.
6 See para **7.3.6** above.

Cheese, fish, fresh fruits and vegetables, meat and poultry

15.3.2 Products controlled by the Weights and Measures Act 1963 (Cheese, Fish, Fresh Fruits and Vegetables, Meat and Poultry) Order 1984 must, generally speaking, be sold by net weight or, subject to maximum container weights, by gross weight when not pre-packed. When pre-packed, the container must usually be marked with an indication of net weight.

Subject to maximum container weights, certain pre-packed cheeses sold by gross weight and soft fruit and mushrooms sold by retail need not be marked with a statement of weight, but the weight must be made known to the buyer before he pays for or takes possession of the food.

There are exemptions in particular for specified meat and fish products, and certain fruits and vegetables may be sold by number or by the bunch.

Quantities of less than 5 g (25 g in the case of cheese) are exempt, as are quantities of more than 5 kg of fresh fruits or vegetables and 10 kg of cheese.

The Order makes special provision for quantity marking in respect of multipacks which contain two or more packs of goods. Different requirements, in particular, apply according to whether the enclosed packs contain different goods, or the same or different quantities of identical goods.

Miscellaneous foods: generally

15.3.3 The Weights and Measures (Miscellaneous Foods) Order 1988 ('the Miscellaneous Foods Order') requires named foods to be sold only in prescribed quantities. It also generally requires pre-packed food (unless exempted) to be marked with an indication of net weight or volume or (in some cases) number and non-pre-packed food to be sold by net weight or (in some cases) by number. Paragraphs **15.3.4–15.3.7** below summarise the provisions respectively on prescribed quantities, quantity marking for prescribed quantity foods, quantity marking for non-prescribed quantity foods and exempted foods and multi-packs.

Miscellaneous foods: prescribed quantities

15.3.4 By provisions which also in part implement Council Directives 75/106/EEC and 80/232/EEC [1], the Miscellaneous Foods Order specifies foods that are, subject to exemptions, required to be pre-packed only in prescribed quantities. The foods are:

15.3.4 *Quantity and price marking requirements*

Foods	*Prescribed Quantities*
Barley kernels, pearl barley, rice (including ground rice and rice flakes), sago, semolina and tapioca	125 g, 250 g, 375 g, 500 g or a multiple of 500 g. Packs of 75 g or less or more than 10 kg exempted
Biscuits, other than wafer biscuits which are not cream-filled	100 g, 125 g, 150 g, 200 g, 250 g, 300 g, or a multiple of 100 g. Packs of 85 g or less or more than 5 kg exempted
Bread in form of a whole loaf	400 g or a multiple of 400 g*
Cereal breakfast foods in flake form, other than cereal biscuit foods	125 g, 250 g, 375 g, 500 g, 750 g, 1 kg, 1.5 kg or a multiple of 1 kg. Packs of 50g or less or more than 10 kg exempted
Chocolate products in bar or tablet form of the following reserved descriptions: chocolate, plain chocolate, gianduja nut chocolate, milk chocolate, white chocolate, filled chocolate, cream chocolate; and skimmed milk chocolate	85 g, 100 g, 125 g, 150 g, 200 g, 250 g, 300 g, 400 g or 500 g. Packs of less than 85 g or more than 500 g exempted
Cocoa products of the following reserved descriptions: cocoa, cocoa powder, fat-reduced cocoa, fat-reduced cocoa powder, sweetened cocoa, sweetened fat-reduced cocoa, sweetened fat-reduced cocoa powder, drinking chocolate, fat-reduced drinking chocolate	50 g, 75 g, 125 g, 250 g, 500 g, 750 g and 1 kg. Packs of less than 50 g or more than 1 kg exempted
Coffee, coffee mixtures and coffee bags (contents)	57 g, 75 g, 113 g, 125 g, 227 g, 250g, 340 g, 454 g, 500g, 680 g, 750 g or a multiple of 454 g or of 500 g. Packs of less than 25 g or more than 5 kg exempted
Coffee extracts and chicory extracts consisting of solid and paste coffee and chicory products	50 g, 100 g, 200 g, 250 g (for mixtures of coffee extracts and chicory extracts only), 300 g (for coffee extracts only), 500 g, 750 g, 1 kg, 1.5 kg, 2 kg, 2.5 kg, 3 kg or a multiple of 1 kg. Packs of 25 g or less or more than 10 kg exempted
Dried fruits of any one or more of the following descriptions – apples (including dried apple rings), apricots, currants, dates figs, muscatels, nectarines, peaches, pears (including dried pear rings), prunes, raisins, sultanas and dried fruit salad	125 g, 250 g, 375 g, 500 g, 1 kg, 1.5 kg, or a multiple of 1 kg. Packs of 75 g or less or more than 10 kg exempted
Dried vegetables of any of the following descriptions – beans, lentils and peas (including split peas)	125 g, 250 g, 375 g, 500 g, 1 kg, 1.5 kg or a multiple of 1 kg. Packs of less than 100 g or more than 10 kg exempted
Edible fats of any of the following descriptions— (a) butter, margarine, any mixture of butter and margarine, and low fat spreads (butter or margarine substitutes); (b) dripping and shredded suet; (c) lard and compound cooking fat substitutes therefor; (d) solidified edible oil (except in gel form)	50 g, 125 g, 250 g, 500 g, or a multiple of 500 g up to and including 4 kg or thereafter a multiple of 1 kg up to and including 10 kg. Packs of 25 g or less or more than 10 kg exempted for (a) only. In other cases – less than 5 g or more than 10 kg

Foods	*Prescribed Quantities*
Flour, ie flour of bean, maize, pea, rice, rye, soya bean or wheat and flour products of any following descriptions – cake flour, other than cake mixtures and sponge mixtures; cornflour, other than blancmange powders and custard powers; self-raising flour	125 g, 250 g, 500 g, or a multiple of 500g and in the case of cornflour, in addition 375g and 750 g. Packs of less than 50 g or more than 10 kg exempted
Honey (other than chunk honey or comb honey)	57 g, 113 g, 227 g, 340 g, 454 g, 680 g or a multiple of 454 g. Packs of less than 50 g exempted
Jam and marmalade other than diabetic jam or marmalade. Jelly preserves	57 g, 113 g, 227 g, 340 g, 454 g, 680 g or a multiple of 454 g. Packs of less than 50 g exempted
Milk other than in a returnable container	189 ml, 200 ml, 250 ml, 284 ml, 500 ml, 750 ml or a multiple of 284 ml or of 500 ml. Packs of 50 ml or less exempted
Milk in a returnable container	(1) ⅓ pt, ½ pt, or a multiple of ½ pt (2) 200 ml, 250 ml, 500 ml, 750 ml or a multiple of 500 ml. Packs of 50 ml or less exempted
Molasses, syrup and treacle	57 g, 113 g, 227 g, 340 g, 454 g, 680 g or a multiple of 454 g. Packs of less than 50 g exempted
Oat products – flour of oats; oatflakes and oatmeal	125 g, 250 g, 375 g, 500 g, 750 g, 1 kg, 1.5 kg, or a multiple of 1 kg. Packs of 50g or less, or more than 10 kg exempted
Pasta	125 g, 250 g, 375 g, 500 g, or a multiple of 500 g. Packs of 50 g or less exempted
Potatoes	500 g, 750 g, 1 kg, 1.5 kg, 2 kg, 2.5 kg, or a multiple of 2.5 kg up to and including 15 kg, 20 kg or 25 kg. Packs of less than 5 g or more than 25 kg and, where the net weight of each potato is not less than 175 g, exempted
Salt	125 g, 250 g, 500 g, 750 g, 1 kg, 1.5 kg or a multiple of 1 kg up to and including 10 kg, 12.5 kg, 25 kg or 50 kg. Packs of 100 g or less exempted
Sugar	125 g, 250 g, 500 g, 750 g, 1 kg, 1.5 kg, 2 kg, 2.5 kg, 3 kg, 4 kg or 5 kg. Packs of 100 g or less, or more than 5 kg exempted
Tea in a tea-bag (contents only)	50 g, 125 g, 250 g, 500 g, 750 g, 1 kg, 1.5 kg, 2 kg, 2.5 kg, 3 kg, 4 kg or 5 kg. Packs of 25 g or less, or more than 5 kg exempted
Tea, other than instant or in tea-bag	50 g, 125 g, 250 g, 500 g, 750 g, 1 kg, 1.5 kg, 2 kg, 2.5 kg, 3 kg, 4 kg or 5 kg or when packed in tins or glass or wooden containers in addition 100 g, 200 g, and 300 g. Packs of 25 g or less or more than 5 kg exempted

* Exempted from the prescribed quantity requirements for loaves of bread are loaves weighing 300 g or less; or any sale in pursuance of a contract for the supply of bread for consumption on the premises of the buyer, if the contract provides for each delivery of bread thereunder to be a specified aggregate quantity of not less than 25 kg and for the weighing of the bread on delivery. (Non pre-packed bread must be made up in the same prescribed quantities but, of course, is exempt from the weight marking requirements.)

1 See para **15.3.1** above.

Miscellaneous foods: quantity marking for prescribed quantity foods

15.3.5 The Miscellaneous Foods Order also makes provision for the quantity marking of foods listed in para **15.3.4** above.

When pre-packed[1], the foods (other than milk) must be marked with an indication of quantity. Packs of less than 5 g or 5 ml are generally exempt. For biscuits, sugar, chocolate and cocoa products the exemption is for 50 g or less. Bread is exempt where the net weight of each loaf is less than 300 g and the number of items if more than one in the container is marked on the container or is clearly visible and capable of being easily counted through the container. Packs of potatoes are exempt where the net weight of each potato is not less than 175 g and there is an indication of the number of potatoes in the pack and the container is marked with a statement of the minimum net weight of each potato.

When not pre-packed, the foods (other than bread, chunk honey, comb honey and milk) if sold by retail must be sold by net weight. Exemptions are provided for eight or less biscuits and for less than 50 g of cocoa products.

1 Or, in specified cases, 'when made up in a container for sale'.

Miscellaneous foods: quantity marking for non-prescribed quantity foods and exempted foods

15.3.6 Most pre-packed foods which are not subject to the prescribed quantity requirements are nevertheless required by the Miscellaneous Foods Order to be marked with an indication of quantity by weight, capacity, volume or number. There are special requirements for certain biscuits, shortbreads, bread, caseins and caseinates, cocoa and chocolate products (not in bar or tablet form), liquid coffee and chicory products, liquid edible oil, milk (when not pre-packed, in small quantities or sold from vending machines), preserved milk and potatoes.

Miscellaneous foods: multipacks

15.3.7 There is special provision for quantity marking in respect of containers holding two or more packs of goods. Different requirements, in particular, apply according to whether the enclosed packs contain different goods, or the same or different quantities of identical goods.

Intoxicating liquor

15.3.8 By provisions which also in part implement Council Directive 75/106/EEC[1], the Weights and Measures (Intoxicating Liquor) Order 1988 requires pre-packed wines and spirits to be sold only in prescribed quantities. Provision is also made for the sale only in prescribed quantities, of draught beer and cider and spirits, wines and made wines for consumption on the premises at which they are sold.

The Order requires pre-packed intoxicating liquors to be marked with an indication of volume.

1 See para **15.3.1** above.

15.4 THE AVERAGE QUANTITY SYSTEM

The system

15.4.1 Any legislation on the quantity of goods has to make allowance for inherent errors in weighing and measuring equipment. In Great Britain controls were traditionally based on the 'minimum system' by which the buyer is expected to receive the stated weight or measure, defences being provided to protect diligent manufacturers and sellers[1]. A different approach was adopted in Directives 75/106/EEC and 76/211/EEC which harmonised rules for intra-Community trade in specified products. This is known as the 'average quantity system' whereby the contents of packages are required to be no less, on average, than their nominal quantity[2]. Compliant goods may bear the prescribed 'e' mark and have free access to all Member States[3]. In Britain these Community rules are implemented by Part V of the W&MA 1985, detailed provisions made under it in the Weights and Measures (Packaged Goods) Regulations 1986 and the Code of Practical Guidance for Packers and Importers, as amended[4], and are obligatory for most packaged food and drink[5].

The DTI's consultation proposals[6] speculate on the simplification of the law so that the whole range of packaged goods of constant quantity has the option of using the average system.

1 W&MA 1985, ss 33–37. See further paras **19.3.1** and **19.6.1** and *Bibby-Cheshire v Golden Wonder Ltd* [1972] 3 All ER 738, [1972] 1 WLR 1487 noted at para **19.3.13** below.
2 See further para **15.4.2** below.
3 See para **15.6.2** below. See also case 96/84 *Vereniging Slachtpluimvee-Export v REWE-Zentral-Aktiengesellschaft* [1985] ECR 1157.
4 See also the *Manual of Practical Guidance for Inspectors*, as supplemented.
5 Weights and Measures (Packaged Goods) Regulations 1986, regs 3, 4 and 5 and Sch 1, Pt I.
6 See para **15.1.1** above.

The duties of packers and importers

15.4.2 Provisions in and under Part V of the W&MA 1985 specify duties which must be performed by packers and importers to ensure that a group of packages selected by an inspector pass the average quantity system reference test. The three rules that must be observed are as follows—

(1) The actual contents of the packages shall not be less, on average, than the nominal quantity[1].
(2) Not more than 2.5% of the packages may be non-standard, ie have a negative error larger than the tolerable negative error (TNE) specified for the nominal quantity[2].
(3) No package may be inadequate, ie have a negative error larger than twice the specified TNE[3].

The DTI's consultation proposals[4] acknowledge that, rather than implementing the Directives by requiring the reference test to be passed, it would be more straightforward to oblige packers and importers to comply with the three rules.

1 W&MA 1985, ss 47(1)(a) and 68(1).

2 W&MA 1985, ss 47(1)(b) and 68(2)(a); and Weights and Measures (Packaged Goods) Regulations 1986, reg 23. (The figure of 2.5% is given not in the Directives but in an interpretation agreed by the Council of Ministers.)
3 W&MA 1985, ss 50(5) and (6) and 68(2)(b); and Weights and Measures (Packaged Goods) Regulations 1986, reg 23.
4 See para **15.1.1** above.

15.5 MANNER OF QUANTITY MARKING AND ABBREVIATIONS OF MEASUREMENT UNITS

15.5.1 The Weights and Measures (Quantity Marking and Abbreviations of Units) Regulations 1987, as amended ('the Quantity Marking Regulations'), prescribe the manner in which quantity information is to be marked on containers and abbreviations and symbols of units of measurement to be used as required in and under Part IV of the W&MA 1985 and for the purposes of the average quantity system[1].

The Regulations implement Community obligations in Directives 75/106/EEC and 76/211/EEC, the general food labelling Directive 79/112/EEC and Directive 80/181/EEC, as amended, on units of measurement.

Detailed requirements of the Quantity Marking Regulations are summarised in paras **15.5.2–15.5.7** below.

1 W&MA 1985, s 48 and Weights and Measures (Packaged Goods) Regulations 1986.

Marking with quantity by measurement

15.5.2 The marking of any container with information as to quantity by measurement (weight, capacity or volume) must comprise the numerical value of the unit of measurement expressed in words or by means of the relevant symbol or abbreviation which may be lawfully used for trade in relation to that unit. Where the numerical value of the unit of measurement is expressed in words, the reference to that unit must be expressed in words and not by means of a symbol or abbreviation.

If the goods are packed by gross weight, the information as to quantity must include the word 'gross' or the words 'including container' or other words which indicate that the marked weight includes the weight of the container. No abbreviation of the word 'gross' is permitted.

It is unnecessary to use the word 'net' where goods are packed by net weight but, if used, the word must not be abbreviated.

Any metric quantity used in the marking may not be expressed as a vulgar fraction.

Legibility and position of marking

15.5.3 Any marking of a container with information as to quantity must be easy to understand, clearly legible and indelible. It must be easily visible to an intending purchaser under normal conditions of purchase and must not in any way be hidden, obscured or interrupted by any other written or pictorial matter. If the information is not on the actual container or on a label securely attached to the container, it must be so placed that it cannot be removed without opening the container.

Size of marking

15.5.4 Except in the case of a catchweight product (ie any product which is not pre-packed according to a pre-determined fixed weight pattern, but is packed in varying quantities), where in any marking of any container the quantity by number or the numerical value of a unit of measurement is expressed in figures, all the relevant figures must be at least of the height specified[1] according to whether the marking is of weight, capacity, volume or number.

1 Weights and Measures (Quantity Marking and Abbreviations of Units) Regulations 1987, Sch 1.

Metric and imperial units

15.5.5 The marking of containers with information as to quantity must be in metric units. However, information as to quantity by measurement may additionally be marked on returnable containers used for milk, by reference to the pint. Moreover, consonant with section 8(5A) of the W&MA 1985, the Quantity Marking Regulations enable any container marked in metric units of measurement to be marked with a supplementary indication.

Regulation 14 of and Schedule 3B to the Units of Measurement Regulations 1986 also authorise the use of the pint in the dispensing of draught beer or cider.

Units of measurement

15.5.6 Subject to the special provision for milk mentioned in para **15.5.5** above, metric units of measurement to be used in marking any container with information as to quantity by measurement are specified. For volume, the units are cubic metre, cubic centimetre, litre, centilitre and millilitre. For capacity the units are litre, centilitre and millilitre. And for mass or weight, the units are kilogram and gram.

Symbols and abbreviations

15.5.7 The following symbols for and abbreviations of relevant units of measurement are permitted by the Quantity Marking Regulations—

Unit of Measurement	*Symbol*
cubic metre	m^3
cubic centimetre	cm^3
litre	l or L
decilitre	dl or dL
centilitre	cl or cL
millilitre	ml or mL
tonne	t
kilogram	kg
hectogram	hg
gram	g
milligram	mg

Where the pint is used in connection with returnable containers for milk or the dispensing of draught beer or cider, the abbreviation 'pt' may be used and the letter 's' may be added, where appropriate, to indicate the plural.

15.6 OTHER MANNER OF MARKING PROVISIONS

15.6.1 Other relevant manner of marking provisions are noted in the following two paragraphs.

The 'e' mark

15.6.2 The Weights and Measures (Packaged Goods) Regulations 1986 prescribe the form of the average quantity system 'e' mark referred to in para **15.4.1** above. When applied to a container it must be at least 3 mm high; be placed in the same field of vision as that of the statement of quantity marked on the package; and be indelible, clearly legible and visible under normal conditions of purchase.

Field of vision

15.6.3 The indication of net quantity on packages of food is required by the Food Labelling Regulations 1996 to appear in the same field of vision (ie to be simultaneously visible) as the name of the food, the indication of minimum durability or 'use by' date, the alcoholic strength and specified cautionary words, as appropriate (see para **6.5.25** above).

15.7 MISLEADING PRICE INDICATIONS

15.7.1 It is an offence to give any indication of price which is misleading[1]. Guidance as to misleading price indications is provided by a statutory Code of Practice[2] which is shortly to be revised to take account of changes arising from Directive 98/6/EC[3] and other legislation. For further comment on the complexities of Part III of the Consumer Protection Act 1987, the reader is referred to Butterworths *Trading and Consumer Law* para **2[3013]** ff.

1 CPA 1987, s 20.
2 Code of Practice for Traders on Price Indications: Department of Trade and Industry 1988.
3 See para **15.8.1** below.

15.8 PRICE MARKING INDICATIONS

15.8.1 The law requiring the price marking of food has changed as a result of European Parliament and Council Directive 98/6/EC on consumer protection in the indication of the prices of products offered to consumers. This in particular repealed and replaced Directive 79/581/EEC on the indication of the prices of foodstuffs. The new Directive aims at simplifying the comparison of products by abandoning the link with prescribed quantities[1] in favour of straightforward indications of the selling price and unit price.

In the United Kingdom, the Directive is implemented by the Price Marking Order 1999[2], which was made under the Prices Act 1974 and is enforced through the penalties it prescribes. The order revoked the Price Marking Order 1991[3] and the Price Marking (Pre-packed Milk in Vending Machines) Order 1976[4]. However, the Price Marking (Food and Drink on Premises) Order 1979[5] remains extant. As its name implies, this requires prices to be displayed on premises where food and drink is or may be for sale for consumption by the public.

1 See section **15.3** above.
2 SI 1999/3042.
3 SI 1991/1382.
4 SI 1976/796.
5 SI 1979/361.

Obligations to indicate the selling price and the unit price

15.8.2 Where, otherwise than in respect of products sold from bulk or during an advertisement, a trader indicates that a product is or may be for sale to a consumer, the 1999 Order requires that he indicate the selling price.

The Order also requires, subject to specified exceptions, that the unit price must be indicated for all products sold from bulk or for pre-packaged products required by or under Parts IV and V of the W&MA 1985 to be marked with the quantity or to be made up in a prescribed quantity. The exceptions relate to—

(a) products offered by aural advertisements, products offered at prices reduced on account of damaged condition or the danger of their deterioration, and products which comprise an assortment of different items sold in single packages;
(b) products of which the unit prices are identical to the selling prices;
(d) products which are pre-packaged in constant quantities and sold in small shops, by itinerant traders or from vending machines;

and to advertisements in which the selling price of the product is not indicated.

Manner of indication of prices and unit price roundings

15.8.3 The 1999 Order also requires that the selling and unit prices be displayed in sterling, but, subject to specified conditions, permits additional indications of price in foreign currency.

The prices and other required indications must be unambiguous, easily identifiable and clearly legible, placed in proximity to the products and so placed as to be visible to consumers without the need for assistance.

In the case of pre-packaged solid food products presented in a liquid medium, the unit price must refer to the product's net drained weight and be clearly distinguished from any indication of the unit price by reference to the net weight.

Prices are required to be inclusive of VAT and other taxes and provision is made in respect of price indications following a change in the rate of VAT.

To ensure accuracy in comparisons, rules are prescribed for calculating decimal places and roundings of unit prices.

Chapter 16

Feeding stuffs

16.1 INTRODUCTION

16.1.1 Fodder and feeding stuffs for animals, birds and fish are excluded from the definition of 'food' in section 1 of the Food Safety Act 1990 (FSA 1990) and thus generally outside the food safety and standards legislation. From 1893[1] separate but related provisions, now located in Part IV of the Agriculture Act 1970 (AA 1970), have been in place to prevent false descriptions of and deleterious substances in feeding stuffs. Since United Kingdom accession to the European Community, feeding stuffs legislation has essentially been made in implementation of Community Directives mostly (see paras **16.3.1** and **16.4.1** below) by regulations under the AA 1970 powers as fortified by the European Communities Act 1972 (ECA 1972)[2].

Provisions necessary for the biological safety of feeding stuffs have been made under the extensive powers of the Animal Health Act 1981 (AHA 1981) (see paras **16.9.2**, **16.9.3** and **16.10.1** below).

Moreover, until recently, the framework established by the Medicines Act 1968 (MA 1968) was used for the control of growth promoters, medicinal feed and similar products, but a switch has now been made to bespoke implementing Regulations under the ECA 1972 (see paras **16.6.1** and **16.8.1** below). The ECA 1972 powers have also been used to implement new Community provisions on the control of establishments and intermediaries and on official inspection of feeding stuffs (see paras **16.5.1** and **16.7.1** below).

A more radical development is the change contemplated by the Food Standards Agency functions in relation to animal feeding stuffs[3] and by section 30 of the Food Standards Act 1999 (FSA 1999). As noted in para **2.3.8***(e)* above, section 30 confers power by order to establish new provisions for the regulation of feed in Great Britain based on the FSA 1990. For feeding stuffs, the general regulatory powers of Part IV of the AA 1970, summarised in section **16.2** below, are thus expected to be superseded. The scope of the changes is awaited with interest, but section 30 evidently affords the opportunity to establish general requirements for the safety of feeding stuffs (similar to those for food in section 8 of the FSA 1990[4]) and otherwise to provide for the regulation of the hygiene as well as the composition of feed. Any such order may reasonably be expected to save current Regulations made under Part IV. Until the coming into force of the first section 30 order, the Secretary of State can make regulations under the 1970 Act, Part IV, either jointly with the minister of Agriculture, Fisheries and Food or alone (see para **2.2.3** above).

It is also necessary to bear in mind that substances and activities relating to the farm production of food sources[5] may be now regulated under the new power, inserted in the FSA 1990 by the FSA 1999[6]. This power evidently gives further scope for control of feeding stuffs although normally it is expected to be invoked only where an adequate alternative does not exist.

Explanation of the devolution of responsibility for feeding stuffs; the power under the

Trade Descriptions Act 1968 (TDA 1968) in respect of feeding stuffs; the Advisory Committee on Feeding stuffs; emergency control orders; emergency orders under the Food and Environment Protection Act 1985; enforcement provisions and defences under the various statutes are at paras **2.1.2**; **2.2.2**; **2.4.11**; **11.6.2**; **11.7.3**; **17.8.1** and **19.6.1** respectively.

It should also be noted that any statement made in respect of, or mark applied to, any material in pursuance of Part IV of the AA 1970 or any name or expression to which a meaning has been assigned under section 70 of that Act when applied to any material in the circumstances specified in that section are deemed not to be trade descriptions and thus not caught by section 1 of the TDA 1968[7].

On the basis that the safety of food from animal origin begins with safe animal feed, the Commission's White Paper on Food Safety[8], proposes a new Regulation to establish animal and public health as the primary objective of animal feed legislation. It is suggested that this should lay down common underlying principles including in particular the scientific basis, the responsibilities of producers and suppliers, the systematic implementation of hazard analysis and critical control points (HACCP), traceability, efficient controls and enforcement. A separate Regulation is proposed for the authorisation of novel feeding stuffs, including in particular genetically modified organisms and products derived from them.

1 Fertilisers and Feeding Stuffs Act 1893.
2 AA 1970, s 74A.
3 See para **2.3.3** above.
4 See section **9.2** above.
5 As to 'food source', see para **4.4.1** above.
6 FSA 1990, Sch 1, para 6A. See further para **4.1.4** above.
7 TDA 1968, s 2(4).
8 COM (1999) 719 final.

16.2 AGRICULTURE ACT 1970, PART IV

16.2.1 With the prospect of changes under section 30 of the FSA 1999[1], it is not appropriate here to offer an extended explanation of the provisions laid down by Part IV of the AA 1970 for the protection of purchasers in Great Britain from feeding stuffs of unsafe or substandard composition. However, a brief summary of its provisions should aid understanding of the transition to the new arrangements. As indicated in para **2.3.8***(e)*, the concepts applied in Part IV for the control of feed are akin to those applied in respect of food by the FSA 1990.

1 See para **16.1.1** above.

16.2.2 The AA 1970 requires a written statutory statement of prescribed compositional information to be given to the purchaser of feeding stuffs and makes provision for the marking of material prepared for sale. Where a feeding stuff is sold under a name or description for which a meaning has been assigned by Regulations, there is an implied warranty that it accords with that meaning and failure of a sample to accord with that meaning renders the seller liable to a fine. Moreover, the seller must give particulars of specified attributes claimed to be present, a warranty being implied that these particulars are correct. A warranty by the seller is also in particular implied as to the suitability of the feeding stuff for use as such. The sale of feeding stuffs containing deleterious ingredients or of dangerous or unwholesome material for use as feeding stuffs is prohibited.

16.2.2 *Feeding stuffs*

Detailed provisions for the operation of these compositional requirements are laid down by Regulations as noted in para **16.3.1** below.

Enforcement is the responsibility, in England, of county, metropolitan district and London borough councils and the Common Council of the City of London and, in Wales, of county and county borough councils. These authorities are required to appoint inspectors and agricultural analysts.

16.2.3 Part IV of the AA 1970 also provides for purchasers to have samples taken and analysed, for inspectors to enter premises and take samples, for the division of samples and analysis by agricultural analysts, for further analysis by the Government Chemist and for regulations prescribing sampling and analysis methods. The 1998 Report on the Review of Public Analyst Arrangements in England and Wales[1] recommended that the provisions for handling samples in the AA 1970 should be aligned with current arrangements for food which allow samples to be passed outside of the current public analyst system if the necessary technology exists elsewhere[2].

The current Regulations prescribing sampling and analysis methods for feeding stuffs are noted in para **16.4.1** below.

1 See para **2.7.1** above.
2 FSA 1990, s 30(4), see para **17.4.6** below.

16.3 COMPOSITIONAL REGULATIONS

16.3.1 The Feeding Stuffs Regulations 1995, as amended, currently lay down the detailed compositional requirements for the operation of Part IV of the AA 1970. In particular they specify the animals to which the definition of 'feeding stuff' applies, the feeding stuffs for which statutory statements must be given, the form and contents of those statements and the meanings assigned to particular feeding stuff names.

The Regulations are the main means by which the substantial body of European Community legislation on the composition of feeding stuffs is implemented in Great Britain. Principal rules enacted by the Council are to be found in Directive 70/524/EEC (concerning additives in feeding stuffs)[1], Directive 79/373/EEC (on the marketing of compound feeding stuffs), Directive 80/511/EEC (authorising in certain cases, the marketing of compound feeding stuffs in unsealed packages and containers), Directive 82/471/EEC (concerning certain protein sources used in animal nutrition), Directive 93/113/EEC (concerning the use and marketing of enzymes, micro-organisms and their preparation in animal nutrition), Directive 93/74/EC (on feeding stuffs intended for particular nutritional purposes), Directive 96/25/EC (on the circulation of feed materials) and Directive 1999/29/EC (on undesirable substances and products in animal nutrition).

In implementation of the Community obligations, the Regulations—

(a) prescribe labelling and marking requirements for pre-mixtures of additives;
(b) provide for the manner of packaging and sealing of compound feeding stuffs, additives and pre-mixtures;
(c) specify the meanings assigned to the names of particular materials, for the purposes of the AA 1970;
(d) regulate the marketing and use of feeding stuffs containing additives and additives intended to be incorporated in feeding stuffs[1];
(e) restrict the marketing and use of feeding stuffs containing specified undesirable substances and the putting into circulation of feed materials containing such substances[2];

(f) restrict the marketing and use of specified protein sources and non-protein nitrogenous compounds in feeding stuffs;
(g) prescribe a minimum iron content for milk replacer feeds;
(h) prohibit the marketing of compound feeding stuffs in which the level of ash insoluble in hydrochloric acid exceeds specified levels;
(i) restrict the marketing of feeding stuffs intended for particular nutritional purposes; and
(j) confer on inspectors appointed under the AA 1970 powers to inspect manufacturers' records relating to compound feeding stuffs.

1 As to the distinction between additives and undesirable substances in feeding stuffs, see case 5/77 *Tedeschi v Denkavit* [1977] 5 ECR 1551, [1978] 1 CMLR 1.
2 In particular, the sale and use of sewage sludge as a compound feeding stuff is prohibited in implementation of Commission Decision 91/516/EEC.

16.3.2 As regards the control of additives in feeding stuffs, it should be noted that Directive 70/524/EEC was almost entirely replaced by amending Directive 96/51/EC. Among other features of the new system thus introduced was the strengthening of safeguards in respect of zootechnical additives by requiring persons putting them into circulation to be specifically authorised. These provisions have been separately implemented in the United Kingdom by the Feedingstuffs (Zootechnical Products) Regulations 1999 described in section **16.6** below. It should also be noted that, to avoid distortions in trade caused by implementation delays by Member States, amending Directive 96/51/EC provides for additives to be authorised in future by Community Regulations rather than Directives[1]. Further amendment of the Feeding Stuffs Regulations 1995 is evidently necessary to provide for the enforcement of a number of such Community additive Regulations, as well as for the full transposition of other changes to Community compositional law such as in Council Directive 96/25/EC (on the circulation of feed materials) and Council Directive 1999/29/EC (on undesirable substances and products in animal nutrition)[2].

Further Commission proposals are under discussion to provide for the strengthening of the rules on the maximum permitted levels for undesirable substances in Directive 1999/29/EC and for the amendment of Directives 96/25/EC and 79/373/EEC to require full ingredient listing.

1 See section **1.5** above.
2 See n 1 to para **16.3.1** above.

16.4 SAMPLING AND ANALYSIS REGULATIONS

16.4.1 The European Community soon found it necessary to provide for the introduction of common sampling and analysis methods for the official control of feeding stuffs. Within the framework established by Council Directive 70/373/EEC, the Commission has prescribed sampling methods by Directive 76/371/EEC and a series of analysis methods by Directives 71/250/EEC, 71/393/EEC, 72/199/EEC, 73/46/EEC, 76/372/EEC, 78/633/EEC, 98/64/EC, and 1999/27/EC[1]. Of particular note is Commission Directive 98/88 which, having in mind enforcement of the Community ban on the use of protein derived from mammalian tissue in feeding stuffs for ruminants[2], establishes guidelines for the microscopic identification and estimation of constituents of animal origin.

16.4.1 *Feeding stuffs*

Under the powers of AA 1970, these provisions are generally implemented in Great Britain by the Feeding Stuffs (Sampling and Analysis) Regulations 1999[3]. However, sampling and analysis methods for zootechnical products are implemented by the Feedingstuffs (Zootechnical Products) Regulations 1999[4]. The Feeding Stuffs (Sampling and Analysis) Regulations also implement the obligation in Council Directive 95/53/EC[5] to ensure that sampling and analysis is carried out in accordance with Community rules, or in their absence, standards recognised by international bodies or scientifically recognised national rules.

1 See also Directive 1999/76/EC.
2 See further para **16.9.2**.
3 The Ministry of Agriculture, Fisheries and Food issued guidance notes to the requirements of the Feedingstuffs (Sampling and Analysis) Regulations 1982, which are consolidated into the 1999 Regulations.
4 See section **16.6** below.
5 See further section **16.7** below.

16.5 ESTABLISHMENTS AND INTERMEDIARIES

16.5.1 Conditions and arrangements for approving and registering establishments and intermediaries operating in the animal feed sector were laid down by Council Directive 95/69/EC. In relation to feeding stuffs and related products which do not contain zootechnical additives[1], this Directive and Articles 6, 8 and 9 of supplemental Commission Directive 98/51/EC are implemented in the United Kingdom by the Feeding stuffs (Establishments and Intermediaries) Regulations 1999 made under the ECA 1972[2]. The Regulations also implement relevant parts of Council Directive 95/53/EC (fixing the principles governing the organisation of official inspections in the field of animal nutrition)[3] and Council Directive 96/51/EC, which substantially replaced the provisions of Directive 70/524/EEC (concerning additives in feeding stuffs)[4].

The Regulations require intermediaries, establishments located in the United Kingdom and establishments located in third countries to be approved or registered. Broadly speaking, 'establishments' are units that manufacture feed additives, premixtures, compound feeds or specified protein sources, while 'intermediaries' are those who wrap, package, store or put into circulation feed additives, premixtures or specified protein sources[5]. The definitions of both terms are to be found in Article 1(3) of Directive 95/69/EC. Generally, approval is required for activities which, under Directive 95/69/EC, are considered potentially hazardous to animals, humans and the environment, whereas registration applies to the use of less sensitive products. In both cases, however, establishments and intermediaries must comply with detailed requirements.

In relation to establishments and intermediaries which must be approved or registered, the Regulations in particular contain provisions which regulate—

(a) the putting into circulation of specified additives, premixtures containing those additives and specified protein sources;
(b) the supply of specified additives, alone or in premixtures; and
(c) the incorporation of specified additives and premixtures containing such additives, in compound feeding stuffs.

1 As to products which contain zootechnical additives, see section **16.6** below.
2 The Ministry of Agriculture, Fisheries and Food has produced guidance to approval and registration of establishments and intermediaries operating in the animal feeding stuffs sector.
3 See section **16.7** below.

4 See section **16.3** above.
5 As to protein sources, see Council Directive 82/471/EEC.

16.6 ZOOTECHNICAL PRODUCTS

16.6.1 'Zootechnical additives' are antibiotics, coccidiostats and other medicinal feed additives and growth promoters listed in Part I of Annex C of Directive 70/524/EEC concerning additives in feeding stuffs. The rules for their control under that Directive were strengthened by amending Directive 96/51/EC because the circulation of poor copies within the Community had been undermining confidence in their safety. As a result, authorisations of zootechnical additives are now to be linked to the persons responsible for putting them into circulation. Authorisations of certain zootechnical additives by Directive 70/524/EEC have also been withdrawn by Commission Regulations 2788/98/EC and Commission Regulation 45/1999/EC and Council Regulation 2821/98/EC[1].

In the United Kingdom, the Feedingstuffs (Zootechnical Products) Regulations 1999, implement these provisions and also, so far as they relate to zootechnical additives and products containing them—

(a) the Community rules on the conditions and arrangements for approving and registering certain establishments and intermediaries operating in the animal feed sector (that is, Council Directive 95/69/EC and Articles 6, 8 and 9 of Commission Directive 98/51/EC[2]);
(b) the sampling methods prescribed by Directive 76/371/EEC and analysis methods prescribed by Directives 71/250/EEC, 71/393/EEC, 72/199/EEC, 73/46/EEC, 76/372/EEC, 78/633/EEC, 81/715/EEC, 84/425/EC, 93/70/EC, 93/117/EC, 98/64/EC and 1999/27/EC[3]; and
(c) the requirements of Council Directive 95/53 fixing the principles governing the organisation of official inspections in the field of animal nutrition[4].

The Regulations make extensive provision for applications for the Community authorisation of zootechnical additives, the approval of establishments located in the United Kingdom, the approval of intermediaries, the approval of establishments located in third countries and the control of zootechnical additives, zootechnical premixtures and zootechnical feeding stuffs.

Fees are set for the examination of dossiers in respect of applications for the Community authorisation of zootechnical additives and for the approval of establishments located in the United Kingdom and intermediaries.

In Great Britain the Royal Pharmaceutical Society of Great Britain is responsible for enforcement.

The application of the MA 1968 to zootechnical additives is excluded except in relation to any advisory function of a committee relating to veterinary medicinal products[5] and to animal test certificates for unauthorised zootechnical additives. In consequence, zootechnical additives are no longer licensed under the MA 1968. Consequential revocations and amendments are made by the Medicated Feedingstuffs and Feedingstuffs (Zootechnical Products) (Consequential Provisions) Regulations 1998.

1 As to the authorisation of additives by Community Regulations rather than Directives, see further para **16.3.2** above.
2 See section **16.5** above.
3 See section **16.4** above.
4 See section **16.7** above.
5 See para **2.4.13** above.

16.7 OFFICIAL INSPECTION OF FEEDING STUFFS

16.7.1 Principles governing the organisation of official inspections in the field of animal nutrition were fixed for the Community by Council Directive 95/53/EC[1]. The Directive is a horizontal measure and a variety of provisions implement it in the United Kingdom. The Feeding Stuffs (Sampling and Analysis) Regulations 1999[2], the Feeding Stuffs (Establishments and Intermediaries) Regulations 1999[3] and the Feeding Stuffs (Zootechnical Products) Regulations 1999[4] each do so as necessary for the specific sectors to which they apply. Moreover, general provisions already existed covering some of the ground. As regards sampling for analysis, for example, section 77 of the AA 1970 anticipated the obligation in Article 18.1 of Directive 95/53/EC to provide for second opinions and for the preservation of reference samples. The Feeding Stuffs (Enforcement) Regulations 1999, which apply to the United Kingdom, complete the implementation process.

The Regulations provide for checks and enforcement action in relation to products brought into the United Kingdom from third countries and products traded within the European Community. The AA 1970 is modified as regards powers of entry, inspections, sampling and analysis and other matters.

1 See also subordinate Commission Directive 98/68/EC.
2 See section **16.4** above.
3 See section **16.5** above.
4 See section **16.6** above.

16.8 MEDICATED FEEDING STUFFS

16.8.1 Animal feeding stuffs with which veterinary medicinal products[1] have been mixed for the purpose of treating or preventing outbreaks of disease in livestock are known as 'medicated feeding stuffs'. The conditions governing their preparation, placing on the market and use in the Community are laid down by Council Directive 90/167/EEC, which is implemented in the United Kingdom by the Medicated Feeding Stuffs Regulations 1998.

The Regulations provide for approval of premises used for manufacturing medicated feeding stuffs and of distributors of medicated feeding stuffs and specify fees in relation to applications. Agricultural merchants are also subject to controls.

The manufacture, retail supply, packaging and labelling of particular products used to make medicated feeding stuffs and the manufacture, packaging, labelling and supply of medicated feeding stuffs are regulated. Subject to an exemption in respect of anthelmintic medicinal products, medicated feeding stuffs and products used to make them may be supplied to stock farmers and holders of animals only against a veterinary surgeon's 'MFS prescription'. The veterinarian must in particular be satisfied that there will be no incompatibility with a previous use, such as administration of an antibiotic or coccidiostat which had already been fed to the animals in a zootechnical feeding stuff.

Specified records must be kept by persons engaged in the manufacture or retail supply of medicated feeding stuffs and the retail supply of products used in their manufacture.

In Great Britain the Royal Pharmaceutical Society of Great Britain is responsible for enforcement.

The application of the MA 1968 is excluded, except in relation to animal test certificates and the retail supply of intermediate products. Consequential revocations are made by the Medicated Feedingstuffs and Feedingstuffs (Zootechnical Products) (Consequential Provisions) Regulations 1998.

1 See Council Directive 81/851/EEC on the approximation of the laws of Member States relating to veterinary products.

16.9 BOVINE SPONGIFORM ENCEPHALOPATHY

16.9.1 Section **13.8** above summarised the legislation to prevent any possible human exposure to bovine spongiform encephalopathy through the consumption of food. This section describes measures taken in respect of feeding stuffs.

It remains to be seen how far the new powers conferred by section 30 of the FSA 1999[1] will be used for the control of biological hazards in feeding stuffs. Until now domestic powers for this purpose have been confined to the AHA 1981. By this means, measures have been taken to prevent the spread of bovine spongiform encephalopathy (BSE) through feeding stuffs containing mammalian meal and specified risk material. These measures are respectively described in paras **16.9.2** and **16.9.3** below. Provision for the identification of ruminant protein in feed for ruminants and other surveillance measures is summarised in para **16.9.4**.

1 See paras **2.2.3**, **2.2.4**, **2.3.8**(*e*) and **16.1.1** above.

Mammalian protein and mammalian meat and bone meal

16.9.2 Very soon after the appearance of BSE, scientists in Britain suspected that the consumption of meat and bone meal by cattle was responsible for the disease. In 1988 a ban was imposed on the feeding to ruminants of rations containing ruminant protein. In 1994, Commission Decision 94/381/EC required Community Member States to prohibit the feeding of protein derived from mammalian tissues to ruminant species. The British provisions were amended in implementation of this requirement.

British measures were further strengthened to prevent contamination of cattle feed with material intended for monogastric animals following the advice of the Government's Spongiform Encephalopathy Advisory Committee in 1996[1]. The sale or supply of mammalian meat and bone meal for the purpose of feeding to all farm animals was banned.

The relevant provisions are now to be found in Part III of the Bovine Spongiform Encephalopathy (No 2) Order 1996, as amended. Subject to specified exceptions, the sale, supply and use of feeding stuffs containing mammalian protein or mammalian meat and bone meal is prohibited, as is the possession of mammalian meat and bone meal on any premises where livestock feeding stuffs are produced or stored or where livestock is kept. Provision is also made for cleansing and disinfection of places where mammalian meat and bone meal and resulting products have been produced, stored or used, for the disposal and recall of meal and products and for the keeping of records.

Amendment of Decision 94/381/EC in the light of recent scientific opinions is proposed by the Commission's White Paper on Food Safety[2].

1 As to the Spongiform Encephalopathy Advisory Committee and its 1996 advice, see respectively paras **2.4.6** and **13.8.1** above.

2 COM (1999) 719 final.

Specified risk material

16.9.3 Paragraph **13.8.2** above explained the legislation forbidding use in food of material which might potentially harbour BSE infectivity, the current ban being in the Specified Risk Material Regulations 1997. In 1990 the food use ban was extended to use in feeding stuffs, for which the rules are now to be found in the Specified Risk Material Order 1997, as amended. As further explained in para **13.8.2**, Commission Decision 97/534/EC prescribed Community-wide controls in respect of specified material from cattle, sheep and goats, but this has been successively deferred, most recently until 30 June 2000. The United Kingdom Government, therefore, acted unilaterally in making the 1997 Regulations and Order to protect public health by prohibiting the material in all food and animal feed, including imported products.

The principal new provision in the Specified Risk Material Order 1997, relates to 'class I specified risk material'. As regards bovine animals, this class comprises, for those aged over 12 months at death outside the United Kingdom, the skull, including the brain and eyes, tonsils and spinal cord, and for those aged over 6 months at death in the United Kingdom, the brains, spinal cord, thymus, tonsils, spleen and intestines and also the skull (including the eyes) of such animals aged over 12 months at death. As regards sheep and goats, the material included in the class is the spleen and, for those animals which at death had a permanent incisor tooth erupted through the gums or were aged over 12 months, the skull (including the brain and eyes), tonsils and spinal cord. The Order prohibits imports of class I specified risk material, except for use in a manufacturing process not producing food or feeding stuffs or cosmetic, pharmaceutical or medical products or products likely to come into contact with any of them[1]. Additionally, specified imported food and feeding stuffs are required to be certified by the veterinary authorities in the place from which they were despatched to the United Kingdom as not containing class I specified risk material.

The Order also—

(a) prohibits the use of specified bovine material derived from animals slaughtered in the United Kingdom in ingredients for cosmetics, pharmaceutical and medical products;
(b) prohibits the use of all specified risk material in feeding stuffs for any creature, subject to an exemption for research purposes;
(c) prohibits the removal of brain and eyes from carcases;
(d) provides for the approval of premises as suitable to process specified risk material in a manufacturing process not producing any food, feeding stuff, cosmetic, pharmaceutical or medical products or any product likely to come into contact with any of them;
(e) makes provision as regards transport, storage and sampling and for the recall and disposal of specified risk material imported, produced or sold in contravention of the Order; and
(f) prohibits the export of specified risk material to other Member States, except in accordance with a licence granted by the minister.

1 The parallel Northern Irish import ban has been challenged by *Eurostock Meat Marketing Ltd* and the NI Court of Appeal has referred questions to the European Court. Meanwhile, the Specified Risk Material (Northern Ireland) Order 1997 continues to apply in all respects except as regards the applicant.

Feeding stuffs and surveillance

16.9.4 For the purpose of routine monitoring, in particular in plants which produce feed for pigs and/or poultry as well as for ruminants, Commission Decision 94/474/EC, as amended by Decision 95/287/EC, requires the United Kingdom to carry out official tests (known as ELISA tests[1]) for the identification of ruminant protein in feed intended for ruminants.

To give early warning of the emergence or occurrence of BSE or scrapie[2], Commission Decision 98/272/EC requires Member States to carry out an annual monitoring programme in accordance with prescribed conditions. These Community obligations are implemented in Great Britain by the Bovine Spongiform Encephalopathy (Feeding Stuffs and Surveillance) Regulations 1999. The Regulations enable samples to be taken for the purpose of enabling the ELISA tests to be carried out and make provision for the investigation by veterinary inspectors of BSE as part of the annual monitoring programme under Decision 98/272/EC.

As regards scrapie, the Decision 98/272/EC monitoring requirement is implemented by the Sheep and Goats Spongiform Encephalopathy Regulations 1998.

1 The enzyme-linked immunosorbent assay test specially developed to detect mammalian protein in animal feed.
2 Scrapie is an animal transmissible spongiform encephalopathy affecting sheep and goats which has been known for more than 250 years.

16.10 ANIMAL WASTE

16.10.1 The protection of feeding stuffs from biological contamination by BSE and other spongiform encephalopathy agents is an aspect of the wider problem of preventing pathogens in feeding stuffs of animal or fish origin. Further Community rules about this are laid down by and under Council Directive 90/667/EEC on veterinary rules for the disposal and processing of animal waste. Supplementary rules (on the approval of alternative heat treatment systems for processing high risk material) are, in particular, contained in Commission Decision 92/562/EEC. These rules, together with those in Council Decision 95/348/EEC (on the treatment of certain types of waste intended to be marketed locally as feeding stuffs for certain animal categories) were implemented in Great Britain by the Animal By-Products Order 1999 made under the AHA 1981. The main parts of the Order make provision for the disposal of high risk and low risk material, catering waste intended for feeding to pigs and poultry and swill for use as feeding stuffs.

By Commission Decision 97/735/EC, Member States are also required to ensure that mammalian animal waste, which has not been processed to guard against transmissible spongiform encephalopathies in accordance with Commission Decision 99/534/EC, cannot enter the feed chain.

To ensure that only animal by-products derived from animals declared fit for human consumption can enter animal feed, the Commission's White Paper on Food Safety[1] proposes amending Directive 90/667/EEC and Directive 92/118/EEC on derived products[2].

1 COM (1999) 719 final.
2 See para **13.1.2** above.

Chapter 17

Enforcement: inspections, sampling, analysis, examination and powers of entry

17.1 INTRODUCTION

17.1.1 No matter how good substantive food laws are, they will be ineffective without sound enforcement. Dating back essentially to 1875[1], British provisions for enforcement by local authority officers have been adapted to serve the purposes of Community official food control. Administrative penalties were considered earlier in this book (see section **9.3** on the inspection, detention and seizure of suspected food; sections **11.2–11.4** on improvement notices, prohibition orders and emergency prohibition notices and orders; and para **12.1.3** on licensing of food premises). Moreover, paras **13.1.1** and **13.1.6** explained the Community control framework and provision for inspection charging in respect of products of animal origin.

This chapter describes the general powers of inspection; chapter 18 deals with prosecutions and evidence, including Code C under the Police and Criminal Evidence Act 1984[2] and the provisions of the Criminal Procedure and Investigations Act 1996. General food inspection is considered below under the following headings—

(a) Community requirements (section **17.2**);
(b) inspections in Great Britain (section **17.3**);
(c) sampling and analysis etc (section **17.4**);
(d) powers of entry, obstruction etc (section **17.5**);
(e) administrative implementation of the official control Directives (section 17.6);
(f) weights and measures enforcement (section **17.7**);
(g) other legislation (section **17.8**).

Before addressing these particular aspects, it should be noted that in its White Paper on Food Safety[3], the Commission contemplates a comprehensive piece of legislation on food and feed safety control which will in particular merge and complete existing rules for national and Community internal and import controls and create a Community approach to financial support for official controls.

1 See para **1.1.1** above.
2 Police and Criminal Evidence Act 1984 (Codes of Practice) (No 3) Order 1995.
3 COM (1999) 719 final.

17.2 COMMUNITY REQUIREMENTS

Official food control Directives

17.2.1 Council Directive 89/397/EEC, as supplemented by Directive 93/99/EEC, lays down the general principles for the performance of official control of foodstuffs in the European Community. 'Official control of foodstuffs' means an inspection by the competent authorities of the compliance of foodstuffs; of food additives, vitamins, mineral salts, trace elements and other additives intended to be sold as such; and of materials and articles intended to come into contact with foodstuffs, with provisions aimed at preventing risks to public health, guaranteeing fair commercial transactions or protecting consumer interests, including provisions on consumer information.

Member States are required to take all necessary measures to ensure that official control is carried out in accordance with Directive 89/397/EEC. As explained in para **4.7.2** above, products consigned to other Member States must be inspected with the same care as those marketed at home and products for export outside the Community must not be excluded.

General inspection requirement

17.2.2 Article 4 of Directive 89/397/EEC requires that inspections shall be carried out regularly and where non-compliance is suspected. The means of inspection must be proportionate to the end to be observed and must cover all stages of production, manufacture, import into the Community, processing, storage, transport, distribution and trade. It should be carried out at the stage most appropriate to achieve the objective. As a general rule, inspections should be carried out without prior warning.

Control operations

17.2.3 By Article 5 of Directive 89/397/EEC, control must include one or more of the following operations, that is to say, inspection; sampling and analysis; inspection of staff hygiene; examination of written and documentary material; and examination of any verification systems set up by the undertaking and of the results obtained.

Inspection subjects

17.2.4 Article 6 of Directive 89/397/EEC requires that the following shall be subject to inspection—

(a) the state and use which is made at the different stages of production and distribution of the site, premises, offices, plant surroundings, means of transport, machinery and equipment;
(b) raw materials, ingredients, technological aids and other products used for the preparation and production of foodstuffs;
(c) semi-finished products;
(d) finished products;
(e) materials and articles intended to come into contact with foodstuffs;
(f) cleaning and maintenance products and processes and pesticides;
(g) processes used for the manufacture or processing of foodstuffs;
(h) labelling and presentation of foodstuffs;
(i) preserving methods.

These operations may be supplemented by interviews with the head of the business under inspection or persons working for it; by the reading of values recorded by measuring instruments installed by the undertaking; and by inspections carried out by the competent authority, with its own instruments, of measurements taken with the instruments installed by the undertaking.

Other provisions of the Directives

17.2.5 Directive 89/397/EEC also provides for the taking of samples and their analysis by official laboratories; hygiene inspections of persons who in their work come into contact, whether directly or indirectly, with the materials and products referred to in para **17.2.4***(b)–(f)*; the noting and copying of written and documentary material; the taking of requisite measures by inspectors; the securing of their powers; their observance of professional secrecy; the drawing up of forward inspection programmes; and notifying the Commission of UK competent authorities and official laboratories[1]. Implementation of the requirements in respect of legal action is dealt with in chapter 18.

Directive 93/99/EEC supplements these principal provisions by requiring authorities to have sufficient suitably qualified and experienced staff; prescribing quality standards and validated analysis mathods for official laboratories; requiring designated Commission food inspectors to be able to accompany national inspectors; and requiring Member States to designate a single liaison body to facilitate co-operation with authorities in other Member States[2].

1 Directive 89/397/EEC, Arts 7–11, 12(2) and 14–15.
2 Directive 93/99/EEC, Arts 2–6.

17.3 INSPECTIONS IN GREAT BRITAIN

Implementation of the food control Directives

17.3.1 In Great Britain, Directives 89/39/EEC and 93/99/EEC are for the most part implemented by, and must in consequence be taken into account in interpreting[1], the enforcement provisions in and under the Food Safety Act 1990 (FSA 1990)[2], including the statutory Codes of Practice[3].

The competent authorities undertaking the inspections are the enforcement authorities specified in section 6 of the Act[4]. Their activities are co-ordinated as described in para **17.3.2** below. The detailed statutory enforcement provisions are considered in sections **17.4** and **17.5** below.

The provisions have now to be seen in the context of the Enforcement Concordat. This was introduced in March 1998 and commits central and local government enforcement agencies to good enforcement policies and procedures. The policy requires each of them to draw up of standards of service and performance, to provide information and advice openly and helpfully, to establish an easily accessible complaints procedure, to ensure that required action is proportionate to the risks and to carry out its duties fairly, equitably and consistently. It remains to be seen how effective these extra-statutory arrangements will be.

Certain administrative arrangements in implementation of Directives 89/397/EEC and 93/99/EEC are described in section **17.6** below.

Directives 89/397/EEC and 93/99/EEC do not apply to metrological controls[5] which are enforced under the Weights and Measures Act 1985 (W&MA 1985) as described in section **17.7** below. The enforcement provisions of other legislation is briefly noted in section **17.8**.

1 See para **1.2.1** above.
2 See in particular FSA 1990, Pt III and ss 40, 41, and 42; Food Safety (Enforcement Authority) (England and Wales) Order 1990; Food Safety (Sampling and Qualifications) Regulations 1990; and Food Safety (Exports) Regulations 1991.
3 See Codes of Practice no 2 (Legal Matters); no 3 (Inspection Procedures – General); no 7 (Sampling for Analysis or Examination); no 8 (Food Standards Inspections); no 9 (Food Hygiene Inspections); Code of Practice no 13 (Enforcement of the Food Safety Act 1990 in relation to Crown premises) – see further para **4.1.6** above; and Code of Practice no 20 (Exchange of information between Member States of the EU on routine food control).
4 See para **2.5.1** above.
5 Directive 89/397/EEC, Art 1(4).

Co-ordination of local authority enforcement

17.3.2 As indicated in para **5.3.11** above, with the removal of war-time controls, it was no longer seen as appropriate for central government to issue extra statutory food rules. For the purpose of assisting with trade codes of practice, local enforcement authorities were instead encouraged to establish a joint committee. This evolved into a means of reconciling conflicts in advice on compliance with food law given by individual local authorities to companies trading nationally. As consumer protection legislation developed in the 1960s, the committee was replaced by the Local Authorities Co-ordinating Body on Food and Trading Standards (LACOTS) with a wider mandate of promoting good law and best practice in trading standards and food safety[1]. In particular LACOTS has devised the 'home authority principle' as the key method of enforcement co-ordination. In summary, this—

- encourages authorities to place special emphasis on goods and services originating within their area;
- provides businesses with a home authority source of guidance and advice;
- supports efficient liaison between local authorities;
- provides a system for the resolution of problems and disputes.

Generally, advice on compliance should be sought by a food manufacturer from the enforcement authority where its decision-making base is located (that is, its 'home authority') and any other authority undertaking inspections, sampling or investigations or dealing with complaints (that is, an 'enforcing authority') should consider liaising with the home authority before pursuing detailed investigation or legal action. Where the manufacturer produces or packs products in an area other than where its decision-making base is located, the authority for that area (an 'originating authority') has particular responsibilities for ensuring that those products conform to legal requirements. In co-operation with the home authority, it will determine those aspects on which it should exercise the home authority functions and advise the manufacturer and enforcing authorities. The home authority principle is intended to help businesses to comply with the law in a spirit of consultation rather than confrontation. It removes neither their obligation to comply with the law, nor the responsibility of the enforcement authority for an area in which a particular contravention is perceived to have taken place[2].

Some formal status has been given to the LACOTS home authority principle by the requirement in statutory Codes of Practice that food authorities should have regard to it[3]. Moreover, in 1996 LACOTS was appointed as the single liaison body for the United

Kingdom for the purposes of supplemental official control Directive 93/99/EEC. By Article 6, the competent authorities of the Member States are required to afford each other administrative assistance in all supervisory procedures and to facilitate this administrative assistance each Member State is required to designate a single liaison body to liaise with the bodies in other Member States. Guidance on the operation of the system is given by Code of Practice no 20 (Exchange of information between Member States of the EU on routine food control matters).

The White Paper 'The Food Standards Agency: a force for change' proposed that there should be detailed discussions between government and local authorities on the improvement of enforcement activity[4]. Among matters suggested for consideration were that the home authority arrangements should be made mandatory and (as recommended by the James Report) that the Agency should take over the LACOTS' role as the single liaison body.

The Agency certainly now has a central role in relation to enforcement of feeding stuffs[5] as well as food legislation. As explained in para **2.3.5** above, section 12 of the Food Standards Act 1999 (FSA 1999) empowers the Agency to monitor, set standards for and audit performance of enforcement authorities.

In the context of enforcement co-ordination it is also right to have in mind the Secretary of State's powers, in section 6(3) of the FSA 1990, to direct that a duty imposed by the FSA 1990 on a food authority shall be discharged by the Secretary of State, the Minister of Agriculture, Fisheries and Food or the Food Standards Agency[6] and, in section 6(5) and (5A), to take over, or direct that the Agency takes over, the conduct of proceedings instituted by some other person[7].

1 For Scotland, the Scottish Food Co-ordinating Committee (SFCC) is the co-ordinating body in those areas where arrangements differ from England and Wales.
2 *Walker's Snack Foods Ltd v Coventry City Council* [1998] 3 All ER 163.
3 See Codes of Practice no 8 (Food Standards Inspections) and no 9 (Food Hygiene Inspections).
4 January 1998 Cm 3830, paras 3.35–3.47.
5 See para **17.8.1** below.
6 See Appendix D, item 6.
7 See Appendix D, items 8 and 9.

17.4 SAMPLING AND ANALYSIS ETC

17.4.1 Article 7 of official control Directive 89/397/EEC provides that samples of products enumerated in items *(b)–(f)* of para **17.2.4** above may be taken for analysis and that analyses must be carried out at official laboratories. In Great Britain these Community provisions are implemented by sections 29–31 of the FSA 1990 and the Food Safety (Sampling and Qualifications) Regulations 1990 considered in the following paragraphs of this section. Guidance on sampling for analysis or examination is given by Code of Practice no 7 (Sampling for Analysis or Examination).

It will be recalled that the FSA 1990 continues in part to treat chemical and biological contamination separately[1]. As noted in para **2.8.1** above, 'analysis' is defined as including microbiological assay and any technique for establishing the composition of food[2], while 'examination' means microbiological examination[3]. The distinct methods of dealing with samples for analysis and examination respectively are described in paras **17.4.3** and **17.4.4** below. Both concepts are, however, embraced by the term 'analysis' as used in Community law[4], and in particular as used in the official control Directives which expressly cover food hygiene and microbiology[5].

1 See in particular paras **1.1.1** and **2.5.2** above.
2 FSA 1990, s 28(2).
3 FSA 1990, s 53(1).
4 For example, as regards the quality of water intended for human consumption, see Directive 98/83/EC, Art 7(5) and Annex III, Pt 1.
5 See in particular Directive 93/99/EEC, Art 2.

Procurement of samples

17.4.2 By section 29 of the FSA 1990, an authorised officer of an enforcement authority may—

(a) purchase a sample of any food, or any substance capable of being used in the preparation of food;
(b) take a sample of any food which—
  (i) appears to him to be intended for sale, or to have been sold, for human consumption; or
  (ii) is found by him on or in any premises which he is authorised to enter[1],
(c) take a sample from any food source, or a sample of any contact material, which is found by him on or in any such premises;
(d) take a sample of any article or substance which is found by him on or in any such premises and which he has reason to believe may be required as evidence in proceedings under any of the provisions of the FSA 1990 or of regulations or orders made under it.

The following points might usefully be noted about section 29.

(1) Samples considered here are to be distinguished from those taken for other purposes (for example, for surveillance under section 11(4) of the FSA 1999[2]). This chapter concerns the powers of sampling for the purposes of enforcement of provisions in and under the FSA 1990.
(2) Although very wide, these sampling powers are not without limit. The words 'take' and 'purchase' are mutually exclusive[3] with the result that, for example, a sample of a food source or contact material cannot be purchased. The term 'procure' is used in the Act to embrace both concepts.
(3) The whole of the food or other material procured will often form the subject of subsequent proceedings: a 'sample' is not confined to a small quantity from which conclusions about the bulk may be inferred. If such conclusions are to be drawn, the sample must certainly be fair, that is, representative of the whole[4]. The uneven distribution of aflatoxins in nuts and dried figs set a particular sampling problem. It is important to be able to detect the isolated 'hot spots' in the food. Special requirements were formerly laid down for this[5] under section 31(2)(b) of the FSA 1990 which enables Regulations made with respect to 'the manner of procuring samples', to include 'the steps to be taken in order to ensure that the samples are fair samples'. These national requirements have now been replaced by those set out in Directive 98/53/EC[6]. Examples of other special sampling procedures are given in paragraph 6 of Code of Practice no 7 (Sampling for Analysis or Examination).
(4) An item of food handed by a complainant purchaser to an authorised officer has by definition not been procured in accordance with section 29 and is neither a sample[7], nor subject to the procedures prescribed by the Food Safety (Sampling and Qualifications) Regulations 1990[8]. This does not, of course, prevent the food from

being submitted by the food authority for analysis or examination, as the purchaser himself might have chosen to do[9]. Guidance on the handling of consumer complaints is given by Code of Practice no 2 (Legal Matters)[10]. Although the Food Safety (Sampling and Qualifications) Regulations 1990 do not apply, it is essential, if criminal or civil proceedings are contemplated, for the authorised officer to protect the integrity of the evidence and the rights of the seller by complying with the spirit of the provisions prescribed for storage, marking and notification.

1 See section **17.5** below.
2 See para **2.3.4** above.
3 *Marston v Wrington Vale Dairies Ltd* (1963) 61 LGR 202.
4 See, for example, *Crawford v Harding* 1907 J 11; *Heatlie v Reid* 1961 JC 70, 1961 SLT 137.
5 By the now revoked Aflatoxins in Nuts, Nut Products, Dried Figs and Dried Fig Products Regulations 1992.
6 See Contaminants in Food Regulations 1997, as amended, and para **10.5.2** above
7 *Arun District Council v Argyle Stores Ltd* (1986) 150 JP 552; *Love v Strickland and Holt Ltd* (3 February 1981, unreported); and *Leach v United Dairies Ltd* [1949] 1 All ER 1023.
8 See paras **17.4.3** and **17.4.4** below.
9 See FSA 1990, s 30(2) and para **17.4.5** below.
10 See para **9.2.5** above.

Procedure where sample is to be analysed

17.4.3 An authorised officer who has procured a sample under section 29 of the FSA 1990 and who considers that it should be analysed, is required by regulation 6(1) of the Food Safety (Sampling and Qualifications) Regulations 1990, forthwith[1] to divide it into three parts.

In the majority of cases the procedure stated in regulation 6(3) must then be followed. The authorised officer must—

(a) if necessary, place each part in a suitable container and seal each container;
(b) mark each part or container;
(c) as soon as it is reasonably practicable to do so, give one part to the owner and give him notice[2] that the sample will be analysed;
(d) submit one for analysis; and
(e) retain one part for future submission for 'checking analysis' as described in para **17.4.8** below;

As to (c), the definition of 'owner' in regulation 1(2) of Food Safety (Sampling and Qualifications) Regulations 1990 does not make clear whether a part given to, for example, a store manager of a corporate body is sufficient compliance.

Different provision is made for two exceptional sets of circumstances. The first relates to certain products in sealed containers. By regulation 6(2), if the sample consists of sealed containers and opening them would, in the opinion of the authorised officer, impede a proper analysis, the authorised officer must divide the sample into parts by putting the containers into three lots, and each lot must be treated as being a part. When considering whether this procedure should be used, it must be borne in mind that analysis of the retained part, noted at (e) above, may be made some considerable time after sampling. Examples where analysis may be affected are foods containing evanescent ingredients (eg vitamins which disappear quickly after opening); foods containing volatile substances such as alcohol; foods packaged in modified atmospheres which require gas analysis or which, if lost, could alter preservative levels; foods packed in aerosols; 'aerated' foods (eg carbonated soft drinks); and products for which an unopened container is necessary for a particular test (eg condensed milk claiming contents equivalent to a specified quantity of whole milk).

Secondly, special provision is made for samples which cannot be divided into parts. By regulation 6(4), if the authorised officer is of the opinion that division of the sample into parts is either not reasonably practicable or is likely to impede a proper analysis, he must, as soon as is reasonably practicable to do so, give to the owner notice that it will be analysed and submit it for analysis.

The 1998 Report on the Review of Public Analyst Arrangements in England and Wales recommended that, although not required by product safety legislation, the three part sampling requirement under the FSA 1990 should be retained[3].

In the normal way, if a prosecution follows the exercise by a sampling officer of the statutory powers, due compliance with regulation 6(1) of the Food Safety (Sampling and Qualifications) Regulations 1990 is a condition precedent to a valid conviction for an offence in or under the Act[4]. *Skeate v Moore* (a case considered under previous legislation) shows the problems in dealing with discrete items like meat pies and sausages. Because of the great difficulties of dividing such products equally, the sampling officer in that case divided six Cornish pasties he had purchased into three lots of two each. Of the two pasties submitted for analysis, the public analyst found that the aggregate of meat was less than was required for one pasty by the relevant Regulations[5]. The shopkeeper's conviction was reversed on appeal. The purpose of the three way division is to give the defendant and the court in due course as good an opportunity as the public analyst had, when he made his analysis, of ascertaining and establishing whether the offence charged has been committed. If the offence charged related exclusively to the part which the public analyst alone had the opportunity to examine, the object of the statutory procedure would be seriously impeded. The sample must be coextensive with the subject of the charge or representative of some larger entity. The Divisional Court took the view that if, as the justices thought, it was possible only to sample in the manner adopted, then the Regulations should be modified.

It is for consideration whether, in the case of any particular class of discrete items, the problems of dividing a sample are so severe that division is 'either not reasonably practicable or likely to impede proper analysis' within the meaning of regulation 6(4). Since the regulation 6(4) procedure denies the trader his part of the sample and the possibility of a future checking analysis, it should evidently be adopted only in exceptional circumstances. One such case is said to be where insufficient product is available. Although not compulsory for this exceptional procedure, it is essential that the sample should be sealed and marked before submission for analysis.

1 Compare *A-G's Reference (No 2 of 1994)* [1994] All ER 1000.
2 The notice must be in writing. See FSA 1990, s 49(1)(b).
3 See para **2.7.1** above.
4 *Skeate v Moore* [1971] 3 All ER 1306, [1972] 1 WLR 110; and compare *National Rivers Authority v Harcros Timber and Building Supplies Ltd* [1993] Crim LR 221.
5 See now Meat Products and Spreadable Fish Products Regulations 1984, reg 4 and Sch 4, para 9.

Procedure where sample is to be examined

17.4.4 By regulation 8 of the Food Safety (Sampling and Qualifications) Regulations 1990, an authorised officer who has procured a sample under section 29 of the FSA 1990 and who considers that it should be examined must—

(a) if necessary place the sample in a suitable container and seal the container;
(b) mark the sample or container;

(c) as soon as it is reasonably practicable to do so, give notice[1] to the owner that the sample will be examined; and
(d) submit it for examination.

Unlike most samples for analysis, those for examination are not required to be divided into three parts because bacterial contamination is not heterogeneously distributed in food and, in a retained part, might be expected to change over time.

1 The notice must be in writing. See FSA 1990, s 49(1)(b).

Submission of samples to public analysts and food examiners

17.4.5 By section 30(1) of the FSA 1990, an authorised officer who has procured a sample must, if he considers that it should be analysed, submit it for analysis by a public analyst or, if he considers that it should be examined, submit it to a food examiner[1]. In section 30, 'sample', in relation to an authorised officer of an enforcement authority, includes any part of a sample retained by him in pursuance of the procedure considered in para **17.4.3** above[2].

The public analyst to whom the sample is submitted can be either one appointed by the food authority for the area where the sample was procured or one appointed for the area of the food authority concerned. The first alternative allows for the submission of a sample procured by an authorised officer outside his own area to the public analyst for the area where the sample was procured.

By section 30(2), a person, other than an authorised officer, who has purchased any food or substance capable of being used in the preparation of food may submit a sample of it to the public analyst for the area where the purchase was made or to a food examiner.

If the office of public analyst for an area is vacant, section 30(3) provides for the sample to be submitted to the public analyst for some other area.

Evidence of analysis or examination is not an essential prerequisite for a prosecution. For example, the presence of a foreign body in food[3] might be proved without analysis or the misdescription of a type of fruit or a cut of meat[4] might perhaps be established by expert testimony from a person other than a public analyst. However, in cases concerning the composition of food, it would seem prudent in all but exceptional cases to refer to the public analyst who is the food authority's scientific adviser for such matters.

The sample must be referred for analysis or examination to one of the laboratories listed as complying with the quality standards and using the validated methods prescribed by Articles 3 and 4 of Directive 93/99/EEC, since they alone are authorised under Community law[5].

1 As to public analysts and food examiners, see sections **2.7** and **2.8** above.
2 See FSA 1990, s 30(9).
3 See para **9.2** above.
4 See para **6.2** above.
5 See para **17.6.3** below.

Analysis and examination of samples

17.4.6 Where a food analyst[1] or examiner is for any reason unable to perform the analysis or examination, the sample must be submitted or, as the case may be, sent by him to another food analyst or examiner[2]. This might evidently arise through lack of specialist equipment, conflict of interest or simply pressure of work. Certainly, the food analyst or food examiner is required to analyse or examine the sample as soon as practicable[3]. This is particularly important in the case of samples of short life foods which should obviously be submitted for analysis or examination without delay.

After an analysis or examination, the food analyst or examiner must give a certificate in the prescribed form[4] to the person by whom the sample was submitted, specifying the result. The certificate must be signed by the food analyst or examiner, but the analysis or examination may be made by a person acting under his direction[5].

1 That is, a public analyst or other person having the requisite qualifications, see section **2.8** above.
2 FSA 1990, s 30(4).
3 FSA 1990, s 30(5).
4 See Food Safety (Sampling and Qualifications) Regulations 1990, reg 9(2) and Sch 3.
5 FSA 1990, s 30(6) and (7).

Evidential status of certificates of analysis and examination

17.4.7 In any proceedings under the Food Safety Act 1990, the production by one of the parties—

(a) of a document purporting to be a certificate given by a food analyst or examiner under the Act; or
(b) of a document supplied to him by the other party as being a copy of such a certificate,

is sufficient evidence of the facts stated in it unless, in a case falling within (a), the other party requires that the food analyst or examiner shall be called as a witness[1]. The evidence of a food analyst or examiner may be rebutted. Where there is doubt in any proceedings about the correctness of the analysis or examination or as to any opinion offered in the certificate relied on by the other party, notice should always be given that the food analyst or examiner is required to give evidence.

Methods of analysis are sometimes laid down by Community law[2]. Where no method is prescribed, up-to-date methods and standards should be employed and observed. Recommendations are issued by relevant committees of the Royal Society of Chemistry on such methods and standards.

1 FSA 1990, s 30(8).
2 See, for example, Erucic Acid in Food Regulations 1977, reg 4A and Animals and Animal Products (Examination for Residues and Maximum Residue Limits) Regulations 1997, reg 18.

Reference to the Government Chemist

17.4.8 Where an authorised officer and the owner of the sample at the time of its procurement agree, or where a court so orders, the authorised officer must submit it for analysis to the Government Chemist or to such other food analyst as the Government Chemist may direct[1]. This 'checking analysis' is used if there is a difference between the public analyst's evidence and that from the defendant's food analyst.

The 1998 Report on the Review of Public Analyst Arrangements in England and Wales[2] recommended that these referee analyst provisions should remain unaltered, that a food analyst should be directly involved in analyses carried out by the Laboratory of the Government Chemist and that the Food Standards Agency should be empowered to nominate a different referee analyst, if the current arrangements with the Government

Chemist (particularly the funding of the service by the Department of Trade and Industry) should change significantly.

1 Food Safety (Sampling and Qualifications) Regulations 1990, reg 7.
2 See para **2.9.1** above.

Supply to owners of copies of certificates of analysis or examination

17.4.9 Where a sample procured under section 29 of the FSA 1990 has been analysed or examined, the owner of food is entitled on request to be supplied with a copy of the certificate of analysis or examination by the enforcement authority[1]. In addition, the defendant charged with an offence triable either way is entitled to advance information of the prosecution case[2] and the rules on disclosure of expert evidence must be complied with[3].

1 Food Safety (Sampling and Qualifications) Regulations 1990, reg 9. See also Code of Practice no 7 (Sampling for Analysis or Examination).
2 See para **18.2.8** below.
3 See para **18.4.6** below.

17.5 POWERS OF ENTRY, OBSTRUCTION ETC

17.5.1 Paragraph **17.2.3** above noted that, besides sampling and analysis, Article 5 of official control Directive 89/397/EEC requires Member States also to carry out Article 6 inspections, inspections of staff hygiene, examinations of written and documentary material and examinations of any verification systems set up by the undertaking and of the results obtained. This general obligation is augmented by certain specific ones.

By Article 8 of official control Directive 89/397/EEC, persons who in the exercise of their activity, come into contact, whether directly or indirectly, with the materials and products referred to in items *(b)–(f)* of para **17.2.4** above are subject to hygiene inspection. The purpose of this inspection is to check that health standards concerning personal cleanliness and clothing are respected. Such inspection is without prejudice to medical examinations.

By Article 9 of official control Directive 89/397/EEC inspectors may take note of written and documentary material held by the natural and legal persons at production, manufacture, import into the Community, processing, storage, transport, distribution and trade. They may also make copies or take extracts of written and documentary material with them for examination.

By Article 11 of official control Directive 89/397/EEC Member States must ensure that inspectors have the right to carry out the operations provided for in the Directive and prescribe that natural and legal persons concerned shall be obliged to undergo any inspection carried out in accordance with the Directive and to assist inspectors in the accomplishment of their tasks.

Article 12(2) of official control Directive 89/397/EEC requires Member States to prescribe that inspectors shall be bound by professional secrecy.

In Great Britain these Community provisions are implemented by sections 32 and 33 of the FSA 1990 which are considered in the following paragraphs of this section. Guidance on powers of entry is given by section B of Code of Practice no 2 (Legal Matters).

Power to enter premises

17.5.2 By section 32(1) of the FSA 1990, an authorised officer of an enforcement authority shall, on producing, if so required, some duly authenticated document[1] showing his authority, have a right at all reasonable hours[2]—

(a) to enter any premises within the authority's area for the purpose of ascertaining whether there is or has been on the premises any contravention of the provisions of the Act, or regulations or orders made under it; and
(b) to enter any business premises, whether within or outside the authority's area, for the purpose of ascertaining whether there is on the premises any evidence of any contravention within that area of any of such provisions; and
(c) in the case of an authorised officer of a food authority, to enter any premises for the purpose of the performance by the authority of their functions under the Act[3].

An authorised officer may thus enter both domestic and business premises within his own authority's area, but outside that area may enter only business premises for the purpose of ascertaining whether there is on the premises any evidence of a contravention within that area. The power to enter business premises in the area of another food authority allows for visits, for example, to a manufacturer as part of an investigation into an offence concerning one of his products found in the area of the visiting officer[4]. However, it is recommended that such visits should be co-ordinated with the home authority. The visiting officer should not advise or propose changes to a company's operating system which properly fall within the remit of the home authority[5].

Entry to premises used only as a private dwelling-house may not be demanded as of right unless 24 hours' notice of the intended entry has been given to the occupier.

1 See FSA 1990, s 49.
2 As to 'reasonable hours', see para **9.3.2** above.
3 As to 'premises' and 'business', see para **4.8.1** above.
4 *Walker's Snack Foods Ltd v Coventry City Council* [1998] 3 All ER 163.
5 Code of Practice no 3 (Inspection Procedures—General), section D.

Refusal of admission

17.5.3 Where admission to premises has been refused, or refusal is apprehended, an authorised officer may, on sworn information in writing and having given notice to the occupier of the premises, apply to a justice of the peace for a warrant, under section 32(2) of the FSA 1990, authorising the officer to enter the premises, if need be by reasonable force. If an application for admission, or the giving of notice, would defeat the object of entry, or in a case of urgency, or where the premises are unoccupied or the occupier is temporarily absent, the justice may nevertheless issue the warrant. Section 32(3) provides for the warrant to continue in force for one month.

Other persons and co-ordination

17.5.4 Authorised officers entering premises may take with them such other persons as they consider necessary and must leave unoccupied premises as effectively secured as they found them[1]. Under this power, the Commission's designated officials are able to accompany British officials as required by supplemental official control Directive 93/99/EEC, article 5(2).

Statutory Codes of Practice[2] recommend co-ordination of inspection visits, and where necessary, the use of multi-disciplinary teams of officers.

1 FSA 1990, s 32(4).
2 Code of Practice no 3 (on Inspection Procedures – General), section C; Code of Practice no 8 (Food Standards Inspections); Code of Practice no 9 (Food Hygiene Inspection).

Inspection of records and computers

17.5.6 On entering premises in accordance with the Act, an authorised officer may inspect any records (in whatever form they are held) relating to a food business and, where such records are kept by means of a computer—

(a) may have access to, and inspect and check the operation of, any computer and any associated apparatus or material which is or has been in use in connection with the records; and
(b) may require any person having charge of, or otherwise concerned with the operation of, the computer, apparatus or material to afford him such assistance as he may reasonably require[1].

The officer may seize and detain any records which may be required as evidence and, where the records are kept by means of a computer, may require the records to be produced in a form in which they may be taken away[2].

1 FSA 1990, s 32(5).
2 FSA 1990, s 32(6).

Examination of verification systems

17.5.7 It will be recalled that Article 5 of official control Directive 89/397/EEC requires Member States to undertake 'examinations of any verification systems set up by the undertaking and of the results obtained'. By 'verification systems' the Directive is understood to mean control systems which are maintained by food businesses and which, if they fail to prevent a contravention, aim in the British context, at least to provide a due diligence defence under the Act[1]. The FSA 1990 gives no specific power for authorised officers to carry out these examinations. However, if an enforcement officer has reason to believe that an offence has been committed he may (and is indeed required by Code of Practice no 2 (Legal Matters) to) satisfy himself as to whether or not the control systems operated by the business would in fact afford a defence[2]. It was held in *Walker's Snack Foods Ltd v Coventry City Council*[3], that the powers to inspect records and computers noted in para **17.5.6** above are available for this purpose.

Leaving aside the Community obligation, the justification for construing the powers in this extended way is evidently to enable the prosecutor, before embarking on what might prove a futile prosecution, to assess whether the defendant is likely to be able to establish a due diligence defence[4]. However, the *Walker*'s judgment has been criticised on the ground that it enables enforcement authorities, before any charges are profferred, to anticipate and defeat a defence. It remains to be seen whether the powers thus used would be incompatible, in any subsequent prosecution, with the defendant's right to a fair trial under Article 6 of the European Convention on Human Rights. The point may reasonably be expected to be tested once the Human Rights Act 1998 is in force[5].

1 See FSA 1990, s 21 and section **19.3** below.
2 Code of Practice no 2 (Legal Matters), paras 15 and 18(c).
3 [1998] 3 All ER 163.
4 See para **18.2.3** below.
5 As from October 2000.

Confidentiality

17.5.8 Section 32(7) of the FSA 1990 makes it an offence, except in the performance of duty, for anyone exercising the FSA 1990 powers of entry to disclose information obtained in the premises with regard to any trade secret[1], including, it would appear, any secret manufacturing process.

1 See official control Directive 89/397/EEC, Art 12(2) and para **17.5.1** above.

Limitations on powers of entry

17.5.9 Two express limitations on the section 32 powers should be noted. First, nothing in the section authorises any person, except with the permission of the local authority under the Animal Health Act 1981[1], to enter any premises—

(a) in which an animal or bird affected with any disease to which that Act applies is kept; and
(b) which is situated in a place declared under that Act to be infected with such a disease[2].

Secondly, by virtue of section 54(4) the powers are not exercisable in relation to any Crown premises[3] which the Secretary of State has certified accordingly in the interests of national security.

1 See para **17.8.1**, n 11 below.
2 FSA 1990, s 32(8).
3 As to application to the Crown, see para **4.1.6** above.

Obstruction etc of officers

17.5.10 It is an offence for any person intentionally[1] to obstruct any person acting in the execution of the Act or, without reasonable cause, to fail to give to any such person any assistance or information which he may reasonably require for the performance of his functions under the Act. It is also an offence for any person responding to a request for information to furnish information which he knows to be false or misleading in a material particular; or recklessly to furnish information which is false or misleading in a material particular[2]. Obstruction need not involve physical violence[3]. Anything which might make the task of the authorised officer more difficult may amount to obstruction[4].

A false statement made to an authorised officer during an interview under caution is a statement to which the criminal sanction applies[5].

The offence of failing, without reasonable cause, to give an authorised officer reasonable assistance or information does not require any person to answer any questions or give any information if to do so might incriminate him[6]. The privilege against self-incrimination does not extend to an employee not authorised to speak for the company in respect of questions asked by authorised officers the answers to which might tend to incriminate the employer[7]. An authorised officer must not be prevented from exercising the statutory power of inspection. On the other hand, it would not be an offence, by virtue of this provision, for a person to refuse to answer questions about his or her alleged failure to comply with company instructions.

1 As to 'intentionally' obstructing, see para **19.1.1** below.
2 FSA 1990, s 33(1) and (2). See also official control Directive 89/397/EEC, Art 11, and para **17.5.1** above.
3 *Borrow v Howland* (1896) 74 LT 787; *Betts v Stevens* [1910] 1 KB 1.
4 *Hinchcliffe v Sheldon* [1955] 3 All ER 406, [1955] 1 WLR 1207; but see *Rice v Connolly* [1966] 2 QB 414, [1966] 2 All ER 649.
5 *R v Page* (1995) 94 LGR 467. As to an interview under caution, see para **18.4.9** below.
6 FSA 1990, s 33(3).
7 *Walker's Snack Foods Ltd v Coventry City Council* [1998] 3 All ER 163.

Reports on inspections

17.5.11 Although there is no statutory requirement for authorised officers to report back to the owner of the food business in writing, Codes of Practice no 8 (Food Standards Inspections) and no 9 (Food Hygiene Inspections) recommend this practice. The food business will wish to consider whether the report calls for adaptation of its verification systems[1].

1 See para **17.5.7** above and section **19.3** below.

17.6 ADMINISTRATIVE IMPLEMENTATION OF THE OFFICIAL CONTROL DIRECTIVES

17.6.1 This section describes other provisions of Directives 89/397/EEC and 93/99/EEC, which are implemented administratively.

Inspection programmes

17.6.2 Article 14 of Directive 89/397/EEC requires Member States to draw up forward programmes of inspections laying down the nature and frequency of inspections. By 1 May in each year the Member States must report to the Commission on implementation during the previous year specifying—

- the criteria applied in drawing up the programmes,
- the number and type of inspections carried out,
- the number and type of infringements established.

By 16 October in each year the Commission, having consulted Member States within the framework of the Standing Committee for Foodstuffs, must send them a recommendation concerning a coordinated programme of inspections for the following year.

Codes of Practice no 8 (Food Standards Inspections) and no 9 (Food Hygiene Inspections) require each food authority to implement and maintain a documented programme of inspections in respect of food standards and food hygiene respectively, according to risk frequency and, so far as practicable, to ensure that inspection visits are carried out in accordance with that programme.

For the purpose of assembling the UK report, the Food Standards Agency can invoke section 41 of the FSA 1990 to call for reports and returns from food authorities[1].

1 See para **2.5.3** above.

Competent authorities and laboratories

17.6.3 Article 15 of Directive 89/397/EEC requires Member States to send to the Commission the names of the competent authorities and the extent of their territorial responsibility and functions, together with the official laboratories authorised by the competent authorities, which are responsible for carrying out analyses in connection with official control. To be authorised, laboratories must comply with the quality standards and use the validated methods prescribed by Articles 3 and 4 of Directive 93/99/EEC[1].

The lists of authorities and laboratories are published in the 'C' series of the Official Journal of the European Communities.

1 See paras **17.2.5** and **17.4.5** above.

17.7 WEIGHTS AND MEASURES ENFORCEMENT

Quantity marking and metrological controls

17.7.1 As noted in para **17.3.1** above, Directives 89/397/EEC and 93/99/EEC do not apply to metrological controls. The requirements in respect of quantity marking (explained in chapter 15) and weighing and measuring equipment are enforced through the W&MA 1985, sections 79–85.

Enforcement is the responsibility of local weights and measures authorities[1]. In England, they are the non-metropolitan county councils, metropolitan district and London borough councils, the Common Council of the City of London, the Inner and Middle Temples and the Council of the Isles of Scilly. In Wales, they are the county and county borough councils. The officers responsible for enforcement are inspectors of weights and measures under the direction of chief inspectors of weights and measures who may have a deputy[2]. They are generally known as trading standards officers and also enforce those functions under the FSA 1990 that are allocated to county councils[3].

1 W&MA 1985, s 69, as amended.
2 W&MA 1985, s 72.
3 See in particular para **2.5.2** above.

Enforcement powers

17.7.2 The powers of inspection, entry and seizure and the provisions in respect of obstruction are similar to those in the FSA 1990[1].

1 W&MA 1985, ss 79–81.

17.8 OTHER LEGISLATION

17.8.1 Enforcement provision like that in the FSA 1990 is also to be found elsewhere in consumer protection legislation relevant to food. Only a brief comparison can be made here of the similarities. Those who exercise or are subject to the respective powers should study them carefully in order to see precisely how they differ.

Orders made under the Prices Act 1974[1] are enforced by local weights and measures authorities who have powers of entry backed by provision in respect of obstruction and are subject to restrictions on disclosure of information.

The Trade Descriptions Act 1968, which overlaps with sections 14 and 15 of the FSA 1990[2], although not with provisions reserving descriptions under the Act[3], is also enforced by local weights and measures authorities and includes powers to make test purchases, to enter premises and to inspect and seize goods and documents, as well as provision in respect of obstruction of authorised officers.

The safety provisions of Part II of the Consumer Protection Act 1987 have limited application in the food context: the regulatory powers in section 11 apply neither to growing crops and things comprised in land by virtue of being attached to it, nor to water, food, feeding stuff and fertiliser. However, regulations have been made under those powers to control goods such as ceramic ware and cooking utensils[4]. Once again enforcement rests with local weights and measures authorities and provision is made for test purchases, powers of search, detention of goods and in respect of obstruction. In addition, there are extensive powers to serve prohibition notices, notices to warn and suspension notices, to forfeit goods and to obtain information. The General Product Safety Regulations 1994[5] draw, as appropriate, on these powers and on those in the FSA 1990 for the purpose of enforcement.

Closer parallels with the FSA 1990 are to be found for feeding stuffs in the enforcement provisions of Part IV of the Agriculture Act 1970. Already summarised in paras **16.2.2** and **16.2.3** above, the provisions include in particular a requirement to appoint agricultural analysts and powers of entry, taking, dividing and analysis of samples, and further analysis by the Government Chemist. As in the case of the FSA 1990, the Food Standards Agency is charged by section 12 of the FSA 1999 with monitoring local authority enforcement[6].

More specialised is the Agriculture and Horticulture Act 1964[7] which, in addition to conferring powers of entry to premises and making provision in respect of obstruction, is enforced by the Horticultural Marketing Inspectorate and includes power to regrade produce.

Even less familiar to those accustomed to the FSA 1990 are the extensive enforcement powers to enter and require information provided by section 19 of the Food and Environment Protection Act 1985 in respect of Regulations, made under section 16 of that Act, on pesticide residues in crops, food and feeding stuffs[8]. The powers may be exercised in England by persons authorised by the Minister of Agriculture, Fisheries and Food or the Secretary of State (in Wales, by the Welsh Assembly[9]) and by authorised officers of local authorities[10]. The Regulations themselves add powers to seize or dispose of non-compliant produce.

More remote still from the FSA 1990 are Orders made under the Animal Health Act 1981 (AHA 1981) to protect animals from unsafe feed such as the Specified Risk Material Order 1997 summarised at para **16.9.3** above. The Order is to be executed and enforced by local authorities[11]. General powers are conferred on inspectors by the Act. The Order itself confers specific powers to take samples and seize and destroy foods and feeding stuffs containing banned material.

For completeness, reference should also be made to regulations providing enforcement mechanisms for food standards specified in Community common agricultural policy Regulations. As explained in para **7.3.1** above, even where it has been found necessary to make these under the European Communities Act 1972, the concepts and enforcement methods of the FSA 1990 have been applied to the food standards aspects. For example, the Common Agricultural Policy (Wine) Regulations 1996[12] provide for enforcement by food authorities at the retail stage and powers of entry akin to those in the FSA 1990, as well as for analysis and examination within the meaning of that Act.

1 See section **15.8** above.
2 As to section 14, see paras **5.3.1** and **5.3.6** above. As to section 15, see paras **6.2.3–6.2.5** above.
3 See para **7.1.2**(1) above.
4 See paras **10.6.1** and **10.6.2** above.
5 See para **9.1.2** above.
6 See paras **2.3.5** and **17.3.2** above.
7 See para **7.3.18** above.
8 See, for example, the Pesticides (Maximum Residue Levels in Crops, Food and Feeding Stuffs) Regulations 1999 considered in para **10.7.1** above.
9 See National Assembly for Wales (Transfer of Functions) Order 1999, art 2 and Sch 1.
10 See Food and Environment Protection Act 1985, s 19(8). In England and Wales, this covers any local authority (other than a parish or community council) as defined in the Local Government Act 1972 or a port health authority.
11 See AHA 1981, s 50. In England and Wales, this means London borough councils, non-metropolitan county councils, county borough councils, metropolitan district councils and the Common Council of the City of London.
12 See para **7.3.8** above.

Chapter 18

Enforcement: prosecutions and evidence

18.1 INTRODUCTION

18.1.1 As indicated in para **17.2.5** above, Article 10 of official control Directive 89/397/EEC requires that where inspectors discover or suspect an irregularity they must take the requisite measures. If in a particular case advice or a warning is not enough, some kind of penalty or formal caution may be called for. Of those available under the Food Safety Act 1990 (FSA 1990) in England and Wales, we have already observed the administrative powers to destroy food[1], to issue improvement notices, prohibition orders and emergency prohibition notices and orders[2] and to cancel, suspend or revoke food premises licences[3]. However, the most obvious penalty is one imposed following a successful criminal prosecution.

This chapter briefly comments first on the prosecutions (including the possibility of a formal caution), before summarising relevant statutory provisions regarding criminal evidence.

Section 20 of the FSA 1990 on offences due to the fault of another person is considered in section **19.2** below. However, the provisions made by the Interpretation Act 1978 (IA 1978) in respect of duplicated offences might usefully be noted here. Where an act or omission constitutes an offence under two or more Acts, or both under an Act and at common law, the offender is, unless the contrary intention appears, liable to be prosecuted and punished under either or any of those Acts or at common law, but is not liable to be punished more than once for the same offence. An example of this duplication is to be found in the overlap, mentioned at para **17.8.1** above, between sections 14 and 15 of the FSA 1990 and the Trade Descriptions Act 1968 (TDA 1968).

1 See section **9.3** above.
2 See sections **11.2–11.4** above.
3 See paras **12.2.2** and **12.3.1** above.

18.2 PROSECUTIONS

The power to prosecute

18.2.1 Paragraph **2.5.2** above explained the responsibilities for enforcement of provisions in and under the FSA 1990. Subject to what is said there, the key provision to be recalled in relation to prosecutions is section 6(5) whereby in England and Wales an enforcement authority may institute proceedings under any provisions of the Act or any regulations or orders made under it[1].

Although persons other than an enforcement authority have the common law right to institute prosecutions under the FSA 1990, this is rarely done. A private citizen does not have the statutory powers to secure evidence and, if injured or damaged through a food product, would no doubt do better to consider civil proceedings as explained in chapter 3.

1 In Scotland the decision on whether to prosecute lies with the Procurator Fiscal.

The decision to prosecute: the Code for Crown Prosecutors

18.2.2 Part C of Code of Practice no 2 (Legal Matters) gives advice on the decision as to whether to prosecute in England and Wales. It advocates recourse to the Code for Crown Prosecutors[1], which is explained in this paragraph, and sets out certain criteria of its own, which are explained in para **18.2.3**. Relevant judicial comment is noted in para **18.2.4**.

Although directed at the Crown Prosecution Service, the Code for Crown Prosecutors (the latest edition of which was published in June 1994) repeats superseded Home Office advice which was more specifically aimed at local authorities[2]. In deciding whether or not to prosecute, the following two tests should be applied—

(a) *the evidential test*, which requires that there be enough admissible and reliable evidence to 'offer a realistic prospect of conviction'; and
(b) *the public interest test*, which requires that there be a consideration of those factors which might operate both in favour of, and against, the need to prosecute.

In considering the evidential test, it will be helpful first to recall the standard of proof incumbent on the prosecution in court. We have already referred at para **3.1.1** to the standard of proof required in criminal proceedings: the prosecution must prove its case 'beyond reasonable doubt'[3]. As will be seen in the next chapter, with 'strict liability' offences such as most of those under the FSA 1990 and other consumer protection legislation, the prosecutor is by definition absolved from having to prove the defendant's criminal intention. On the other hand, regard must be had as to whether the defendant is likely to be able to establish a due diligence or other statutory defence, having in mind that, where the defence bears the legal burden of proof, the standard required is the civil one of the balance of probabilities[4]. However, for proof beyond reasonable doubt to be required for prosecution decisions would be excessive and would tend to usurp the function of the court. 'A realistic prospect of conviction', according to the Code for Crown Prosecutors, 'means that a jury or bench of magistrates, properly directed in accordance with the law is more likely than not to convict the defendant of the charge alleged'. While not attempting to anticipate lines of defence in the absence of an indication on the face of the papers, a prosecutor in relation to food law offences will obviously need to have in mind whether a due diligence defence[5] might be established, as well as more general possibilities of a breach of the Codes of Practice under the Police and Criminal Evidence Act 1984 (PACE)[6].

Turning to the public interest test, the Code for Crown Prosecutors lists some public interest factors both for and against prosecution. They are not exhaustive and, of course, are aimed at the work of the Crown Prosecution Service. For food authorities, the main importance of the Code is no doubt the analytical method advocated by the two test approach.

1 Copies of the Code can be obtained from the Crown Prosecution Service.
2 Home Office circular 29/1983.
3 *Miller v Minister of Pensions* [1947] 2 All ER 372 at 373–374.

4 See para **19.3.4** below.
5 See section **19.3** below generally.
6 See paras **18.4.8–18.4.10** below.

The decision to prosecute: Food Safety Act Code of Practice no 2

18.2.3 Part C of Code of Practice no 2 (Legal Matters) also lists a number of factors that food authorities should consider before deciding whether a prosecution should be taken. These may include—

(a) the seriousness of the alleged offence;
(b) the previous history of the party concerned;
(c) the likelihood of the defendant being able to establish a due diligence defence (see section **19.3** below);
(d) the ability of any important witnesses and their willingness to cooperate;
(e) the willingness of the party to prevent a recurrence of the problem;
(f) the probable public benefit of a prosecution and the importance of the case – eg whether it might establish legal precedent in other companies or in other geographical areas;
(g) whether other action, such as issuing a formal caution in accordance with Home Office circular 59/1990[1] (except in Scotland) or an improvement notice, or imposing a prohibition, would be more appropriate or effective (it is possible in exceptional circumstances to prosecute as well as issuing a notice; failure to comply with a notice would be an additional offence);
(h) any explanation offered by the affected company.

It will be seen that this list includes factors relevant both to the evidential test (eg item (c)) and to the public interest test (eg item (a)) referred to in the last paragraph, while some of the latter may be in favour of prosecution (eg item (f)) and others may be against (eg item (g)). Obviously there is no point in considering the public interest in a prosecution, unless there appears to be sufficient evidence to sustain it.

1 Home Office circular 59/1990 has been revised and replaced by circular 18/1994. See para **18.2.10** below.

The decision to prosecute: judicial comment

18.2.4 The courts have frowned on the prosecution of trivial cases[1]. In *Smedleys Ltd v Breed*, which was an appeal against conviction, under what is now section 14 of the FSA 1990, for selling a tin of peas containing a caterpillar, the House of Lords was critical of the enforcement authority for bringing proceedings in what it regarded as a trivial case. Pointing out that the authority had no duty to automatically prosecute every case, Viscount Dilhorne stated that 'where it is apparent that a prosecution does not serve the general interests of consumers the justices may think fit, if they find that the Act has been contravened, to grant an absolute discharge'.

Had the case arisen under the present Act, the appellants would probably have been able to establish the due diligence defence[2] that is now available.

1 *Smedleys Ltd v Breed* [1974] AC 839, [1974] 2 All ER 21, at 33, HL; *Sunblest Bakeries Ltd v Andrews* (1985) unreported.
2 FSA 1990, s 21, see section **19.3**.

Responsibility for the decision to prosecute and conduct of proceedings

18.2.5 Prosecutions for the police are conducted by the Crown Prosecution Service set up for the purpose by the Prosecution of Offences Act 1985 as a result of the recommendation in the 1981 Report of the Royal Commission on Criminal Procedure that the roles of the investigator and the lawyer should be separated. In addition to the perceived need for legal input into prosecutions, an important reason for this recommendation was the belief that it is unsatisfactory that the person responsible for the decision to prosecute should be the person who had carried out or been concerned in the investigation. An officer who carries out an investigation, inevitably and properly, forms a view of the guilt of the suspect. Having done so, without any kind of improper motive, he may be inclined to shut his mind to other evidence telling against the guilt of the suspect or to overestimate the strength of the evidence he has assembled. Although the Royal Commission did not advocate that the Crown prosecutors should take on central and local government prosecutions, it acknowledged that there were similar arguments of principle for their doing so[1]. It would therefore be imprudent for those concerned with such prosecutions not to have regard to the spirit of the Royal Commission proposals.

As to the prosecution decision, delegation by the authority to a senior council officer should generally be capable of meeting this objective. However, acting by committee in open session is an unacceptable way of making the decision, since it may well prejudice the food business and its right to a fair trial.

As to the conduct of proceedings, any authorised member or officer of a local authority may appear for them although not a qualified lawyer[2]. Such officers have played a long and honourable part in prosecuting offences under food legislation which is specialised and unfamiliar to many lawyers. It would appear that the separation of functions advocated by the Royal Commission can be honoured by arrangements under which the prosecutor is a senior officer who has played no part in the investigation.

Prosecuting, however, is itself an increasingly specialist task which, for example, demands a knowledge of evidence[3] and procedure beyond the confines of the FSA 1990. As a result, there is evidently an increasing trend by enforcement authorities to the use of legally qualified prosecutors.

1 Cmnd 8092, in particular, at paras 6.23, 6.24 and 7.41.
2 Local Government Act 1972, s 223.
3 See section **18.4** below.

Time limits for prosecutions

18.2.6 Prosecutions for offences triable either way under the FSA 1990 (including regulations and orders) cannot be begun after the expiry of three years from the commission of the offence, or one year from its discovery by the prosecutor, whichever is the earlier[1]. In respect of prosecutions for offences triable only summarily, such as those under section 33(1)[2] of the FSA 1990 and those under regulation 44 of the Food Labelling Regulations 1996[3], the time limit is six months as specified by section 127 of the Magistrates' Courts Act 1980 (MCA 1980)[4].

It should also be noted that offences under food hygiene Regulations are continuing offences, committed afresh each day that the Regulations are not complied with[5].

Unreasonable delay in bringing proceedings may be an abuse of process notwithstanding the fact that they have been commenced within the statutory time limits[6]. Part C of Code of Practice no 2 (Legal Matters) recommends that prosecutions should be brought without unnecessary delay.

1 FSA 1990, s 34.
2 See para **17.5.10** above.
3 See para **6.5.2** above.
4 As to offences triable either way and summarily, see para **18.2.8** below.
5 *R v Thames Metropolitan Stipendiary Magistrate, ex p Hackney London Borough Council* (1993) 92 LGR 392.
6 *Daventry District Council v Olins* (1990) 154 JP 478, DC; *R v Telford Justices, ex p Badhan* [1991] 2 QB 78, [1991] 2 All ER 854.

Commencement of proceedings

18.2.7 Legal proceedings are commenced by laying an information at the offices of the clerk to the justices for the relevant area[1] and the issue of a summons in accordance with the Magistrates' Courts Rules 1981, SI 1981/552. It is essential that charges are laid correctly. For example, to charge an offence as to false description of food without stating whether the offence was under section 15(1) of the FSA 1990 or section 1 of the TDA 1968 would be bad for uncertainty because the defendant would not know which enactment he was alleged to have contravened[2]. Moreover, an information must not charge more than one offence[3]. An information that charged the defendant under what is now section 14 of the FSA 1990 with selling food 'not of the nature or of the substance or of the quality demanded' was held to be for more than one offence and bad for duplicity[4].

1 *R v Manchester Stipendiary Magistrate, ex p Hill* [1983] 1 AC 328, sub nom *Hill v Anderton* [1982] 2 All ER 963.
2 As to FSA 1990, s 15(1) and TDA 1968, s 1, see further paras **6.2.3–6.2.5** above.
3 Magistrates' Courts Rules 1981, r 12.
4 *Bastin v Davies* [1950] 2 KB 579, [1950] 1 All ER 1095. See further para **5.3.5** above.

Mode of trial

18.2.8 In relation to the provision for punishment of offences made by section 35 of the FSA 1990, it is desirable first to consider the mode of trial. All but one of the offences against the FSA 1990 itself are triable either way; that is, they are triable either on indictment (by jury in the Crown Court) or summarily (by magistrates)[1]. Obstruction offences under section 33(1) alone are triable summarily only.

For regulations under the FSA 1990, the enabling power in section 26(3) allows a choice of trial mode to be specified. For the most part[2], provision for trial either way has been confined to hygiene regulations[3].

The procedure for offences triable either way is laid down by sections 18–23 of the MCA 1980. If the defendant does not plead guilty, the magistrates' court hears the parties and considers whether the case should be dealt with summarily or in the Crown Court. In deciding which mode of trial is appropriate, the court must, in particular, have regard to the nature of the case, whether the circumstances make the offence one of a serious character and whether summary powers, including the prescribed maximum penalties, would be adequate. It must not, however, be informed of any previous conviction of the defendant[4]. A decision by the magistrates in favour of summary trial is subject to the consent of the defendant who, by not consenting, elects to be tried in the Crown Court.

At the time of writing, consideration is being given to a Criminal Justice (Mode of Trial) Bill, which would leave to magistrates the decision as to where either way offences are heard. This is a highly contentious measure, since it would remove the right of trial by jury which many defendants choose. Although sentences tend to be heavier in the event of a guilty verdict, 40% of people who plead not guilty are acquitted, compared with only 25% in the magistrates' court[5].

It should also be noted that a defendant charged with an offence triable either way has a right to advance information of the prosecution case[6].

1 See IA 1978, Sch 1.
2 But see, for example, the Plastic Materials and Articles in Contact with Food Regulations 1998, reg 10(13).
3 See chs 12 and 13 and the Food Safety (Temperature Control) Regulations 1995 in ch 14.
4 *R v Colchester Justices, ex p North Essex Building Co Ltd* [1977] 3 All ER 567, [1977] 1 WLR 1109.
5 Sunday Telegraph, 6 December 1998.
6 See Magistrates' Courts (Advance Information) Rules 1985, SI 1985/601.

Maximum penalties

18.2.9 Section 35 of the FSA 1990 also specifies maximum penalties. On conviction on indictment, they are an unlimited fine or imprisonment for up to two years or both.

The maximum penalties on summary conviction are more complex. Subject to separate provision for obstruction offences explained below, the penalties are a fine of specified maximum amount or imprisonment for a term not exceeding six months or both. In the case of offences under section 7, 8 or 14[1] food safety may be at issue and the maximum fine is £20,000. In any other case, the maximum fine is the 'statutory maximum', which (by virtue of Schedule 1 to the IA 1978 and section 32 of the MCA 1980[2]), in relation to England and Wales, is currently £5000. As noted in the previous paragraph, obstruction offences under section 33(1) are triable summarily only. The penalties which may be imposed are a fine not exceeding a specified maximum or imprisonment for a term of three months or both. The specified maximum for a fine is level 5 on the 'standard scale' which (by virtue of Schedule 1 to the IA 1978 and section 37 of the Criminal Justice Act 1982[3]), is currently £5000.

The previous paragraph also explained that, of regulations made under the FSA 1990, in general it is the hygiene regulations that provide for trial either way. Normally[4], the maximum penalties in those regulations are, on summary conviction, a fine not exceeding the statutory maximum and, on conviction on indictment, a fine or imprisonment for a term not exceeding two years or both. In other regulations under the FSA 1990, contraventions generally[5] render defendants liable on summary conviction to a fine not exceeding level 5 on the standard scale.

1 See sections **5.2**, **9.2** and **5.3** above respectively.
2 As amended by s 17(2) of the Criminal Justice Act 1991 (CJA 1991).
3 As amended by s 17(1) of the CJA 1991.
4 But see, for example, Fresh Meat (Hygiene and Inspection) Regulations 1995, reg 21(1), which prescribes a fine not exceeding level 3 on the standard scale (ie currently £1000)
5 But again see, for example, Plastic Materials and Articles in Contact with Food Regulations 1998, reg 10(13).

Formal cautions

18.2.10 It has been the practice for many years for enforcement authorities to issue a letter of caution where it was felt that an offence had been committed but, for whatever reason, a prosecution was inappropriate. Such cautions had no status in law and could not be cited in any subsequent proceedings. In 1985 the Home Office drew the attention of prosecuting local authorities to a more formal system of cautioning which was updated and improved in 1990[1]. The current guidance is in Home Office circular 18/1994. This stresses that a formal caution is a serious matter. It is recorded and should influence the decision whether or not to prosecute if the person offends again. Moreover, it may be cited in any subsequent court proceedings. In order to safeguard the offender's interests, three conditions must be met before a caution can be administered. There must be evidence of the offender's guilt sufficient to give a realistic prospect of conviction; the offender must admit the offence; and the offender must understand the significance of the caution and give informed consent to being cautioned. If the first two of these requirements are met, consideration should be given as to whether a caution is in the public interest, taking into account the principles described in the Code for Crown Prosecutors[2].

This system is used by food authorities. LACOTS has issued guidance[3] which recommends that a formal caution should not be cited in court in relation to an offence committed more than three years after the offence for which it was issued.

1 Home Office circulars 14/1985 and 59/1990.
2 See para **18.2.2** above.
3 'Formal cautions': LACOTS CO11945.

Offences by bodies corporate

18.2.11 Section 36 of the FSA 1990 makes special provision in respect of offences by bodies corporate. A body corporate or 'corporation' is a legal entity distinct from the individuals who constitute it from time to time. A company formed and registered under the Companies Act 1985 (CA 1985)[1] is the main but by no means the only sort. Another example, that is, 'a body corporate established by or under any enactment for the purpose of carrying on under national ownership any industry or part of an industry or undertaking', is the subject of section 36(2).

A body corporate can be prosecuted and punished in its own name. Offences are customarily applied to persons and a 'person' includes a body of persons corporate or unincorporate[2]. However, where its offence is proved to have been committed with the consent or connivance of, or to be attributable to, any neglect on the part of any director, manager, secretary or other similar officer, or any person who was purporting to act in any such capacity, that person as well as the body corporate must be deemed to be guilty of the offence, and is liable to be prosecuted and punished accordingly[3].

1 CA 1985, ss 1 and 735(1).
2 IA 1978, Sch 1.
3 FSA 1990, s 36(1).

18.3 OTHER LEGISLATION

18.3.1 Sections **17.7** and **17.8** above compared enforcement provisions in consumer protection and other legislation relevant to food. For the most part, these other statutes also make provision parallel to the FSA 1990 for punishment of offences, time limits[1] and bodies corporate.

In most cases, the penalty specified is a fine on summary conviction not exceeding level 5 on the standard scale[2]. Additionally the Weights and Measures Act 1985

(W&MA 1985) and Part II of the Consumer Protection Act 1987 (CPA 1987) provide for a maximum of six months' imprisonment. Either way offences[3] allowing for a fine on conviction on indictment are provided by the Prices Act 1974 (PA 1974), section 20 of the CPA 1987 and Part III of the Food and Environment Protection Act 1985 (F&EPA 1985). Section 76(2) of the Animal Health Act 1981 (which applies in respect of import of class I specified risk material by the Specified Risk Material Order 1997[4]) also provides the possibility of imprisonment for a maximum of 12 months. The F&EPA 1985 (in respect of emergency orders[5]) and the Trade Descriptions Act 1968 (TDA 1968) afford the possibility of still more severe punishment in specifying a maximum term of two years.

Regulations made under the European Communities Act 1972 (ECA 1972) to enforce food standards specified in Community common agricultural policy Regulations[6] generally contain provisions similar to regulations under the FSA 1990. The criminal penalties prescribed cannot exceed the limits specified in paragraph 1(1)(d) of Schedule 2 to the ECA 1972.

Prosecution under the TDA 1968 does not permit evasion of the protection afforded by the FSA 1990 in respect of samples procured for analysis. Where an act or omission constitutes an offence under both statutes[7], section 22(2) of the TDA 1968 provides that evidence on behalf of the prosecution concerning any such sample will not be admissible in proceedings under the TDA 1968 unless section 31 of the FSA 1990 and regulations made under it have been complied with[8].

It should be noted that proceedings may be instituted under the PA 1974[9] and the W&MA 1985 only by or on behalf of a local weights and measures authority or, in the latter case, the chief officer of police for a police area[10]. Proceedings under Part III of the Agriculture and Horticulture Act 1964 (A&HA 1964) may be instituted only by or with the consent of the Minister (or the Welsh Assembly, in Wales) or with the consent of the Attorney General[11].

1 As to time limits, see further MCA 1980, s 127.
2 See para **18.2.9** above.
3 See para **18.2.8** above.
4 See para **16.9.3** above.
5 See section **11.7** above.
6 See paras **7.3.1** and **17.8.1** above.
7 See para **17.8.1** above.
8 See paras **17.4.2** and **17.4.3** above.
9 PA 1974, Schedule, para 8(1).
10 W&MA 1985, s 83.
11 A&HA 1964, s 20(3).

18.4 EVIDENCE

Introduction

18.4.1 Paragraph **18.2.5** above considered responsibility for the decision to prosecute. Sound decisions depend on good reports from investigating officers. These should include the identity of the person alleged to have committed the offence, any previous convictions and other relevant facts, followed by the admissible evidence set out in logical and chronological sequence. Opinions and recommendations as to appropriate action may be helpful but should be separate from the main body of the report.

Although many food law cases are simple, others are very complex. A food product may have to be traced from source, through a chain of distribution to the point where the primary offence has been committed and, at each stage, the necessary evidence established and the culpability assessed of every company, director and manager involved.

Authorised officers thus need a variety of qualities. In addition to investigative and reporting skills, a knowledge of food law and a grasp of the scientific and technical issues, they require some understanding of the relevant law relating to evidence. Food cases may be lost through failure to adduce the necessary evidence or to follow correct procedures.

Prosecution evidence may be excluded by the court either at common law or under section 78 of PACE[1]. In general, it must be admissible and be obtained fairly and impartially.

A full consideration of the law of evidence must be sought elsewhere[2]. This section summarises some important statutory rules on witness statements, other documentary evidence, questioning suspects and disclosure of unused material.

1 See further para **18.4.7** below. See also section 25 of the Criminal Justice Act 1988 (CJA 1988), noted in para **18.4.4**.
2 See *Cross and Tapper on Evidence* (9th edn, 1999), Butterworths.

Hearsay evidence in criminal proceedings

18.4.2 In criminal proceedings, there is a general common law rule[1] against 'hearsay evidence'. This has been expressed in one learned work as—

> 'any statement other than one made by a person while giving oral evidence in the proceedings is inadmissible as evidence of any fact or opinion stated'[2].

The rule applies to what was written as well as what was spoken, but among the exceptions to it are the helpful statutory provisions concerning witness statements and other documentary evidence summarised in paras **18.4.3–18.4.6** below.

Provisions on evidence from computer records in section 69 of the PACE were repealed by the Youth and Criminal Evidence Act 1999 as from 1 April 2000.

1 As to proposals for legislation, see Law Commission No 245 'Evidence in Criminal Proceedings: Hearsay and related topics' Cm 3670 1997.
2 See *Cross and Tapper on Evidence* (9th edn, 1999), Butterworths, p 530.

Proof by written statement

18.4.3 Section 9 of the Criminal Justice Act 1967 provides a very useful procedure whereby agreed written statements of facts may be received in evidence with the same effect as oral evidence[1] if specified conditions are met. In particular, the statement must be signed by the witness, must contain a declaration of his knowledge that it is subject to penalties if false, must be served on the other party and must not have been objected to within seven days.

It is common practice in food cases to take advantage of this procedure. A written witness statement is, for example, useful to set out a consumer's complaint about a food product.

1 *Ellis v Jones* [1973] 2 All ER 893.

Criminal Justice Act 1988: first-hand hearsay

18.4.4 Significant exceptions to the rule against hearsay in relation to documentary evidence were made by the CJA 1988. Section 23 specifically relates to 'first-hand hearsay', that is, where the information has passed through no more than one person before being recorded in the document presented to the court. Subject to specified provisions[1], the section allows, in two categories of cases, for a statement made by a person in a document to be admissible in criminal proceedings as evidence of any fact of which direct oral evidence by him would be admissible. The first category is where—

(a) the person who made the statement in the document is dead, or by reason of his bodily or mental condition unfit to attend as a witness; or
(b) the person who made the statement is outside the United Kingdom and it is not reasonably practicable to secure his attendance; or
(c) all reasonable steps have been taken to find the person who made the statement, but he cannot be found.

The second category is where the statement was made to a police officer or some other person charged with the duty of investigating offences or charging offenders, and the person who made it does not give oral evidence through fear or because he is kept out of the way.

The admission of statements under section 23 is subject to specified safeguards. Section 25 enables the court, in the interests of justice, to direct that the statement shall not be admitted. Section 26 provides that statements in documents which appear to have been prepared for purposes of criminal proceedings or investigations shall not be given in evidence in criminal proceedings without the leave of the court, which is not to be given unless their admission is in the interests of justice.

1 CJA 1988, s 23(4); Criminal Appeal Act 1968 (CAA 1968), Sch 2, para 1A; and PACE, s 69.

Criminal Justice Act 1988: business etc documents

18.4.5 The CJA 1988 also enables business and similar documents to be put in evidence. Subject to specified provisions[1], section 24 allows for a statement in a document to be admissible in criminal proceedings as evidence of any fact of which direct oral evidence would be admissible if—

(a) the document was created or received by a person in the course of a trade or business, profession or other occupation, or as the holder of a paid or unpaid office; and
(b) the information contained in the document was supplied by a person (whether or not the maker of the statement) who had, or may reasonably be supposed to have had, personal knowledge of the matters dealt with.

Section 24 applies whether the information contained in the document was supplied directly or indirectly, in other words, it may include 'multiple hearsay'. However, if the information was supplied indirectly, the section applies only if each person through whom it was supplied received it—

(a) in the course of trade, business, profession or other occupation; or
(b) as the holder of a paid or unpaid office.

As with section 23, the admission of statements under section 24 is subject to the section 25 and 26 safeguards mentioned in the previous paragraph.

1 CJA 1988, s 24(3) and (4); CAA 1968, Sch 2, para 1A; and PACE, s 69.

Criminal Justice Act 1988: expert reports

18.4.6 We have already observed, in para **17.4.7** above, the circumstances in which the production of a certificate of analysis or examination is sufficient evidence of the facts stated in it. Paragraph **17.4.5** noted that prosecutors in food cases might wish to put in to the court expert evidence other than that which is provided by public analysts and food examiners. Similarly, a food company may wish to use reports from experts on food science or technology in defence of proceedings. Section 30 of the CJA 1988 provides that an expert report is admissible whether or not the person making it attends to give oral evidence, but only with the leave of the court. For the purpose of determining whether to give leave, the court is required to have regard to the contents of the report, to the reason why the person making the report shall not give oral evidence, to any risk of unfairness to the accused and to any other relevant circumstances. An expert report when admitted is evidence of any fact or opinion of which the person making it could have given oral evidence.

For these purposes, an 'expert report' means a written report by a person dealing wholly or mainly with matters of which he is (or would if living be) qualified to give expert evidence.

Also to be borne in mind are the requirements on disclosure of expert evidence in the Crown Courts (Advance Notice of Expert Evidence) Rules 1987, SI 1987/716 and the Magistrates' Courts (Advance Notice of Expert Evidence) Rules 1997, SI 1997/705. These provide for mutual disclosure of expert evidence between parties to proceedings respectively in Crown Courts and, in the event of a not guilty plea, in magistrates' courts. A party failing to comply may not adduce the evidence without leave of the court.

Police and Criminal Evidence Act 1984: exclusion of unfair evidence

18.4.7 Part VII of PACE makes general provision in respect of evidence in criminal proceedings. In particular, section 78 enables a court to refuse to allow evidence on which the prosecution proposes to rely if it appears that, having regard to all the circumstances, including circumstances in which the evidence was obtained, the admission of the evidence would have such an adverse effect on the fairness of the proceedings that the court ought not to admit it.

In food cases, care must be taken that documents, such as recipes, production records, staff instructions, invoices and correspondence, which are often necessary as evidence, have been obtained and used fairly[1].

1 *Walker's Snack Foods Ltd v Coventry City Council* [1998] 3 All ER 163.

Police and Criminal Evidence Act 1984: codes of practice

18.4.8 Part VI of PACE provides for the issue of codes of practice in relation to statutory powers of search and seizure and detention, treatment and questioning. Although these provisions are directed primarily at police officers, other persons who are charged with the duty of investigating offences or charging offenders must, in the discharge of that duty, have regard to any relevant provisions of a PACE code of practice[1]. Thus, a routine inspection by a trading standards officer has been held to be a search within the ordinary meaning of the word so that the provisions of PACE Code B (search of premises and seizure of property) applied[2]. On the other hand, a request for information from environmental health officers carrying out their statutory duty under section 32(1)(b) of the FSA 1990[3] was held to be governed neither by PACE Code C (detention, treatment and questioning of persons), nor, since the officers were relying on their statutory powers rather than on consent to enter premises, by PACE Code B[4].

Failure to comply with the provisions of any relevant code of practice does not render the officer liable to civil or criminal proceedings[5] but any evidence so obtained may be inadmissible[6].

For authorised officers investigating offences against food law PACE Code C will be the most important. PACE Codes C and E (tape recording of interviews with suspects) are addressed further in paras **18.4.9** and **18.4.10** respectively below.

The latest editions of the PACE Codes B, C, D and E codes were issued by the Police and Criminal Evidence Act 1984 (Codes of Practice) (No 3) Order 1995.

1 PACE, s 67(9).
2 *Dudley Metropolitan Borough Council v Debenhams plc* (1994) 159 JP 18.
3 See para **17.5.2** above.
4 *Walker's Snack Foods Ltd v Coventry City Council* [1998] 3 All ER 163.
5 PACE, s 67(10).
6 See *Dudley Metropolitan Borough Council v Debenhams plc* (1994) 159 JP 18. For a wider discussion, see *Butterworths Trading and Consumer Law*, Div 2 para 3047.

Police and Criminal Evidence Act 1984 Code C: questioning of suspected persons

18.4.9 The modern rules to secure the fair questioning of suspected persons are to be found in PACE and PACE Code C made under it. The parts most relevant[1] to questioning for the purposes of food law are noted below. In application they must, of course, be adapted to the particular circumstances. For example, the need to search in exercise of powers of stop and search are not relevant to food cases.

Cautions

1. A person of whom there are grounds to suspect of an offence must be cautioned before any questions about it (or further questions if it is his answers to previous questions which provide the grounds for suspicion) are put to him regarding his involvement or suspected involvement in that offence if his answers or silence (ie failure or refusal to answer a question or to answer satisfactorily) may be given in evidence to a court in a prosecution. He therefore need not be cautioned if questions are put to him for other purposes, for example, solely to establish his identity or his ownership of any vehicle or to obtain information in accordance with any relevant statutory requirement or in furtherance of the proper and effective conduct of a search, (for example to determine the need to search in exercise of powers of stop and search or to seek co-operation while carrying out a search) or to seek verification of a written record.
2. The caution shall be in the following terms—

> 'You do not have to say anything. But it may harm your defence if you do not mention when questioned something which you later rely on in court. Anything you do say may be given in evidence.'

Minor deviations do not constitute a breach of this requirement provided that the sense of the caution is preserved.

3. Where there is a break in questioning under caution the interviewing officer must ensure that the person being questioned is aware that he remains under caution. If there is any doubt, the caution shall be given again in full when the interview resumes.

Interviews

4. As soon as a police officer who is making enquiries of any person about an offence believes that a prosecution should be brought against him and that there is sufficient evidence for it to succeed, he shall ask the person if he has anything further to say. If the person indicates that he has nothing more to say the officer shall without delay cease to question him about that offence.
5. (a) An accurate record must be made of each interview with a person suspected of an offence, whether or not the interview takes place at a police station.
   (b) The record must state the place of the interview, the time it begins and ends, the time the record is made (if different), any breaks in the interview and the names of those present; and must be made on the forms provided for this purpose or in the officer's pocket book or in accordance with the code of practice for tape recording police interviews with suspects (Code E)[2].
   (c) The record must be made during the course of the interview, unless in the investigating officer's view it would not be practicable or would interfere with conduct of the interview, and must constitute either a verbatim record of what has been said or, failing this, an account of the interview which adequately and accurately summarises it.
6. If an interview record is not made during the course of the interview it must be made as soon as practicable after its completion.
7. Written interview records must be timed and signed by the maker.
8. If an interview record is not completed in the course of the interview the reason must be recorded in the officer's pocket book.
9. Unless it is impracticable the person interviewed shall be given the opportunity to read the interview record and to sign it as correct or to indicate the respects in which he considers it inaccurate. If the interview is tape-recorded the arrangements set out in Code E apply. If the person concerned cannot read or refuses to read the record or to sign it, the senior police officer present shall read it to him and ask him whether he would like to sign it as correct (or make his mark) or to indicate the respects in which he considers it inaccurate. The police officer shall then certify on the interview record itself what has occurred.
10. If the appropriate adult or the person's solicitor is present during the interview, he shall also be given an opportunity to read and sign the interview record (or any written statement taken down by the police officer).
11. Any refusal by a person to sign an interview record when asked to do so in accordance with the provisions of the Code must itself be recorded.
12. A written record shall also be made of any comments made by a suspected person, including unsolicited comments, which are outside the context of an interview but which might be relevant to the offence. Any such record must be timed and signed by the maker. Where practicable the person shall be given the opportunity to read that record and to sign it as correct or to indicate the respects in which he considers it inaccurate. Any refusal to sign shall be recorded.

The caution set out in PACE Code C relates to section 34 of the Criminal Justice and Public Order Act 1994. This enables a court to draw such inferences 'as appear proper' from the accused's failure, at specified times, to mention any fact relied on in his defence which in the circumstances existing at the time he could reasonably have been expected to mention. The specified times are any time before being charged on being questioned under caution, or on being charged with the offence or officially informed he might be prosecuted for it.

1 The selection is derived from *Butterworths Law of Food and Drugs*, Vol I, para A 35.
2 See para **18.4.10** below.

Police and Criminal Evidence Act 1984 Code E: tape recording of interviews with suspects

18.4.10 PACE Code E relates to the tape recording of interviews with suspects. Authorised officers must have regard to the Code and the practice direction on it[1], if tape recording is used for this purpose.

1 *Practice Note (Criminal Evidence) (Tape Recording of Police Interviews)* [1989] 2 All ER 415, [1989] 1 WLR 631.

Criminal Procedure and Investigations Act 1996 (CP&IA 1996): disclosure

18.4.11 The law requiring disclosure of unused material by the prosecution[1] was strengthened by the CP&IA 1996.

From 1 April 1997[2], Part I of the CP&IA 1996 and statutory instruments under it[3] have made provision in relation to disclosure of information, by the prosecutor and the accused, in criminal proceedings relating to alleged offences which have not hitherto been subject to criminal investigation. Part I covers investigations which police officers or other persons have a duty to conduct, with a view to it being ascertained whether a person should be charged with an offence, or whether a person charged with an offence is guilty of it. Criminal investigations by authorised officers investigating contraventions of food law are thus included.

The prosecutor has a duty (of 'primary disclosure') either to disclose to the accused any material which has not previously been disclosed and which in the prosecutor's opinion might undermine the case for the prosecution, or to give to the accused a written statement that there is no such material. Where material does not consist of information (for instance, a food sample) the prosecutor discloses it by allowing the accused to inspect it at a reasonable time and a reasonable place. This requirement supersedes the guidance, in Part A of Food Safety Act Code of Practice no 2 (Legal Matters)[4], that food authorities should 'try to comply' with any reasonable request by a person under investigation to have access to consumer complaint samples provided that this 'does not impede the proper storage, analysis, examination or evidential value of the samples'.

Part I of the CP&IA 1996 also provides for compulsory disclosure by the accused in relation to indictable offences (and voluntary disclosure in relation to summary ones) of a written 'defence statement' to the court and the prosecutor. The statement must set out in general terms the nature of the defence, indicate the matters on which issue is taken with the prosecution case and set out, in the case of each such matter, the reason why this is. Where a defence statement is given, the prosecutor has a duty (of 'secondary disclosure') either to disclose to the accused any material which has not previously been disclosed and which might be reasonably expected to assist the accused's defence, or to give to the accused a written statement that there is no such material.

Further provisions of Part I, in particular, enable the accused, in specified circumstances, to make application for disclosure and impose on the prosecutor a continuing duty to disclose.

Paragraph **9.2.5** above has already explained that the accused in criminal proceedings also has a right to know who has made the accusation.

1 See, for example, *R v Leyland Justices, ex p Hawthorn* [1979] QB 283, [1979] 1 All ER 209; *R v Maguire* [1992] QB 936, [1992] 2 All ER 433; *R v Ward* [1993] 2 All ER 577, [1993] 1 WLR 619.
2 Criminal Procedure and Investigations Act 1996 (Appointed Day No 3) Order 1997, SI 1997/682.
3 Criminal Procedure and Investigations Act 1996 (Defence Disclosure Time Limits) Regulations 1997, SI 1997/684; Magistrates' Courts (Criminal Procedure and Investigations Act 1996) (Disclosure) Rules 1997, SI 1997/703; Magistrates' Courts (Criminal Procedure and Investigations Act 1996) (Confidentiality) Rules 1997, SI 1997/704.
4 See, paras **9.2.5** and **17.4.2** above.

Police and Criminal Evidence Act 1996: criminal investigations

18.4.12 Part II of the CP&IA 1996 provides for a code of practice designed to secure—

(a) that the police take all reasonable steps in criminal investigations;
(b) that unused material is revealed to the prosecutor;
(c) that where the prosecutor so requests, unused material is disclosed to the accused; and
(d) that the prosecutor is given a statement that the activities required by the code have been carried out.

Like Part I of the CP&IA 1996, authorised officers investigating contraventions of food law are bound by the code since it applies to persons, other than police officers, who are charged with the duty of conducting criminal investigations. By section 26 of the CP&IA 1996, they must, in discharging the duty, have regard to any relevant provisions of the code which would apply if the investigation were conducted by police officers. Failure to comply with this obligation does not, however, in itself render the officer liable to criminal or civil proceedings.

Police and Criminal Evidence Act 1996: code of practice

18.4.13 The code was brought into operation by the Criminal Procedure and Investigations Act 1996 (Code of Practice) (No 2) Order 1997, SI 1997/1033. Those responsible for investigating food law offences should consult the full code, but a summary of relevant provisions[1] is set out below. Of the definitions in the code it might, in particular, be noted here that 'disclosure officer' is defined as the person responsible for examining material retained by the police during the investigation; revealing material to the prosecutor during the investigation and any criminal proceedings resulting from it, and certifying that he has done this; and disclosing material to the accused at the request of the prosecutor.

General responsibilities

Separate functions are specified for investigators, officers in charge of investigations and disclosure officers. In conducting an investigation, the investigator should pursue all reasonable lines of inquiry, whether these point towards or away from the suspect. What is reasonable in each case will depend on the particular circumstances. If the officer in charge of an investigation believes that other persons may be in possession of material that may be relevant to the investigation, and if this has not already been obtained he should ask the disclosure officer to inform them of the existence of the investigation and to invite them to retain the material in case they receive a request for disclosure.

Recording of information

If material which may be relevant to the investigation consists of information which is not recorded in any form, the officer in charge of an investigation must ensure that it is recorded in a durable or retrievable form. Negative information is often relevant to an investigation. If it may be relevant it must be recorded.

Retention of material

The investigator must retain material obtained in a criminal investigation which may be relevant to the investigation. This includes not only material coming into the possession of the investigator but also material generated by him.

Where material has been seized in exercise of the powers, the duty to retain it under this code is subject to the provisions on retention of seized material in section 22 of PACE.

The following are categories of material which may be relevant to the investigation and must be retained—

- final versions of witness statements and draft versions where their content differs from the final version (including any exhibits mentioned), interview records (written records, or audio or video tapes, of interviews with actual or potential witnesses or suspects);
- communications between the police and experts such as forensic scientists, reports of work carried out by experts, and schedules of scientific material prepared by the expert for the investigator, for the purposes of criminal proceedings;
- any material casting doubt on the reliability of a confession;
- any material casting doubt on the reliability of a witness;
- any other material which may fall within the test for primary prosecution disclosure in the Act.

All material which may be relevant to the investigation must be retained until a decision is taken whether to institute proceedings against a person for an offence.

Preparation of material for prosecutor

The Code sets out in detail how material should be prepared.

Revelation of material to prosecutor

The disclosure officer must give the schedules to the prosecutor. Wherever practicable this should be at the same time as he gives him the file containing the material for the prosecution case. He should also draw the attention of the prosecutor to any material an investigator has retained.

Certification by disclosure officer

The disclosure officer must certify to the prosecutor that to the best of his knowledge and belief, all material which has been retained and made available to him has been revealed in accordance with the code.

Disclosure of material to the accused

If material has not already been copied to the prosecutor, and he requests its disclosure to the accused, on the ground that—

- it falls within the test for primary or secondary prosecution disclosure, or
- the court has ordered its disclosure after considering an application from the accused,

the disclosure officer *must* disclose it to the accused.

1 The selection is derived from *Butterworths Law of Food and Drugs*, Vol I, para **A [34]**.

Chapter 19

Strict liability, defences etc

19.1 STRICT LIABILITY

19.1.1 The normal rule of English criminal law is that 'a man's deed does not make him guilty unless his mind be guilty': he must have a criminal intention (*mens rea*) in order to be guilty of the offence in question. There are, however, exceptions to this rule where the legislature has thought it so important to prevent a particular act from being committed that it forbids it absolutely to be done in any case. In such circumstances if the act is done, the offender is liable to the prescribed penalty whether or not he has any *mens rea*[1]. Modern food legislation has since its inception generally been of this kind[2]. Although a few offences in the Food Safety Act 1990 (FSA 1990) contain the word 'knowingly'[3] or depend on the intention of the defendant[4], liability under most of them do not require proof of criminal intent. Since the mere commission of the unlawful act or failure to do something required by law is sufficient for conviction in these cases, they are known as offences of 'strict liability'.

To relieve the harshness of strict liability offences, Parliament has customarily added provisions which enable liability to be passed on to the person truly responsible for a contravention and afford honest traders statutory defences. These provisions in the FSA 1990 are considered in sections **19.2–19.5** below.

1 See *Pearks, Gunston & Tee v Ward* [1902] 2 KB 1.
2 *Betts v Armstead* (1888) 20 QBD 771.
3 See FSA 1990, ss 9(3), 11 (5), 12(5), 12(6) and 13(2) considered respectively in paras **9.3.2**, **11.3.6**, **11.4.2**, **11.4.3** and **11.6.2** above.
4 See FSA 1990, ss 7(1) and 33(1)(a) considered respectively in paras **5.2.2** and **17.5.10** above.

19.2 OFFENCES DUE TO FAULT OF ANOTHER PERSON

19.2.1 Section 20 of the FSA 1990 provides that where the commission by any person of an offence is due to the act or default of some other person, that other person is guilty of the offence; and a person may be charged with and convicted of the offence whether or not proceedings are taken against the first-mentioned person. This is what is known as the 'by-pass procedure' through which a food authority may bring proceedings against a manufacturer[1], importer, supplier, agent or employee[2] in addition to or instead of the principal offender who may well be the retailer seller. So that the food authority are in a position, if necessary, to bring proceedings under this procedure against whoever was essentially responsibility for the breach of food law, it is important that investigating officers should in each case identify and interview all potential 'other persons'. Proceedings against the other person alone would be appropriate where it appears that, unlike the principal offender, the other person cannot establish a statutory defence[3].

1 See, for example, *Birds Eye Wall's Ltd v Shropshire County Council* (1994) 158 JP 961.
2 *Tesco Supermarkets Ltd v Nattrass* [1972] AC 153, [1971] 2 All ER 127, HL.
3 See sections **19.3–19.5** below.

19.3 DEFENCE OF DUE DILIGENCE

The statutory provision

19.3.1 At the time that the FSA 1990 was in preparation, the main defences in the then food legislation were manifestly either too impractical for defendants or too generous to importers[1]. They were outmoded by comparison with the defence of 'all reasonable precautions and all due diligence' that, for some 30 years, had been developing in parallel consumer protection legislation[2]. The opportunity was therefore seized in 1990 to replace unsatisfactory specific provisions[3] with a comprehensive due diligence defence tailored to modern food manufacturing and distribution practice. Very much on the lines of recent statutes like the Consumer Protection Act 1987 (CPA 1987), section 21(1) of the FSA 1990 stated the basic defence thus—

> '. . . it shall . . . be a defence for the person charged to prove that he took all reasonable precautions and exercised all due diligence to avoid the commission of the offence by himself or by a person under his control.'

Special provision was, however, made by section 21(2) for persons who are charged with offences under section 8 (food not complying with the food safety requirement), section 14 (food not of the nature or substance or quality demanded) or section 15 (false or misleading labelling or advertising of food)[4] and who neither prepared the food in respect of which the offence is alleged to have been committed, nor imported it into Great Britain. They are 'taken to have established the defence if they satisfy the requirements' of either section 21(3) or section 21(4).

A person satisfies the requirements of section 21(3) if he proves—

> '(a) that the commission of the offence was due to an act or default of another person who was not under his control, or to reliance on information supplied by such a person;
> (b) that he carried out all such checks of the food in question as were reasonable in all the circumstances, or that it was reasonable in all the circumstances for him to rely on checks carried out by the person who supplied the food to him; and
> (c) that he did not know and had no reason to suspect at the time of the commission of the alleged offence that his act or omission would amount to an offence under the relevant provision.'

A person satisfies the requirements of section 21(4) if he proves—

> '(a) that the commission of the offence was due to an act or default of another person who was not under his control, or to reliance on information supplied by such a person;
> (b) that the sale or intended sale of which the alleged offence consisted was not a sale or intended sale under his name or mark; and
> (c) that he did not know, and could not reasonably have been expected to know, at the time of the commission of the alleged offence that his act or omission would amount to an offence under the relevant provision.'

Before moving on in the next paragraph to consider these due diligence provisions, it should be noted that conditions are imposed if the defence involves the allegation that the commission of the offence was due to the act or default of another person. The person charged will not, without leave of the court, be entitled to rely on the defence unless, in accordance with section 21(5), he gives the prosecution such information identifying or assisting in the identification of that other person as is in his possession.

1 See Food Act 1984 (FA 1984), ss 100 and 102 respectively.
2 See further section **19.6** below.
3 For example, the now repealed FA 1984, s 3 which, in particular, allowed a defence where the presence of extraneous matter 'was an unavoidable consequence of the process of collection or preparation'. The defendant failed to prove this in the notorious case of *Smedleys Ltd v Breed* [1974] AC 839, [1974] 2 All ER 21, noted at paras **5.3.7** and **18.2.4** above.
4 See sections **9.2, 5.3** and **6.2** above.

The philosophy of the defence

19.3.2 The qualifications to the simple due diligence defence respectively laid down by section 21(3) and section 21(4) impose a lesser burden of proof on persons who neither prepared the food nor imported it. The aim is that those who are at the head of the British marketing chain and have the greatest influence over the final product should bear the greatest responsibility.

Persons who prepare food are subject to the full rigour of the due diligence defence. It will be recalled from para **12.4** above that 'preparation' includes the manufacture and any form of processing or treatment; and that 'treatment' includes subjecting food to heat or cold[1]. These wide definitions would appear to catch manufacturers, processors, caterers and retailers who, for example, bake bread and flour products themselves; who heat pies or other products, or who chill or freeze products. On the other hand, they do not extend to the secondary activity of slicing meat which does nothing to change its physical condition[2].

Importers were considered at para **4.7.1** above. Like those preparing food, they are responsible for placing food on the British market[3] and are allowed no special dispensation in pleading the due diligence defence.

Persons other than those described above can take advantage of the provisions of section 21(3) or (4) in respect of offences against section 8, 14 or 15 of the Act. The conditions with which they must comply depend on whether or not they were marketing the food product under their own name or mark. Where the food is an 'own-label' product of the kind often manufactured for and sold by major supermarket chains, there is a higher level of responsibility because all three limbs of section 21(3) must be proved. Where, however, the food is a manufacturer's branded product, the seller will by definition satisfy section 21(4)(b) and have only to prove (a) and (c). This, as explained below, is an easier task.

As to application of these provisions by Regulations under the FSA 1990, see section **19.5** below.

1 FSA 1990, s 53(1).
2 *Leeds City Council v J H Dewhurst Ltd* [1990] Crim LR 725.
3 See case 25/88 *Ministère Public v Esther Renée Bouchara, née Wurmser and Norlaine* [1989] ECR 1105, [1991] 1 CMLR 173.

Case law on due diligence

19.3.3 Although there have as yet been few judicial decisions on section 21 of the FSA 1990, a substantial body of case law in relation to the concept of 'all reasonable precautions and all due diligence' has built up over the years under the kindred provisions in trade descriptions, weights and measures and consumer protection legislation. From the decisions it is possible to identify principles which food traders should take into account in establishing systems for the purpose of providing a due diligence defence if, despite their best endeavours, an offence is committed.

Paragraphs **19.3.4–19.3.8** below consider the principles deriving from the case law.

The defendant's burden of proof

19.3.4 Whether all reasonable precautions have been taken and all due diligence exercised are essentially questions of fact which in each case must be proved by the defendant on whom the burden rests[1]. As noted in para **4.3.4** above, he must meet the civil law standard of proof and satisfy the court 'on the balance of probabilities'[2].

1 *Amos v Melcon (Frozen Foods) Ltd* (1985) 149 JP 712, DC.
2 *R v Carr-Briant* [1943] KB 607, [1943] 2 All ER 156, CCA; *Robertson v Watson* 1949 JC 73; *R v Jenkins* (1923) 39 TLR 458, CCA; *Cant v Harley & Sons Ltd* [1938] 2 All ER 768.

All reasonable precautions and all due diligence

19.3.5 In considering the scope of the concept of 'all reasonable precautions and all due diligence', it is instructive to compare, with section 21(1) of the FSA 1990, the duty of care which citizens owe to their fellows if the tort of negligence is to be avoided[1]. In his famous judgment in *Donaghue v Stevenson*[2], Lord Atkin expressed this duty in the following terms: 'you must take reasonable care to avoid acts or omissions which you can reasonably foresee would be likely to injure your neighbour'. In a civil law context, an obligation to exercise due diligence has been construed as indistinguishable from this obligation to exercise reasonable care[3].

Nevertheless, although the duty of care in negligence indicates the extent of the section 21 due diligence duty, the parallel with civil law cannot be carried too far. Thus, the presence of a small piece of bone in a jar of baby food that created an offence under section 14 of the FSA 1990, could not of itself also be sufficient to negative the statutory defence. The maxim *res ipsa loquitur* (the thing speaks for itself) relates to the burden of proof in civil cases, not criminal cases[4].

The case law certainly emphasises that sitting back and doing nothing would be most unwise for a trader hoping to maintain that he has been duly diligent. Courts have regularly rejected the defence where they have identified reasonable precautions that defendants have failed to take. It has been held, for example, that samples of defective 'waterproof' watches could have been checked by a simple immersion test[5] and that a detector at the end of the production line would have prevented metal in chocolate[6]. Moreover, in a further case[7] concerning the sale of goods falsely described as complying with a BS standard, Lloyd LJ stated that—

> 'reasonable diligence required the appellants to establish some kind of system, whether by random sampling of the goods or whatever, to ascertain whether the goods conformed to the description. That does not mean that the system had to be foolproof – no system could be that. Nor did the appellants have to examine every article. But they did have to do something.'

In practice, then, the prudent food business should establish and keep up a system to ensure that all reasonable precautions are taken and all due diligence exercised.

What such action entails in any particular case will depend on the facts including the size and resources of the defendant's business. Precautions that might be reasonable for a large retailer might not be reasonable for the village shop[8].

That a system does not have to be foolproof to establish the defence is confirmed by a recent case[9]. The fact that the prosecutor could suggest something else that a defendant supermarket might have done to have avoided mistaken sales by its staff of food after expiry of the 'use by' date did not mean that it had failed to take all reasonable precautions and to exercise all due diligence.

1 See section **3.3** above.
2 [1932] AC 562 at 580.
3 *Riverstone Meat Co v Lancashire Shipping Co* [1960] 1 All ER 193 at page 219. See also *Tesco Supermarkets Ltd v Nattrass* [1972] AC 153 at page 199.
4 *Cow and Gate Ltd v Westminster City Council* (1995) Independent, 27 April.
5 *Sherratt v Geralds the American Jewellers Ltd* (1970) 68 LGR 256/114 Sol Jo 147.
6 *R v F & M Dobson Ltd* (1995) 16 Cr App 957.
7 *Texas Homecare Ltd v Stockport Metropolitan Borough Council* (1987) 152 JP 83.
8 *Garrett v Boots Chemists Ltd* (16 July 1980, unreported).
9 *Lincolnshire County Council v Safeway Stores plc* (1999) unreported. See further para **19.3.12** below.

Testing and supplier's assurances

19.3.6 Much of the case law on due diligence systems has been concerned with the adequacy or otherwise of testing and supplier's assurances.

In 1977 the Divisional Court decided that it would have been possible for a wholesaler to have had toys analysed for excess lead in paint: it was not enough to get a written assurance from the manufacturers and invite Trading Standards Officers to sample for analysis[1]. But in a more recent case concerning pencils containing unsafe amounts of hexavalent chromium, other wholesalers, who dealt in about 10,000 lines, satisfied the magistrates that it would not have been reasonable for them to have carried out random sampling. In the event, the due diligence defence was still denied them because, although they had dealt with reliable suppliers for 15 years, they had failed to get from them a positive assurance of compliance with the specific Regulations that were contravened[2].

Importation has posed particular problems for defendants. A foreign agent's verbal assurance and past satisfactory record has been held to be insufficient to meet the requirements of the defence[3] and, even where analyses and random sampling were arranged, the defendants had to show that tests abroad were actually being carried out[4] and that tests within the jurisdiction were adequate and (preferably in the form of independent statistical evidence) sufficient in number[5].

1 *Taylor v Lawrence Fraser (Bristol) Ltd* [1978] Crim LR 43, 121 Sol Jo 757.
2 *Riley v Webb* (1987) 151 JP 372.
3 *Hicks v SD Sullam Ltd* (1983) 147 JP 493, 3 Tr L 129.
4 *Rotherham Metropolitan Borough Council v Raysun (UK) Ltd* (1988) 153 JP 37, [1989] CCLR 1.
5 *P & M Supplies (Essex) Ltd v Devon County Council* (1991) 156 JP 328; *Dudley Metropolitan Council v Firman* (15 October 1992, unreported).

Official testing of products

19.3.7 The decision in *Taylor v Lawrence Fraser (Bristol) Ltd* referred to in the previous paragraph made clear that defendants cannot simply transfer to the enforcement authority the responsibility for taking precautions. However, two more recent decisions indicate that defendants, who carried out no specific checks of their own, may nevertheless sometimes be able to establish the due diligence defence through their reliance on official testing.

In the first[1], the Divisional Court upheld the justices' decision that the defence was made out by retailers of Piesporter wine which had been incorrectly labelled as to alcoholic strength by the German producer. The retailers had two shops only but sold some 1,200 different types of wine. In view of the tight German control regime, it was held to be reasonable for them to have relied on the assurances of their suppliers.

The second case[2] was more controversial. The Divisional Court confirmed that a meat trader, charged with consigning beef which was unfit for human consumption contrary to section 8(1)(b) of the FSA 1990, was not prevented from relying on a Government meat hygiene inspector's certificate, if it was otherwise reasonable to do so, to show he had taken all reasonable precautions and exercised all due diligence.

In each of these cases the food was an agricultural product for the purposes of the common agricultural policy for which official testing was undertaken before it was put into circulation on the market. The decisions are, it is submitted, of limited application and, even in relation to agricultural products, traders would generally be acting at their peril if they were to assume that official tests will absolve them from the need to consider and take positive precautions.

1 *Hurley v Martinez & Co Ltd* (1990) 154 JP 821.
2 *Carrick District Council v Taunton Vale Meat Traders Ltd* (1994) 158 JP 347.

Directing mind or will of the company

19.3.8 It was noted, in para **19.2.1** above, that an employee may be 'another person' for the purposes of proceedings under the by-pass procedure in section 20 of the FSA 1990 and, in para **19.3.1**, that section 21 specifically contemplates circumstances in which the due diligence defence involves the allegation that the commission of the offence was due to the act or default of 'another person'. In the leading case of *Tesco Supermarkets Ltd v Nattrass*[1], employers established a due diligence defence on the ground that the offence was actually the fault their employee. The House of Lords decided that in instituting, by means of a chain of command, an effective system of control to avoid the commission of offences under the Trade Descriptions Act 1968 (TDA 1968), the supermarket company had taken all reasonable precautions and exercised all due diligence. This was not a delegation of the duty to exercise due diligence but the performance of that duty. The store manager, whose default had led to the commission of the offence, could not be identified with the company: he was 'another person' for the purposes of the Act.

However, the due diligence defence was not made out by another company which failed to carry out regular checks and undertake adequate supervision or to give shop managers sufficient training and instructions[2].

1 [1972] AC 153, [1971] 2 All ER 127, HL.
2 *Baxters (Butchers) Ltd v Manley* (1985) 4 Tr L 219.

Control systems

19.3.9 In the light of the case law each proprietor needs to devise a control system suitable to his business.

Following the enactment of the FSA 1990, some simple guidance was issued which outlined for farmers, growers, food processors, wholesalers, importers, distributors and retailers what systems might satisfy a court that all steps have been taken to avoid committing an offence. These 'Guidelines on the Statutory Defence of Due Diligence' were published jointly in 1991 by the National Consumer Council, LACOTS, the Institution of Environmental Health Officers, the National Farmers Union, the Retail Consortium and the Food and Drink Federation, with the support of the then Parliamentary Secretary to the Ministry of Agriculture, Fisheries and Food[1]. This publication is referred to below as the 'Due Diligence Guidelines'. The following notes on control systems draw on the guidance which it contains, taking account of subsequent case law. Readers are recommended to consult other detailed sources[2].

In general, the following points should be considered in establishing a control system—

(a) Subject to what was said in para **19.3.7**, positive steps to set up a system are essential to satisfy the defence.
(b) To prove that all reasonable precautions have been taken and all due diligence exercised, it must be shown not only that the control system has been set up, but also that it is working.
(c) If there is a precaution which can be reasonably taken, then it must be taken.
(d) The control system must be capable of dealing with perceived risks, but does not have to be foolproof.
(e) The extent of the control system depends on the size and resources of the business. What is required for a large corporate body may not be appropriate for a small private business.
(f) The control system must cover every aspect of the company's business. Because the defence in the FSA 1990 is similar to those in other relevant statutes, a common control system can be established to deal with all matters subject to that Act, plus quantity controls, price checks and general product descriptions.

    A non-exhaustive list of subjects which might be covered is—
    (i) hygiene of premises, equipment and staff;
    (ii) bought-in stock, raw materials, food sources and packaging;
    (iii) production, processing, handling and storage;
    (iv) recipes, product specifications;
    (v) labelling and advertising;
    (vi) quantity marking, weighing and measuring;
    (vii) price marking, misleading indications of price;
    (viii) staff training;
    (ix) monitoring of customer complaints.
(g) All staff participating in the system must be given written instructions and be asked to acknowledge them in writing. If possible, their duties should be identified in their job specifications.
(h) The system must be pro-active and re-active. It must be capable of identifying and preventing risks and of correcting them if they occur.
(i) The system must be kept under review and updated as necessary.
(j) The adequacy of the control system will be judged by the nature of the products, the manufacturing, processing or retailing techniques involved, and all other relevant

factors. Although there are many common matters in due diligence defences, there is no such thing as a standard due diligence system. Every system must be fitted to the business which operates it.

Further matters of concern are addressed in the remainder of this section including, in para **19.3.13**, some points (supplemental to what is said in the 'Due Diligence Guidelines') on specific food trade sectors.

1 A copy is obtainable from the Food and Drink Federation.
2 See in particular, 'A Guide to Good Manufacturing Practice: A Guide to its Responsible Management' (4th edn), Institute of Food Science and Technology, 5 Cambridge Court, 210 Shepherd's Bush Road, London W6 7NL.

Hazard analysis, quality control and codes of practice

19.3.10 The 'Due Diligence Guidelines' note particular elements which may well need to be covered by a control system.

The first is the Hazard Analysis and Critical Control Points ('HACCP') approach to food control which is widely used and, as explained in para **12.2.2** above, must now be applied for the purposes of the Food Safety (General Food Hygiene) Regulations 1995. As indicated, the HACCP approach involves identifying and weighting each risk that the business will fail to meet any safety or other imperative, and then devising and implementing appropriate control measures. Although perhaps best suited to food manufacturing, HACCP is applicable for all stages in the food supply chain.

As well as HACCP, the business might usefully consider the adoption of a Quality Assurance scheme, the most obvious instance of which is provided by British Standard BS 5750 (ISO 9000 series). It should be noted, however, that the statutory defence will not be established solely by observance of quality assurance techniques, which are not as such directed at securing the legality of products.

Additionally, the prudent proprietor will wish to take account of trade and government codes of good practice for and guidance on the preparation of food and for its labelling, storage, handling and distribution[1].

1 For information on current publications, see *Butterworths Law of Food and Drugs*, in particular, Vol 3, Div D.

Assuring test standards

19.3.11 The 'Due Diligence Guidelines' also point out that sample testing should be undertaken by accredited laboratories and that, where in-house facilities are used, steps should be taken to verify the methodology and accuracy of results by obtaining independent accreditation (eg under the UK Accreditation Service scheme), by conducting paired audit tests with other laboratories or by some other appropriate method. It would, for example, be possible to arrange an audit by a company offering quality systems and due diligence control services. The contractor should have the necessary professional qualifications, accreditation and operate quality systems to BS 5750, as well as being covered by professional indemnity insurance.

It should also be borne in mind that agents involved in the operation of due diligence systems by whose act or default an offence is committed may be subject to prosecution[1].

1 See para **19.2.1** above.

Records and written assurances from suppliers

19.3.12 Written records of the control system will be required if the due diligence system has to be proved in court. The text laying down the basic procedures should be adopted by those having the directing mind or will of the business, and checks and other actions carried out within this framework should be recorded and signed by the staff involved. Ideally, defect reports and remedial action should be recorded in writing, but oral reporting may be sufficient, for example within a supermarket, if errors are traceable to the person concerned and are followed by warnings, additional training and extra checks[1].

For bought-in products, the system must manifestly be able to confirm by way of suppliers' written assurances, test data or otherwise that every reasonable effort has been taken to secure compliance with legal requirements.

Evidence of a carefully devised and run system which stands scrutiny by enforcement officers may, if a contravention does occur, persuade the prosecution that there will be a sound defence if the matter is taken to court.

1 *Lincolnshire County Council v Safeway Stores plc* (1999) unreported.

Specific food trade sectors

19.3.13 It will be apparent from what has already been said, that some indication can be gathered from the case law as to the sorts of control systems that might be adequate for particular sectors of the food trade.

Subject to the special circumstances noted in para **19.3.7** above, section 21 of the FSA 1990 imposes a heavy burden on those, like manufacturers and importers, who do not get the benefit of section 21(3) or (4). Paragraph **19.3.6** cited examples of failures to meet the strict obligations in respect of imports. However, in *Bibby-Cheshire v Golden Wonder Ltd*[1], a manufacturer managed to meet the onerous requirements of the due diligence defence. The case concerned an under-weight packet of crisps. The magistrates found that the best available machines had been used; that it was economically impossible to weigh individually the 20 million packets produced every week; and that there was an efficient system of random checking which ensured that no machine consistently produced under-weight bags. Although demanding, the requirements of the defence can be met. Paragraph **3.6.1***(a)* above has already noted the need for manufacturers to ensure that their food control and management systems take account of the possibility of civil as well as criminal liability.

Subject to what is said below, further examples in para **19.3.6** show that the burden on wholesalers is scarcely less heavy. They too will normally be in a large way of business and will seldom be able to rely simply on written assurances from their suppliers.

Judicial interpretation of the bespoke provisions of section 21(3) and (4) of the FSA 1990 is for the moment still awaited. As noted above, the provisions in section 21(3) for own-labellers include specific requirements that they should have carried out all such checks of the food in question as were reasonable in all the circumstances, or that it was reasonable in all the circumstances to rely on checks by their suppliers. This requirement is a halfway-house between the full due diligence obligation required of manufacturers and importers and lesser one required of sellers of branded goods. The ratio of self-checking to reliance on a supplier's checks must depend on the confidence the retailer has in the checking system operated by the supplier. This confidence can be achieved by regular checks on the supplier's due diligence system by the retailer's staff or agents. In effect, the supplier and retailer must in combination have implemented a full due diligence system.

Sellers of other products (also generally speaking retailers) have the advantage of section 21(4). It should be noted that the threshold imposed by this provision is lower than that in section 21(3) not only because it will be self evident that the sale was not 'under his own name or mark', but also because section 21(4)(c) is less taxing in practice than section 21(3)(c). The seller of a manufacturer's branded product has to prove that he 'could not reasonably have been expected to know' that his act or omission would amount to an offence. The obligation of the own-labelling business to prove that it 'had no reason to suspect' this will be no easy task if, as will normally be the case, it has imposed precise product requirements on the manufacturer.

The size and resources of the seller's business will determine what section 21(4) demands of him. Large retailers must organise and operate effective systems throughout their stores[2], as well as taking steps to assure themselves as to the reliability of their purchases. Apart from himself complying with relevant legislation, the small retailer could in general be expected to do no more than buy from reputable suppliers, to obtain from them positive assurances as to the legality of the products and to check that the supplies conform with what was ordered. Exceptionally, butchers, bakers and other small businesses 'preparing' food, are subject to the full rigour of the due diligence defence[3].

1 [1972] 3 All ER 738, [1972] 1 WLR 1487.
2 See, for example, *Tesco Supermarkets Ltd v Nattrass* [1972] AC 153, [1971] 2 All ER 127, HL and *Lincolnshire County Council v Safeway Stores plc* (1999) unreported.
3 See para **19.3.2** above.

19.4 DEFENCE OF PUBLICATION IN THE COURSE OF BUSINESS

19.4.1 The FSA 1990 repeats the now common defence for persons who innocently publish advertisements. It provides that it is a defence for the defendant to prove that he is a person whose business it is to publish or arrange for the publication of advertisements and that he received the offending advertisement in the ordinary course of his business and did not know, and had no reason to suspect, that its publication would amount to an offence[1].

An advertising agency which designed an offending advertisement, is unlikely be able to sustain this defence and would have to consider the possibilities of recourse to section 21.

1 FSA 1990, s 22.

19.5 DEFENCES IN REGULATIONS

Due diligence and publishing defence

19.5.1 The defences of due diligence and publication in the course of business are customarily applied to Regulations under the FSA 1990 as they apply for the purposes of section 8, 14 or 15. Persons other than those who prepared or imported the food in question are therefore eligible to claim the benefit of section 21(3) and (4) in respect of offences enacted by the Regulations.

Special defences

19.5.2 Regulations under the FSA 1990 commonly contain the defence in relation to exports explained in para **4.7.2** above and often make transitional provision by means of defences[1].

Special defences are, moreover, sometimes provided by Regulations to meet particular circumstances. Thus, there are defences in relation to contraventions of chill and hot holding requirements[2], in case of alteration of the appropriate durability indication[3] and in respect of various offences under the Plastic Materials and Articles in Contact with Food Regulations 1998[4]. Since section 21 applies only to food, the 1998 Regulations also prescribe their own due diligence defence[5].

Food businesses whose products are affected by any special defence, will need to ensure that their control systems are adapted to take advantage of it.

1 See, for example, Food Labelling Regulations 1996, reg 50.
2 Food Safety (Temperature Control) Regulations 1995, regs 6(1), 7(1), 7(2) and 9.
3 Food Labelling Regulations 1996, reg 46.
4 See regs 4(7) and 5(2).
5 See reg 10(8)–(12).

19.6 OTHER LEGISLATION

19.6.1 Provision of the kind described in this chapter is not exclusive to the FSA 1990, since other relevant legislation operates through strict liability offences.

Provision in respect of offences due to the fault of another person (the by-pass procedure described in para **19.2.1** above) is also included in the Trade Descriptions Act 1968 (TDA 1968), the Weights and Measures Act 1985 (W&MA 1985), the CPA 1987, the Agriculture and Horticulture Act 1964 (A&HA 1964) and the Agriculture Act 1970.

Likewise, as indicated in para **19.3.3** and in the case law cited above, the due diligence defence appears in different guises in the TDA 1968, Parts IV and V of the W&MA 1985 and the CPA 1987. Forms of it are also to be found in the A&HA 1964, the Agriculture Act 1970, the Food and Environment Protection Act 1985 and subordinate legislation like the Common Agricultural Policy (Wine) Regulations 1996.

The Prices Act 1974 applies the by-pass and due diligence provisions of the TDA 1968.

Defences in respect of advertisements published in the course of business, like section 22 of the FSA 1990, are included in the TDA 1968 and, in respect of misleading price indications, in the CPA 1987.

The A&HA 1964 and Parts IV and V of the W&MA 1985 include defences, of the kind in section 102 of the now repealed FA 1984, where the defendant bought with a warranty that the produce complied with relevant legislation.

Other defences relating to special circumstances are to be found in sections 35–37 and 50 of the W&MA 1985 and in section 24 of the CPA 1987.

Traders subject to any such other legislation will need to ensure that their control systems are sufficiently comprehensive in scope.

Appendix A

Digest of food and feeding stuffs legislation relating to England and Wales

Notes

1. Measures concerning the presence in food and feeding stuffs of, such as, pesticides and veterinary medicines and genetically modified organisms are included in this Appendix, but those concerning the approval of such substances are outside the scope of this book.
2. Emergency control orders under section 13 of the Food Safety Act 1990 and emergency orders under section 1 of the Food and Environment Protection Act 1985 are normally of short duration and are not included.
3. For amended and annotated texts of the majority of the statutes and statutory instruments listed below, see as appropriate, *Butterworths Law of Food and Drugs*, *O'Keefe's Law of Weights and Measures*, *O'Keefe's Law of Trade Descriptions*, *Miller's Product Liability and Safety*, *Butterworths Trading and Consumer Law*; *Halsbury's Statutes* (4th edn) and *Halsbury's Statutory Instruments*. For up-to-date information as to new or amended legislation, see Butterworths monthly *Consumer Law Bulletin*.

PART I: STATUTES APPLICABLE IN WHOLE OR IN PART TO FOOD OR FEEDING STUFFS

Amendments to statutes contained in this Part have not been listed: for fuller coverage see *Halsbury's Statutes* (4th edn).

Agriculture Act 1970, Pt IV, fertilisers and feeding stuffs.

Agriculture and Horticulture Act 1964 (c 28), Pt III, grading of horticultural produce.

Agricultural Produce (Grading and Marking) Act 1928 (18 & 19 Geo 5, c 19), grading and marking of agricultural produce.

Animal Health Act 1981 (c 22) consolidated various enactments relating to diseases of animals and in particular, in section 29, provided for the control of zoonoses.

Consumer Protection Act 1987 (c 43), Pt I, product liability; Pt II, consumer safety; Pt III, misleading indications of price.

Deregulation and Contracting Out Act 1994 (c 40), in particular, made provision for the amendment of statutory provisions and rules of law in order to remove or reduce certain burdens affecting persons in the carrying on of trades, businesses or professions or otherwise.

European Communities Act 1972 (c 68) made provision in connection with the enlargement of the European Communities to include the United Kingdom.

European Economic Area Act 1993 (c 51) made provision in relation to the European Economic Area established under the Agreement signed at Oporto on 2 May 1992 as adjusted by the Protocol signed at Brussels on 17 March 1993.

Food and Environment Protection Act 1985 (c 48), Pt I, contamination of food; Pt III, pesticides etc.

Food Safety Act 1990 (c 16), Pt I, Preliminary; Pt II, main provisions – food safety, consumer protection, regulations, defences etc, miscellaneous and supplemental; Pt III, administration and enforcement – administration, sampling and analysis etc, powers of entry and obstruction etc, offences, appeals; Pt IV, miscellaneous and supplemental—powers of ministers, protective provisions, financial provisions, instruments and documents, amendments of other Acts, supplemental.

Food Standards Act 1999 (c 28) established the Food Standards Agency and made provisions as to its functions; amended the law relating to food safety and other interests of consumers in relation to food; enabled provision to be made in relation to the notification of tests for food-borne diseases; and enabled provision to be made in relation to animal feeding stuffs.

Government of Wales Act 1998 (c 38) in particular established and made provision for the transfer of functions to the National Assembly for Wales.

Horticultural Produce Act 1986 (c 20) conferred on authorised officers (within the meaning of Pt III of the Agriculture and Horticulture Act 1964) powers in relation to the movement of horticultural produce.

Prices Act 1974 (c 24) in particular made provision for requiring prices to be indicated on or in relation to goods offered or exposed for sale by retail.

Sale of Goods Act 1979 (c 54) consolidated the law of sale of goods in the amended Sale of Goods Act 1893.

Scotch Whisky Act 1988 (c 22) made provision as to the definition of Scotch whisky and as to the production and sale of whisky.

Scotland Act 1998 (c 46) in particular provided for the establishment and legislative competence of a Scottish Parliament and for the establishment of and transfer of functions to a Scottish Administration.

Trade Descriptions Act 1968 (c 29), in particular, replaced the Merchandise Marks Acts 1887 to 1953 by fresh provisions prohibiting misdescriptions of goods, services, accommodation and facilities provided in the course of trade.

Unfair Contract Terms Act 1977 (c 50) imposed further limits on the extent to which civil liability for breach of contract, or for negligence or other breach of duty, can be avoided by means of contract terms or otherwise.

Weights and Measures Act 1985 (c 72) consolidated enactments relating to weights and measures.

PART IIA: SUBORDINATE LEGISLATION APPLICABLE IN WHOLE OR IN PART TO FOOD

Animal by-products

Animal By-Products (Identification) Regulations 1995, SI 1995/1086, as amended by SIs 1995/1763, 1996/1499, 1699, 1997/1729, 1998/2424 and 2000/656.

Animal By-Products Order 1999, SI 1999/646.

Food additives, contaminants, residues and other substances

Additives

Colours in Food Regulations 1995, SI 1995/3124, as amended by SI 2000/481.

Miscellaneous Food Additives Regulations 1995, SI 1995/3187, as amended by SIs 1997/1413 and 1999/1136.

Sweeteners in Food Regulations 1995, SI 1995/3123, as amended by SIs 1996/1477, 1997/814, and 1999/982.

Additives: Labelling

Food Additives Labelling Regulations 1992, SI 1992/1978, as amended by SIs 1995/3123, 3124, 3187, 1996/1499 and 1999/1136.

Flavourings

Flavourings in Food Regulations 1992, SI 1992/1971, as amended by SIs 1994/1486 and 1996/1499.

Other added substances

Chloroform in Food Regulations 1980, SI 1980/36, as amended by SIs 1982/1727, 1990/2486 and 1991/1476, and by virtue of the Criminal Justice Act 1988, s 52 in relation to penalties.

Erucic Acid in Food Regulations 1977, SI 1977/691, as amended by SIs 1982/264, 1727, 1990/2486 and 1991/1476, and by virtue of the Criminal Justice Act 1988, s 52 in relation to penalties.

Extraction Solvents in Food Regulations 1993, SI 1993/1658, as amended by SIs 1995/1440 and 1998/2257.

Mineral Hydrocarbons in Food Regulations 1966, SI 1966/1073, as amended by SIs 1982/1727, 1990/2486, 1991/1476, 1992/2597 and 1995/3187, and by virtue of the Criminal Justice Act 1988, s 52 in relation to penalties.

Tryptophan in Food Regulations 1990, SI 1990/1728, as amended by SI 1990/2486.

Contaminants

Arsenic in Food Regulations 1959, SI 1959/831, as amended by SIs 1960/2261, 1973/1052, 1982/1727, 1990/2486, 1991/1476 and 1992/1971, and by virtue of the Criminal Justice Act 1988, s 52 in relation to penalties.

Contaminants in Food Regulations 1997, SI 1997/1499, as amended by SIs 1999/1603 and 1999/3221.

Lead in Food Regulations 1979, SI 1979/1254, as amended by SIs 1982/1727, 1985/912, 1990/2486, 1991/1476, 1992/1971, 1995/3124 and 1995/3267, and by virtue of the Criminal Justice Act 1988, s 52 in relation to penalties.

Tin in Food Regulations 1992, SI 1992/496, as amended by SI 1992/2596.

Food contact materials

Ceramic Ware (Safety) Regulations 1988, SI 1988/1647.

Cooking Utensils (Safety) Regulations 1972, SI 1988/1957, as amended by SI 1987/1680.

Materials and Articles in Contact with Food Regulations 1987, SI 1987/1523, as amended by SIs 1990/2487, 1991/1476 and 1994/979, and by virtue of the Criminal Justice Act 1988, s 52 in relation to penalties.

Plastic Materials and Articles in Contact with Food Regulations 1998, SI 1998/1376.

N-nitrosamines and N-nitrosatable Substances in Elastomer or Rubber Teats and Dummies (Safety) Regulations 1995, SI 1995/1012.

Pesticide residues

Pesticides (Maximum Residue Levels in Crops, Food and Feeding Stuffs) (England and Wales) Regulations 1999, SI 1999/3483.

Veterinary Residues

Animals and Animal Products (Examination for Residues and Maximum Residue Limits) Regulations 1997, SI 1997/1729.

Food enforcement

Exports

Food Safety (Exports) Regulations 1991, SI 1991/1476, as amended by SIs 1995/1086, 3116, 3123, 3124, 3187, 3267, 1996/1499, 1998/2424 and 1999/1540.

Food Authorities

Food Safety (Enforcement Authority) (England and Wales) Order 1990, SI 1990/2462.

Forms

Detention of Food (Prescribed Forms) Regulations 1990, SI 1990/ 2614.

Food Safety (Improvement and Prohibition—Prescribed Forms) Regulations 1991, SI 1991/100.

Improvement Notices

Deregulation (Improvement of Enforcement Procedures) (Food Safety Act 1990) Order 1996, SI 1996/1683.

Meat Hygiene Appeals

Meat Hygiene Appeals Tribunal (Procedure) Regulations 1992, SI 1992/2921, as amended by SIs 1995/539, 2148, 2000/225 and 656.

Registration

Food Premises (Registration) Regulations 1991, SI 1991/2825, as amended by SIs 1993/2022, 1994/3082, 1995/539, 540, 1086, 1763, 2148, 3205, 1996/1499, 1997/723 and 1998/994.

Food Premises (Registration) (Welsh Form of Application) Regulations 1993, SI 1993/1270.

Revision of penalties

Food (Revision of Penalties) Regulations 1985, SI 1985/67.

Food (Revision of Penalties) Regulations 1982, SI 1982/1727, as amended by SIs 1991/1231, 1993/1520, 1995/1763, 2200, 3116, 3124, 3187, 3267 and 1996/1499.

Milk and Dairies (Revision of Penalties) Regulations 1982, SI 1982/1703, as amended by SI 1998/2424.

Sampling and qualifications

Authorised Officers (Meat Inspection) Regulations 1987, SI 1987/133, as amended by SI 1990/2486.

Food Safety (Sampling and Qualifications) Regulations 1990, SI 1990/2463, as amended by SIs 1995/1086, 1997/1729, 1998/1376, 1999/1540 and 1999/1603.

Food: fees and charges

Charges for Inspections and Controls Regulations 1997, SI 1997/2893, as amended by SI 1998/2880.

Dairy Products (Hygiene) (Charges) Regulations 1995, SI 1995/ 1122, as amended by SI 2000/656.

Meat (Hygiene and Inspection) (Charges) Regulations 1998, SI 1998/2095, as amended by SIs 2000/224 and 656.

Novel Foods and Novel Food Ingredients (Fees) Regulations 1997, SI 1997/1336, as amended by SIs 1999/1756, 2000/253 and 656.

Food hygiene and preparation

Food: bovine spongiform encephalopathy

Beef and beef products
Beef Labelling (Enforcement) Regulations 1998, SI 1998/616.

Beef on the bone
Beef Bones Regulations 1997, SI 1997/2959, as amended by SIs 1999/3371 (in relation to England only), 3464 (making identical amendments in relation to Wales only) and 2000/656.

Export of Bovine Products
Bovines and Bovine Products (Trade) Regulations 1999, SI 1999/1103, as amended by SI 1999/1554.

Meat from cattle over thirty months old
Fresh Meat (Beef Controls) (No 2) Regulations 1996, SI 1996/2097, as amended by SIs 1996/2522 and 2000/656.

Specified Risk Material
Specified Risk Material Regulations 1997, SI 1997/2965, as amended by SIs 1997/3062, 1998/2405, 1999/539 and 2000/656.

Food Irradiation

Food (Control of Irradiation) Regulations 1990, SI 1990/2490, as amended by SI 2000/656.

Heat treatment of ice-cream

Ice-Cream (Heat Treatment etc) Regulations 1959, SI 1959/734, as amended by SIs 1963/1083, 1982/1727, 1990/2486, 1995/1086 and 1763, and by virtue of the Criminal Justice Act 1988, s 51 in relation to penalties.

Hygiene of foodstuffs

Dairy Products

Dairy Products (Hygiene) Regulations 1995, SI 1995/1086, as amended by SIs 1995/1763, 1996/1499, 1699, 1997/1729, 1998/2424 and 2000/656.

Milk and Dairies (General) Regulations 1959, SI 1959/277, as amended by SIs 1982/1703, 1990/2486, 1992/3143, 1995/1086, 1998/2424 and 2000/656, and by virtue of the Criminal Justice Act 1988, s 52.

Eggs and Egg Products
Egg Products Regulations 1993, SI 1993/1520, as amended by SIs 1995/1763, 1996/1499 and 2000/656.

Ungraded Eggs (Hygiene) Regulations 1990, SI 1990/1323, as amended by SI 1990/2486.

Fishery Products and Live Shellfish
Food Safety (Fishery Products and Live Shellfish) (Hygiene) Regulations 1998, SI 1998/994, as amended by SIs 1999/399, 1999/1585 and 2000/656.

Fresh meat

Fresh Meat (Hygiene and Inspection) Regulations 1995, SI 1995/539 as amended by SIs 1995/731, 1763, 2148, 2200, 3124, 3189, 1996/1148, 2235, 1997/1729, 2074, 2000/225 and 656.

Fresh Meat (Import Conditions) Regulations 1996, SI 1996/3125.

General food hygiene
Food Safety (General Food Hygiene) Regulations 1995, SI 1995/1763, as amended by SIs 1995/2148, 2200, 3205, 1996/1699, 1997/2537, 1998/994, 1999/1360, 1540, 2000/656 and 930.

Imports: general

Imported Food Regulations 1984, SI 1984/1918, as amended by SIs 1990/2486, 1997/2537 and 2000/656, and by virtue of the Criminal Justice Act 1988, s 51.

Imported Food Regulations 1997, SI 1997/2537.

Products of Animal Origin (Import and Export) Regulations 1996, SI 1996/3124, as amended by SIs 1997/3023, 1998/994, 1999/683, 2000/225.

Animals and Animal Products (Import and Export) Regulations 1998, SI 1998/190.

Meat: enforcement
Meat (Enhanced Enforcement Powers) (England) Regulations 2000, SI 2000/225.

Meat Products
Meat Products (Hygiene) Regulations 1994, SI 1994/3082 as amended by SIs 1995/539, 1995/1763, 1995/2200, 1995/3205, 1996/1499, 1999/683 (partially revoked by SI 2000/790), 2000/225, 656 and 790.

Minced Meat and Meat Preparations
Minced Meat and Meat Preparations (Hygiene) Regulations 1995, SI 1995/3205, as amended by SIs 1996/3124, 2000/225 and 656.

Poultry Meat, Farmed Game Bird Meat and Rabbit Meat

Poultry Meat, Farmed Game Bird Meat and Rabbit Meat (Hygiene and Inspection) Regulations 1995, SI 1995/540 amended by SIs 1995/1763, 2148, 2200, 3205, 1997/1729, 2000/225 and 656.

Snails, frogs' legs and honey
Miscellaneous Products of Animal Origin (Import Conditions) Regulations 1999, SI 1999/157.

Temperature Control
Food Safety (Temperature Control) Regulations 1995, SI 1995/2200, as amended by SIs 1995/3205, 1996/1499, 1998/994 and 1398
International Carriage of Perishable Foodstuffs Regulations 1985, SI 1985/1071, as amended by SIs 1992/2682, 1995/1716, 1996/2765 and 1997/1673.

Wild Game Meat

Wild Game Meat (Hygiene and Inspection) Regulations 1995, SI 1995/2148, as amended by SIs 1995/3205 and 2000/656.

Food labelling etc

General labelling

Food Labelling Regulations 1996, SI 1996/1499, as amended by SIs 1998/141, 1398, 2424, 1999/747, 1136, 1483, 1540, 1603 and 2000/768.

Genetically Modified and Novel Foods

Genetically Modified and Novel Foods (Labelling) (England) Regulations 2000, SI 2000/768.

Lot marking

Food (Lot Marking) Regulations 1996, SI 1996/1502.

Misleading advertisements

Control of Misleading Advertisements Regulations 1988, SI 1988/915, as amended by virtue of the Criminal Justice Act 1988, s 52, by the Broadcasting Act 1990, s 203(1), (3), Sch 20, para. 51, Sch 21 (subject to transitional provisions and savings listed therein), and by SIs 1995/1537 and 2000/914.

Food standards

Main food quality standards

Bananas
(See under *Fruit and Vegetables*)

Bread and Flour
Bread and Flour Regulations 1998, SI 1998/141, as amended by SI 1999/1136.

Caseins and Caseinates
Caseins and Caseinates Regulations 1985, SI 1985/2026, as amended by SIs 1989/2321, 1990/2486, 1991/1476, 1992/2596 and 1996/1499, and by virtue of the Criminal Justice Act 1988, s 52 in relation to penalties.

Cocoa and Chocolate Products
Cocoa and Chocolate Products Regulations 1976, SI 1976/541, as amended by SIs 1982/17, 1982/1727, 1990/2486, 1991/1476, 1992/2596, 1995/3187, 3267 and 1996/1499, and by virtue of the Criminal Justice Act 1988, s 52 in relation to penalties.

Coffee and Coffee Products
Coffee and Coffee Products Regulations 1978, SI 1978/1420, as amended by SIs 1982/254, 1727, 1987/1986, 1990/2486, 1991/1476, 1992/2596, 1995/3187 and 1996/1499, and by virtue of the Criminal Justice Act 1988, s 52 in relation to penalties.

Condensed Milk and Dried Milk
Condensed Milk and Dried Milk Regulations 1977, SI 1977/928, as amended by SIs 1982/1066, 1727, 1986/2299, 1989/1959, 1990/2486, 1991/1476, 1992/2596, 1995/3187 and 1996/1499, and by virtue of the Criminal Justice Act 1988, s 52 in relation to penalties.

Eggs
Eggs (Marketing Standards) Regulations 1995, SI 1995/1544, as amended by SIs 1996/1725, 1997/1414, 1998/1665.

Eggs (Marking and Storage) Regulations 1965, SI 1965/1000, as amended by SI 1978/1248.

Fishery and aquaculture products
Sea Fish (Marketing Standards) Regulations 1986, SI 1986/1272 as amended by SIs 1989/687 and 1994/452, and by virtue of the Criminal Justice Act 1988, s 52 in relation to penalties.

Preserved Sardines (Marketing Standards) Regulations 1990, SI 1990/1084, as amended by SI 1990/2486.

Preserved Tuna and Bonito (Marketing Standards) Regulations 1994, SI 1994/2127, as amended by SIs 1996/1008 and 1499.

Fruit and Vegetables
Grading of Horticulture Produce (Amendment) Regulations 1973, SI 1973/22.

Grading of Horticultural Produce (Amendment) Regulations 1983, SI 1983/1053 (These Regulations amend the Agriculture and Horticulture Act 1964).

Grading of Horticultural Produce (Forms of Labels) Regulations 1982, SI 1982/387.

Fruit Juices and Fruit Nectars
Fruit Juices and Fruit Nectars Regulations 1977, SI 1977/927, as amended by SIs 1979/1254, 1982/1311, 1727, 1990/2486, 1991/1284, 1476, 1992/2596, 1995/236, 3187, 3267, 1996/1499 and 1997/1413, and by virtue of the Criminal Justice Act 1988, s 52 in relation to penalties.

Honey
Honey Regulations 1976, SI 1976/1832, as amended by SIs 1982/1727, 1990/2486, 1991/1476, 1992/2596 and 1996/1499, and by virtue of the Criminal Justice Act 1988, s 52 in relation to penalties.

Jam and Similar Products
Jam and Similar Products Regulations 1981, SI 1981/1063, as amended by SIs 1982/1727, 1990/2085, 2486, 1991/1476, 1992/2596, 1995/3123, 3124, 3187, 1996/1499 and 1998/1398, and by virtue of the Criminal Justice Act 1988, s 52 in relation to penalties.

Meat and Meat Products
Meat Products and Spreadable Fish Products Regulations 1984, SI 1984/1566, as amended by SIs 1986/987, 1990/2486, 1991/1476, 1992/2596, 1995/3123, 3124, 3187, 1996/1499 and 1998/1398, and by virtue of the Criminal Justice Act 1988, s 52 in relation to penalties.

Milk and milk products
Drinking Milk Regulations 1998, SI 1998/2424.

Milk and Milk Products (Protection of Designations) Regulations 1990, SI 1990/607, as amended by SIs 1990/2486, 1995/3267 and 1996/1499.

Olive Oil
Olive Oil (Marketing Standards) Regulations 1987, SI 1987/1783, as amended by SIs 1990/2487, 1992/2590 and 1998/2410, and by virtue of the Criminal Justice Act 1988, s 52, in relation to penalties.

Olive Oil (Designations of Origin) Regulations 1999, SI 1999/1513.

Poultrymeat
Poultrymeat (Water Content) Regulations 1984, SI 1984/1145, as amended by SI 1990/2486, and by virtue of the Criminal Justice Act 1988, s 52 in relation to penalties.

Quick-Frozen Foodstuffs
Quick-Frozen Foodstuffs Regulations 1990, SI 1990/2615, as amended by SIs 1992/2596, 1994/298 and 1996/1499.

Spirit Drinks
Spirit Drinks Regulations 1990, SI 1990/1179, as amended by SIs 1990/2486 and 1995/732.

Scotch Whisky Order 1990, SI 1990/998.

Spreadable Fats
Spreadable Fats (Marketing Standards) (England) Regulations 1999, SI 1999/2457.

Sugar Products
Specified Sugar Products Regulations 1976, SI 1976/509, as amended by SIs 1982/255, 1727, 1990/2486, 1991/1476, 1992/2596, 1995/3124, 3187 and 1996/1499, and by virtue of the Criminal Justice Act 1988, s 52 in relation to penalties.

Water
Natural Mineral Water, Spring Water and Bottled Drinking Water Regulations 1999, SI 1999/1540, as amended by SI 2000/656.

Whisky
(See under *Spirit drinks*)

Wine
Common Agricultural Policy (Wine) Regulations 1996, SI 1996/696, as amended by SIs 1997/542, 1998/453, 1999/482 and 672.

Novel Foods

Novel Foods and Novel Food Ingredients Regulations 1997, SI 1997/1335, as amended by SIs 1999/1756, 2000/83, 656, and 768.

Organic products

Organic Products Regulations 1992, SI 1992/2111, as amended by SIs 1993/405, 1994/2286, 1997/166.

Foodstuffs for particular nutritional uses

Infant Formula and Follow-on Formula Regulations 1995, SI 1995/77, as amended by SIs 1995/3267, 1996/1499 and 1997/451.

Processed Cereal-based Foods and Baby Foods for Infants and Young Children Regulations 1997, SI 1997/2042, as amended by SI 1999/275.

Foods Intended for Use in Energy Restricted Diets for Weight Reduction Regulations 1997, SI 1997/2182.

Medical Food (England) Regulations 2000, SI 2000/845.

Food Standards Act 1999

Food Standards Act 1999 (Commencement No 1) Order 2000, SI 2000/92.

Food Standards Act 1999 (Commencement No 2) Order 2000, SI 2000/1066.

Food Standards Act 1999 (Transitional and Consequential Provisions and Savings) (England and Wales) Regulations 2000, SI 2000/656.

Food: revocations and amendments

Those of particular importance include:

Food (Miscellaneous Revocations) Regulations 1991, SI 1991/1231.

Food (Miscellaneous Revocations and Amendments) Regulations 1995, SI 1995/3267.

General safety

General Product Safety

General Product Safety Regulations 1994, SI 1994/2328, as amended by SIs 1994/3142 and 3144.

Food Imitation

Food Imitation (Safety) Regulations 1989, SI 1989/1291.

Quantity and price marking of food

Quantity marking

Units of Measurement Regulations 1986, SI 1986/1082, as amended by SIs 1994/2867 and 1995/1804.

Weights and Measures Act 1963 (Cheese, Fish, Fresh Fruits and Vegetables, Meat and Poultry) Order 1984, SI 1984/1315, as amended by SIs 1985/988 and 1985/1980, and by virtue of the Criminal Justice Act 1988, s 52.

Weights and Measures (Packaged Goods) Regulations 1986, SI 1986/2049, as amended by SIs 1987/1538, 1992/1580, 1994/1258 and 1852.

Weights and Measures (Quantity Marking and Abbreviations of Units) Regulations 1987, SI 1987/1538, as amended by SIs 1988/627 and 1994/1852.

Weights and Measures (Intoxicating Liquor) Order 1988, SI 1988/2039, as amended by SIs 1990/1550, 1994/1883 and 1994/2868.

Weights and Measures (Miscellaneous Foods) Order 1988, SI 1988/2040, as amended by SIs 1990/1550 and 2868.

Price marking

Price Marking (Food and Drink on Premises) Order 1979, SI 1979/361.

Price Marking Order 1999, SI 1999/3042.

Unfair contract terms

Unfair Terms in Consumer Contracts Regulations 1999, SI 1999/2083.

PART IIB: SUBORDINATE LEGISLATION APPLICABLE TO FEEDING STUFFS

(See further Part IIA of this Appendix.)

Composition

Feeding Stuffs Regulations 1995, SI 1995/1412 as amended by SIs 1996/1260, 1998/104, 2072, 1999/1528 and 2325.

Establishments and intermediaries

Feeding Stuffs (Establishments and Intermediaries) Regulations 1999, SI 1999/1872.

Feeding stuffs: bovine spongiform encephalopathy

Feeding stuffs and surveillance

Bovine Spongiform Encephalopathy (Feeding Stuffs and Surveillance) Regulations 1999, SI 1999/882.

Mammalian protein and mammalian meat and bone meal

Bovine Spongiform Encephalopathy (No 2) Order 1996, 1996/3183, as amended by SIs 1997/2387, 1998/3071, 1999/646 and 921.

Specified risk material

Specified Risk Material Order 1997, SI 1997/2964.

Medicated feeding stuffs

Medicated Feeding stuffs Regulations 1998, SI 1998/1046.

Sampling and analysis

Feeding Stuffs (Sampling and Analysis) Regulations 1999, SI 1999/1663.

Zootechnical products

Feedingstuffs (Zootechnical Products) Regulations 1999, SI 1999/1871.

Appendix B

Digest of European Community food and feeding stuffs legislation

Notes

1. National implementing legislation is listed in Appendix A.
2. Note 1 to Appendix A applies also to this Appendix.
3. Of EC Regulations concerning agricultural products subject to market organisation, only those setting market standards for foodstuffs are included.
4. For amended texts of many of these Community instruments, see, as appropriate, Butterworths *Law of Food and Drugs*, O'Keefe's *Law of Weights and Measures*, O'Keefe's *Law of Trade Descriptions*, Miller's *Product Liability and Safety* and Butterworths *Trading and Consumer Law*. For up-to-date information as to new or amended legislation, see Butterworths monthly *Consumer Law Bulletin*.

PART I: COMMUNITY LEGISLATION APPLICABLE IN WHOLE OR IN PART TO FOOD

Animal waste

Council Directive 90/667/EEC (disposal and processing of animal waste, for its placing on the market and for the prevention of pathogens in feeding stuffs of animal or fish origin) (OJ L 363 27.12.90, p 51) as amended by Directive 92/118 (OJ L 62 15.3.92, p 49)

Commission Decision 92/562/EEC (approval of alternative heat treatment systems for processing high-risk material) (OJ L 359 9.12.92, p 23)

Commission Decision 97/735/EC (protection measures with regard to trade in certain types of mammalian animal waste) (OJ L 294 28.10.97, p 7) as amended by Directive 1999/534 (OJ L 204 4.8.99, p 37)

Commission Decision 1999/534/EC (measures applying to the processing of certain animal waste to protect against transmissible spongiform encephalopathies) (OJ L 204 4.8.99, p 37).

Consumer protection: general

Council Directive 85/374/EEC (liability for defective products) (OJ L 210 7.8.85, p 29), as amended by Directive 1999/34 (OJ L 141 4.6.1999, p 20)

Council Directive 84/450/EEC (misleading advertising) (OJ L 250 19.9.84, p 17) as amended by Directive 97/55/EC (OJ L 290 23.10.97, p 18)

Council Directive 87/357/EEC (products which, appearing to be other than they are, endanger the health or safety of consumers) (OJ L 192 11.7.87, p 49)

Council Directive 92/59/EEC (general product safety) (OJ L 228 11.8.92, p 24)

Council Directive 93/13/EEC (unfair terms in consumer contracts) (OJ L 95 21.4.93, p 29)

European Parliament and Council Directive 98/27/EC (injunctions for the protection of consumers' interests) (OJ L 166 11.6.98, p 51).

European Community committees concerning food

Council Decision 69/414/EEC (Standing Committee for Foodstuffs) (OJ (SE) 1969 (II) p 500)

Commission Decision 97/579/EC (scientific committees in the field of consumer health and food safety) (OJ L 237 28.8.97, p 18).

Food additives, contaminants, residues and other substances

Food additives

Additives framework Directive
Council Directive 89/107/EEC (OJ L 40 11.2.89, p 27) as amended by Directive 94/34 (OJ L 237 10.9.94, p 1)

Decision of the European Parliament and Council 292/97/EC (maintenance of national laws prohibiting the use of certain additives in the production of certain specific foodstuffs) (OJ L 48 19.2.97, p 13) as amended by Directives 98/72 (OJ L 295 4.11.98, p 18) and 96/85 (OJ L 86 28.3.96, p 4).

Additives other than colours and sweeteners
European Parliament and Council Directive 95/2/EEC (food additives other than colours and sweeteners) (OJ L 61 18.3.95, p 1)

Commission Directive 96/77/EC (specific criteria of purity concerning sweeteners for use in food stuffs) (OJ L 339 30.12.96, p 1) as amended by Directive 98/86 (OJ L 334 9.12.98, p 1).

Colours
European Parliament and Council Directive 94/36/EC (colours for use in foodstuffs) (OJ L 237 19.9.94, p 13)

Commission Directive 95/45/EC (specific criteria of purity concerning sweeteners for use in food stuffs) (OJ L 226 22.9.95, p 1) as amended by Directive 1999/75/EC (OJ L 205 5.8.1999, p 19).

Sweeteners
European Parliament and Council Directive 94/35/EC (sweeteners for use in foodstuffs) (OJ L 237 19.9.94, p 3)) as amended by Directive 96/83 (OJ L 48 19.2.97, p 16)

Commission Directive 95/31/EC (specific criteria of purity concerning sweeteners for use in food stuffs) (OJ L 178 28.7.95, p 1) as amended by Directive 98/66 (OJ L 257 19.9.98, p 35).

Restrictions on additives in traditional foodstuffs
Decision of the European Parliament and the Council 292/97/EC (maintenance of national laws prohibiting the use of certain additives in the production of certain specified foodstuffs) (OJ L 48 19.2.97, p 13).

Food contaminants

Council Regulation 315/93/EEC (Community procedures for contaminants in food) (OJ L 37 13.2.93, p 1)

Commission Regulation 194/97/EC (maximum levels for certain contaminants in foodstuffs) (OJ L 31 1.2.97, p 48) as amended by Regulations 1525/98 (OJ L 201 17.7.98, p 43), 864/1999 (OJ L 108 27.4.99, p 16), 1566/1999 (OJ L 184 17.7.99, p 17)

Commission Directive 98/53/EC (sampling and analysis methods for certain aflatoxins) (OJ L 201 17.7.98, p 93).

Food flavourings

Council Directive 88/388/EEC (flavourings for use in foodstuffs and source materials for their production) (OJ L 184 15.7.88, p 61) as amended by Directive 91/71/EEC (OJ L 42 15.2.91, p 25)

Council Decision 88/389/EEC (establishment of an inventory of the source materials and substances used in the preparation of flavourings) (OJ L 184 15.7.88, p 67)

Council Regulation 2232/96/EC (laying down a Community procedure for flavouring substances used or intended for use in or on foodstuffs) (OJ L 299 23.11.96, p 1)

Commission Decision 1999/217/EC (adopting a register of flavouring substances used in or on foodstuffs drawn up in application of Regulation 2232/96) (OJ L 84 27.3.99, p 1).

Materials and articles in contact with food

General material and articles
Council Directive 89/109/EEC (OJ L 40 11.2.89, p 38)

Commission Directive 80/590/EEC (symbol that may accompany materials and articles) (OJ L 151 19.6.80, p 21).

Vinyl chloride
Council Directive 78/142/EEC (materials and articles which contain vinyl chloride monomer and are intended to come into contact with foodstuffs) (OJ L 44 15.2.78, p 15)

Commission Directive 80/766/EEC (Community method of analysis for the official control of the vinyl chloride monomer in materials and articles) (OJ L 213 16.8.80, p 42)

Commission Directive 81/432/EEC (Community method of analysis for the official control of vinyl chloride released by materials and articles) (OJ L 167 24.6.81, p 6).

Ceramic articles
Council Directive 84/500/EEC (ceramic articles intended to come into contact with foodstuffs) (OJ L 277 20.10.84, p 12).

Regenerated cellulose film
Commission Directive 93/10/EEC (materials and articles made of regenerated cellulose film intended to come into contact with foodstuffs) (OJ L 93 17.4.93, p 27)) as amended by Directive 93/111 (OJ L 310 14.12.93, p 41).

Elastomer or rubber teats and soothers
Commission Directive 93/11/EEC (concerning the release of the N-Nitrosamines and N-Nitrosatable substances from elastomer or rubber teats and soothers) (OJ L 93 17.4.93, p 37).

Plastics materials and articles
Commission Directive 90/128/EEC (plastics materials and articles intended to come into contact with foodstuffs) (OJ L 349 13.12.90, p 26) as amended by Directives 92/39 (OJ L 168 23.6.92, p 21), 93/09 (OJ L 90 14.4.93, p 26), 95/03 (OJ L 41 23.2.95, p 44), 96/11 (OJ L 61 12.3.96, p 26) and 1999/91 (OJ L 310 4.12.99, p 41)

Council Directive 82/711EEC (basic rules necessary for testing migration of the constituents of plastics materials and articles) (OJ L 297 23.10.82, p 26) as amended by Directives 93/8 (OJ L 7 13.1.93, p 11), 97/48 (OJ L 222 12.8.97, p 10)

Council Directive 85/572/EEC (list of simulants to be used for testing migration of the constituents of plastics materials and articles) (OJ L 372 31.12.85, p 14).

Other substances added to food

Erucic acid
Council Directive 76/621/EEC (OJ L 202 28.7.76, p 35) as amended

Commission Directive 80/891/EEC (Community method of analysis for determining the erucic acid content of oils and fats intended to be used as such for human consumption and foodstuffs containing added oils and fats) (OJ L 254 27.9.80, p 35).

Extraction solvents
Council Directive 88/344/EEC (on extraction solvents used in the production of foodstuffs and food ingredients) (OJ L 157 24.6.88, p 28) as amended by Directives 92/115 (OJ L 409 31.12.99, p 31), 94/52 (OJ L 331 21.12.94, p 10), 97/60 (OJ L 331 3.12.97, p 7).

Pesticide residues

Cereals
Council Directive 86/362/EEC (maximum levels for pesticide residues in and on cereals) (OJ L 221 7.8.86, p 37) as amended by Directives 88/298 (OJ L 126 20.5.88, p 53), 93/57 (OJ L 211 23.8.93, p 1), 94/29 (OJ L 189 23.7.94, p 67), 95/39 (OJ L 197 22.8.95, p 29), 96/33 (OJ L 144 18.6.96, p 35), 97/41 (OJ L 184 12.7.97, p 33), 97/71 (OJ L 18.12.97, p 42), 98/82 (OJ L 290 29.10.98, p 25), 1999/65 (OJ L 172 8.7.99, p 40), 1999/71 (OJ L 194 27.7.99, p 36).

Fruit and vegetables and other products of plant origin
Council Directive 76/895/EEC (maximum levels for pesticide residues in and on fruit and vegetables) (OJ L 340 9.12.76, p 26) as amended by Directives 80/428 (OJ L 102 19.4.80, p 26), 81/36 (OJ L 46 19.2.81, p 33), 82/528 (OJ L 234 9.8.82, p 1), 85/3768 (OJ L 362 31.12.85, p 8), 88/298 (OJ L 126 20.5.88, p 53), 89/106 (OJ L 66 10.3.89, p 36), 93/58 (OJ L 211 23.8.93, p 6), 96/32 (OJ L 144 18.6.96, p 12), 97/41 (OJ L 184 12.7.97, p 33).

Council Directive 90/642/EEC (maximum levels for pesticide residues in and on certain products of plant origin including fruit and vegetables) (OJ L 350 14.12.90, p 71) as amended by Directives 93/58 (OJ L 211 23.8.93, p 6), 94/30 (OJ L 189 23.7.94, p 70), 95/38 (OJ L 197 22.8.95, p 14), 95/61 (OJ L 292 7.12.95, p 27), 96/32 (OJ L 144 18.6.96, p 12), 97/41 (OJ L 184 12.7.97, p 33), 97/71 (OJ L 347 18.12.97, p 42), 98/82 (OJ L 290 29.10.98, p 25), 99/65 (OJ L 172 8.7.99, p 40), 1999/71 (OJ L 194 27.7.99, p 36)

Commission Directive 79/700/EEC (Community methods of sampling for the official control of pesticide residues in and on fruit and vegetables) (OJ L 207 15.8.79, p 26).

Foodstuffs of animal origin
Council Directive 86/363/EEC (maximum levels for pesticide residues in and on foodstuffs of animal origin) (OJ L 221 7.8.86, p 43) as amended by Directives 93/57 (OJ L 211 23.8.93, p 1), 94/29 (OJ L 189 23.7.94, p 67), 95/39 (OJ L 197 22.8.95, p 67), 96/33 (OJ L 144 18.6.96, p 35), 97/41 (OJ L 184 12.7.97, p 33), 97/71 (OJ L 347 18.12.97, p 42), 98/82 (OJ L 290 29.10.98, p 25), 1999/71 (OJ L 194 27.7.99, p 36).

Veterinary residues

Council Regulation 2377/90/EEC (maximum residue limits of veterinary medicinal products in foodstuffs of animal origin) (OJ L 224 18.8.90, p 1) as amended by Regulations 92/762 (OJ L 83 28.3.92, p 14), 94/2701 (OJ L 287 8.11.94, p 7), 94/2703 (OJ L 287 8.11.94, p 19), 94/3059 (OJ L 323 16.12.94, p 15), 95/1102 (OJ L 110 17.5.95, p 9), 95/1441 (OJ L 143 27.6.95, p 22), 95/1442 (OJ L 143 27.6.95, p 26), 95/1798 (OJ L 174 26.7.95, p 20), 95/2796 (OJ L 290 5.12.95, p 1), 95/2804 (OJ L 291 6.12.95, p 8), 96/281 (OJ L 37 15.2.96, p 9), 96/282 (OJ L 37 15.2.96, p 12), 96/1140 (OJ L 151 26.6.96, p 6), 96/1147 (OJ L 151 26.6.96, p 26), 96/1311 (OJ L 170 9.7.96, p 4), 96/1312 (OJ L 170 9.7.96, p 8), 96/143 (OJ L 184 24.7.96, p 21), 96/1742 (OJ L 226 7.9.96, p 5), 96/1798 (OJ L 236 18.9.96, p 23), 96/2010 (OJ L 269 22.10.96, p 5), 96/2017 (OJ L 270 23.10.96, p 2), 96/2034 (OJ L 272 25.10.96, p 2), 97/17 (OJ L 5 9.1.97, p 12), 97/211 (OJ L 35 5.2.97, p 1), 97/270 (OJ L 45 15.2.97, p 8), 97/434 (OJ L 67 7.3.97, p 1), 97/716 (OJ L 106 24.4.97, p 10), 97/748 (OJ L 110 26.4.97, p 21), 97/749 (OJ L 110 26.4.97, p 24), 97/1836 (OJ L 263 25.9.97, p 6), 97/1837 (OJ L 263 25.9.97, p 9), 97/1838 (OJ L 263 25.9.97, p 14), 97/1850 (OJ L 264 26.9.97, p 12), 98/121 (OJ L 11 17.1.98, p 11), 98/426 (OJ L 53 24.2.98, p 3), 98/613 (OJ L 82 19.3.98, p 14), 98/1000 (OJ L 142 14.5.98, p 18), 98/1076 (OJ L 154 28.5.98, p 14), 98/1191 (OJ L 165 10.6.98, p 6), 98/1568 (OJ L 205 22.7.98, p 1), 98/1569 (OJ L 205 22.7.98, p 7), 98/1570 (OJ L 205 22.7.98, p 10), 98/1916 (OJ L 250 10.9.98, p 8), (8/1917 (OJ L 250 10.9.98, p 13), 98/1958 (OJ L 254 16.9.98, p 7), 98/2560 (OJ L 320 28.11.98, p 28), 98/2686 (OJ L 337 12.12.98, p 20), 98/2692 (OJ L 338 15.12.98, p 5), 98/2728 (OJ

L 343 18.12.98, p 8), 1999/508 (OJ L 60 9.3.99, p 16), 1999/804 (OJ L 102 17.4.99, p 58), 1999/953 (OJ L 118 6.5.99, p 23), 1999/954 (OJ L 118 6.5.99, p 28), 99/997 (OJ L 122 12.5.99, p 24), 99/998 (OJ L 122 12.5.99, p 30), 1999/1308 (OJ L 156 23.6.99, p 1), 1999/1931 (OJ L 240 10.9.99, p 3), 1999/1942 (OJ L 241 11.9.99, p 4), 1999/1943 9OJ L 214 11.9.99, p 9), 1999/2385 (OJ L 288 11.11.99, p 14), 1999/2393 (OJ L 290 12.11.99, p 5), 1999/2593 (OJ L 315 9.112.99, p 26), 1999/2728 (OJ L 328 22.12.99, p 23), 1999/2757 (OJ L 331 23.12.99, p 45), 1999/2758 (OJ L 331 23.12.99, p 49)

Council Directive 96/22/EC (prohibition on the use in stockfarming of certain substances having a hormonal or thyrostatic action and of beta-agonistes) (OJ L 125 23.5.96, p 3)

Council Directive 96/23/EC (on measures to monitor certain substances and residues thereof in live animals and animal products) (OJ L 125 23.5.96, p 10).

Food hygiene and treatment

Bovine spongiform encephalopathy etc

General

Commission Decision 94/381/EC (protection measures with regard to bovine spongiform encephalopathy and the feeding of mammalian derived protein) (OJ L 172 7.7.94, p 23) as amended by Decisions 95/60 (OJ L 55 11.3.95, p 43), 1999/129 (OJ L 41 16.2.99, p 14)

Commission Decision 94/474/EC (protection measures relating to bovine spongiform encephalopathy) (OJ L 194 29.7.94, p 96) as amended by Decisions 95/287, (OJ L 181 1.8.95, p 40), 98/256 (OJ L 113 15.4.98, p 32), 98/272 (OJ L 122 24.4.98, p 59)

Commission Decision 96/385/EC (approving the plan for the control and eradication of bovine spongiform encephalopathy in the United Kingdom) (OJ L 151 26.6.96, p 39) as amended by Decision 97/870 (OJ L 353 24.12.97, p 45)

Commission Decision 97/534/EC (prohibition of use of material presenting risks as regards transmissible spongiform encephalopathies) (OJ L 216 8.8.97, p 95) as amended by Decision 1999/881 (OJ L 331 23.12.99, p 78)

Commission Decision 98/256/EC (emergency measures to protect against bovine spongiform encephalopathy) (OJ L 113 15.4.98, p 32) as amended by Decisions 98/564/EC (OJ L 273 9.10.98, p 37), 98/692/EC (OJ L 328 4.12.98, p 28)

Commission Decision 98/272/EC (epidemio-surveillance for transmissible spongiform encephalopathies) (OJ L 122 24.4.98, p 59)

Commission Decision 98/351/EC (setting the date on which dispatch from Northern Ireland of bovine products under the Export Certified Herds scheme may commence under Decision 98/256) (OJ L 157 3.5.98, p 110)

Commission Decision 1999/514/EC (setting the date on which dispatch from the United Kingdom of bovine products under the date-based scheme may commence under Decision 98/256) (OJ L 195 28.7.1999, p 42).

Labelling of beef and beef products

Council Regulation 820/97/EC (identification of bovine animals and labelling of beef and beef products) (OJ L 117 7.5.97, p 9)

Commission Regulation 1141/97/EC (detailed rules as regards the labelling of beef and beef products) (OJ L 165 24.6.97, p 7) as amended by Regulations 2406/97 (OJ L 332 4.12.97, p 36), 824/98 (OJ L 117 21.4.98, p 4)

Commission Regulation 2628/97/EC (detailed rules as regards transitional provisions for the start-up period of the system for the identification and registration of bovine animals) (OJ L 354 30.12.97, p 17) as amended by Regulations 2105/98 (OJ L 267 2.10.98, p 4), 2729/98 (OJ L 343 18.12.98, p 12)

Commission Regulation 2629/97/EC (detailed rules as regards ear tags, holding registers and passports) (OJ L 354 30.12.97, p 19) as amended by Regulations 1177/98 (OJ L 163 6.6.98, p 19), 2194/98 (OJ L 276 13.10.98, p 4) , 331/1999 (OJ L 40 13.2.99, p 27), 1663/1999 (OJ L 197 29.7.99, p 27)

Commission Regulation 2630/97/EC (minimum level of controls to be carried out) (OJ L 354 30.12.97, p 23) as amended by Regulation 132/1999 (OJ L 17 22.1.99, p 20)

Commission Regulation 494/98/EC (application of administrative sanctions) (OJ L 60 28.2.98, p 78).

Food irradiation

Directive 1999/2/EC of the European Parliament and of the Council (foods and food ingredients treated with ionising radiation) (OJ L 66 13.3.1999, p 16)

Directive 1999/3/EC of the European Parliament and of the Council (establishment of a Community list of foods and food ingredients treated with ionising radiation) (OJ L 66 13.3.1999, p 24).

General food hygiene

Council Directive 93/43/EEC (OJ L 175 19.7.93, p 1)

Commission Directive 96/3/EC (derogation for transport by sea of bulk liquid oils and fats) (OJ L 21 27.1.96, p 42)

Commission Directive 98/28/EC (derogation for transport by sea of bulk raw sugar) (OJ L 140 12.5.98, p 10).

Hygiene of specific products of animal origin

Eggs and Egg products

Council Directive 92/118/EEC Annex II, Chapter 2 (OJ L 62 15.3.93, p 49) as amended

Council Directive 89/437/EEC (hygiene and health in relation to egg products) (OJ L 212 22.7.89, p 87) as amended by Directives 89/662 (OJ L 395 30.12.89, p 13), 91/684 (OJ L 376 31.12.91, p 38)

Commission Decision 97/38/EC (public health requirements for imports of egg products) (OJ L 14 17.1.97, p 61).

Decision 94/371/EC (laying down specific public health conditions for the putting on the market of certain types of eggs) (OJ L 168 2.7.94, p 34).

Fishery products and live bivalve molluscs
Council Directive 91/492/EEC (production and placing on the market of live bivalve molluscs) (OJ L 268 24.9.91, p 1) as amended by Directives 97/61 (OJ L 295 29.10.97, p 10), 97/79 (OJ L 24 30.1.98, p 31)

Council Directive 91/493/EEC (production and placing on the market of fishery products) (OJ L 268 24.9.91, p 15) as amended by Directives 95/71 (OJ L 332 30.12.95, p 40), 97/79 (OJ L 24 30.1.98, p 31).

Fresh meat
Council Directive 64/433/EEC (production and marketing of fresh meat) (OJ L 121 28.7.64, p 2012) as amended by Directives 66/601 (OJ L 192 27.10.66, p 3302), 75/379 (OJ L 172 3.07.75, p 17), 83/90 (OJ L 059 05.03.83, p 10), 85/586 (OJ L 372 31.12.85, p 44), 768/85 (OJ L 362 31.12.85, p 8), 3805/85 (OJ L 357 19.12.87, p 1), 89/662 (OJ L 395 30.12.89, p 13), 91/497 (OJ L 268 24.09.91, p 69), 92/5 (OJ L 057 02.03.92, p 1), 95/23 (OJ L 243 11.10.95, p 7)

Directive 72/461/EEC (health problems affecting intra-Community trade fresh meat) (OJ (SE) 31 December 1972, p 24) as amended by Directives 73/358 (OJ L 326 27.11.73, p 17), 75/379 (OJ L 1722 3.7.75, p 17), 77/98 (OJ L 26 31.1.77, p 81), 80/1099 (OJ L 47 21.2..80, p 1), 82/893 (OJ L 378 31.12.82, p 57), 84/336 (OJ L 177 4.7.84, p 22), 84/643 (OJ L 339 27.12.84, p 27), 85/322 (OJ L 168 28.6.85, p 41), 3768/85 (OJ L 362 31.12.85, p 8), 87/231 (OJ L 99 11.4.87, p 18), 87/489 (OJ L 280 3.10.87, p 28), 89/662 (OJ L 395 30.12.89, p 13), 91/266 (OJ L 134 29.5.91, p 45), 91/687 (OJ L 377 31.12.91, p 16), 92/118 (OJ L 62 15.3.93, p 49)

Directive 72/462/EEC (health and veterinary inspection problems upon importation of bovine, ovine and caprine animals and swine and fresh meat or meat products from third countries) (OJ (SE) 31 December 1972, p 28) as amended by Directives 73/358 (OJ L 326 27.11.73, p 17), 75/379 (OJ L 172 3.7.75, p 17), 77/98 (OJ L 26 31.1.7, p 81), 83/91 (OJ L 59 5.3.83, p 34), 3768/85 (OJ L 362 31.12.85, p 8), 88/289 (OJ L 124 18.5.88, p 31), 89/227 (OJ L 93 6.4.89, p 25), 89/662 (OJ L 395 30.12.89, p 13), 90/423 (OJ L 224 18.8.90, p 13), 90/425 (OJ L 224 18.8.90, p 29), 91/69 (OJ L 46 19.2.91, p 37), 91/266 (OJ L 134 29.5.91, p 45), 91/496 (OJ L 268 24.9.91, p 56), 91/497 (OJ L 268 24.9.91, p 69), 91/688 (OJ L 377 31.12.91, p 18), 3763/91 (OJ L 356 24.12.91, p 1), 1601/92 (OJ L 173 27.6.92, p 13), 96/91 (OJ L 13 16.1.97, p 26), 97/76 (OJ L 10 16.1.98, p 25), 97/79 (OJ L 24 30.1.98, p 31).

Fresh poultrymeat
Council Directive 71/118/EEC (trade in fresh poultry meat) (OJ L 55 8.3.71, p 23), as amended and re-issued by Directive 92/116 (OJ L 62 15.3.92, p 1)

Council Directive 91/494/EEC (conditions governing intra-Community trade in and imports from third countries of fresh poultry meat) (OJ L 268 24.9.91, p 35) as amended by Directives 92/116 (OJ L 62 15.3.92, p 1), 93/121 (OJ L 340 31.12.93, p 39), 1999/89 (OJ L 300 23.11.99, p 17).

Meat products
Council Directive 77/99/EEC (Community trade in meat products) (OJ L 26 31.1.77, p 85) as amended by Directives 81/476 (OJ L 186 8.7.81, p 20), 85/327 (OJ L 168 28.6.85, p 49), 3768/85 (OJ L 362 31.112.85, p 8), 88/658 (OJ L 382 31.12.88, p 15), 89/227 (OJ L 93 6.4.89, p 25), 89/662 (OJ L 395 30.12.89, p 13), 92/5 (OJ L 57 2.3.92, p 1),

92/116 (OJ L 62 15.3.93, p 1), 92/118 (OJ L 62 15.3.93, p 49), 95/68 (OJ 332 30.12.95, p 10), 97/76 (OJ L 10 16.1.98, p 25)

Council Directive 80/215/EEC (intra-Community trade in meat products) (OJ L 47 21.2.80, p 4 as amended by Directives 80/1100 (OJ L 325 1.12.80, p 16), 81/476 (OJ L 186 8.7.81, p 20), 85/321 (OJ L 168 28.6.85, p 39), 3768/85 (OJ L 362 31.12.85, p 8), 87/491 (OJ L 279 2.10.87, p 27), 88/660 (OJ L 382 31.12.88, p 35), 89/662 (OJ L 395 30.12.89, p 13), 91/687 (OJ L 377 31.12.91, p 16)

Commission Decision 97/221/EC (conditions and model veterinary certificates in respect of imports of meat of meat products from third countries) (OJ L 89 4.4.97, p 32)

Council Directive 92/118/EEC (animal health and public health requirements governing trade in and imports into the Community) (OJ L 62 15.3.93, p 49) as amended by Decisions 94/466 (OJ L 190 26.7.94, p 26), 94/723 (OJ L 288 9.11.94, p 48), 95/338 (OJ L 200 24.8.95, p 35), 95/339 (OJ L 200 24.8.95, p 36), 96/90 (OJ L 13 16.1.97, p 24), 96/103 (OJ L 24 31.1.96, p 28), 96/340 (OJ L 129 30.5.96, p 35), 96/405 (OJ L 165 4.7.96, p 40), 97/79 (OJ L 24 30.1.98, p 31), 1999/72 (OJ L 290 12.11.99, p 32)

Commission Decision 97/41/EC (health conditions and a public health certificate for the importation from third countries of meat products from poultrymeat, farmed game meat, wild game meat and rabbit meat) (OJ L 17 21.1.97, p 34).

Milk and milk-based products

Council Directive 92/46/EEC (production and placing on the market of raw milk, heat treated milk and milk-based products) (OJ L 268 14.9.92, p 1) as amended by Directives 92/118 (OJ L 62 15.3.93, p 49), 94/71 (OJ L 368 31.12.94, p 33)

Commission Directive 89/362/EEC (hygiene in milk production holdings) (OJ L 156 8.6.89, p 30)

Commission Decision 95/165/EEC (uniform criteria for the grant of derogations to certain establishments manufacturing milk-based products) (OJ L 108 13.5.95, p 84)

Commission Decision 95/340/EC (provisional list of third countries from which Member States authorise imports of milk and milk based products) (OJ L 200 24.8.95, p 38) as amended by 96/106 (OJ L 24 31.1.96, p 3), 96/325 (OJ L 123 23.5.96, p 24), 96/571 (OJ L 250 2.10.96, p 19), 96/584 (OJ L 255 9.10.96, p 20)

Commission Decision 95/342/EC (treatment where there is a risk of foot-and-mouth disease) (OJ L 200 24.8.95, p 50)

Commission Decision 95/343/EC (health certificate specimens for importation from third countries of heat-treated milk, milk-based products and raw milk intended to be accepted at a collection centre, standardisation centre, treatment establishment or processing establishment) (OJ L 200 24.8.95, p 52) as amended by Directives 96/106 (OJ L 24 31.1.96, p 3), 97/115 (OJ L 42 13.2.97, p 16).

Minced meat and meat preparations

Council Directive 94/65/EC (production and placing on the market of minced meat and meat preparations) (OJ L 368 31.12.94, p 10)

Commission Decision 97/29/EC (health conditions and public health certification for the importation of minced meat and meat preparations from third countries) (OJ L 12 15.1.97, p 33).

Miscellaneous products of animal origin
Council Directive 92/118 (animal health and public health requirements governing trade in and imports into the Community) (OJ L 62 15.3.93, p 49) as amended by Decisions 94/466 (OJ L 190 26.7.94, p 26), 94/723 (OJ L 288 9.11.94, p 48), 95/338 (OJ L 200 24.8.95, p 35), 95/339 (OJ L 200 24.8.95, p 36), 96/90 (OJ L 13 16.1.97, p 24), 96/103 (OJ L 24 31.1.96, p 28), 96/340 (OJ L 129 30.5.96, p 35), 96/405 (OJ L 165 4.7.96, p 40), 97/79 (OJ L 24 30.1.98, p 31), 1999/72 (OJ L 290 12.11.99, p 32).

Rabbit meat and farmed game meat
Council Directive 91/495/EEC (production and placing on the market of rabbit meat and farmed game meat) (OJ L 268 24.9.91, p 35) as amended by Directive 92/116 (OJ L 62 15.3.92, p 1).

Council Directive 92/118 (animal health and public health requirements governing trade in and imports into the Community) (OJ L 62 15.3.93, p 49) as amended by Decisions 94/466 (OJ L 190 26.7.94, p 26), 94/723 (OJ L 288 9.11.94, p 48), 95/338 (OJ L 200 24.8.95, p 35), 95/339 (OJ L 200 24.8.95, p 36), 96/90 (OJ L 13 16.1.97, p 24), 96/103 (OJ L 24 31.1.96, p 28), 96/340 (OJ L 129 30.5.96, p 35), 96/405 (OJ L 165 4.7.96, p 40), 97/79 (OJ L 24 30.1.98, p 31), 1999/72 (OJ L 290 12.11.99, p 32)

Commission Decision 97/219/EC (animal and public health conditions and veterinary certification for imports of farmed game meat and rabbit meat from third countries) (OJ L 88 3.4.97, p 45) as amended by Decision 2000/160 (OJ L 51 24.2.200, p 37).

Wild game meat
Council Directive 92/45/EEC (killing of wild game and placing on the market of wild game meat) (OJ L 268 14.9.92, p 35) as amended by the Fourth Act of Accession

Commission Decision 97/218/EC (animal and public health conditions and veterinary certification for imports of wild game meat, excluding meat of wild swine, from third countries) (OJ L 88 3.4.97, p 25)

Commission Decision 97/220/EC (animal and public health conditions and veterinary certification for imports of meat of wild swine from third countries) (OJ L 88 3.4.97, p 70).

Trade in products of animal origin: general

Council Directive 89/662/EEC (veterinary checks in intra-Community trade) (OJ L 395 30.12.89, p 13) as amended by Directives 91/496 (OJ L 268 24.9.91, p 56), 92/67 (OJ L 268 14.9.92, p 73), 92/118 (OJ L 62 15.3.93, p 49)

Council Directive 97/78/EC (principles governing the organisation of veterinary checks on products entering the Community from third countries) (OJ L 24 3.1.98, p 9).

Food labelling

Alcoholic beverages

Commission Directive 87/250/EEC (indication of alcoholic strength by volume in the labelling of alcoholic beverages for sale to the ultimate consumer) (OJ L 113 30.4.87, p 57).

Foodstuffs produced from genetically modified organisms

Council Regulation 1139/98/EC (compulsory indication on the labelling of certain foodstuffs produced from genetically modified organisms) (OJ L 159 3.6.98, p 4) [Corrigenda, see OJ L 190 4.7.98, p 86; OJ L 94 9.4.99, p 27] as amended by Regulation 49/2000/EC (OJ L 6 11.1.2000, p 17)

Commission Regulation 50/2000/EC (labelling of foodstuffs and food ingredients containing additives and flavourings that have been genetically modified or have been produced from genetically modified organisms) (OJ L 6 11.1.2000, p 15).

General labelling

Council Directive 79/112/EEC (labelling, presentation and advertising of food) (OJ L 33 8.2.79 p 1) as amended by Directives 86/197 (OJ L 144 29.5.86, p 38), 89/395 (OJ L 186 30.6.89, p 17), 91/72 (OJ L 42 15.2.91, p 27), 93/102 (OJ L 291 25.11.93, p 14), 97/4 (OJ L 4 14.2.97, p 21)

Commission Directive 1999/10/EC (derogations from Article 7 of Directive 79/112/EEC) (OJ L 69 16.3.1999, p 22).

Lot marking

Council Directive 89/396/EEC (OJ L 186 30.6.89, p 21) as amended by Directives 91/238 (OJ L 107 27.4.91, p 50), 92/11 (OJ L 65 11.3.92, p 32).

Nutrition labelling

Council Directive 90/496/EEC (nutrition labelling for foodstuffs) (OJ L 276 6.10.90, p 40).

Protective gases

Commission Directive 94/54/EC (compulsory indication of the labelling of certain foodstuffs) (OJ L 300 23.11.94, p 14) as amended by Directive 96/21 (OJ L 88 5.4.96, p 5).

Food standards

Common agricultural policy marketing standards

Bananas
Council Regulation 404/93/EEC (common organisation of the market in bananas) (OJ L 47 25.2.93, p 1) as amended by Regulations 3518/93 (OJ L 320 22.12.93, p 15), 3290/94 (OJ L 349 31.112.94, p 105), 1637/98 (OJ L 210 28.7.98, p 28), 1257/1999 (OJ L 160 26.6.99, p 8)

Commission Regulation 2257/94/EEC (quality standards for bananas) (OJ L 245 20.9.94, p 6).

Drinking Milk
Council Regulation 2597/97/EC (OJ L 351 23.12.97, p 13) amended by Regulation 1602/1999 (OJ L 189 22.7.99, p 43).

Eggs
Council Regulation 1907/90/EEC (marketing standards for eggs) (OJ L 173 06.07.90, p 5) as amended by Regulations 2617/93 (OJ L 240 25.9.93, p 1), 31174/94 (OJ L 330 21.112.94, p 4), 818/96 (OJ L 111 4.5.96, p 1)

Commission Regulation 1274/91/EEC (detailed rules for implementing the above Regulation) (OJ L 121 16.05.91, p11) as amended by Regulations 3540/91 (OJ L 335 6.12.91, p 12), 2221/92 (OJ L 218 1.8.92, p 81), 3300/93 (OJ L 296 1.12.93, p 52), 1259/94 (OJ NO L 137 1.6.94, p 52), 3239/94 (OJ L 338 28.12.94, p 48), 786/95 (OJ L 79 7.4.95, p 12), 2401/95 (OJ L 246 13.10.95, p 3), 505/98 (OJ L 63 4.3.98, p 16).

Fishery and aquaculture products
Council Regulation 3759/92/EEC (common organisation of the market in fishery and aquaculture products) (OJ L 388 31.12.92, p 1) as amended. As from 1 January 2001, Regulation 3759/92 is replaced by Council Regulation 104/2000/EC (common organisation of the market in fishery and aquaculture products) (OJ L 17 21.1.2000, p 22)

Council Regulation 2406/96/EC (common marketing standards for certain fishery products) (OJ L 334 23.12.96, p 1) as amended by Regulation 323/97 (OJ L 52 22.2.97, p 8)

Commission Regulation 3703/85/EEC (detailed rules for applying common marketing standards for certain fish or chilled fish) (OJ L 351 28.12.85, p 63) as amended by Regulation 3506/89 (OJ L 342 24.11.89, p 11)

Commission Regulation 3863/91/EEC (determining a minimum marketing size for crabs applicable to certain coastal areas of the United Kingdom) (OJ L 363 31.12.91, p 1)

Council Regulation 2136/89/EEC (marketing standards for preserved sardines) (OJ L 212 22.07.89, p 79)

Council Regulation 1536/92/EEC (marketing standards for preserved tuna and bonito) (OJ L 163 17.6.92, p 1).

Fruit and vegetables
Council Regulation 2200/96/EC (common organisation of the market in fruit and vegetables) (OJ L 297 21.11.96, p 1) as amended by Regulations 2520/96 (OJ L 346 17.12.97, p 41), 857/1999 (OJ L 108 27.4.99, p 7), 1257/1999 (OJ L 160 26.6.99, p 8)

Note: Under Article 2 of this Regulation marketing standards have been laid down for dessert apples and pears, apricots, artichokes, asparagus, aubergines, avocados, beans, Brussels sprouts, cabbages, carrots, cauliflowers, ribbed celery, cherries, citrus fruit, courgettes, cucumbers, garlic, kiwifruit, leeks, lettuces, curled-leaved endives and broad-leaved (Batavian) endives, melons, onions, peaches and nectarines, peas for shelling, plums, spinach, strawberries, sweet peppers, table grapes, tomatoes, water melons and witloof chicory

Commission Regulation 2251/92/EEC (quality inspection of fresh fruit and vegetables) (OJ L 219 4.8.92, p 9) as amended by Regulations 3720/92 (OJ L 378 23.12.92, p 32), 785/93 (OJ L 79 1.4.93, p 55), 3148/94 (OJ L 332 22.12.94, p 28), 766/97 (OJ L 112 29.4.97, p 10).

Milk and milk product designations
Council Regulation 1898/87/EC (protection of designations used in the marketing of milk and milk products) (OJ L 182 3.7.87, p36) as amended by Regulation 222/88 (OJ L 28 1.2.88, p 1)

Commission Regulation 577/97/EC (detailed rules) (OJ L 87 2.4.97, p 3) as amended by Regulations 1278/97 (OJ L 175 3.7.97, p 6), 2181/97 (OJ L 299 4.11.97, p 1), 623/98 (OJ L 85 20.3.98, p 3), 2521/98 (OJ L 315 25.11.98, p 12), 1298/98 (OJ L 180 24.6.98, p 5), 568/1999 (OJ L 70 17.3.99, p 11).

Olive oil
Council Regulation 136/66/EEC (common organisation of the market in oils and fats) (OJ L 172 1.1.66 p 3025) as amended by Regulations 2146/68 (OJ NO L 314 31.12.68, p 1), 1253/70 (OJ L 143 1.7.70, p 1), 1547/72 (OJ L 165 21.7.72, p 1), 73/101 (OJ L 2 1.1.73, p 1), 73/1707 (OJ L 175 29.6.73, p 5), 2560/77 (OOJ L 303 28.11.77, p 1), 1562/78 (OJ L 185 7.7.78, p 1), 1585/80 (OJ L 160 26.6.80, p 2), 3454/80 (OJ L 360 31.12.80, p 16), 1413/82 (OJ L 162 12.6.82, p 6), 2260/84 (OJ L 208 3.8.84, p 1), 231/85 OJ L 26 31.1.85, p 12), 3768/85 (OJ L 362 31.12.85, p 8), 1454/86 (OJ L 133 21.5.86, p 8), 1915/87 (OJ L 183 3.7.87, p 7), 3994/87 (OJ L 377 31.12.87, p 31), 1098/88 (OJ L 110 29.4.88, p 10), 2210/88 (OJ L 197 26.7.88, p 1), 1225/89 (OJ L 197 26.7.88, p 1), 1225/89 (OJ L 128 11.5.89, p 15), 3499/90 (OJ L 338 5.12.90, p 1), 3577/90 (OJ L 353 17.12.90, p 23), 1720/91 (OJ L 162 26.6.91, p 27), 356/92 (OJ L 15.2.92, p 1), 2046/92 (OJ L 215 30.7.92, p 1), 3179/93 (OJ L 285 20.11.93, p 9), 32390/94 (OJ L 349 31.12.94, p 105), 1581/96 (OJ L 206 16.8.96, p 11), 1638/98 (OJ L 210 28.7.98, p 32), 2702 /1999 (OJ L 327 14.12.99, p 7)

Commission Regulation 2568/91/EEC (characteristics of olive oil and olive-residue oil and relevant methods of analysis) (OJ L248 5.9.91, p 1) as amended by Regulations 3682/91 (OJ L 349 18.12.91, p 36), 1429/92 (OJ L 150 2.6.92, p 17), 1683/92 (OJ L 176 30.6.92, p 27), 3288/92 (OJ L 327 13.11.92, p, 28), 183/92 (OJ L 22 30.1.93, p 58), 177/94 (OJ L 69 29.3.95, p 1), 2527/95 (OJ L 258 28.10.95, p 49), 2472/97 (OJ L 341 12.12.97, p 25), 282/98 (OJ L 4.2.98, p 5), 2248/98 (OJ L 282 20.10.98, p 55), 379/1999 (OJ L 46 20.2.99, p 15)

Commission Regulation 2815/98/EC (marketing standards for olive oil) (OJ L 349 24.12.98, p 56) as amended by Regulation 640/1999 (OJ L 82 26.3.1999, p 8).

Poultrymeat
Council Regulation 1906/90/EEC (marketing standards for poultry) (OJ L 173 6.7.90, p 1) as amended by Regulations 317/93 (OJ L 37 13.2.93, p 8), 3204/93 (OJ L 289 24.11.93, p 3)

Commission Regulation 1538/91/EEC (detailed rules for implementing the above Regulation) (OJ L 143 7.6.91, p 1) as amended by Regulations 2988/91 (OJ NO L 284 12.10.91, p 26), 315/92 (OJ L 34 11.2.92, p 23), 1980/92 (OJ L 198 17.7.92, p 31), 2891/93 (OJ L 263 22.10.93, p 12), 1026/94 (OJ LLL 112 3.5.94, p 32), 3239/94 (OJ L 338 28.12.94, p 48), 2390/95 (OJ L 244 12.10.95, p 60), 205/96 (OJ L 27 3.2.96, p 6), 1000/96 (OJ L 134 5.6.96, p 9).

Spirit drinks
Council Regulation 1576/89/EEC (OJ L 160 12.6.89, p 1) as amended by Regulations 3280/92 (OJ L 327 13.11.92, p 3), 3378/94 (OJ L 366 31.12.94, p 1)

Commission Regulation 1014/90/EEC (OJ L 105 25.4.90, p 9) as amended by Regulations 1180/92 (OJ L 115 8.5.91, p 5), 1781/91 (OJ L 160 25.6.91, p 5), 3458/92 (OJ NO L 350 1.12.92, p 5), 1712/95 (OJ L 163 14.7.95, p 4), 2626/95 (OJ L 269 11.11.95, p 5), 2523/97 (OJ L 346 17.12.97, p 46), 2140/98 (OJ L 270 7.10.98, p 9)

Commission Regulation 1267/94/EC (OJ L 138 2.6.94, p 7), as amended by Regulation 1434/97 (OJ L 196 24.7.97, p 56).

Spreadable fats
Council Regulation 2991/94/EC (standards for spreadable fats) (OJ L 316 19.12.94, p 2)

Commission Regulation 577/97/EC (detailed rules) (OJ L 87 2.4.97, p 3) as amended by Regulations 1278/97 (OJ L 175 3.7.97, p 6), 2181/97 (OJ L 299 4.11.97, p 1), 623/98 (OJ L 85 20.3.98, p 3), 1298/98 (OJ L 180 24.6.98, p 5), 2521/98 (OJ L 315 25.11.98, p 12), 568/1999 (OJ L 70 17.3.99, p 11).

Wine
Council Regulation 822/87/EEC (common organisation of the market in wine) (OJ L 84 27.3.87, p 1), as replaced by Regulation 1493/1999/EC (OJ L 179 14.7.99, p 1) with effect from 1 August 2000

Council Regulation 823/87/EEC (special provisions for quality wines produced in specified regions (psr)) (OJ L 84 27.3.87, p 59), as replaced by Regulation 1493/1999/EC with effect from 1 August 2000

Commission Regulation 881/98/EC (detailed rules for the protection of the additional traditional terms used to designate certain types of quality wines (psr)) (OJ L 124 25.4.98, p 22), as amended by Regulations 2215/98 (OJ L 279 16.10.98, p 4), 2253/1999 (OJ L 275 26.10.99, p 9)

Council Regulation 2392/89/EEC (general rules for the description and presentation of wines and grape musts) (OJ L 232 9.8.89, p 13) as replaced by Regulation 1493/1999/EC with effect from 1 August 2000

Council Regulation 2333/92/EEC (general rules for the description and presentation of sparkling wines and aerated sparkling wines) (OJ L 231 13.8.92, p 9) as replaced by Regulation 1493/1999/EC with effect from 1 August 2000

Commission Regulation 554/95/EEC (detailed rules) (OJ L 56 14.3.95, p 3) as amended by Regulation 1915/96 (OJ L 252 4.10.96, p 10)

Council Regulation 3895/91/EEC (rules for the description and presentation of liqueur wines, semi-sparkling wines and aerated semi-sparkling wines) (OJ L 368 31.12.91, p 1) as replaced by Regulation 1493/1999/EC with effect from 1 August 2000

Commission Regulation 3901/91/EEC (detailed rules) (OJ L 368 31.12.91, p 15)

Council Regulation 4252/88/EEC (preparation and marketing of liqueur wines) (OJ L 373 31.12.88, p 59) as replaced by Regulation 1493/1999/EC with effect from 1 August 2000

Council Regulation 1601/91/EEC (general rules on the definition, description and presentation of aromatised wines, aromatised wine-based drinks and aromatised wine product cocktails) (OJ L 149 14.6.91, p 1) as amended by Regulations 3279/92 (OJ L 327 13.11.92, p 1), 3378/94 (OJ L 366 31.12.94, p 1).

Foodstuffs intended for particular nutritional uses

Council Directive 89/398/EEC (foodstuffs intended for particular nutritional uses) (OJ L 186 30.6.98, p 27) as amended by Directives 96/84 (OJ L 48 19.2.97, p 20), 1999/41 (OJ L 172 8.7.99, p 38)

Commission Directive 91/321 (infant formulae and follow-on formulae) (OJ L 175 4.7.91, p 35) as amended by Directives 96/4 (OJ L 49 28.2.96, p 12), 99/50 (OJ L 139 2.6.99, p 29)

Commission Directive 96/5/EC (processed cereal-based foods and baby foods for infants and young children) (OJ L 49 28.2.96, p 12) as amended by Directives 98/36 (OJ L 167 12.6.98, p 23), 1999/39 (OJ L 124 18.5.99, p 8)

Commission Directive 96/8/EC (foods intended for use in energy-restricted diets for weight reduction) (OJ L 55 6.3.96, p 22)

Commission Directive 1999/21/EC (dietary foods for special medical purposes) (OJ L 91 7.4.99, p 29).

Internal market and environmental standards

Caseins and caseinates
Council Directive 83/417/EEC (OJ L 237 26.8.83, p 25).

Cocoa and chocolate products
Council Directive 73/241/EEC (OJ L 228 16.8.73, p 23) as amended by Directives 74/411 (OJ L 221 12.8.74, p 17), 74/644 (OJ L 349 28.12.74, p 63), 75/155 (OJ L 64 11.3.75, p 21), 76/628 (OJ L 223 16.8.76, p 1), 78/609 (OJ L 197 22.7.78, p 10), 78/842 (OJ L 291 17.10.78, p 15), 80/608 (OJ L 170 1.3.80, p 33), 85/7 (OJ L 2 3.1.85, p 22), 89/344 (OJ L 142 25.5.89, p 19).

Coffee and coffee extracts
Council Directive 77/436/EEC (OJ L 172 12.7.77, p 20) as amended by Directives 85/7 (OJ L 2 3.1.85, p 22), 85/573 (OJ L 372 31.12.85, p 22).

Note: European Parliament and Council Directive 1999/4/EC (OJ L 66 13.3.99, p 26) repeals and replaces Directive 77/436 as from 13 September 2000.

Dehydrated preserved milk
Council Directive 76/118/EEC (OJ L 24 30.1.76, p 49) as amended by Directives 78/630 (OJ L 206 29.7.78, p 12), 83/635 (OJ L 357 21.12.83, p 37).

Fruit juices and similar products
Council Directive 93/77/EEC (OJ L 244 30.9.93, p 23).

Honey
Council Directive 74/409/EEC (OJ L 221 12.8.74, p 10).

Jams, jellies, marmalades and chestnut puree
Council Directive 79/693/EEC (OJ L 205 13.8.79, p 5) as amended by Directive 88/593 (OJ L 318 25.11.88, p 44).

Natural mineral waters and spring water
Council Directive 80/777/EEC (OJ L 229 30.8.80, p 1) as amended by Directives 80/1276 (OJ NO L 375 31.12.80, p 72), 85/7 (OJ L 2 3.1.85, p 22), 96/70 (OJ L 299 23.11.96, p 26).

Quick frozen foodstuffs
Council Directive 89/108/EEC (quick frozen foodstuffs) (OJ L 40 11.2.89, p 34)

Commission Directive 92/1/EEC (monitoring temperatures) (OJ L 34 11.2.92, p 28)

Commission Directive 92/2/EEC (sampling and analysis) (OJ L 34 11.2.92, p 30).

Sugars
Council Directive 73/437/EEC (OJ L 356 27.12.73, p 71).

Water
Council Directive 80/778/EEC (quality of water intended for human consumption) (OJ L 229 30.8.80, p 11) as amended by Directives 81/858 (OJ L 319 7.11.81, p 19), 91/692 (OJ L 377 31.12.91, p 48)

Note: Council Directive 98/83/EC (quality of water intended for human consumption) (OJ L 330 5.12.98, p 32), which must be transposed into national law by 25 December 2000, will repeal and replace Directive 80/778 as from 25 December 2003.

Novel foods and novel food ingredients

European Parliament and Council Regulation 258/97/EC (novel foods and novel food ingredients) (OJ L 43 14.2.97, p 1)

Commission Recommendation 97/618/EC (scientific aspects and presentation of information necessary to support applications for the placing on the market of novel foods and novel food ingredients and the preparation of initial assessment reports under Regulation 258/97) (OJ L 253 16.9.97, p 1).

Organic products

Council Regulation 2092/91/EEC (organic production of agricultural products and indications referring thereto on agricultural products and foodstuffs) (OJ L 198 22.7.91, p 1) as amended by Regulations 1535/92 (OJ L 11 17.1.92, p 14), 2083/92 (OJ L 208 24.7.92, p 15), 207/93 (OJ L 25 2.2.93, p 5), 2608/93 (OJ L 239 24.9.9, p 10) 2381/94 (OJ L 255 1.10.94, p 84), 529/95 (OJ L 54 10.3.95, p 10), 1201/95 (OJ L 119 30.5.95, p 9), 1202/95 (OJ L 119 30.5.95, p 11), 1935/95 (OJ L 186 5.8.95, p 1), 1488/97 (OJ L 202 30.7.97, p 12), 1900/98 (OJ L 247 5.9.908, p 6), 330/1999 (OJ L 40 13.2.99, p 23), 1804/1999 (OJ NO L 222 24.8.99, p 1), 331/2000 (OJ L 48 19.2.2000, p 1)

Commission Regulation 207/93/EEC (defining the context of Annex VI to Regulation 2092/91/EEC and laying down detailed rules for implementing the provisions of Article 5(4)) (OJ L 25, 2.2.93, p 1) as amended by Regulation 345/97 (OJ L58 27.2.97, p 38)

Commission Regulation 94/92/EEC (detailed rules for implementing the arrangements for imports from third countries) (OJ L 11 17.1.92, p 14) as amended by Regulations 314/97 (OJ L 51 21.2.97, p 34), 548/2000 (OJ L 67 15.3.2000, p 12)

Commission Regulation 3457/92/EEC (detailed rules concerning the inspection certificate for imports from third countries into the Community) (OJ L 1.12.92, p 56)

Commission Regulation 529/95/EC (deferring for imports from third countries the date of application of Article 11(1) of Regulation 2092/91) (OJ L 54 10.3.95, p 10) as amended by Regulation 522/96 (OJ L 77 27.3.96, p 10).

Protected food names

Geographical indications and designations of origin
Council Regulation 2081/92/EEC (protection of geographical indications and designations of origin for agricultural products and foodstuffs) (OJ L 208 24.7.92, p 1) as amended by Regulations 535/97, 1068/97

Commission Regulation 2037/93/EEC (detailed rules of application of Regulation 2081/92) (OJ L 185 28.7.93, p 5) as amended by Regulations 1428/97 (OJ L 196 24.7.97, p 39), 1726/98 (OJ L 22 11.8.98, p 1)

Commission Regulation 1107/96/EC (registration of geographical indications and designations of origin under the procedure in Article 17 of Regulation 2081/92) (OJ L 148 21.6.96, p 1) as amended by Regulations 1263/96 (OJ L 163 2.7.96, p 19), 123/97 (OJ L 22 24.1.97, p 19), 1065/97 (OJ L 156 13.6.97, p 5), 2325/97 (OJ L 322 25.11.97, p 33), 644/98 (OJ L 87 21.3.98, p 8), 134/98 (OJ L 15 21.1.98, p 6), 1548/98 (OJ L 202 18.7.98, p 24), 83/1999 (OJ L 8 14.1.99, p 17), 590/1999 (OJ L 74 19.3.99, p 8), 1070/1999 (OJ L 130 26.5.99, p 18)

Council Regulation 2400/96/EC (entry of certain names in the 'Register of protected designation of origin and protected geographical indications' provided for in Council Regulation 2081/92) (OJ L 327 18.12.96, p 11) as amended 13.21.1.93, p 16

Commission Decision 93/53/EEC (setting up a scientific committee for designations of origin, geographical indications and certificates of specific character) (OJ L 13 21.1.93, p 16) as amended by Decisions 94/437 (OJ L 180 14.7.94, p 47), 97/656 (OJ L 277 10.10.97, p 30)

Certificates of specific character for agricultural products and foodstuffs
Council Regulation 2082/92/EEC (certificates of specific character for agricultural products and foodstuffs) (OJ L 208 24.7.92, p 9)

Commission Regulation 1848/93/EEC (detailed rules for the application of Regulation 2082/92) (OJ L 168 10.7.93, p 35) as amended by Regulations 2515/94 (OJ L 275 26.10.94, p 1).

Commission Regulation 2301/97/EC (entry of certain names in the 'Register of certificates of specific character') (OJ L 319 21.11.97, p 8), as amended

(See also Decision 93/53EEC under *Geographical indications and designations of origin.*)

Food: official control

Council Directive 89/397/EEC (official control of foodstuffs) (OJ L 186 30.6.89)

Council Directive 93/99/EEC (additional measures concerning the official control of foodstuffs) (OJ L 290 24.11.93, p 18).

Meat inspection charges

Council Directive 85/73/EEC (financing of health inspections and controls of fresh meat and poultrymeat) (OJ L 32 5.2.85, p 14), a consolidated text of which is annexed to Council Directive 96/43/EC (OJ L 162 1.7.96, p 1), as subsequently amended.

Notification of technical standards

Directive 98/34/EC of the European Parliament and Council (procedure for the provision of information in the field of technical standards and regulations and of rules on information society services) (OJ L 204 21.7.98, p 37) as amended by Directive 98/48/EC (OJ L 217 5.8.98, p 18).

Radioactive contamination of foodstuffs and feeding stuffs

Export conditions

Council Regulation 2219/89/EEC (special conditions for exporting foodstuffs and feeding stuffs following a nuclear accident or any other case of radiological emergency) (OJ L 211 22.7.89, p 4).

Import conditions for agricultural products from third countries

Council Regulation 737/90/EEC (conditions governing imports of agricultural products originating in third countries following the accident at the Chernobyl nuclear power-station) (OJ L 82 29.3.90, p 1) as extended by Council Regulation 686/95/EC and amended by Regulation 616/2000 (OJ L 75 24.3.2000, p 1)

Commission Regulation 1661/1999/EEC (detailed rules for the application of Regulation 737/90) (OJ L 197 29.7.1999, p 17)

Commission Regulation 727/97/EEC (establishing a list of products excluded from the application of Regulation 737/90) (OJ L 108 25.4.97, p 16).

Maximum permitted levels of contamination

Council Regulation (Euratom) 3954/87 (maximum permitted levels of radioactive contamination of foodstuffs and feeding stuffs following a nuclear accident or any other case of radiological emergency) (OJ L 371 30.12.87, p 11) as amended by Regulation 2218/89 (OJ L 211 22.7.89, p 1)

Commission Regulation (Euratom) 944/89 (maximum permitted levels of radioactive contamination in minor foodstuffs following a nuclear accident or any other case of radiological emergency) (OJ L 101 13.4.89, p 17)

Commission Regulation (Euratom) 770/90 (maximum permitted levels of radioactive contamination of feeding stuffs following a nuclear accident or any other case of radiological emergency) (OJ L 83 30.3.90, p 78).

Quantity and price marking of food

Quantity marking

Average quantity
Council Directive 75/106/EEC (making up by volume of certain prepackaged liquids) (OJ L 42 15.2.75, p 1) as amended by Directives 79/1005 (OJ L 308 4.12.79, p 25), 85/10 (OJ L 44 5.1.85, p 20), 88/316 (OJ L 143 10.6.88, p 26), 89/676 (OJ L 398 30.12.89, p 18)

Council Directive 76/211/EEC (making up by volume of certain prepackaged products) (OJ L 46 21.2.76, p 1) as amended by Directive 78/891 (OJ L 311 4.11.78, p 21).

Units of measurement
Council Directive 80/181 (units of measurement) (OJ L 39 15.280, p 40) as amended by Directives 85/1 (OJ L 2 3.1.85, p 11), 89/617 (OJ L 357 7.12.89, p 28), 1999/103 (OJ L 34.9.2.99, p 17).

Price marking

Directive 98/6/EC of the European Parliament and the Council (consumer protection in the indication of the prices of products offered to consumers) (OJ L 80 18.3.98, p 27).

PART II: COMMUNITY LEGISLATION APPLICABLE TO FEEDING STUFFS

(See further Part I of this Appendix.)

Additives in feeding stuffs

Council Directive 70/524/EEC (concerning additives in feedingstuffs) (OJ L 270 14.12.70, p 1) as amended by Directives 82/471 (OJ L 213 21.7.82, p 8), 84/587 (OJ L 319 8.12.85, p 8), 3768/85 (OJ L 362 31.12.85, p 8), 95/69 (OJ 1332 30.12.95, p 32), 96/25 (OJ L 125 23.5.96, p 35), 96/51(OJ L 235 17.9.96, p 39), 96/66 (OJ L 272 25.10.96, p 32), 97/6 (OJ L 35 5.2.97, p 11), 97/72 (OJ L 351 23.12.97, p 55), 98/19 (OJ L 96 28.3.98, p 39), 98/92 (OJ L 346 22.12.98, p 49), 2786/98 (OJ L 347 23.12.98, p 25), 2788/98 (OJ L 347 23.12.98, p 31), 2821/98 (OJ L 351 29.12.98, p 14), 20/1999 (OJ LL 80 25.3.99, p 20), 45/1999 (OJ L 6 12.1.99, p 3)

Council Directive 87/153/EEC (guidelines for the assessment of additives in animal nutrition) (OJ L 064 07.3.87, p 19) as amended by Directives 94/40 (OJ L 208 11.8.94, p 15), 95/11 (OJ L 106 11.5.95, p 23)

Commission Regulation 1436/98/EC (authorising certain additives in feeding stuffs) (OJ L 191 7.7.98, p 15)

Commission Regulation 2316/98/EC (authorisation of new additives and amending conditions for authorisation of certain additives already authorised) (OJ L 289 28.10.98, p 4)

Commission Regulation 2374/98/EC (authorisation of new additives in feedingstuffs) (OJ L 295 4.11.98, p 3)

Commission Regulation 639/1999/EC (authorisation of a new additive in feedingstuffs) (OJ L 82 26.3.99, p 6)

Commission Regulation 866/1999/EC (authorisation of new additives and new additive uses in feedingstuffs) (OJ L 108 27.4.99, p 21)

Commission Regulation 1245/1999/EC (authorisation of new additives in feedingstuffs) (OJ L 150 17.6.99, p 15)

Commission Regulation 1411/1999/EC (authorisation of new additives and new additive uses in feedingstuffs) (OJ L 164 30.6.99, p 56)

Commission Regulation 1594/1999/EC (amending the conditions for the authorisation of an additive in feedingstuffs) (OJ L 188 21.7.99, p 35)

Commission Regulation 1636/99/EC (authorisation of new additive uses in feeding stuffs) (OJ L 194 27.7.1999, p 17)

Commission Regulation 2233/1999/EC (extending the provisional authorisations of certain additives in feeding stuffs) (OJ L 284 6.11.1999, p 1).

Circulation of feed materials

Council Directive 96/25/EC (circulation of feed materials) (OJ L 125 23.5.96, p 35) as amended by Directive 98/67 (OJ L 261 24.9.98, p 10), 1999/61 (OJ L 162 22.6.99, p 67)

Compound feeding stuffs

Council Directive 79/373/EEC (marketing of compound feeding stuffs) (OJ L 086 06.4.79, p 30) as amended by Directives and Regulations 3768/85 (OJ L 362 31.12.85, p 8), 86/354 (OJ L 212 2.8.86, p 27), 90/44 (OJ L 27 31.1.90, p 35), 95/69 (OJ L 332 30.12.95, p 15, p 33), 96/24 (OJ L 125 23.5.96, p 33), 97/47 (OJ L 211 .8.97, p 45), 98/87 (OJ L 318 27.11.98, p 43), 99/61 (OJ L 162 26.6.99, p 67)

Commission Directive 80/511/EEC (compound feeding stuffs in unsealed packages) (OJ L 126 21.5.80, p 14) as amended by Directive 98/67 (OJ L 261 24.9.98, p 31)

Commission Directive 82/475/EEC (categories of ingredients which may be used for the purposes of labelling compound feeding stuffs for pet animals) (OJ L 213 21.7.82, p 27) as amended by Directives 91/334 (OJ L 184 10.7.91, p 27), 98/67 (OJ L 261 24.9.98, p 31)

Commission Directive 91/357/EEC (categories of ingredients which may be used for the purposes of labelling compound feeding stuffs for animals other than pet animals) (OJ L 193 17.7.91, p 34) as amended by Directives 97/47 (OJ L 211 5.8.97, p 45), 98/67 (OJ L 261 24.9.98, p 31)

Commission Decision 91/516/EEC (list of ingredients whose use is prohibited in compound feeding stuffs) (OJ L 281 09.10.91, p 23) as amended by Decision 92/508 (OJ

L 312 29.10.92, p 36), 95/274 (OJ L 167 18.7.95, p 24), 97/582 (OJ L 237 28.8, p 39), 1999/420 (OJ L 162 26.6.99, p 69).

Enzymes, micro-organisms and their preparations

Council Directive 93/113/EC (use and marketing of enzymes, micro-organisms and their preparations in animal nutrition) (OJ L 334 31.12.93, p 17) as amended by Directive 97/40 (OJ L 180 9.7.97, p 21).

Establishments and intermediaries

Council Directive 95/69/EC (conditions and arrangements for approving and registering certain establishments and intermediaries operating in the animal feed sector) (OJ L 332 30.12.95, p 15) as amended by Directives 98/92 (OJ L 346 22.12.98, p 49), 1999/20 (OJ L 80 25.3.99, p 22)

Commission Directive 98/51 (measures for implementing Directive 95/69) (OJ NO L 208 24.7.98, p 43).

Medicated feedingstuffs

Council Directive 90/167/EEC (preparation placing on the market and used of medicated feedingstuffs in the Community) (OJ L 92.7.90, p 42).

Official inspections

Council Directive 95/53/EC (principles governing the organisation of official inspections in the field of animal nutrition) (OJ L 265 08.11.95, p 17) as amended by Directive 1999/20 (OJ L 80 25.3.99, p 22)

Commission Directive 98/68/EC (standard document referred to in Article 9(1) of Directive 95/53 and certain checks at the introduction into the Community of feeding stuffs from third countries) (OJ L 261 24.9.98, p 32).

Particular nutritional purposes

Council Directive 93/74/EEC (feeding stuffs intended for particular nutritional purposes) (OJ L 237 22.9.93, p 35) as amended by Directive 96/25/EC (OJ L 125 23.5.96, p 35).

Commission Directive 94/39/EC (list of intended uses of animal feeding stuffs for particular nutritional purposes) (OJ L 207 10.8.94, p 20) as amended by Directive 95/39 (OJ L 197 22.8.95, p 29)

Commission Directive 95/10/EC (method of calculating the energy value of dog and cat food intended for particular nutritional purposes) (OJ L 091 22.4.95, p 39) as amended by Directives 98/67 (OJ L 261 24.9.98, p 10), 1999/78 (OJ L 209 7.8.99, p 23).

Protein sources

Council Directive 82/471/EEC (certain products used in animal nutrition) (OJ L 213 21.7.82, p 8) as amended by Directives and Regulations 84/443 (OJ L 245 14.9.84, p 21), 85/509 (OJ L 314 23.11.85, p 25), 3768/85 (OJ L 362 31.12.85, p 8), 86/530 (OJ L 312 7.11.86, p 39), 88/485 (OJ L 239 30.8.88, p 36), 89/520 (OJ L 270 19.9.89, p 13), 90/439 (OJ L 227 21.8.90, p 33), 93/26 (OJ L 179 22.7.93, p 2), 93/56 (OJ L 206 18.8.93, p 13), 95/33 (OJ L 167 18.7.95, p 17), 95/69 (OJ L 332 30.12.95, p 15), 96/25 (OJ L 125 23.5.96, p 35), 1999/20 (OJ L 80 25.3.99, p 20)

Council Directive 83/228/EEC (guidelines for assessment of certain products used in animal nutrition) (OJ L 126 13.5.83, p 23).

Sampling and analysis

Community methods of sampling and analysis for feeding stuffs

Council Directive 70/373 (introduction of Community methods of sampling and analysis for the official control of feeding stuffs) (OJ L 170 03.8.70, p 21) as amended by Directives and Regulations 72/275 (OJ L 171 29.7.72, p 39), 73/101 (OJ L 2 1.1.73), 3768/85 (OJ L 362 31.12.85, p 8).

Guidelines for the microscopic examination of constituents of animal origin for the official control of feedingstuffs

Commission Directive 98/88/EC (guidelines for the microscopic examination of constituents of animal origin for the official control of feedingstuffs) (OJ L 318 27.11.98, p 45).

Specific analysis methods for feeding stuffs

First Commission Directive 71/250 (on analysis methods) (OJ L 155 12.7.71, p 13) as amended by Directives 74/203 (OJ L 108 22.4.77, p 7), 81/680 (OJ L 246 29.8.81, p 32), 98/54 (OJ L 208 24.7.98, p 30)

Second Commission Directive 71/393 (on analysis methods) (OJ L 279 20.12.71, p 7) as amended by Directives 73/047 (OJ L 083 30.3.73, p 35), 81/680 (OJ L 246 29.8.81, p 32), 84/004 (OJ L 015 18.1.84, p 28), 98/64 (OJ L 257 19.9.98, p 45)

Third Commission Directive 72/199 (on analysis methods) (OJ L 123 24.9.72, p 6) as amended by Directives 81/680 (OJ L 246 29.8.81, p 32), 84/004, (OJ L 015 18.1.84, p 28), 93/28 (OJ L 179 22.7.93, p 8), 98/54 (OJ L 208 24.7.98, p 49), 1999/79, (OJ L 209 7.8.1999, p 23)

Fourth Commission Directive 73/46 (on analysis methods) (OJ L 083 30.3.73, p 21) as amended by Directives 81/680 (OJ L 246 29.8.81, p 32), 92/89 (OJ L 344 26.11.92, p 35), 98/54 (OJ L 208 24.7.98, p 49), 1999/27 (OJ L 118 6.5.99, p 36)

Seventh Commission Directive 76/372 (on analysis methods) (OJ L 102 15.4.76, p 8) as amended by Directives 81/680 (OJ L 246 29.8.81, p 32), 92/95 (OJ L 327 13.11.92, p 54), 94/14 (OJ L 94 13.4.94, p 30)

Eighth Commission Directive 78/633 (on analysis methods) (OJ L 206 29.7.78, p 43) as amended by Directives 81/680 (OJ L 246 29.8.81, p 32), 84/004 (OJ L 015 18.1.84, p 28)

Ninth Commission Directive 81/715 (on analysis methods) (OJ L 257 10.9.81, p 38)

Tenth Commission Directive 84/425 (on analysis methods) (OJ L 238 06.9.84, p 34) as amended by Directive 93/70 (OJ L 234 17.9.93, p 17)

Eleventh Commission Directive 93/70 (on analysis methods) (OJ L 234 17.9.93, p 17)

Twelfth Commission Directive 93/117 (on analysis methods) (OJ L 329 30.12.93, p 54)

Commission Directive 98/64/EC (on analysis methods for amino-acids, crude oils and fats, and olaquindox) (OJ L 257 19.9.98, p 14)

Commission Directive 1999/27 (on analysis methods for amprolium, diclazuril and carbadox) (OJ L 118 6.5.1999, p 36)

Commission Directive 1999/76 (on analysis methods for lasalocid sodium) (OJ L 207 6.8.1999, p 13).

Specific sampling methods for feeding stuffs

First Commission Directive 76/371 (on sampling methods) (OJ L 102 15.4.76, p 1).

Standing committee for feeding stuffs

Council Decision 70/372 (setting up a standing committee for feeding stuffs) (OJ L 170 03.8.70, p 1).

Undesirable substances and products

Council Directive 1999/29/EC (undesirable substances and products in animal nutrition) (OJ L 115 4.5.1999, p 32).

Appendix C

Some useful addresses

Advertising Standards Authority
Brook House, 2 Torrington Place, London WC1E 7HW
Tel: 020 7580 5555; **Fax**: 020 7631 3051
E-mail: enquiry@asa.co.uk; **Website**: http://www.asa.org.uk/

Association of Public Analysts
Honorary Secretary, Analytical Services (South Wales)
54 The Parade, Cardiff CF2 3AB
Tel: 44 (+0)1222 820800; **Fax**: 44 (+0)1222 820801
E-mail: secretary@the-apa.org.uk; **Website**: http://www.the-apa.org.uk/

British Meat Manufacturers' Association
11/12 Buckingham Gate, London SW1E 6LB
Tel: 020 7828 1224; **Fax**: 020 7828 1237
E-mail: enquiries@BMMA.org.uk; **Website**: http://www.bmma.org.uk/

British Retail Consortium
5 Grafton Street, London W1X 3LB
Tel: 020 7647 1500; **Fax**: 020 7647 1599
E-mail: info@brc.org.uk

British Standards Institution
389 Chiswick High Road, London W4 4AL
Tel: 020 8996 9000; **Fax**: 020 8996 7400
E-mail: info@bsi.org.uk; **Website**: http://www.bsi.org.uk/bsi/

Butterworths Limited
Halsbury House, 35 Chancery Lane, London WC2A 1EL
Tel: 020 7400 2500; **Fax**: 020 7400 2842
E-mail: webmaster@butterworths.com (internet enquires)
Customer services e-mail: customer.services@butterworths.com
Website: http//www.butterworths.com

Campden & Chorleywood Food Research Association Group
Chipping Campden, Gloucestershire GL55 6LD
Tel: (0)1386 842000; **Fax**: (0)1386 842100
E-mail: information@campden.co.uk; **Website**: http://www.campden.co.uk/

Crown Prosecution Service
50 Ludgate Hill, London EC4M 7EX
Tel: 020 7796 8000
E-mail: enquiries@cps.gov.uk; **Website**: http://www.cps.gov.uk

Department of the Environment, Transport and the Regions
Biotechnology Safety Unit, 123 Victoria Street, London SW1E 6DE
Tel: 020 7890 5275; **Fax**: 020 7890 5259
E-mail: biotech@detr.gsi.gov.uk;
Website: http://www.environment.
detr.gov.uk/acre/index.htm

Department of Health
Public Enquiry Office, Richmond House, 79 Whitehall, London SW1A 2NL
Tel: 020 7210 4850
E-mail: dhmail@doh.gsi.gov.uk; **Website**: http://www.doh.gov.uk/

Department of Trade and Industry
DTI Enquiry Unit, 1 Victoria Street, London SW1H 0ET
Tel: 020 7215 5000
Website: http://www.dti.gov.uk/

European Commission
Rue de la Loi, B-200, Brussels, Belgium
Tel: + 32-2. 299 11 11
Website: http://www.europa.eu.int

European Commission: Representation in the United Kingdom
8 Storey's Gate, London SW1P 3AT
Tel: 020 7973 1992; **Fax**: 020 7973 1907
E-mail: EU-UK-Press@cec.org.uk; **Website**: http://www.cec.org.uk

European Information Association
EIA Manager, Central Library, St Peter's Square, Manchester M2 5PD
Tel: (0)161 228 3691; **Fax**: +(0)161 236 6547
E-mail: eia@manchestergb.demon.co.uk; **Website**: www.eia.org.uk

Food and Agriculture Organisation of the United Nations (FAO)
Viale delle Terme di Caracalla, 00100 Rome, Italy
Tel: +39.0657051; **Fax**: +39.0657053152
E-mail: Codex@fao.org; **Website**: http://www.fao.org

Food and Drink Federation
6 Catherine Street, London WC2B 5JJ
Tel: 020 7836 2460
E-mail: fdnto@fdf.org.uk; **Website**: http://www.foodanddrinknto.org.uk/

Food Standards Agency
PO Box 30080
Hannibal House, Elephant and Castle, London SE1 6YA
(*Different specialisations are dealt with at different sites—please ring helpline to obtain most relevant contact.*)
Food Standards Helpline Tel: 0845 757 3012
Website: http://www.foodstandards.gov.uk/

Food Standards Agency
Welsh Executive
Southgate House, Wood Street
Cardiff
Tel: 029 2067 8999; **Fax**: 029 2067 8919

Health and Safety Executive
Health and Safety Laboratory, Broad Lane, Sheffield S3 7HQ
Tel: 0541 545500; **Fax**: 0114 2892333
E-mail: public.enquiries@hse.gov.uk; **Website**: http://www.hse.gov.uk/

Home Office Publications
Public Enquiry Team, Room 856, 50 Queen Anne's Gate, London SW1H 9AT
Tel: 020 7273 3072; **Fax**: 020 7273 2191
Website: http://www.homeoffice.gov.uk/

Horticultural Marketing Inspectorate (MAFF)
Ergon House, c/o Nobel House, 17 Smith Square, London SW1P 3JR
Tel: 020 7238 6000
http://www.maff.gov.uk/hort/hortindx.htm

Institute of Food Science and Technology
5 Cambridge Court, 210 Shepherd's Bush Road, London W6 7NJ
Tel: 020 7603 6316; **Fax** 020 7602 9936.
E-mail: ifst@ifst.org; **Website**: http://www.ifst.org/

Institute of Trading Standards Administration
3/5 Hadleigh Business Centre, 351 London Road, Hadleigh, Essex SS7 2BT
Tel: 01702 559922; **Fax**: (01702) 551161
E-mail: institute@itsa.org.uk; **Website**: http://www.tradingstandards.gov.uk/

Institution of Environmental Health Officers
Chadwick Court, 15 Hatfields, London SE1 8DJ
Tel: 020 7928 6006; **Fax**: 020 7827 5865
E-mail: cieh@dial.pipex.com; **Website**: http://www.cieh.org.uk

Laboratory of the Government Chemist
Queen's Road, Teddington, Middlesex TW11 0LY
Tel: 020 8943 700; **Fax** 020 8943 2767.
E-mail: info@lgc.co.uk; **Website**: http://www.lgc.co.uk

Law Laboratories Ltd
Lawlabs House, Shady Lane, Great Barr, Birmingham, B44 9ET
Tel: 0121 344 6000; **Fax**: 0121 344 6060 (advisory), 0121 344 6262 (analytical)
E-mail: market@lawlabs.com; **Website**: http://www.lawlabs.com/

Leatherhead Food Research Association
Randalls Road, Leatherhead, Surrey KT22 7RY
Tel: 01372 376761; **Fax**: 01372 386228
E-mail: help@lfra.co.uk; **Website**: http://www.lfra.co.uk/

Local Authorities Co-ordinating Body on Trading Standards (LACOTS)
10 Albert Embankment, London, SE1 7SP
Tel: 020 7840 7200; **Fax**: 020 7735 9977
Website: http://www.lacots.org.uk

Meat Hygiene Service
Room 366, Foss House, Kingspool,
1–2 Peasholme Green, York YO12XP
Tel: 01904 45 3000; **Fax**: 01904 45 5502

Ministry of Agriculture, Fisheries and Food (MAFF)
Nobel House, 17 Smith Square, London SW1P 3JR
Tel: 020 7238 3000 (general switchboard); **Fax**: 020 7238 6591
MAFF Helpline Tel: 0645 33 55 77
E-mail: helpline@inf.maff.gov.uk; **Website**: http://www.maff.gov.uk/
(The Joint Food Safety and Standards Group (JFSSG) Consumer Helpline is based within MAFF, see that entry above.)

National Consumer Council
20 Grosvenor Gardens, London SW1W 0DH
Tel: 020 7730 3469; **Fax**: 020 7730 0191
Minicom: 020 7730 3469
E-mail: info@ncc.org.uk; **Website**: http://cgi.www.ncc.org.uk/

National Farmers' Union
164 Shaftesbury Avenue, London WC2H 8HL
Tel: 020 7331 7200; **Fax** : 020 7331 7313
E-mail: NFU@nfu.org.uk; **Website**: http://www.nfu.org.uk/

National Weights and Measures Laboratory
Stanton Avenue, Teddington, Middlesex TW11 0JZ
Tel: 020 8943 7272; **Fax**: 020 8943 7270
E-mail: info@nwml.dti.gov.uk; **Website**: http://www.nwml.gov.uk/

Office of Fair Trading
Fleetbank House, 2–6 Salisbury Square, London EC4Y 8JX
Tel: 020 7211 8000 (switchboard); 0345 22 44 99 (general enquiries); **Fax**: 020 7211 8800
E-mail: enquiries@oft.gov.uk; **Website**: http://www.oft.gov.uk/

Pesticides Safety Directorate (MAFF),
Mallard House, Kings Pool, York, YO1 7PX
Tel: 01904 455775; **Fax:** 01904 455733
E-mail: p.s.d.information@psd.maff.gsi.gov.uk; **Website:** pesticides.gov.uk

Stationery Office
Customer Services, PO Box 29, St Crispins House, Duke Street, Norwich NR3 1GN
Tel: 0870 600 5522; **Fax**: 0870 600 5533
E-mail: customer.services@theso.co.uk; **Website**: http://www.the-stationery-office.co.uk/

United Kingdom Register of Organic Food Standards (UKROFS)
Nobel House, 17 Smith Square, London SWIP 3JR
Tel: 020 7238 5915; **Fax** 020 7238 6553

Veterinary Medicines Directorate (MAFF)
Woodham Lane, New Haw, Addlestone, Surrey KT15 3LS
Tel: 01932 336911; **Fax**: 01932 336618

Appendix D

Powers of the Secretary of State for Health under the Food Safety Act 1990 (FSA 1990), as amended

	Power	*Enabling provision*
1	To provide exemptions from the definition of 'food'.	section 1(2)(d)
2	To extend the definition of 'premises' to any ship or aircraft as specified.	section 1(3)
3	To extend the meaning of 'sale'.	section 2(1)(b)
4	To provide by order that concurrent functions under the FSA 1990 be exercised solely by a particular food authority.	section 5(4)
5	To prescribe qualifications for food authority authorised officers.	section 5(6)
6	To direct that any duty imposed on food authorities shall be discharged by the Secretary of State, Minister of Agriculture, Fisheries and Food or the Food Standards Agency.	section 6(3)
7	To specify which authorities shall enforce and execute regulations and orders.	section 6(4)
8	To take over conduct of proceedings which have been instituted by another person.	section 6(5A)
9	To direct the Food Standards Agency to take over conduct of proceedings which have been instituted by another person.	section 6(5B)
10	To prescribe qualifications for 'authorised officers' of enforcement authorities.	section 6(6)
11	To make emergency control orders.	section 13(1)
12	To consent to the doing of anything prohibited by an emergency control order (shared with the Food Standards Agency).	section 13(3)
13	To give directions to prevent commercial operations with respect to food, food sources or food contact materials to which an emergency control order applies (shared with the Food Standards Agency).	section 13(5)
14	To recover certain expenses incurred in respect of emergency control orders (shared with the Food Standards Agency).	section 13(7)

	Power	Enabling provision
15	To make regulations as to safety and consumer protection in relation to food, food sources and food contact materials.	section 16
16	To make regulations for the enforcement of Community provisions in relation to food, food sources and food contact materials.	section 17
17	To make regulations as to commercial operations with respect to novel foods and food sources, genetically modified foods and food sources and prohibiting the importation of food of a specified class.	section 18(1)
18	To make regulations as to the licensing of producers and sellers of milk authorising the use of special designations of milk.	section 18(2)
19	To make regulations requiring the registration or licensing of food premises.	section 19
20	To make regulations prohibiting or regulating commercial operations with respect to non-compliant food, food sources or food contact materials and providing that food certified as non-compliant may be treated as failing to comply with food safety requirements for the purposes of section 9 of the FSA 1990.	section 26(1)
21	To make regulations requiring the keeping of records and registers, prescribing licence conditions and providing for appeals against decisions.	section 26(2)
22	To prescribe by regulations or otherwise approve the qualifications of persons appointed as public analysts.	section 27(2)
23	To make regulations defining arrangements prohibited between the public analyst for a particular area and food businesses carried on in that area.	section 27(5)
24	To prescribe by regulations or otherwise approve the qualifications of food analysts and food examiners for the purposes of analysis and examination.	section 30(9)
25	To make regulations as to sampling, dealing with samples, analysis and examination.	section 31
26	To issue codes of practice for the guidance of food authorities.	section 40(1)
27	To order the duties of a defaulting food authority to be discharged by another food authority or the Food Standards Agency.	section 42(1)
28	To cause a local inquiry to be held for the purpose of determining whether the power at 27 above is exercisable.	section 42(2)
29	To recover expenses from a defaulting food authority.	section 42(4)
30	To make regulations authorising charges to be imposed by enforcement authorities.	section 45
31	To direct that expenses incurred by county councils in the enforcement or execution of any provision of the FSA 1990 be defrayed as expenses for special county purposes.	section 46(2)

	Power	Enabling provision
32	To determine the remuneration and allowances to be paid to the chairman of any tribunal constituted under regulations.	section 47
33	In regulations or orders to make further provision, including application with modifications or adaptions, of other enactments to those regulations or orders.	section 48(1)
34	By regulations to prescribe the form of documents.	section 49(2)
35	To certify that the powers of entry conferred by section 32 of the FSA 1990 should not be exercisable in relation to Crown premises.	section 54(4)
36	By order to modify local Acts and subordinate legislation in consequence of the provisions of the FSA 1990.	section 59(2)

Appendix E

Statutory Codes of Practice under section 40 of the Food Safety Act 1990

Code of Practice no 1: Responsibility for Enforcement of the Food Safety Act 1990

Code of Practice no 2: Legal Matters

Code of Practice no 3: Inspection Procedures – General

Code of Practice no 4: Inspection, Detention and Seizure of Suspect Food (Section 9 of the Food Safety Act 1990)

*Code of Practice no 5: The use of Improvement Notices (Revised April 1994)

*Code of Practice no 6: Prohibition Procedures

*Code of Practice no 7: Sampling for Analysis or Examination

*Code of Practice no 8: Food Standards Inspections (Revised July 1996)

*Code of Practice no 9: Food Hygiene Inspections (Revised September 1995) (Annex I Revised August 1997)

Code of Practice no 10: Enforcement of the Temperature Control Requirements of Food Hygiene Regulations: enforcement of temperature monitoring and temperature measurement (Revised February 1994)

Code of Practice no 11: Enforcement of the Food Premises (Registration) Regulations

Code of Practice no 12: Quick-Frozen Foodstuffs: division of enforcement responsibilities; enforcement of temperature monitoring and temperature measurement (Revised February 1994)

Code of Practice no 13: Enforcement of the Food Safety Act 1990 in relation to Crown Premises

Code of Practice no 14: Enforcement of the Food Safety (Live Bivalve Molluscs and Other Shellfish) Regulations 1992

Code of Practice no 15: Enforcement of the Food Safety (Fishery Products) Regulations 1992

Code of Practice no 16: Enforcement of the Food Safety Act 1990 in relation to the Food Hazard Warning System (Revised August 1997)

Code of Practice no 17: Enforcement of the Meat Products (Hygiene) Regulations 1994 (Guidance Notes to be read in conjunction with Code of Practice no 17 on the Enforcement of the Meat Products (Hygiene) Regulations 1994) (February 1995)

Code of Practice no 18: Enforcement of the Dairy Products (Hygiene) Regulations 1995 and the Dairy Products (Hygiene) (Scotland) Regulations 1995

*Code of Practice no 19: Qualifications and Experience of Authorised Officers and Experts

Code of Practice no 20: Exchange of Information between Member States of the EU on Routine Food Control Matters

* At the time of writing these Codes are due to be further revised.

Appendix F

Permitted food additives

The following lists of permitted food additives have been extracted from the specified Regulations. It is important to note that they are lists only of the permitted additives: they do *not* show the restrictions on use of the additives and cannot serve as a substitute for the Regulations.

PART 1: PERMITTED SWEETENERS

In the Sweeteners in Food Regulations 1995, as amended, 'permitted sweetener' means any sweetener specified in column 2 below which satisfies the specific purity criteria for that sweetener set out in the Annex to Directive 95/31/EC.

EC No	*Permitted sweetener*	
E 420	Sorbitol	
	(i)	Sorbitol
	(ii)	Sorbitol syrup
E 421		Mannitol
E 953		Isomalt
E 965		Maltitol
	(i)	Maltitol
	(ii)	Maltitol syrup
E 966		Lactitol
E 967		Xylitol
E 950		Acesulfame K
E 951		Aspartame
E 952		Cyclamic acid and its Na and Ca salts
E954		Saccharin and its Na, K and Ca salts
E 957		Thaumatin
E 959		Neohesperidine DC

PART II: PERMITTED COLOURS[1]

In the Colours in Food Regulations 1995, as amended, 'permitted colour' means any colour listed below which satisfies the specific purity criteria for that colour set out in the Annex to Directive 95/45/EC.

EC No	*Colour*	*Colour index No*[2] *or description*
E 100	Curcumin	75300
E 101	(i) Riboflavin (ii) Riboflavin-5'-phosphate	
E 102	Tartrazine	19140
E 104	Quinoline Yellow	47005
E 110	Sunset Yellow FCF Orange Yellow S	15985
E 120	Cochineal, Carminic acid, Carmines	75470
E 122	Azorubine, Carmoisine	14720
E 123	Amaranth	16185
E 124	Ponceau 4R, Cochineal Red A	16255
E 127	Erythrosine	45430
E 128	Red 2G	18050
E 129	Allura Red AC	16035
E 131	Patent Blue V	42051
E 132	Indigotine, Indigo carmine	73015
E 133	Brilliant Blue FCF	42090
E 140	Chlorophylls and Chlorophyllins: (i) Chlorophylls (ii) Chlorophyllins	75810 75815
E 141	Copper complexes of chlorophylls and chlorophyllins: (i) Copper complexes of chlorophylls (ii) Copper complexes of chlorophyllins	75815
E 142	Green S	44090
E 150a	Plain caramel[3]	
E 150b	Caustic sulphite caramel	
E 150c	Ammonia caramel	
E 150d	Sulphite ammonia caramel	
E 151	Brilliant Black BN, Black PN	28440
E 153	Vegetable carbon	
E 154	Brown FK	
E 155	Brown HT	20285

EC No	*Colour*	*Colour index No[2] or description*
E 160a	Carotenes:	
	(i) Mixed carotenes	75130
	(ii) Beta-carotene	40800
E 160b	Annatto, bixin, norbixin	
E 160c	Paprika extract, capsanthin, capsorubin	
E 160d	Lycopene	
E 160e	Beta-apo-8′-carotenal (C 30)	40820
E 160f	Ethyl ester of beta-apo-8′-carotenic acid (C 30)	40825
E 161b	Lutein	
E 161g	Canthaxanthin	
E 162	Beetroot Red, betanin	
E 163	Anthocyanins	Prepared by physical means from fruit and vegetables
E 170	Calcium carbonate	77220
E 171	Titanium dioxide	77891
E 172	Iron oxides and hydroxides	77491 77492 77499
E 173	Aluminium	
E 174	Silver	
E 175	Gold	
E 180	Litholrubine BK	

Notes

1 Aluminium lakes prepared from colours listed above are also permitted.
2 Colour index numbers are taken from the third edition 1982 of the Colour Index, volumes 1 to 7, 1315. Also amendments 37 to 40 (125), 41 to 44 (127–50), 45 to 48 (130), 49–52 (132–50), 53 to 56 (135).
3 The term caramel relates to products of a more or less intense brown colour which are intended for colouring. It does not correspond to the sugary aromatic obtained from heating sugars and which is used in the flavouring of food (eg confectionery, pastry, alcoholic drinks.)

PART III: PERMITTED MISCELLANEOUS ADDITIVES

In the Miscellaneous Food Additives Regulations 1995, as amended—

'permitted miscellaneous additive' means any miscellaneous additive listed below which satisfies the specific purity criteria (if any) for that miscellaneous additive; and

'purity criteria', in relation to a miscellaneous additive, means—

(a) in the case of a miscellaneous additive for which purity criteria are set out in the Annex to Directive 96/77/EC, those purity criteria;

(b) in any other case, the purity criteria specified or referred in Schedule 5 to the Regulations.

1. Miscellaneous additives generally permitted for use in foods not referred to in Schedule 6, 7 or 8

Schedule 6 to the Miscellaneous Food Additives Regulations 1995 lists foods in which miscellaneous additives listed in Part III.1 of this Appendix are generally prohibited; Schedule 7 lists foods in which a limited number of miscellaneous additives listed in Part III.1 of this Appendix may be used; and Schedule 8 lists miscellaneous additives permitted in foods for infants and young children.

EC No	*Name*
E 170	Calcium carbonates
	(i) Calcium carbonate
	(ii) Calcium hydrogen carbonate
E 260	Acetic acid
E 261	Potassium acetate
E 262	Sodium acetates
	(i) Sodium acetate
	(ii) Sodium hydrogen acetate (sodium diacetate)
E 263	Calcium acetate
E 270	Lactic acid
E 290	Carbon dioxide
E 296	Malic acid
E 300	Ascorbic acid
E 301	Sodium ascorbate
E 302	Calcium ascorbate
E 304	Fatty acid esters of ascorbic acid
	(i) Ascorbyl palmitate
	(ii) Ascorbyl stearate
E 306	Tocopherol-rich extract
E 307	Alpha-tocopherol
E 308	Gamma-tocopherol
E 309	Delta-tocopherol
E 322	Lecithins
E 325	Sodium lactate
E 326	Potassium lactate
E 327	Calcium lactate

EC No	*Name*
E 330	Citric acid
E 331	Sodium citrates
	(i) Monosodium citrate
	(ii) Disodium citrate
	(iii) Trisodium citrate
E 332	Potassium citrates
	(i) Monopotassium citrate
	(ii) Tripotassium citrate
E 333	Calcium citrates
	(i) Monocalcium citrate
	(ii) Dicalcium citrate
	(iii) Tricalcium citrate
E 334	Tartaric acid (L(+)–)
E 335	Sodium tartrates
	(i) Monosodium tartrate
	(ii) Disodium tartrate
E 336	Potassium tartrates
	(i) Monopotassium tartrate
	(ii) Dipotassium tartrate
E 337	Sodium potassium tartrate
E 350	Sodium malates
	(i) Sodium malate
	(ii) Sodium hydrogen malate
E 351	Potassium malate
E 352	Calcium malates
	(i) Calcium malate
	(ii) Calcium hydrogen malate
E 354	Calcium tartrate
E 380	Triammonium citrate
E 400	Alginic acid
E 401	Sodium alginate
E 402	Potassium alginate
E 403	Ammonium alginate
E 404	Calcium alginate
E 406	Agar
E 407*	Carrageenan
E 407a	Processed eucheuma seaweed

EC No	Name
E 410	Locust bean gum
E 412	Guar gum
E 413	Tragacanth
E 414	Acacia gum (gum arabic)
E 415	Xanthan gum
E 417	Tara gum
E 418	Gellan gum
E 422	Glycerol
E 440*	Pectins
	(i) pectin
	(ii) amidated pectin
E 460	Cellulose
	(i) Microcrystalline cellulose
	(ii) Powdered cellulose
E 461	Methyl cellulose
E 463	Hydroxypropyl cellulose
E 464	Hydroxypropyl methyl cellulose
E 465	Ethyl methyl cellulose
E 466	Carboxy methyl cellulose
	Sodium carboxy methyl cellulose
E 469	Enzymatically hydrolysed carboxy methyl cellulose
E470a	Sodium, potassium and calcium salts of fatty acids
E 470b	Magnesium salts of fatty acids
E 471	Mono- and diglycerides of fatty acids
E 472a	Acetic acid esters of mono- and diglycerides of fatty acids
E 472b	Lactic acid esters of mono- and diglycerides of fatty acids
E 472c	Citric acid esters of mono- and diglycerides of fatty acids
E 472d	Tartaric acid esters of mono- and diglycerides of fatty acids
E 472e	Mono- and diacetyl tartaric acid esters of mono- and diglycerides of fatty acids
E 472E	Mixed acetic and tartaric acid esters of mono- and diglycerides of fatty acids
E 500	Sodium carbonates
	(i) Sodium carbonate
	(ii) Sodium hydrogen carbonate
	(iii) Sodium sesquicarbonate
E 501	Potassium carbonates
	(i) Potassium carbonate
	(ii) Potassium hydrogen carbonate

C No	*Name*
E 503	Ammonium carbonates
	(i) Ammonium carbonate
E	(ii) Ammonium hydrogen carbonate
E 504	Magnesium carbonates
	(i) Magnesium carbonate
	(ii) Magnesium hydroxide carbonate (syn: Magnesium hydrogen carbonate)
E 507	Hydrochloric acid
E 508	Potassium chloride
E 509	Calcium chloride
E 511	Magnesium chloride
E 513	Sulphuric acid
E 514	Sodium sulphates
	(i) Sodium sulphate
	(ii) Sodium hydrogen sulphate
E 515	Potassium sulphates
	(i) Potassium sulphate
	(ii) Potassium hydrogen sulphate
E 516	Calcium sulphate
E 524	Sodium hydroxide
E 525	Potassium hydroxide
E 526	Calcium hydroxide
E 527	Ammonium hydroxide
E 528	Magnesium hydroxide
E 529	Calcium oxide
E 530	Magnesium oxide
E 570	Fatty acids
E 574	Gluconic acid
E 575	Glucono-delta-lactone
E 576	Sodium gluconate
E 577	Potassium gluconate
E 578	Calcium gluconate
E 640	Glycine and its sodium salt
E 920	L-Cysteine
E 938	Argon
E 939	Helium
E 941	Nitrogen
E 942	Nitrous oxide
E 948	Oxygen

EC No	Name
E 1103	Invertase
E 1200	Polydextrose
E 1404	Oxidised starch
E 1410	Mono starch phosphate
E 1412	Distarch phosphate
E 1413	Phosphated distarch phosphate
E 1414	Acetylated distarch phosphate
E 1420	Acetylated starch
E 1422	Acetylated distarch adipate
E 1440	Hydroxy propyl starch
E 1442	Hydroxy propyl distarch phosphate
E 1450	Starch sodium octenyl succinate
E 1451	Acetylated oxidised starch

* The substances listed under numbers E407 and E440 may be standardised with sugars, on condition that this is stated in addition to the number and designation.

2. Conditionally permitted preservatives and antioxidants

A Sorbates, Benzoates and P-Hydroxybenzoates

EC No	Name
E 200	Sorbic acid
E 202	Potassium sorbate
E 203	Calcium sorbate
E 210	Benzoic acid
E 211	Sodium benzoate
E212	Potassium benzoate
E 213	Calcium benzoate
E 214	Ethyl p-hydroxybenzoate
E 215	Sodium ethyl p-hydroxybenzoate
E 216	Propyl p-hydroxybenzoate
E 217	Sodium propyl p-hydroxybenzoate
E 218	Methyl p-hydroxybenzoate
E 219	Sodium methyl p-hydroxybenzoate

B Sulphur dioxide and sulphites

EC No	Name
E 220	Sulphur dioxide
E 221	Sodium sulphite
E 222	Sodium hydrogen sulphite
E 223	Sodium metabisulphite
E 224	Potassium metabisulphite
E 226	Calcium sulphite
E 227	Calcium hydrogen sulphite
E 228	Potassium hydrogen sulphite

C Other preservatives

EC No	Name
E 230	Biphenyl, diphenyl
E 231	Orthophenyl phenol
E 232	Sodium orthophenyl phenol
E 234	Nisin
E 235	Natamycin
E 239	Hexamethylene tetramine
E 242	Dimethyl dicarbonate
E 284	Boric acid
E 285	Sodium tetraborate (borax)s
E 249	Potassium nitrite
E 250	Sodium nitrite
E 251	Sodium nitrate
E 252	Potassium nitrate
E 280	Propionic acid
E 281	Sodium propionate
E 282	Calcium propionate
E 283	Potassium propionate
E 1105	Lysozyme

D Other antioxidants

EC No	Name
E 310	Propyl gallate
E 311	Octyl gallate
E 312	Dodecyl gallate
E 320	Butylated hydroxyanisole (BHA)
E 321	Butylated hydroxytoluene (BHT)
E 315	Erythorbic acid
E 316	Sodium erythorbate

3. Other permitted miscellaneous additives

EC No	Name
E 297	Fumaric acid
E 338	Phosphoric acid
E 339	Sodium phosphates
	(i) Monosodium phosphate
	(ii) Disodium phosphate
	(iii) Trisodium phosphate
E 340	Potassium phosphates
	(i) Monopotassium phosphate
	(ii) Dipotassium phosphate
	(iii) Tripotassium phosphate
E 341	Calcium phosphates
	(i) Monocalcium phosphate
	(ii) Dicalcium phosphate
	(iii) Tricalcium phosphate
E 343	Magnesium phosphates
	(i) Monomagnesium phosphate
	(ii) Dimagnesium phosphate
E 450	Diphosphates
	(i) Disodium diphosphate
	(ii) Trisodium diphosphate
	(iii) Tetrasodium diphosphate
	(v) Tetrapotassium diphosphate
	(vi) Dicalcium diphosphate
	(vii) Calcium dihydrogen diphosphate
E 451	Triphosphates
	(i) Pentasodium triphosphate
	(ii) Pentapotassium triphosphate

EC No	Name
E 452	Polyphosphates
	(i) Sodium polyphosphate
	(ii) Potassium polyphosphate
	(iii) Sodium calcium polyphosphate
	(iv) Calcium polyphosphates
E 431	Polyoxyethylene (40) stearate
E 353	Metatartaric acid
E 355	Adipic acid
E 356	Sodium adipate
E 357	Potassium adipate
E 363	Succinic acid
E 385	Calcium disodium ethylene diamine tetra-acetate (Calcium disodium EDTA)
E 405	Propane-1,2-diol alginate
E 416	Karaya gum
E 420	Sorbitol
	(i) Sorbitol
	(ii) Sorbitol syrup
E 421	Mannitol
E 953	Isomalt
E 965	Maltitol
	(i) Maltitol
	(ii) Maltitol syrup
E 966	Lactitol
E 967	Xylitol
E 425	Konjac*
	(i) Konjac gum
	(ii) Konjac glucomannane

* These substances may not be used to produce dehydrated foods intended to rehydrate on ingestion.

E 432	Polyoxyethylene sorbitan monolaurate (polysorbate 20)
E 433	Polyoxyethylene sorbitan monooleate (polysorbate 80)
E 434	Polyoxyethylene sorbitan monopalmitate (polysorbate 40)
E 435	Polyoxyethylene sorbitan monostearate (polysorbate 60)
E 436	Polyoxyethylene sorbitan tristearate (polysorbate 65)
E 442	Ammonium phosphatides
E 444	Sucrose acetate isobutyrate
E 445	Glycerol esters of wood rosins
E 459	Beta-cyclodextrine

EC No	*Name*
E 468	Crosslinked sodium carboxy methyl cellulose
E 473	Sucrose esters of fatty acids
E 474	Sucroglycerides
E 475	Polyglycerol esters of fatty acids
E 476	Polyglycerol polyricinoleate
E 477	Propane-1,2-diol esters of fatty acids
E 479b	Thermally oxidised soya bean oil interacted with mono- and diglycerides of fatty acids
E 481	Sodium stearoyl-2-lactylate
E 482	Calcium stearoyl-2-lactylate
E 483	Stearyl tartrate
E 491	Sorbitan monostearate
E 492	Sorbitan tristearate
E 493	Sorbitan monolaurate
E 494	Sorbitan monooleate
E 495	Sorbitan monopalmitate
E 512	Stannous chloride
E 520	Aluminium sulphate
E 521	Aluminium sodium sulphate
E 522	Aluminium potassium sulphate
E 523	Aluminium ammonium sulphate
E 541	Sodium aluminium phosphate, acidic
E 535	Sodium ferrocyanide
E 536	Potassium ferrocyanide
E 538	Calcium ferrocyanide
E 551	Silicon dioxide
E 552	Calcium silicate
E 553a	(i) Magnesium silicate
	(ii) Magnesium trisilicate**
E 553b	Talc**

** Asbestos free.

E 554	Sodium aluminium silicate
E 555	Potassium aluminium silicate
E 556	Calcium aluminium silicate
E 559	Aluminium silicate (Kaolin)
E 579	Ferrous gluconate
E 585	Ferrous lactate
E 620	Glutamic acid
E 621	Monosodium glutamate
E 622	Monopotassium glutamate
E 623	Calcium diglutamate

EC No	Name
E 624	Monoammonium glutamate
E 625	Magnesium diglutamate
E 626	Guanylic acid
E 627	Disodium guanylate
E 628	Dipotassium guanylate
E 629	Calcium guanylate
E 630	Inosinic acid
E 631	Disodium inosinate
E 632	Dipotassium inosinate
E 633	Calcium inosinate
E 634	Calcium 5′-ribonucleotides
E 635	Disodium 5′ ribonucleotides
E 900	Dimethyl polysiloxane
E 901	Beeswax, white and yellow
E 902	Candelilla wax
E 903	Carnauba wax
E 904	Shellac
E 905	Microcrystalline wax
E 912	Montan acid esters
E 914	Oxidised polyethylene wax
E 927b	Carbamide
E 950	Acesulfame-K
E 951	Aspartame
E 957	Thaumatin
E 959	Neohesperidine DC
E 999	Quillaia extract
E 1201	Polyvinylpyrrolidone
E 1202	Polyvinylpolypyrrolidone
E 1505	Triethyl citrate
E 1518	Glyceryl triacetate (triacetin)

4. Permitted carriers and carrier solvents

EC No	Name
	Propan-l 2-diol (propylene glycol)
E 422	Glycerol
E 420	Sorbitol
E 421	Mannitol
E 953	Isomalt
E 965	Maltitol

EC No	Name
E 966	Lactitol
E 967	Xylitol
E 400–404	Alginic acid and its sodium, potassium, calcium and ammonium salts
E 405	Propan-1.2-diol alginate
E 406	Agar
E 407	Carrageenan
E 410	Locust bean gum
E 412	Guar gum
E 413	Tragacanth
E 414	Acacia gum (gum arabic)
E 415	Xanthan gum
E 440	Pectins
E 432	Polyoxyethylene sorbitan monolaurate (polysorbate 20)
E 433	Polyoxyethylene sorbitan monooleate (polysorbate 80)
E 434	Polyoxyethylene sorbitan monopalmitate (polysorbate 40)
E 435	Polyoxyethylene sorbitan monostearate (polysorbate 60)
E 436	Polyoxyethylene sorbitan tristearate (polysorbate 65)
E 442	Ammonium phosphatides
E 460	Cellulose (microcrystalline or powdered)
E 461	Methyl cellulose
E 463	Hydroxypropyl cellulose
E 464	Hydroxypropyl methyl cellulose
E 465	Ethyl methyl cellulose
E 466	Carboxy methyl cellulose
	Sodium carboxy methyl cellulose
E 322	Lecithins
E 470b	Magnesium salts of fatty acids
E 471	Mono-and diglycerides of fatty acids
E 472a	Acetic acid esters of mono- and diglycerides of fatty acids
E 472c	Citric acid esters of mono- and diglycerides of fatty acids
E 472e	Mono-and diacetyl tartaric acid esters of mono-and diglycerides of fatty acids
E 473	Sucrose esters of fatty acids
E 475	Polyglycerol esters of fatty acids
E 491	Sorbitan monostearate
E 492	Sorbitan tristearate
E 493	Sorbitan monolaurate
E 494	Sorbitan monooleate
E 495	Sorbitan monopalmitate
E 1404	Oxidised starch
E 1410	Monostarch phosphate
E 1412	Distarch phosphate

EC No	Name
E 1413	Phosphated distarch phosphate
E 1414	Acetylated distarch phosphate
E 1420	Acetylated starch
E 1422	Acetylated distarch adipate
E 1440	Hydroxy propyl starch
E 1442	Hydroxy propyl distarch phosphate
E 1450	Starch sodium octenyl succinate
E 170	Calcium carbonates
E 263	Calcium acetate
E 331	Sodium citrates
E 332	Potassium citrates
E 341	Calcium phosphates
E 501	Potassium carbonates
E 504	Magnesium carbonates
E 508	Potassium chloride
E 509	Calcium chloride
E 511	Magnesium chloride
E 514	Sodium sulphate
E 515	Potassium sulphate
E 516	Calcium sulphate
E 517	Ammonium sulphate
E 577	Potassium gluconate
E 640	Glycine and its sodium salt
E 1505	Triethyl citrate
E 1518	Glyceryl triacetate (triacetin)
E 551	Silicon dioxide
E 552	Calcium silicate
E 553b	Talc
E 558	Bentonite
E 559	Aluminium silicate (Kaolin)
E 901	Beeswax
E 1200	Polydextrose
E 1201	Polyvinylpyrrolidone
E1202	Polyvinylpolypyrrolidone
E 322	Lecithins
E 432–E 436	Polysorbates
E 470a	Sodium potassium and calcium salts of fatty acids
E 471	Mono and diglycerides of fatty acids
E 491–E 495	Sorbitans
E 570	Fatty acids
E900	Dimethylpolysiloxane

EC No	*Name*
	Polyethyleneglycol 6000
E 425	Konjac
	(i) Konjac gum
	(ii) Konjac glucomannae
E 459	Beta-cyclodextrine
E 1451	Acetylated oxidised starch
E 468	Cross linked sodium carboxy methyl cellulose
E 469	Enzymatically hydrolysed carboxy methyl cellulose

Index

Location references are to paragraph numbers, figures in bold type indicating chapters. References to text in the appendices are prefixed by the abbreviation 'App'. References to tables or diagrams are in italics. Abbreviations used in the index are as follows:

AA	Agriculture Act 1970
CEA	Civil Evidence Act 1968
CJA	Criminal Justice Act 1988
CPA	Consumer Protection Act 1987
CPIA	Criminal Procedure and Investigations Act 1988
EC	European Community
ECA	European Communities Act 1972
ECJ	European Court of Justice
EEA	European Economic Area
EPA	Environment Protection Act 1990
FEPA	Food and Environment Protection Act 1985
FSA	Food Safety Act 1990
FSTA	Food Standards Act 1999
LGA	Local Government Act 1992
PACE	Police and Criminal Evidence Act 1984
PHA	Public Health Act 1875
SA	Scotland Act 1998
SEA	Single European Act
SFDA	Sale of Food and Drugs Act 1875
TDA	Trade Descriptions Act 1968
WMA	Weights and Measures Act 1985